The Practice of Faith

Karl Rahner

THE PRACTICE OF FAITH

A Handbook of Contemporary Spirituality

CROSSROAD · NEW YORK

1983

The Crossroad Publishing Company
370 Lexington Avenue, New York, N.Y. 10017

Originally published as *Praxis des Glaubens: Geistliches Lesebuch*,
edited by Karl Lehmann and Albert Raffelt
© Verlag Herder Freiburg im Breisgau 1982

Translation of the Introduction and Sections 7, 8, 14, 19,
20, 21, 26, 34, 35, 40, 41, 42, 43, 44, 47, 52, 57, and 58
Copyright © 1983 by The Crossroad Publishing Company
See also pages 313–16 which constitute an extension of
this copyright page.

Printed in the United States of America

Library of Congress Cataloging in Publication Data

Main entry under title:

The Practice of faith.

Translation of: Praxis des Glaubens.
1. Christian life—Catholic authors.   2. Spiritual
life—Catholic authors.   I. Rahner, Karl, 1904–
BX2350.2.P64713 1983   248.4′82   83–18897
ISBN 0-8245-0603-0

Contents

LOVE

HOPE

Introduction

Karl Rahner is not only one of the architects of modern Catholic theology, he is also a master of the practice of the Christian life. His spiritual-practical publications nearly equal the number of his scientific, scholarly ones. As a Jesuit priest, he has not only exercised his ministry in extensive retreat work and preaching but has sought, throughout practically his whole career, to achieve a rapprochement between theology and spirituality. His elder brother, the ascetical and mystical theologian Hugo Rahner, may well have exerted a telling influence in this respect. And so, even as a young theologian, Karl Rahner carried out many of his historical investigations on questions and problems in the history of Christian spirituality, and we find some of this work reprinted in *Theological Investigations XVI* and *XVII*. In a later period his interests lay principally in the area of the early history of penance and confession, as indicated by *Theological Investigations XV: Penance in the Early Church*. His German edition of a standard French work, M. Viller's *Ascesticism and Mysticism in the Patristic Era*, is further evidence of our theologian's long-standing preoccupation with the fonts of Christian spirituality.

It goes without saying that Rahner's interest in these studies is more than purely historical. Precisely his recent works bear abundant testimony to the extent to which his spiritual impulse—the legacy, especially, of his order's founder, Ignatius Loyola—and his theological reflection compenetrate to form a living, vital whole.

Karl Rahner's Work

This is not the place for a detailed examination of the unity that obtains between Rahner's spiritual roots and his scientific theology, especially as we have attempted just such an examination elsewhere.* Still, in as brief

---

*See Karl Lehmann and Albert Raffelt, eds., *Rechenschaft des Glaubens: Karl Rahner—Lesebuch*, 2nd ed. (Freiburg i. Br.: Verlag Herder, 1982), pp. 13–53; also Karl Lehmann, "Karl Rahner," in H. Vorgrimler and R. Vander Gucht, eds., *Bilanz der Theologie im 20. Jahrhundert*, vol. 4: *Bahnbrechende Theologen* (Freiburg i. Br.: Verlag Herder, 1970), pp. 143–81.

a space as one may hope to achieve anything of the kind, we wish to call the reader's attention to certain of the salient elements in a general view of that intimate linkage, seeing that such a consideration may be of some advantage for a comprehension of the material in the present collection.

1. Not the least of the reasons why Karl Rahner's theology has met with such broad acceptance and recognition is that it springs from a profound faith experience. At the origins of Rahner's theological thought—with all the learning it displays along with an extraordinary philosophical gift— we find a deep and simple faith, penetrated alike with a rare passion for the incomprehensible God and a subdued (but all the more genuine for that) human intimacy and goodness.

It is out of the living store of an experience of a God who grows ever greater that Rahner's theology draws its whole, inexhaustible dynamic, shattering again and again the stubborn shell of our concepts and falling back once more into the bottomless fund of thought, meditation, and indeed language that renews that dynamic's freshness and youth. Here the philosophical experience of a far-away, silent, inaccessible God and the Christian experience of the ineffable nearness of that same God's mystery in the forgiving and sheltering grace of Jesus Christ run together, form a mutually complementary totality, and bear fruit. We have a theology here that is no stranger to the human lot of finitude, and one that surely knows of catastrophe in this world and the need of the cross. Yet it has never fled the world. Everywhere, in all life situations, as indeed in the hour of death, there is a place where one can find and accept God's inescapable tender of salvation. For at the basis of this theology stands the all but invincible hope for grace, a hope that the human being cannot and will not at the last utterly reject God's salvific invitation. Not that the bitter earnest of eternal perdition need be denied: only, it is the urgency and strength of the hope of salvation that receives the emphasis.

These are the grounds on which, without any wavering regarding the radical core of a Christianity altogether sure of its central tenets, Karl Rahner has been able to fashion a new rapport with men and women outside the Catholic Church and outside the Christian churches, including those called atheists. Precisely in virtue of the openness and frankness of his faith is Rahner all the more reliable and brotherly a witness. Thus he has become, for so many, an unobtrusive guide in finding the meaning of life in God. Here speaks someone whom countless persons can believe, because he has actually experienced that of which he tells in his prayers and meditations—someone whose own existence is warranty for his doctrine. Without self-consciousness or constraint, without the least tinge of ideology, Karl Rahner convincingly demonstrates that God can be found in everything. His faith is a brotherly one in the best sense, for he is willing to come to grips with all the questions a human being asks, indeed he shares them, sees them through to the end, and responds to no genuine need with subterfuge or evasion.

2. This fellowship in faith is not the cozy security of those who "already know one another." It is the very antithesis of an introverted or exclusivistic piety, since the passion for inquiry is a basic ingredient of this theology. God's response never fails to transcend our capacity to ask questions, and the spiritually alert Christian, indeed the human being as human being, must continue to swing the hard, sober hammer of inquiry. There are no forbidden questions, then, nor any false pride in some inviolable, final "possession" of understanding. To be sure, no self-centered, self-circling thinking is ever implied in such an attitude, no posture of hollow questioning for questioning's sake, no idle "intellectual one-upmanship." There are no foolish questions. Everything is addressed with the greatest possible freedom of approach. Surely, no discussion sends the reader away with a superficially reassuring answer. But neither does it ever end by exhausting itself in vain inquiry. In many a line of questioning, doubtless, there will be boulders to be pried loose, and theology and its history laboriously to be mined. But there will unfailingly be gold nuggets when the work is done, some abiding insight, some perception full of spiritual strength—sometimes in just a few powerful sentences. At times some insight will have to struggle to break through the hard soil in order to find its path to the light, and then the sentences will be long, complicated, and chock-full of distinctions. But it is only via the passion of such substantive inquiry that thought can be possessed of the inner strength to escape hasty systematization.

> This person is at once bold and measured, audacious and chary. Each proposition is protected, shielded, staked out, and roped off—not only showing that he knows the ojection beforehand, for he has already thought of everything, but also showing, by mapping out such narrow boundaries, how much else there is to think about when that which has already been treated has created enough trouble for the reader.... Never, not even for a moment, is his attitude presumptuous or arrogant. No, rather, it is convinced of the relative insufficiency of what it has to give. (Hans Urs von Balthasar)

3. A boldness like that, the boldness of the boundless inquiry, can only be the trait of one who knows that he does not produce the truth, but that truth is given him as a gift, after all his creative searching. Theology can never be anything but the endlessly renewed question, the rumination of the Word given in the Church as confession and commitment.

> Theology never leaves off looking for what it has already found. The
> totality of the human being's truth, unlike its piecemeal questions and
> particular answers, is always at hand. This is why it must ever be
> called into question and rediscovered all over again. (Karl Rahner)

Precisely where it is whole and all-embracing, truth can scarcely be
purely subjective. The truth of faith, then, with all its personal basic
structuring, is ultimately withdrawn from the sphere of mere private
preference to attain to its plenitude only in intercommunication. Dialogue
is its lifeblood. And so the truth must in some wise be institutionalized.
Karl Rahner has no fear of this intimate bond between truth and the institution. Not that he entertains any antipathy for true individual freedom;
only, he shies away from the arbitrariness so often demonstrated by subjectivity—in full recognition, of course, of the benefit of truth's "otherness"
and the redeeming quality of its foreignness, its strangeness, provided it not
be allowed to lapse into sheer incomprehensibility and naked facticity.
This essential, incurable conflict between truth and institution has taken
hold of Karl Rahner by his very being, and his efforts to grapple with it are
by no means the least of the elements composing the new "ecclesiality" of
Karl Rahner the theologian. Rahner's critique of the Church is steeped in
an ever greater assent to and endorsement of that Church. It is a wounded
love, battling for more breadth and vitality in its Church. This must not
be forgotten as we frequently read, in the later Rahner, quite a few "hard
words" for the institutional Church and a considerable number of its official personnel.

4. To many, Rahner seems a free-floating thinker, easily inclined to di-
gress onto less than promising tangents. But this can be the judgment only
of someone who is ignorant of Rahner's biblical grounding, the abiding
nearness, for him, of the world of human beings, and a lifework steeped
in history. His knowledge of the fonts of the Christian faith is bottomless.
And yet he never struts, never demonstrates an idle complacency in a
plump sackful of learning. For over twenty years—and this should not be
forgotten—he lived and worked immersed in the great sources of Christian
tradition. Much of what he absorbed there has become a solid store and
reservoir of theological experience that he seems almost to take for granted.
He never explicitly treats his enormous background in the history of tradition. But it is there, ready at a moment's notice, the instant he has need
of the unexcelled thinking of the theology of Christian history's morning.
A great deal has settled to the placid depths of an ocean of knowledge.
And there it waits. But it comes like lightning when called up by some
particular question, summoned to the present and put to the test. Then
they surface: Irenaeus, Origen, the Cappadocians, Augustine, Thomas
Aquinas, Bonaventure, Suarez, and—of course—the great mystics.

Here is someone with almost an incredible knowledge of historical
and systematic theology. But he only makes use of it as of a divining
rod, as he goes in search of the fonts. Sometimes it is a long, slow way
around, and seemingly a fruitless one—when suddenly it twitches,
that divining rod, and then it is infallible. Rahner only speaks when he
has discovered something. (Hans Urs von Balthasar)

5. One who has built a theology on a boundless communion of brothers
and sisters in faith and on a concrete universality of thought may not,
after all, keep a genuine insight all to himself and his elite, "learned" circle. The practical and pastoral element of Rahner's theology is not part of
any consequences or post-theological "application." It belongs to the
basic thrust and torque of the theology itself, as it seeks to be of help to the
humblest parish on the edge of the rain forest and its solitary missionary.
And here we have a prime reason why Karl Rahner has renounced his plans
and opportunities to avail himself of such enormous power of creativity in
order to compose a great systematic summa, perhaps on the order of Karl
Barth's *Church Dogmatics*. Instead, he has devoted himself to the "menial
labor" of preparing the theological knowledge of his times for assimilation
by a wider audience; hence his work as editor (or co-editor) of great international standard works such as *Lexicon für Theologie und Kirche, Sacra-
mentum Mundi, Handbuch der Pastoraltheologie, Quaestiones Disputa-
tae, Wörterbuch der Pastoraltheologie, Christlicher Glaube in moderner
Gesellschaft*, and the journal *Concilium*.

Here again we recognize the Rahner literature as a corpus of spiritual
theology. Not incapable of an occasional ironical sideswipe at pure learning—for which he is a match "any day of the week," of course—now and
then Rahner will drop a remark to the effect that his "works of piety" are
just as close to his heart as are his scholarly publications.

The wealth of his publications on the practice of the spiritual life is,
however, manageable, even in overview, by very few connoisseurs of the
Rahnerian corpus. For this reason, in order to open the door to hard-to-
find and hence less well known or forgotten treasures of this corpus, we
now present the following collection.

About This Book

It is difficult today to find present spiritual writing in such a way that it
meets the reader's expectations and yet concentrates on what is essential
in the Christian life. For some, Christian praxis will mean, above all, explicitly religious activity—in the sacraments, the liturgy, even in custom
and religious convention. For others it will mean, first and foremost, involvement with the cause of the oppressed—participation in the social
struggles of our times. With the necessary distinctions made, neither

misses the mark, and Karl Rahner's work is no stranger to the tension between them.

When we consult the classic manuals of the spiritual life, such as those in ascetical theology, we see at once that their scholastic theological approach is not up to the management of this tension, at least not without further "translation." In our original rationale for the selection of the pieces to be presented in this volume, we attempted to organize all the material along the lines of the seven sacraments as constituting the matrix of the Christian life. It proved impossible, however, to carry out our plan without artificiality, although this motif still appears everywhere in the following pages, stamped on the "scaffolding" of our structure. The framework we finally settled on is that of the three theological virtues of faith, hope, and love. As the reader takes up the individual essays in our collection, he or she will easily remark how frequently they explicitly fall into one or another of these categories of the Christian life. On the other hand, the mutual compenetration of the three theological virtues is manifest in the fact that many of our selections could have been positioned elsewhere, without violence to the thematic structure of the book. We are not suggesting a rigid structural correspondence between each selection and its respective thematic category.

The present volume is intended for a specific, but not necessarily homogeneous, readership. It is addressed less to persons seeking theoretical knowledge than to those concerned with the practical molding of their faith, and who wish to make use of reflection and meditation in order to do so. Members of religious orders, people in secular professional callings, homemakers wishing to reflect on their own religiousness or that of their families, all should have access to readable, but rich material.

The selections in this volume are intended to minister to this purpose. They have, we think, all the indicated breadth. Their content represents a deliberate distribution across the whole span of traditional doctrine, without, however, being intended to replace a manual of systematic theology, if indeed such a manual is desirable at all. Certain key themes will at times be represented by more complicated, theoretical pieces (§ 14, for example). In general, however, readability has been an important criterion of our selectivity. First we chose material from works already published; then, when this was laid out according to our structure as described above, we were able to complement our list with a number of ad hoc, unpublished essays.

Our work in preparing this volume has convinced us that it is precisely in the area of spiritual literature that the theological upheaval of recent decades is more palpable and perceptible. The so-called abstract theological disciplines reflect this turbulence less strikingly. This observation applies as well to style as to subject matter. It will scarcely be a surprise, then, for the reader to discover that relatively little of our author's older writing has been the object of our selection. At the same time, however, the editors have been careful not to select material that is readily available elsewhere, even when it is thematically apposite. As a result, some Rahnerian subject matter will be underrepresented or even missing. Of course, this was indeed a help in keeping the scope of this volume within reasonable limits.

Readers with a broader interest in the theology of Karl Rahner will want to examine several other books as well: particularly his *Foundations of Christian Faith: An Introduction to the Idea of Christianity*, which is the most comprehensive and systematic of the author's writings; also *A Rahner Reader*, the earlier anthology edited by Gerald McCool; and, finally, as a useful introduction to Rahner's theology as a whole, *A World of Grace: An Introduction to the Themes and Foundations of Karl Rahner's Theology*, edited by Leo O'Donovan.

Any editing of the material collected here has been limited, with the author's approval, to a few changes in wording with a view to stylistic smoothness or uniformity, some breaking up of paragraphs, an occasional reformulation of a transition, and the deletion or insertion of references and crossreferences. No special attention has been called to an occasional condensation or abridgment. Scholars will find our index of sources an easy guide to the original publications for purposes of comparison, and will want to use our collection only as a "jumping-off point."

The compilation of a volume of selections from the works of Karl Rahner on the spiritual life has been a publishing ambition of long-standing. The editors hope that the finished product does not fall too short of original expectations, and that they will have succeeded in communicating to a wider audience something of the excitement and enthusiasm with which they themselves have been infected through the writings of Karl Rahner.

Karl Lehmann
Albert Raffelt

The Practice of Faith

1 · Why Am I a Christian Today?

I shall try to report what I am trying to say and be when I say: "I would like to be a Christian." One has to say here, "I would like to be." In the Christian view, one must in the end leave it to God to decide whether one really is—in theory and, above all, in practice—what one claims to be and automatically is in social life and in the Church on the surface of everyday life.

I would like to be a person who is free and can hope, who understands and shows by his actions that he himself is at the mercy of his freedom, a freedom which throughout life is creating itself and making him finally what he should be according to his original pattern of human nature, a person who is faithful, who loves, who is responsible. I am well aware that such words can very easily sound very lofty and theoretical, that they create a feeling that real life is being shrouded in a haze of fine words, but also that in their meaning they are far from "clear." We can ignore the first difficulty because no one, not even the most primitive materialist, can do without ideals which, because they have not yet been reached, draw one on and keep one's life moving. As to the second difficulty, the vagueness of the "ideals" just mentioned, this must be admitted. All words which express or invoke the totality of human existence are "unclear": that is, they cannot be defined by being assigned a place in an intrinsically clear system of coordinates distinct from them. They are "unclear" because they point to the one, most real, absolutely single totality which we call "God." For us, however, this "unclarity" has an absolutely positive and irreplaceable function, and a person who does not accept this "unclarity" as a good and a promise drifts into trivial stupidity.

I am convinced that such a free history of real self-determination takes place in and through all the impenetrable details, and uncertainties, perplexities, inadequacies, all the starts that never reach a tangible goal, and all the internal and external determinisms which fill our lives and make them, even for ourselves, almost a meaningless accident. I am convinced that a human being's historical life moves in freedom toward a

3

point of decision, that it contains this decision in itself, that life as a whole must be answered for and does not simply run away into a void in these details. Of course, this outlook on which my life is based, which is almost inescapable and yet required of me, is nothing but breathtaking optimism, so terrifying that everything in me trembles with the sheer audacity of it.

Yet I cannot give up this attitude, cannot let it decay into the triviality of the everyday or the cowardice of scepticism. Of course philosophers and other theorists of human life can talk forever about the meaning of freedom, responsibility, love, selflessness, and so forth. Nor do I find such terms clear and transparent. Nevertheless they have a meaning and guide choices in the thousand and one trivia of life. It may seem that such words can be analysed psychoanalytically, biologically and sociologically and revealed as an avoidable or unavoidable superstructure on much more primitive things, which alone can count as true reality. I also constantly discover cases in which, to my consolation or my horror, such detailed analyses are in fact correct. And yet because in such attempts at analysis as elsewhere it is always the same responsible subject which is at work, and is responsible even for this destruction of its own subjectivity because it is the subjectivity that does the work, in the end, on the whole, such attempts at destruction are in my view false.

I am not trying to escape from myself and have no desire to escape from my responsible freedom as a true subject. Will this being left to oneself end in my case in a final protest or a final acceptance? Since I exist and an acceptance is so firmly planted in me and my freedom, my acceptance seems to me in one sense so obvious an implication of the ground of reality that I often feel that all protests against one's own existence in its full particularity are no more than passing incidents in a fundamentally universal acceptance of oneself and the whole of one's existence. On the other hand I cannot escape the knowledge that a subject's freedom cannot be directed simply to this or that particularity alone, but existence as such, and that therefore the temptation to straightforward rejection, to a total protest (which is the essence of true sin), always exists and can become a reality in the triviality of a banal existence.

I accept myself. I accept myself without protest with all the accidents of my biological and historical existence, even though I have the right and duty to change and improve those elements in it which I feel oppressive. It is this very critical desire to change my existence in all its dimensions which is the form and the proof of the fact that in the end I really accept this existence. But for all the hope of really changing something, this existence (my own and that of others, for which I also feel responsible) remains opaque, burdensome, will not dissolve into controllable transparency; it remains short and full of pains and problems, subject to death, to which all generations remain exposed.

I accept this existence, accept it in hope. I accept it in the one hope which includes and supports everything, which one can never know that one really has (or only pretends to have because at a particular moment one feels marvellous). This hope, whose inner light is its only justification, is the hope that the incomprehensibility of existence (for all the obvious beauty it also contains) will one day be revealed in its ultimate meaning and will be this finally and blissfully. It is a total hope, which I cannot replace with a vague mixture of a little hope and unadmitted despair, though this may always also be present in the deepest core of existence when the foreground of my life seems to be occupied by nothing but meaninglessness and despair. This all-embracing and unconditional hope is what I want to have. I declare my allegiance to it; it is my supreme possibility and what I must answer for as my real task in life. Who will convince me that this is utopia, that such a hope is false and cowardly, worse than if I let myself fall into a radical scepticism which is theoretically possible, but in the reality of life where we take responsiblity and love is impossible to maintain? This ultimate basic trust in the complete and comprehensive meaning of existence is not a free-floating ideology; it not only supports everything else, but is also supported by all the other experiences of life. It includes (at least partial) experience of meaning, light, joy, love and faithfulness, which make an absolute claim.

These specific experiences which support ultimate hope just as they are supported by it will have to be discussed later. For the present, I take it for granted that we are above the dull naiveté which thinks (as even sophisticated scientists sometimes do) that matter is more real than mind or spirit, which floats over matter as no more than a sort of exhalation or side effect of physical constructions. These "materialists" do not see that they cannot come into contact with this matter except through mind, or they are totally unable to say what matter as such really and fundamentally is.

This free fundamental act of existence, which can only be described haltingly and of course does not exist only where it is explicitly talked about, moves towards what or, better, the person, we call God. I know that this word is obscure, by definition the most obscure word there can be, the word which it is genuinely impossible to include among the other words of human language as one more word. I know that what is meant by the word may be present in a person's life even if its name is never spoken by the person. (Anonymous theists do exist because in the totality of reality God is not a particular entity like Australia or a blackbird, which one really doesn't need to know anything about, but supports everything, is the origin of everything, permeates everything and therefore exists and rules anonymously but genuinely as the unexpressed condition of possibility for all knowledge and all freedom wherever mind is at work.) I know that today what we mean by God is very difficult to imagine by means of the image of a great architect of the world (which was still acceptable in the period of the Enlightenment). I know that the word "God" has been used to do any number of terrible and stupid things. I know that it is very easy to keep on finding, in oneself and in others, stupid misunderstandings which do their mischief under cover of the word "God." And yet I say that the ultimate basis of my hope in the act of unconditional acceptance of the meaningfulness of my existence is promised to me by God. This does not make him the projection of my hope into a void for in the instant that I envisage God as my projection, "God" becomes meaningless and ineffective for me. Equally, I can no more abandon the basis of my hope than abandon the hope or identify it with my powerless, finite self, which has to hope, no more make myself God than I can simply think of this God as outside me and one thing alongside others. God must be what is most real and what embraces all things in its support for him to be at once the basis and goal of the unbounded and unconditional hope which becomes a basic acceptance in trust of existence.

On the other hand, this God is incomprehensible mystery. This hope (in which reason and freedom are still united) transcends any possible explanation because every detail which can be understood and included as an element in the equation of life is and always remains influenced and threatened by others which have not been included. Even in everyday life we experience the unboundedness of our transcendence of what is nevertheless not subject to our transcendence.

In addition, human transcendence in knowledge and freedom also shows this. It can neither be made to stop at a particular point nor derive power from any "nothingness" (because "nothing" can do nothing), and moves towards mystery as such inasmuch as by its own power it is completely unable to fill the infinite sphere of consciousness. But the miracle of existence is not so much that there is this mystery (who can really deny it except by obstinately refusing to take an interest in it?), but that we can and may become involved with it without being tossed back in that very instant into our own nothingness (to the point where atheism becomes the only form of recognition worthy of God).

The act of accepting existence in trust and hope is therefore, if it does not misinterpret itself, the act of letting oneself sink trustfully into the incomprehensible mystery. Therefore my Christianity, if it is not to misinterpret itself, is my letting myself sink into the incomprehensible mystery. It is therefore anything but an "explanation" of the world and my existence, much more an instruction not to regard any experience, any understanding (however good and illuminating they may be) as final, as intelligible in themselves.

Even less than other people do Christians have "final" answers, which they can endorse with a "solves everything" label. Christians cannot include their God as a specific understood element in the equations of their lives, but only accept him as the incomprehensible mystery, in silence and adoration, as the beginning and end of their hope and so as their only ultimate and universal salvation.

The movement of finite mind towards God in such a way that God becomes the content and the goal of this movement and not just the initiator of a movement which in the end remains far from him in the finite must be supported by God himself. Because Christians know that this fundamental trust of theirs, because it is really absolute and desires God himself, is supported by God himself, they call this most intimate movement of their existence towards God by the power of God "grace," "the Holy Spirit," and express this single movement towards the immediate presence of God in faith, hope and love.

Christians believe that anyone who is faithful to the dictates of his or her conscience is following this intimate movement in God towards God. They believe that this movement takes place even if a person does not recognise it for what it is, and has been unable to see its historical manifestation in Jesus Christ, even in the descriptions of an explicitly Christian faith. Christians fear in their own case (and therefore in the case of others) that in the final balance of their lives they may freely say No to this deepest movement of their existence in an open or concealed unbelief or lack of hope. However, at the same time they hope for all others and so also for themselves that this movement may find its way through all the darkness and superficiality of life to its final "eternal" goal. Christians accept this ultimate threat to themselves from themselves (to freedom from freedom, which can say no to God). They keep on overcoming it in the hope that the human race's history of freedom, which is in turn contained by the freedom of the incomprehensible mystery and by the power of his love, will on balance have a happy outcome through God. It makes no difference to this that no theoretical statements can be made about the salvation of individuals—in other words, that in the present absolute hope is the ultimate.

All that has been said so far forms for me, as a Christian, a mysterious synthesis with the encounter with Jesus of Nazareth. In this synthesis primal hope and knowledge of Jesus form a circle which is in the end unbreakable and give each other mutual support and justification before the intellectual conscience of a person who wants to be honest—but with an intellectual honesty which includes what we Christians call "humility." Through the mediation of the message of Christianity and the Church in the gospel of Jesus, and also supported by that ultimate hope in grace, the Christian encounters Jesus. The experience of this synthesis between ultimate primal trust in grace and the encounter with Jesus is naturally somewhat different in the lives of different people, and there is a difference in particular between those who throughout their conscious lives have been Christians and those whose explicit encounter with Jesus for their salvation took place only at a later stage in their lives. However, since the grace which moves all human beings is the grace of Jesus Christ even if the person who receives grace is not consciously aware of this, and since all love of neighbour is, by Jesus' own statement, love for him even if a person is not consciously aware of it, this synthesis (at least as an offer made to freedom) is present in every human being. As far as this synthesis is concerned, therefore, the distinction between Christians and non-Christians (a distinction the importance of which should be neither underestimated nor overestimated) relates, not to its presence, but to its conscious realisation in explicit faith. So in this synthesis whom does a Christian recognise Jesus as?

This experience in which Jesus becomes for a particular person the event of the unique and qualitatively unsurpassable and irreversible approach of God, is always affected by the totality of its elements as a single entity even if each of the elements is not necessarily immediately present explicitly and clearly in conscious awareness. There is Jesus, a human being who loves, who is faithful unto death, in whom all of human existence, life, speech and action, is open to the mystery which he calls his Father and to which he surrenders in confidence even when all is lost. For him the immeasurable dark abyss of his life is the Father's protecting hand. And so he holds fast to love for human beings and also to his one hope even when everything seems to be being destroyed in death, when it no longer seems possible to love God and human beings. But in Jesus all this was supported and crowned by the conviction that with him, his word and his person the "kingdom of God" was made finally and irreversibly present. Christians believe that in Jesus God himself was triumphantly promising himself directly in love and forgiveness to human beings. In Jesus God, on his own initiative, was bringing about and also proclaiming his victory in the human history of freedom, and so of course creating a new and ultimate radical situation of choice for the person who hears this message.

In Christianity this experience of Jesus includes the assurance that this is a man in whom reality does not lag behind the demands of human nature, despite the scepticism produced by the rest of our experience of human beings we can here really rely on a human being. This does not mean that we have to have a stylised picture of Jesus as a superman. He had his limitations, even in his teaching and its presentation, because this is an inevitable part of being a real human being. But he was the person he was supposed to be, in life and in death. His disciples, who witnessed his downfall on Good Friday without illusions, discovered in themselves, as something given by him, a certainty that life was not destroyed, that death in reality was his victory, that he was taken into the protection of the mystery of God, that he "rose." Resurrection here of course does not mean a return into our spatio-temporal and biological reality, but the definitive rescue of the whole human being ("in body and soul") in God. Because this resurrection is being accepted by the mystery which, in its incomprehensibility, is called God, how it happened is impossible to imagine. However, where our absolute hope and the experience of this life and death meet we can no longer think in terms of Jesus' destruction without also denying our own absolute hope, without, whether we admit it or not, allowing ourselves to fall in despair into bottomless emptiness and ultimate nullity.

When, in our own hope for ourselves, we try to find somewhere in the history of the human race a person of whom we can dare to believe that here the hope that embraces all the dimensions of our existence is fulfilled and that this fulfilment itself makes itself known to us, that is, appears in history, this search can find no identifiable figure without the apostolic witness to Jesus. In the first place at least, amazing as it may seem, we simply can find no one who, according to the testimony of their disciples, made this claim. (If we also accept this claim as the guarantee of our own salvation, it then becomes even more unusual.) If, through the witness of the apostles, we have experienced the risen Christ, that experience gives us then the power and the courage to say from the centre of our own existence, "He is risen." The fundamental structure of human hope and its historical experience form a unity: he is the one who has been accepted by God. The question which human beings constitute for the limitlessness of incomprehensibility has been answered by God in Jesus.

Here human existence has finally achieved happiness in the victory achieved from both sides, the victory of grace and of freedom. Here the sceptical doubts about human beings in their uselessness and sin have been left behind. Jesus regarded himself in life and word as the irrevocable coming of God's kingdom, God's victory in human freedom achieved by the power of God, and his self-understanding, which derived from the unbreakable unity of his unconditional solidarity with God and with the world, is confirmed by what we call his resurrection. He is now both the question and the answer present in human life. He is the ultimate answer which cannot be bettered, because every other conceivable question for human beings is made superfluous by death and in him this all-consuming question has been answered if he is the risen one and irrevocably promises us the incomprehensible boundlessness of God himself, alongside which there is nothing else which could be question or answer. He is the word of God to us, the answer to the one question which we ourselves are, a question no longer about a particular detail, but the universal question, about God.

From this position, the statements of traditional ecclesiology and theology about Jesus Christ can be recapitulated and at the same time protected against misunderstandings. We can say what is meant by his "metaphysical divine sonship," by the hypostatic union of the eternal word of God, by the complete and unimpaired human reality in Jesus, by the communication of idioms. This Christology, which is more than fifteen hundred years old and even today for the most part shared by all the main Christian churches, is still valid and will continue to be so, because it expresses, remorselessly and correctly, what the Christian faith experiences in Jesus, God's irrevocable promise of himself to the world, which is historically accessible in its irrevocablity.

On the other hand, it is possible for these official Christological formulas of the Christian churches to be misunderstood and then rightly rejected. They do not simply need repeating to be immediately understood; and the orthodox believer, while he may explain them, may still admit that what they say can also be said in other ways. Anyone who says in the orthodox sense that Jesus is God has stated the Christian truth, provided that he correctly understands this statement, which cannot be taken for granted. This also implies the converse, that anyone who accepts Jesus as the insurpassable word of God to himself or herself, as the final confirmation of their own hope, is a Christian even if he or she cannot reproduce, or can reproduce only with difficulty, these traditional Christological formulas, which derive from a conceptual framework which it is hard for us to recover.

The cross and the resurrection belong together in any authentic faith in Jesus. The cross means the no longer obscured requirement that human beings must surrender completely before the mystery of existence, which human beings can no longer bring under their control because they are finite and sinful. The resurrection means the content of the absolute hope that in this surrender there takes place the forgiving and blissful and final acceptance of a human being by this mystery, that when we let go completely we do not fall. The cross and resurrection of Jesus together mean that precisely this letting go without falling took place in an exemplary way through God's act in Jesus and that we too are irrevocably promised this possibility (including that of being able to let go, which is the most difficult task of our lives) in Jesus.

Here, in Jesus, we have the "absolutely particular." We need only to rely on this particular person lovingly and absolutely. (In the end the interposition of time is no more an obstacle to this than that of a body. We only have to take a chance.) Then we have everything. True, we have to die together with him, but no one can escape this fate. We should not try to squeeze past death until others—emphatically not ourselves—can no longer notice whether we accept our own death. So why not die with Jesus, saying in unison with him, "My God, why have you abandoned me?" and "Into your hands I commend my spirit"?

Only here does all the metaphysics about human beings become real. And it is no longer so important what the metaphysics is or might be like "in itself." By the time it has arrived at Jesus, it contains very little, and therefore everything. Because it treats reaching death as reaching life, and there we have the answer to the question, all or nothing! Not in talking about death, but in death, his and ours. Not until this moment, which for oneself is still to come, has one finally embraced Christianity.

Nevertheless, even beforehand we can prepare to be open to this event. This training for dying does not destroy the splendour of the life we lead now. Let those who can and want to enjoy this glorious life. But let them enjoy it with an eye on death. Only in death does everything acquire its ultimate importance and so become the "light burden." Christianity is for me the simplest way because it embodies the single totality of existence, plunges this totality calmly and hopefully with the dying Jesus into God's incomprehensibility and leaves all the details of life to us as they are, but without giving us a formula.

Nevertheless the simplest is also the most difficult. It is grace, the grace offered to all, which can be accepted and (this is Christian hope) is accepted, even where absolute hope has still not explicitly found the person it is looking for as its embodiment, Jesus of Nazareth. Perhaps it is ordained that many "find" him more easily by looking for him in anonymous hope without being able to call him by his historical name. If the conscious personal history of the human race forms a unity, everything in it is important for all and for that reason the original sacrament which is Jesus Christ has been established from the beginning above all the periods and spaces of this one history, but over it as over a history in which necessarily not everything can be at the same historical distance from everything else or have the same explicit closeness. Nevertheless, anyone who has met Jesus with sufficient clarity must acknowledge him because otherwise he or she would be denying his or her own hope.

If the resurrection of Jesus is mystery victoriously promising itself to us by the power of God as the mystery of our definitive life, it is certain and understandable that his resurrection would not exist if Jesus did not also rise in the belief in his eternal validity. It is for that reason that there exists the community of people who believe in him as the one who was crucified and rose from the dead. This community is called a Church all the more because those who believe in Jesus Christ, simply because of their shared reference to the one Jesus just cannot simply be religious individualists. Nor can this faith in Jesus be transmitted without active witness, which again ultimately requires a social structure in the community of faith which gathers round Jesus.

For this and many other reasons Christianity means Church. Human beings are social beings always driven even by the history of their ultimate freedom from a socially constituted community and toward one. Even the most radical religious individualist is still related to the Church by language, holy scripture, tradition, and so on even if he or she wants to make himself or herself totally independent of it. Truth, too, is connected with an open and yet critical relationship to society and therefore to institutions, though this does not mean that an individual's "own" truth can be something arbitrary. Truth which is not constantly seeking to communicate itself to others in unity and love, and which is not constantly given to the individual by a community, is not truth, because in religion truth is the consciousness of the person who gives himself or herself to others in love.

Nor can this truth in community escape the solidity inherent in the social nature of a community. The various Christian churches and denominations may not attach exactly the same value to the Church, but throughout Christianity there are institutions, and therefore in principle there is a desire for the Church. Where individual freedom and uniqueness (which are essential to a Christian) exist as the individual's immediate relation to God, and yet because of them religious groups and a Church are necessary, there will always be the permanent tension, which constantly takes different forms and must always be resolved afresh, between Christian freedom and the Christian need for the Church. This tension cannot be resolved either by an ecclesiastical totalitarianism (a genuine danger easily underestimated by ecclesiastics) or by a Christian anarchism, nor can there ever be such specific rules for dealing with it in particular cases that a solution could be merely an administrative matter of applying the rules. In the end it is only in hope that the individual Christian can endure this tension in patience, in the hope that one day the eternal kingdom of love will exist and not the Church. Nevertheless the recognition more or less everywhere in the Christian world of baptism as the rite of initiation into the Christian community in the confession of the divine Trinity is a universal admission in principle that membership in the Church is an essential feature of Christianity.

I do not want to say much here about what in the Christian world is the bitter topic of the divisions between the Christian churches, this problem which has produced the most terrible events in Christian history, religious wars between Christians. Today this question, which has existed throughout almost the whole history of Christianity, exists perhaps primarily as the question whether and in what way the Christian religious conscience has to make a distinction of religious significance between the different Christian denominations and churches. In the past the question did not take this form. Hitherto (and quite properly, on their terms) all the Christian denominations were convinced that the diversity of creeds and the ecclesial institutions which held them were not simply purely accidental and ultimately unimportant variations of the one Christian faith, but that they raised a genuine religious question for the conscience of each individual. It was held that true Christianity, which alone led to salvation, was to be found only in one or other of the denominations and churches. Today, whether we like it or not, the situation in this respect has certainly become more difficult for the average Christian. On many issues at least, it is no longer so easy to say whether the various Christian creeds are really in direct contradiction or whether they are all (or many of them) simply expressions of the same Christian truth and reality within different conceptual frameworks and with different linguistic resources and different, historically conditioned, emphases, and would therefore certainly all find a place in the one Church.

Christians throughout the world have come to realise that the diversity of church laws, rights, customs and spiritualities can be much greater than that which European Christendom was previously used to. It has at least become clear in principle that one Church does not mean the same canon law in all its detail. The historical accidents, which in themselves have nothing to do with the unity of faith and the unity of the Church and yet have played a very important part in the division, are well known.

Everywhere there is a growing understanding of the need for ecumenism. In such a situation it is certainly no longer so easy to regard one of the Christian confessions and churches, to the exclusion of all the others, as the only legitimate one and the only route to salvation. There has of course been progress in this difficult situation, even where (as in the Roman Catholic Church) there is not yet a willingness to recognise all the churches with their different creeds and institutions as in principle equal in status. The title "Church" is given on all sides, the universal validity of baptism is stressed, there is a recognition of the genuine religious value of many doctrines, institutions, and forms of spirituality in the various churches, rejoicing at the identity of holy scripture throughout the Christian world, and so on. However, these very attempts at ecumenical rapprochement have made it much more difficult in practice, at least for Catholic Christians, to still allow their Church the unique status which, even at the Second Vatican Council, it claimed for itself as opposed to all the other Christian churches.

Today there are also all the difficulties of historical knowledge which affect the precise connection between even the most primitive stage of the Church and the historical Jesus and also the impossibility (at least for the average Christian) of deciding rationally which developments in subsequent church history are legitimate and which are illegitimate (or at least not binding in faith)—and there certainly have been both. In this situation even Catholic Christians have to distinguish between the content and absoluteness of their assent in faith to their Church, if they can give such assent, which is in principle possible and required, and the arguments from fundamental theology which justify this assent but are in themselves external to it. The two are not the same, as every traditional fundamental theology knows. The true assent of faith accepts the actual Church as it understands itself.

On the other hand, as regards fundamental theology and the external justification for this assent, the average Catholic will answer yes to a double question and thus legitimise his or her relationship in faith to the Roman Catholic Church. A Catholic will ask whether he or she can find in this Church the liberating spirit of Jesus, his truth, without at the same time encountering obstacles in the shape of the Church itself or its doctrine or an absolutely binding practice. A Catholic will ask whether he or she, despite and through all historical and unavoidable change, can find in this Church the clearest and strongest possible connection in historical continuity with the beginnings of the Church and so with Jesus.

An affirmative answer to this double question seems to me, a born Catholic, to give me the right and duty to maintain an unqualified relationship with my Church, a relationship which naturally, by its nature, includes a critical attitude to it as the locus of evangelical freedom. How a non-Catholic can come to the Catholic Church, something which is in principle possible, is a different question and one which cannot be explored further here.

Every true Christian naturally suffers because of the social and historical structure of the Church. In its empirical reality the Church always lags behind its essence. It proclaims a message by which its own empirical reality is always called in question. The Church is also always the Church of sinners, whose members by their actions deny what they profess. In fact the Church cannot in this connection rely totally on the argument that it is made up of human beings and therefore, like every other historical community or association, reveals human nature. The Church's role is to be *par excellence* the place in which the power of grace demonstrates its victory over the depths of malice and narrowness in human beings.

Of course the Church can point to people in whom this power of grace is really made manifest, but are such people that much easier to see in the Church than outside it? How is one expected to prove that without becoming pharisaical and arrogant when one really honestly looks "outside" the Church for such people? A difficult question. Quite enough terrible and base things have happened in the history of the Church. There is so much that is terrible and base that the only helpful answer is this: where else would we go if we left the Church? Would we then be more faithful to the liberating spirit of Jesus if, egotistical sinners that we are, we distanced ourselves as the "pure" from this poor Church? We can do our part to remove its meanness only if we help to bear the burden of this wretchedness (for which all of us too bear some guilt), if we try to live in the Church as Christians, if we help to bear the responsibility of constantly changing it from inside. The Church in all denominations must always be the Church of the "reformation."

If we believe we can discover some element of genuine Christianity in ourselves and understand what it really means, how then can we refuse to graft it unselfishly into this community of sinners? Are they not in fact, through the power of the spirit of Jesus, moving through all the wretchedness of history towards that fulfilment promised by the death and resurrection of Jesus to all of us and not just to a small élite among the human race?

Christians have always known, in theory at least, that they can only know, make real and credible their relationship of hope and love to the imcomprehensible mystery of their lives in unconditional love for their neighbour, which is the only way we can really break out of the hell of our egotism. This love for others in all the varied forms which it can take is by no means so straightforward, even without being distorted into a method of covert egotism; it is the liberating grace of God. Where this love is real, the spirit of Jesus is at work, even if it is not named, as Matthew 25 clearly teaches us. We can only say in trembling: Let us hope that the grace of God is working this miracle somewhere in ourselves! Everything depends on this, absolutely everything.

Of course in a period such as ours it has to be realised that this love of neighbour cannot possibly be itself if it lends grace and dignity merely to the private relations of individuals. Today it must also be practised particularly (though not only) as the responsibility of every person and every

Christian for the social domain as such. It must take the form of justice and peace because in the end justice cannot be sought by a compromise of merely rational calculation, but only by the occurrence often enough in society and history of the absurd miracle of selfless love.

And the other way around, this miracle is concealed in sober calculations of justice. Social and political responsibilities have a particular form for the individual Christian, individual Christian groups and the Church as such. The Church must make its love of neighbour credible through its commitment to action in society and against it. There is a horrifying amount of injustice, violence, alienation and war in the world and all this injustice adopts the disguise of inevitability, cold reason and legitimate interest. Because sinful Christians in a sinful Church are beneficiaries of this injustice, whether they know and admit it or not, the critical function of the Church in society cannot have as its true and own responsibility the defence of a socio-political status quo. If it gives the average person the impression that it is a support of a conservative system, if it wants to be on good terms with everyone instead of like Jesus, preferring the poor and rootless, if it receives more sympathy from the socially secure and the rich than from the poor and from the oppressed, then there is something wrong with this Church.

The Church must carry out its critical commitment in society under the guidance of the spirit which has been given to it, the spirit of Jesus, and in the hope of eternal life. The memory of the death and resurrection of Jesus gives the Church a critical distance from society which allows it not to treat as absolute (explicitly or covertly) either the future already achieved or the nearest feasible future. If the Church were to develop into a merely "humanitarian concern" it would be betraying its responsibility because its task is to proclaim to human beings the ultimate seriousness and incomprehensible dignity of this love for human beings. But even today the greater danger seems to be that love of neighbour, and our neighbours today are mainly secular society, is not taken sufficiently seriously by Christians. And yet this is the only place where the God whom the Christians are looking for can be found, with Jesus, not even he dissolved the incomprehensible mystery, but accepted it in faith and love by refusing to make a choice between love of God and love of human beings.

Christianity and the churches are slowly acquiring new and much more complex relationships with the non-Christian world religions than they had in the past, when these religions were outside the cultural orbit of Christianity. Christianity cannot withdraw the claim to have heard and to preach the universal and unrepeatable word of grace in Jesus, who was crucified and rose from the dead. But Christianity does not for that reason deny that the Spirit of God is carrying out its liberating work throughout history in the middle of human limitations and culpable confusion, the Spirit in whom Jesus surrendered himself to God in death.

The non-Christian world religions also bear witness in their own way to this spirit and not merely to human limitations. Many of their provisional and important experiences may be included as elements of an answer in the all-embracing answer which is Jesus because the history of the Christian message is by no means yet at an end. Nor can Christianity treat atheism, which today has become a mass-phenomenon on a world scale, simply as a manifestation of rejection on the part of human beings who refuse to submit to the incomprehensible mystery of God, rather also as an element in the history of the experience of God in which God is seen in an ever more radical way as the mystery to be adored, to which we give ourselves in hope.

Both in my life and in my thinking I keep finding myself in situations of confusion which cannot be "cleared up." At first even I feel that one just has to carry on, even if one doesn't know where it's all leading. I feel that one must just keep quiet when one can't speak clearly, that carrying on in ordinary honesty is the only appropriate attitude for human beings, and the most that can be expected of us. But then I find I cannot avoid or keep silent about the question of what underlies this carrying on. What I find when I ask that question is the hope which accepts no limits as final. This hope concentrates all our experience into two words, "mystery" and "death." "Mystery" means confusion in hope, but "death" orders us not to disguise the confusion, but to endure it. I look at Jesus on the cross and know that I am spared nothing. I place myself (I hope) in his death and so hope that this shared death is the dawn of the blessed mystery. I must interpret death, and interpreting it as final emptiness and darkness has no more justification. But in this hope, even in all the darkness and disappointment, life already begins to emerge in its beauty and everything becomes promise. I find that being a Christian is the simplest task, the utterly simple and therefore heavy-light burden, as the Gospel calls it. When we carry it, it carries us. The longer one lives the heavier and the lighter it becomes. At the end we are left with mystery, but it is the mystery of Jesus. One can despair or become impatient, tired, sceptical and bitter because time goes by and the mystery still does not dawn as happiness, but it is better to wait in patience for the day that knows no ending.

2 · The Spirituality of the Future

For a Catholic the *first* thing to be said about a future spirituality is quite obviously that, despite all change coming or to come, it is and will remain, albeit in a mysterious identity, the old spirituality of the Church's history up to the present time. Consequently the spirituality of the future will be one related to the living God, who has revealed himself in the history of humanity, who has established himself in his most intimate reality—even as basic ground, as innermost dynamism and final end—at the very heart of the world and the humanity created by him.

Christian spirituality of the future also will be about the God of Abraham, Isaac and Jacob, the God and Father of Jesus Christ. This spirituality can never and may never degenerate into a mere humanism of a horizontal type. It will always be a spirituality of adoration of the incomprehensible God in spirit and in truth. This spirituality will always be related to Jesus Christ, the Crucified and Risen, as to the ultimate, victorious and irreversible self-promise of God, historically manifested to the world; it will be a discipleship of Jesus and will receive from him and from the concreteness of his life a norm, an internal structural principle, that can no longer disintegrate into a theoretical morality; it will always be an acceptance of the death of Jesus who, without any reassurance and yet absolutely openly, allowed himself in his death to fall into the abyss of God's incomprehensibility and incalculable decrees, in faith, hope and love, so that in this way and no other we attain to the infinite truth, freedom and salvation of God.

The spirituality of the future will also always be one living in the Church, receiving from it, giving itself to the Church, founded in it and sustaining it, even though it is as yet perhaps very uncertain what this implies exactly and concretely in the future. Such a spirituality of the future will also always be one that finds concrete expression and an ecclesial manifestation historically and sociologically in the sacraments of the Church, even though the concreteness of the relationship between the existentiality and the sacramentality of the self-realization of the Christian as such is in principle very variable even now and consequently can change considerably in the course of history. The Church's spirituality in the future—for the Church must always have a spirituality—will also have a sociological, political dimension facing on to the world, bearing a responsibility for this merely apparently secular world; and it may be said at once that this very dimension—which also pertains to spirituality as such—will in the future presumably be more clearly possessed and filled up by the latter.

The spirituality of the future will be a spirituality of the Sermon on the Mount and of the evangelical counsels, continually involved in renewing its protest against the idols of wealth, pleasure and power. The spirituality of the future will be a spirituality of hope, awaiting an absolute future, enabling man to be grimly realistic and continually to break down the illusion that he could himself, by his own power and shrewdness, produce in this world and in its continuing history the eternal kingdom of truth and freedom. The spirituality of the future will always preserve the memory of the past history of piety, will regard as stupid, inhuman and unChristian the view that man's piety is continually making a fresh start—unhistorically—at zero and consists in nothing but wild revolutions.

This future spirituality therefore will learn over and over again positively and negatively from the Church's past. On the one hand therefore it will always, as in the past, be open for new pentecostal beginnings emerging from the base, not organized and regulated from the outset by authority from above, but bursting out charismatically where the Spirit breathes as he wills, even though such new charismatic departures prove in the discernment of spirits to be truly produced by the Spirit, since, apparently hoping desperately and almost self-destructively, they also establish themselves humbly in the institutional Church without having first negotiated legalistically principles to ensure that they do not perish in this Church of institutions. The spirituality of the future will always be lovingly and familiarly immersed in the documents of the history of the piety of past times, since this is its own history. It will never leave aside as of no interest to itself the history of the saints, of the liturgy, of mysticism; in the future it will perhaps also develop quite new forms of evangelical fellowship and yet have love and sympathy for the spirit and concrete form of older religious orders which are still alive. The spirituality of the future will preserve the history of the Church's piety and will continually discover afresh that what is apparently old and past can offer the true future to our present time. That was the *first* thing to be said about the spirituality of the future. This first statement of course does not exclude but includes the possibility that many individual forms and shapes of the piety of the past in their concreteness are no more than what has been and the Church must have the sober courage forthrightly to abandon them.

A *second* thing can certainly be predicted of the spirituality of the future: compared to the spirituality of former times, it will certainly have to concentrate very clearly on what is most essential to Christian piety. Since what is essential and decisive in the Christian faith was more or less taken for granted and undisputed in our cultural group of the western Church, during the past 1500 years, in public opinion and in society even in its secular fields, that faith was of course living and found expression in spirituality, but really became interesting and attractive only when it ceased to be merely obvious and took concrete shape in the most varied individual types of piety, often in competition with one another. Devout people were deeply interested in the most diverse forms of devotion, particular religious practices, greatly varying styles of the religious life, each clearly distinguished from the others. For example (and all this is merely by way of example), succeeding one another and alongside one another, there were devotion to the Precious Blood, devotion to the Child Jesus and to Mary's Seven Dolours, a thoroughly organized intercession for the Holy Souls, an intensively cultivated practice of indulgences, etc.; clearly distinguished from one another were the very diverse spiritualities of the individual religious orders, the varying trends and tendencies in mysticism and their theological interpretation, a widespread practice of pilgrimage, the veneration of certain sanctuaries and miraculous pictures, and interest—sometimes scarcely intelligible today—in particular dogmas and theological opinions reflected in the piety of the time, etc.

All this will certainly not simply disappear from the consciousness and the life of the Church as such. For it can be observed that Rome even today is trying to keep alive some of these concrete individual forms of devotion. It would also be deplorable if everything were to disappear in a grey homogeneous spirituality and no one can say whether new and surprising concrete forms and practices of spirituality may not take shape in the future. But in a bleak age of worldwide secularism and atheism it may be presumed that far fewer individual flowers of Christian spirituality will be able to bloom. In this situation, even in the field of spirituality, concentration on the essential Christian beliefs is unavoidable and indispensable. There will certainly be Marian devotion and the veneration of saints in the future. And we can certainly only wish—and indeed in the light of the ultimate grounds of faith—that something of this kind will exist and even take on a new life. But we shall speak of Jesus and not of the Infant of Prague. We shall speak of Mary but have less to do with Lourdes and Fatima. In the future also there will be a eucharistic piety, including (we may hope) adoration of our Lord under the sacramental species. But this does not mean that the eucharistic cult with all its developments will retain in a living spirituality of the future the same position as in the past. I do not think that the piety of the future will have the same interest in new dogmas as was the case—for example, in the field of Mariology—up to our own time.

The spirituality of the future will be concentrated on the ultimate data of revelation: that God is, that we can speak to him, that his ineffable incomprehensibility is itself the very heart of our existence and consequently of our spirituality; that we can live and die with Jesus and properly with him alone in an ultimate freedom from all powers and authorities; that his incomprehensible cross is set up above our life and that this scandal reveals the true, liberating and beatifying significance of our life. These and similar things were not lacking of course even in the spirituality of former times, but they will make their impact more clearly, more forcefully and with a certain exclusiveness on the future spirituality of a bleaker age. Why should not this be so, if man and the Church actively realize that they are not masters of their history, but must so shape their spirituality that it is adapted to the historical situation imposed on us and not made by us and consequently should be credible even for non-Christians. Even this statement is of course burdened with all the reservations that are involved in the unforeseeability of the future.

There is a *third* point to be made. The spirituality of the future will not be supported or at any rate will be much less supported by a sociologically Christian homogeneity of its situation; it will have to live much more clearly than hitherto out of a solitary, immediate experience of God and his Spirit in the individual. Of course as such and in principle *fides qua*, which stamps all spirituality, has always been understood as an event involving personal responsibility, the decision and freedom of the individual. For this decision of faith in particular is less than anything else in a person's existence something for which he can shift responsibility to others, to other causes or to other causes preceding it. But formerly this act of faith on the part of the individual took place within a homogeneously Christian milieu, even though of the secular and bourgeois society; it was possible to believe what was believed by more or less everyone at least in the public sphere and in verbal communication, so that it almost seemed as if a person was relieved—particularly in the dimension of faith—from the supposedly untransferable burden of responsibility, of the decision of faith against unbelief, of hope against all hope, of unrewarded love; and in the area of spirituality it was a question only of the intensity by which we ourselves choose on a particular occasion what is taken for granted by everyone. Today it is different. Christian faith today (and consequently spirituality) must be continually freshly realized: in the dimension of a secularized world, in the dimension of atheism, in the sphere of a technical rationality, declaring from the very outset that all statements which cannot be justified in the light of this rationality are meaningless or amount (in Wittgenstein's words) to "mysticism" about which we can only be silent if we want to retain our integrity and sobriety.

In such a situation the lonely responsibility of the individual in his or her decision of faith is necessary and required in a way much more radical than it was in former times. That is why the modern spirituality of the Christian involves courage for solitary decision contrary to public opinion, the lonely courage analogous to that of the martyrs of the first century of Christianity, the courage for a spiritual decision of faith, drawing its strength from itself and not needing to be supported by public agreement, particularly since even the Church's public opinion does not so much sustain the individual in his or her decision of faith, but is itself sustained by the latter. Such a solitary courage, however, can exist only if it lives out of a wholly personal experience of God and his Spirit.

It has already been pointed out that the Christian of the future will be a mystic or he or she will not exist at all. If by mysticism we mean, not singular parapsychological phenomena, but a genuine experience of God emerging from the very heart of our existence, this statement is very true and its truth and importance will become still clearer in the spirituality of the future. For, according to Scripture and the Church's teaching, rightly understood, the ultimate conviction and decision of faith comes in the last resort, not from a pedagogic indoctrination from outside, supported by public opinion in secular society or in the Church, nor from a merely rational argumentation of fundamental theology, but from the experience of God, of his Spirit, of his freedom, bursting out of the very heart of human existence and able to be really experienced there, even though this experience cannot be wholly a matter for reflection or be verbally objectified. Possession of the Spirit is not something of which we are made factually aware merely by pedagogic indoctrination as a reality beyond our existential awareness (as great theological schools, especially of post-Tridentine theology, asserted), but is experienced inwardly. This cannot be explained here in detail and at length. But the facts are there: the solitary Christian makes the experience of God and his liberating grace in silent prayer, in the final decision of conscience, unrewarded by anyone, in the unlimited hope which can no longer cling to any particular calculable assurance, in the radical disappointment of life and in the powerlessness of death—if these things are only voluntarily borne and accepted in hope, in the night of the senses and the spirit (without, as the mystics say, being able in this respect to claim a special privilege), etc. All this, however, assumes that he or she accepts the experiences merely indicated here and does not run away from them in what is in the last resort a culpable fear; under these circumstances he or she really has the experience, even though he or she cannot attempt to interpret it or give it a theological label. It is only in the light of this experience of God, which is the real basic phenomemon of spirituality, that theological indoctrination by Scripture and the Church's teaching acquires its ultimate credibility and existential enforceability.

As we said, this personal experience of God cannot be more precisely explained, described or—better—invoked. In so far, on the one hand, as it is the very heart of all spirituality, while we on the other hand are asking here about the peculiarities of the spirituality of the future, we shall examine some typical characteristics of this orginal human experience of God in both transcendence and grace which will belong (or belong even now) to this spirituality of the future.

We may now attempt to describe a *fourth* characteristic of the spirituality of the future which is part of a singular dialectical unity with the third, the solitary experience of God on the part of the individual. What we mean is the fraternal fellowship in which the same all-sustaining experience of the Spirit becomes possible: fraternal community as a real and essential element of the spirituality of tomorrow. By this is meant a phenomenon perhaps only slowly becoming clear, something of which we older people can speak only hesitantly and cautiously while still awaiting its future. I think that we older people did not formerly perceive what is meant by this phenomenon or at best perceived only traces of it, even though in looking back over the whole course of the history of spirituality it is possible frequently to discover something of the kind. By origin and education we older people were spiritually individualists, even though we gladly carried out the communal liturgy as our obvious, objective duty. Even though the phenomenon we mean, apparently being revived occasionally today, might also be discovered as existing in former times, on the whole the experience of the Spirit properly so called, spirituality in its true sense, "mysticism," was understood and lived as obviously a purely individual occurrence for one person and for himself alone occasionally in solitary meditation, in the individual experience of conversion, in the course of a retreat, in the monastic cell, etc.

Where was there a communal experience of the Spirit, clearly conceived, desired and experienced in a general way—as it evidently was at the Church's first Pentecost—that was not presumably an accidental local gathering of a number of individualistic mystics, but an experience of the Spirit on the part of a community as such? Such a "collective experience" cannot and of course is not meant to take away from the individual Christian his radical decision for faith coming from his solitary experience of God nor to spare him this, since human individuality and solidarity are not factors to be balanced against each other nor can they replace each other. But this is not to say that an experience of the Spirit in a small community is as such *a priori* inconceivable, even though we older clerics at least never or scarely ever experienced anything of this kind and still less attempted to practice it. Why should it not happen? Why should not younger people and clergy now and even more in the future have easier access to such a communal experience of the Spirit? Why should not—as part of the spirituality of the future—phenomena like joint consultation among

Christians, genuinely human communication in truly human and not merely external technical dimensions, events in group dynamics, etc., be embraced, exalted and sanctified by a communal experience of the Spirit of God and thus become a truly fraternal fellowship in the Holy Spirit? For this kind of thing in the last resort does not need to take place under extravagant accompanying circumstances apparently almost of a parapsychological character, such as are seen occasionally in American enthusiastic groups of the Pentecostal movements. There is no need to speak in tongues, no need to attempt to produce any phenomenon of healing by laying on of hands. In tomorrow's spirituality also sound psychology with all its critical conclusions must remain valid. But even if this factor is not naively ignored, even if not every kind of singular eruption from consciousness or subconsciousness, not every transmission of insights and feelings from one person to another, is immediately interpreted as an inspiration of the Holy Spirit, this is far from saying that there cannot be anything like a communitarian experience of the Spirit at all.

Why could there not also be jointly a really spiritual discernment of spirits? Is the prayer to the Holy Spirit at the beginning of a consultation between Christians concretely and practically merely a pious opening ceremony, after which everything goes on as otherwise at a secular board meeting with the management making use of purely rational arguments? In the spirituality of the future can there not be a kind of guru, a spiritual father giving to another person an instruction filled with the Spirit, which cannot be completely broken down into psychology, theoretical, dogmatic and moral theology? In the spirituality of the future as such, I suspect anyway that the element of a fraternal, spiritual fellowship, of a communally lived spirituality, can play a greater part and be slowly but courageously acquired and developed. I have no recipes to offer as to how exactly all this might happen. But this certainly does not mean that there are no starting points and ways of access for such a spirituality in fellowship as such, even though a critical transposition of group-dynamics and similiar occurrences into a truly spiritual happening is still to be sought, even though communal prayer as an external rite and communal Scripture reading as the study of exegesis by several people together and an instructive sermon in the traditional sense do not constitute that communal spiritual event which is here envisaged as an important element of future spirituality.

In conclusion, a *fifth* element of the spirituality of the future may be mentioned here: it will have a new ecclesial aspect. Regarded abstractly and in principle, this ecclesial character of Catholic spirituality is in itself something that must be taken for granted at all times, since we are talking about a spirituality rooted in a common faith and always to be sacramentally realized. But there is no need to deny or conceal the fact that this ecclesial aspect of a Catholic spirituality in the future will take a form somewhat different from that to which we were accustomed, especially in the last century and a half of the Pian epoch of the Church. At least once in this period the Church was the object of an almost fanatical love, regarded as our natural home, sustaining and sheltering us in our spirituality, where whatever we needed was available as a matter of course and had only to be willingly and joyfully appropriated. The Church supported us, it did not need to be supported by us.

Today all this is different. We do not see the Church so much as the *signum elevatum in nationes*, as it was acclaimed at the First Vatican Council. What we now see is the poor Church of sinners, the tent of the pilgrim people of God, pitched in the desert and shaken by all the storms of history, the Church laboriously seeking its way into the future, groping and suffering many internal afflictions, striving over and over again to make sure of its faith; we are aware of a Church of internal tensions and conflicts, we feel burdened in the Church both by the reactionary callousness of the institutional factor and by the reckless modernism that threatens to squander the sacred heritage of faith and to destroy the memory of its historical experience. The Church can be an oppressive burden for the individual's spirituality by doctrinalism, legalism and ritualism, to which true spirituality, if it really is authentic and genuine, can have no positive relationship. But none of this can dispense the spirituality of the individual from having an ecclesial character, least of all at a time when solidarity and sociability in the secular field are obviously bound in the future to increase and cannot decline. Why then could not the spirituality of the future take the form of a superior, duplicate naivety, marked by wisdom and patience, which has an ecclesial character because of the fact and in the very fact that it bears and endures as a matter of course the misery and inadequacy of the Church? Even Origen in his day knew that the Pneumatomachians could not be allowed to leave the Church, but, in patience, humility, bringing about the descent of God into the flesh of the world and the Church, and in love, would have to establish their possession of the Spirit in the concrete Church just as it is and as, in spite of all necessary and due reforms, it will remain.

This kind of attachment to the Church must be part also of the spirituality of the future. Otherwise it is élitist arrogance and a form of unbelief, failing to grasp the fact that the holy Word of God has come into the flesh of the world and sanctifies this world by taking on himself the sin of the world and also of the Church. The ecclesial aspect of the spirituality of the future will be less triumphalist than formerly. But attachment to the Church will also in the future be an absolutely necessary criterion for genuine spirituality: patience with the Church's form of a servant in the future also is an indispensable way into God's freedom, since, by not following this way, we shall eventually get no further than our own arbitrary opinions and the uncertainties of our own life selfishly caught up in itself.

Allowing for all reservations about the unforeseeability of the concrete shape of future Catholic spirituality, have I succeeded in naming some few perhaps arbitrarily selected particular characteristics of this spirituality? I can't be certain, but may I hope so?

F·A·I·T·H

3 · The Situation of Faith Today

We are living in a world in which the historical fields—formerly more or less separated culturally, socially and politically—have grown or are growing together into a unity. The result is that each has become everybody's neighbour, even though in varying degrees, and therefore also the "foreign policy" of a "regional Church" and her "home policy" have and are bound to have such an influence on each other that one can scarcely be distinguished from the other.

We are living in a world in which the general consciousness of society and of each individual is fundamentally and deeply stamped by the sciences, that is, by the historical sciences which, despite their function of summing up general trends, tend to make historical realities relative, by the autonomous, exact, and functional natural sciences and by the empirical social sciences thinking likewise almost in the same terms. Man's "metaphysical" and religious consciousness can exist openly and have the chance of a future only by entering without hesitation into a symbiosis with this scientific consciousness and its sceptical rationality and by not placing God where the scientist with his own methods would be expected to find him but cannot.

We are living in an age of the mass society where authority is regarded as merely functional, and in which, by an odd juxtaposition, freedom and interdependence have become key concepts and mutually both threaten and substantiate each other.

We are living in a world in which man in the most diverse dimensions has become the object of his own power to manipulate and change. The result is that he can scarely continue to regard himself as a finished image of God but see himself rather as *the* point of the cosmos at which its journey, guided by Utopian plans, begins into the wholly undefined future.

We are living in a world in which depth-psychology is discovering in man abysses which, on the one hand, it seeks to control, not through an appeal to the rational freedom of the subject, but through psychotechnics conceived in terms of natural science and, on the other hand, undertakes to resolve man into the anonymous forces of his biological and social origin.

We are living in a world which is a society under the direction of the mass media, where no one can know any longer who directs the media themselves.

We are living in a world in which the ideal types, in the light of which man understands his own nature, have become mobile and plural, so that in any particular cultural sphere there is no longer an ideal accepted publicly and by everyone which the individual with good will can take for granted as that which he must strive to realize in himself.

Finally, we are living in a world whose society is pluralistic: that is, in which, even in the individual historical spheres, there is no longer a society which sets up concrete guidelines for all its groups.

To describe the religio-sociological situation of the Church in the light of this summary characterization, we would have to speak of what might be called the "remnants" of the past. There are still considerable remnants of a socially constituted, traditional Christianity, a Christianity possessing a certain official status in society. This was formerly taken for granted as a social factor and therefore could be rejected only by an act of unbelief, which remained essentially private, or by a protest—which could be dangerous—against the homogeneous public opinion of society. Such remnants of traditional and socially constituted Christianity in this sense certainly still exist; we need not be ashamed of them, nor have we *a priori* in virtue of any sort of formally democratic principles the duty of demolishing them. But they *are* remnants and they are sustained by those other remnants of a secular historical period, which also persist to the present time and are, up to a point, effective in it. This former society was in fact in its secular culture also homogeneous, hierarchically structured, and with a common public opinion, which was prior to the individual's decision and shaping of his life in a much more unambiguous way than it is today. It is important therefore to see clearly that the formerly homogeneous Christian character of society as such was the result of and an element in the unity and homogeneousness of secular society, thus making it necessary for us to investigate what were the grounds and factors of this secular, social homogeneousness.

The homogeneous Christian character of our Western civilization throughout a thousand years was not the effect of a miracle of God's grace, external and additional to the intramundane causes and elements of a secular-homogeneous culture and society, nor was it really constituted by the free decision of faith on the part of all individuals, which was directed to the same end but could then be understood only as miraculous; the homogeneous Christian character of that former culture and society was simply of one piece with the homogeneousness of secular culture and society.

For the men of that passing and largely past age, this can certainly be interpreted theologically as grace, through which God placed the decision of faith—necessary also for them—before men in a particular form but without absolving them from the necessity of making it. But we certainly no longer have this grace in so far as we live and make our decision of faith in the light of the special conditions of our own time and do not live and act in the light of the remnants of a past age still effective in our time.

We cannot rely on this "grace" for today or for any forseeable future, nor do we need to do so. The "grace" is denied us of a homogeneous Christian society which itself provides for all strictly Christian patterns of behaviour and in this respect marks out a place for the decision of Christian faith and in a certain sense facilitates it. We need have no regrets for this external, (in theological terms) "medicinal" grace of faith, as it is more and more withdrawn from us with the passing away of a secular-homogeneous culture and society. For in a sense at least it was contrary to the ultimate nature of faith, since the latter means a decision for God and his call which in the last resort must be made always in a critical dissociation from the "world": that is, from the current ways of thinking and behaviour in the person's social environment.

The situation of Christians and thus of the Church today is therefore one of transition from a people's Church,* corresponding to the former homogeneous, secular society and culture, to a Church as that community of believers who critically dissociate themselves, in virtue of a personal free decision in every case, from the current opinions and feelings of their social environment, and who also find and imprint on properly theological faith its special character, perhaps precisely in and through a critical attitude to their society and its ruling forces. Against these, no fearful clinging to the remnants we have mentioned of a homogeneous secular and Christian society of former times is of any use; no return of the Church's missionary activity to the so-called "little flock" is of any use, although this flock still exists among the remnants and thus presents an opportunity —constantly shrinking—for the Church to go on in the old style, until the very last bourgeois and rural oases from these remnants of an historical epoch, moving towards its end, will have more or less entirely disappeared.

This does not mean that it is forbidden—indeed, there is an obligation —to prevent by every means an overrapid decline of whatever still exists

*There is no exact English equivalent for *Volkskirche*, which signifies the Church of the country or area, providing for its spiritual needs, just as the national or local government provides for its temporal needs.

and can be preserved of these remnants. It is of course always the Church's task to carry over that which remains forever and which has hitherto been authentically represented in these declining forms of a secular and religious culture and society, into a new form more appropriate to the present and future than the form now slowly but inevitably crumbling and thus to hand on this permanent reality authentically and effectively to the coming age.

None of this alters the fact that our present situation is one of transition from a Church sustained by a homogeneously Christian society and almost identical with it, from a people's Church, to a Church made up of those who have struggled against their environment in order to reach a personally clearly and explicitly responsible decision of faith. This will be the Church of the future or there will be no Church at all. But we believe in the permanence of the Church in the world and history, and hope for this permanence also for the history of *our* people; nevertheless we have to strive for the greatest possible number of members of the Church and thus cannot be content to set our hopes on a little heap called Church, trusting to be sheltered from the winds in history and society. That is why the clear, frank and bold acceptance of the situation is a basic question for the Church today.

The often lamented decline of Christian ways and faith is not the work or effect of sinister forces nor even primarily a decline of really necessary, saving faith (whether and to what extent there is such a thing, we can never know). It is simply the disappearance of the preconditions of that very special kind of faith and Christianity, by no means identical with the essence of faith and Christianity, which was involved in social conditions which are now disappearing and could not be assumed as permanent by Christian faith, since they are not all necessary for a true and ecclesial Christianity.

4 · Fraternal Faith

The word "fraternal" implies a relationship. It refers the individual to another person, whom he should regard as his brother. Christian brotherly love implies that in the exercise of his faith the priest in particular should approach his fellow man as brothers, and that this relationship, consciously and existentially, should form a part of his faith today. The "brother" in question is first of all the layman, and then any man, even one who does not think he believes, indeed even one who rejects faith.

This relationship, whether consciously achieved or not, belongs primarily to the nature of faith and above all to the nature of the faith of a priest. Christian faith is in fact, whether we realise it or not, an essential link with the Church, with the "faithful." It is fundamentally the acceptance of God's message, in which, quite apart from his unique call to each individual, God addresses his spiritual creatures as a whole, establishes a kingdom, a union which embraces mankind as a whole, and then manifests himself to each individual, communicating his message through the agency of man. Faith both presupposes the community and creates it; the courage to believe is always born of a pentecostal event, where many are gathered together in unity of purpose. Faith is our confidence in the personal experience of others, a conviction gained through the power of the Spirit which is at work in others, our personal experience of the Spirit given to us for the sake of others. This permanent characteristic of faith which I have sketched out should be one of the most notable characteristics of the form of faith today. It cannot be sufficiently stressed, however, that this brotherly love is not directed towards an abstract but towards our actual brother here and now, our "neighbour."

In fact we priests, in particular, run the unspoken and unconscious danger—a danger which for that reason is all the more real, ineradicable and fateful—of believing that we have a different faith from the layman. Naturally we don't consciously believe this in theory, but we constantly run the risk of living as though it were so. And today it is more difficult than it ever was to reconcile such an attitude with the real faith that is in us and in the other members of the Church. Of course we are God's messengers, heralds of his mysteries. But because of this we easily forget the real meaning of faith: that we are first and foremost believers like all the rest, believers with all the burdens, risks, dark hours, and temptations that faith involves, and the need constantly to achieve it anew. Without meaning to, we think or act as though we were God's magistrates or the civil servants in his government of the world. We see ourselves as God's experts and unconsciously it is ourselves that we are defending when we think we are defending or spreading the Church and God's work of salvation. We often act as though we had a private view of God's plans, as though everything were clear to us, whereas others had better merely do what we tell them, since we are the experts in heavenly affairs. This is why we often fail to engage in real dialogue with other Christians, why we are often not genuinely convinced that we can learn from them, from their faith and their crises of faith.

Today our faith must be a faith of brotherliness. It must be humble; it is only a real faith when it is not that of the *beati possidentes*. We must truly share our faith with others, put ourselves in the ranks of those who believe with difficulty and in spite of temptation; those who wonder what they really mean when they repeat the formulas of faith; those who ask what these formulas have to do with the real business of living; those who are tortured by the nagging suspicion that the edifice of faith is nothing more than a traditional superstructure covering up other attitudes which really control their lives, because they are unwilling to admit publicly what they really feel.

If we have a fraternal faith, we will not masquerade as what we are not, we will not bear witness to anything we are not carrying out, or trying to carry out in practice in our lives, painfully and prayerfully. Fraternal faith means a daily struggle against the routine of the theological terms and the countless moral recipes we have learned and continue to hand on to others often without having fully understood them. Theology is good, necessary, and we shall never have finished studying it. Yet how second-rate theological subtlety is where real problems are concerned, when compared with the qualities of mind or heart which we will have to rely on to solve the ultimate questions of faith. At this level we priests have no advantage over the laity. Let us be to ourselves and to the layman what we are: men who seek, who ask, who are tempted and are filled with anxiety, just as they are; men who pray: "Lord, I believe; help my unbelief!" Let us not play-act steadfastness and serenity of faith if we do not possess them. Let us not pretend that we find everything in the world of faith equally important, or equally easy to put into practice with equal fervour, simply because it is all part of God's revelation. Our brothers, the laity, are unable to do this, and we shouldn't pretend that we can manage it. We may not be selective in our formal assent, in some cases only implicit, to the things revealed by God and taught by the Church with absolute authority. But as regards the things which we put into practice explicitly and existentially, the things by which we live and to which our lives bear witness, then we can and must distinguish between degrees of concern, of practice, of intensity of witness. Let us believe as our brothers in the Church do. Let us put our trust in the fact that we as priests today do not need to believe any differently from lay people, who believe as they do because they have no alternative. Let us have a fraternal faith, sharing in the crisis of faith today; let us become involved in whatever storms faith today has to weather, for they too are sent from God. Then our message will be credible and acceptable and can be an example which gives strength to others.

What I have tentatively suggested above about a fraternal faith, is also true of our relations with those who think they do not believe and those— the distinction between the two groups is not wholly clear—who really don't believe. If Christ redemed us by suffering in himself a world empty of God, then the priest's fraternal faith must include the sharing of the contemporary crisis of faith. We cannot believe in the only proper and ultimately certain way which is required of us today, unless our faith is anchored in our time in the spiritual climate of our age.

It would be foolish and ridiculous to see the real or apparent loss of faith today, the contemporary crisis of faith, as being simply the result of human malevolence. There are objective reasons for all this: the inevitable and intrinsically valuable pluralism of culture for one thing—though we may note that it is precisely Catholic, anti-fideistic teaching that culture should spring from several sources and not, that is to say, from revelation alone. This pluralism has brought with it a variety of spiritual doctrines and trends which is almost impossible for the individual to come to terms with objectively and which, viewed subjectively, he cannot be blamed for leaving unresolved. In addition there is the increasing freedom from sociological constraint in fundamental questions of truth: this again in the final analysis is of positive value for Christianity, since a real faith requires a personal decision and a personal freedom which have too often been compromised by such sociological links, whatever supporters of the "national church" idea or of a more or less moderate *compelle intrare* may say. Finally there is another tendency, in itself proper and of positive value, but often not fully understood or integrated: the growing accent on the unworldliness of God, which is connected with fundamental changes in man's view of himself and the world today. These and many other similar reasons create a climate for faith which, although it does not justify the apparent disappearance of faith today, nevertheless makes it comprehensible and allows us to see it very often as a merely apparent reluctance to believe; a reluctance which, seen in wider historical perspective, is simply a critical adolescent stage in the faith of mankind and does not precede its decline.

What does this mean for us? As priests today we need a fraternal faith towards our apparently unbelieving brothers. How can we hope to be heralds of the gospel for them, how can we be a fruitful example of faith, how can we share the agonies of their lack of faith and pray in Christ for the grace of faith for them—how can we do this if we act, in their eyes or even in our own, as though we were different from them? We have the duty, the right, and the grace to see our faith in Christ as part of the same world that they live in, that made them what they are: an unimaginably vast world of science, continually developing; a world in which man is still searching for himself; a world of rational planning and technology; a sober rational world, where miracles do not happen every day, a world of hard and fast laws and precise calculations; a world without God, in which such elements of the miraculous as remain must be discovered and experienced afresh. They, like us, come from a world in which God's power seems almost always concealed behind the workings of the world itself; in which religion itself is subject to a thousand earthly laws; in which the inevitability and burden of death is felt as more immediate than the happiness of eternal life. Our faith too must come from this world. If we are in truth men of today, if in our faith we do not run away from ourselves out of a mistaken and misplaced fear, then our faith will face up to our situation in the world of today. This situation must affect the form of our faith, penetrate it, purify it and test it, make it humble and modest, ready to face up to this one situation again and again. Our faith must be such that the so-called unbeliever cannot deny that there stands before him a man like himself, a man of today, who does not utter the word "God" easily or unthinkingly, who does not presume to have penetrated this mystery, a modest, coolly sceptical man of today like himself, and who nevertheless—no, not *nevertheless*—who *for that very reason* believes. Our faith must be seen by unbelievers to be a fraternal faith.

But if this were always and everywhere the case, how different the form of our faith would have to be. Not different for reasons of cunning apologetical tactics, but because we ourselves aspire to a full and pure Christian faith. We must overcome all the traits of an unfraternal faith in ourselves: that bogus tone of superficial conviction, and a manner of speaking in which the message of Christianity becomes an easy remedy for all the evils of the age; habits of mind and speech which suggest we do not feel the alienation from God which characterises our age, but imply that we know everything, have understood everything, that Christianity is a formula which contains the explanation of the world rather than the grace-bearing commandment to abandon ourselves completely to the incomprehensible mystery of ineffable love. It is not without value to warn against the dangers and misunderstandings in the writings of Teilhard de Chardin. But it would be still more valuable if theologians instead concentrated on building up a balanced faith on the basis of modern knowledge and experience. This does not involve an unconditional acceptance of the way in which our contemporary non-Christian world regards human existence. Indeed it can just as well involve a fundamental transformation of modern conceptions of life. But whenever warnings against diluting the Christian message take on a clerical tone of superiority, the tone which implies: we know all about this, all these new problems are basically either a muddying of permanent clarity achieved long ago, or belong to the category of sciences which have no religious significance, then such warnings are completely unconvincing and ineffectual.

If we had a fraternal faith, always and everywhere, the "unbelievers" would not so easily be able to suspect that we were ultimately only safeguarding ourselves and the Church and bourgeois values, rather than safeguarding them, our brothers, as well as ourselves, from the descent into the depths of despair or weary resignation. May God grant us a fraternal faith, a faith which is real and true in his sight.

5 · The Simplicity of Faith

A charcteristic of faith today is its radical simplicity. In saying this, I do not intend to defend fundamentalism, nor the simplified theology of the Enlightenment, nor yet the modernist reduction of the tenets of faith simply to religious feeling interpreted naturalistically. What I do mean is the whole, permanent, revealed Christian and Catholic faith, as it has developed through the history of revelation and of dogma. Nothing more than this. But precisely here we are confronted with the question and the problem of radical simplicity and unity in our faith and in our experience of faith. Why?

Let us ignore for a moment, though it might seem to help us in our enquiry, the traditional Catholic teaching on *fides implicita*. According to this doctrine, it is not necessary to have an explicit knowledge of the entire content of faith proclaimed by the Church; indeed it may sometimes be preferable to know only a little. In fact, the limitations of man's mind and heart are such that the essentials of faith have a better chance of being realised, if faith itself is based on a few fundamental elements rather than a host of abstract concepts. Leaving this possible approach to the problem on one side, let us consider instead the content of faith, in all its developments and all its details, as it has been handed on to us in religious and theological teaching, a permanent treasure of unquestionable value. We are still left with the same problem. Why?

The courage to believe and the capacity for making faith meaningful in our lives presuppose today, more than ever before, that the content of faith is not seen as a vast, almost incalculable number of propositions which, collectively and severally, are guaranteed, from outside so to speak, by the formal authority of a God who reveals himself. Faith built up in such a way is threatened by the modern questioning —itself formal and abstract—of the reality of divine revelation quite apart from its content. A formally abstract and extrinsic view of revelation and a dogmatic positivism in matters of faith cannot, in fact, hope to combat the present threat to our faith. Man's picture of God today is of a being too transcendental, too absolute, too incomprehensible for him to accept that this God would have wished to instruct him by drawing from the inexhaustible treasure of divine knowledge an arbitrary collection of unconnected propositions, to which, had he so wished, he might well have added others; propositions which apparently have to be accepted blindly, since neither knowing nor understanding them seems to have any significance for man's life as he lives it. Modern man's picture of God and his experience of historical religion make it impossible for him to accept that apart from a very specific history, such as that of Israel or the Christian Church, or the generally unsuccessful essays of natural philosophy in the religious sphere, man's search for the ultimate meaning of existence should have produced no more than errors or unanswered questions.

In consequence, Christian faith today can only be genuinely and uninhibitedly acceptable, can only answer the real questions and the legitimate viewpoints of our time, if it show itself to be the authentic supernatural revelation of God acting in history and be seen to be God's sole, total, and fundamentally simple answer to the sole, total question which man asks of his own existence. The progress and the content of revelation, its different states of development in history, must appear in their true and genuine unity and simplicity. This is an enormous task which theology still has to carry out. It is easy enough, of course, to talk in general terms of tasks which have still not been tackled, but any more precise reference to an unsolved or urgent probem merely seems to upset ecclesiastical and theological dignitaries. Those who cling anxiously to the peaceful atmosphere of earlier times regard all the really important questions as having been solved or explained away long ago, and see those who raise them as malcontents who are wilfully confusing settled issues.

The unification and simplification of theological statements which I have in mind, and which on the whole is still lacking, should not simply stop at presenting the unity of the objective content of faith in a clearer and more radical way than before. It should also work out, on a generous scale, a kind of maieutic process to show how in religious experience, where grace is present, the reality proclaimed through the official historical channels of revelation can be realised and experienced existentially from within. For grace is given to every man and this absolute self-communication of the triune God does not lie outside existence lived effectively, consciously, and freely. Just as grace, however, cannot be understood objectively by individual reflection, neither can the individual's simple reflection on grace objectivise any particular development of Christian dogma clearly expounded in the ministerial proclamation of the word. The unified presentation of the Christian message should, therefore, offer a bold synthesis of our present-day image of the world and the basic historical situation of modern man: his caution, his common sense and realism, his distrust of big words, his feeling for the development and unification of the world, and his consciousness of the gulf between reality and high-flown sentiments.

Obviously I cannot here attempt to suggest how such a task could be carried out. But perhaps I can very tentatively indicate some guidelines. To achieve this simplification in the presentation of dogma, we must realise that fundamentally there are only three absolute mysteries in Christianity: the trinity, incarnation, and sanctifying grace; and we must be aware of the internal relationships among these mysteries and especially of the essential unity of incarnation and sanctifying grace. We must grasp that this unity is already immanent in the trinitarian economy, since in Christ and his grace we have God's absolute communication to man. We must show that man is absolutely open, radically accessible to this absolute mystery of God; we must make sure it is understood, in the unity of the exterior message and the interior experience of grace, that this absolute mystery brings man absolute forgiveness and love by its complete and radical communication of itself; that God is not in fact remote, silent and unheeding, even though he remains a mystery and only becomes real to us in this communication of himself. Finally it is essential that the *a posteriori* christology of Jesus of Nazareth should be joined to an *a priori* existential christology of the humanity of God, based on metaphysical anthropology. This christology would explain how God's absolute and definitive revelation involves the divinised humanity of the God-Man, and how the absolute saviour and the definitive eschatological acceptance by humanity of God's self-communication necessarily leads us to the teaching of Chalcedon. If this were done, a great deal would have been achieved, in my opinion, towards a simplification of the dogmatic conception of the content of revelation. I am, of course, very conscious that what I propose may at first sight—but only at first sight—appear to be even more difficult to understand than traditional dogmatic statements.

What Christian dogma teaches over and above this lies on the social plane, the plane of historical accidents, of liturgy and cult. But our contemporaries are not worried by the fact that this absolute religion, historically the most highly developed religion, has great richness and complexity in these dimensions and carries both the inheritance and the burden of its past. They are conditoned to accept such historical facts without undue concern. If only the essentials of Christianity, everything in it that has been freely ordained and revealed by God, could be seen to be divinely simple and self-explanatory. Surely the one thing which man finds immediately comprehensible is that the absolute mystery of God is the foundation of his own existence, and that the easiest and at once the most difficult existential act is the acceptance of this ineffably loving and forgiving presence. This is the essence of Christianity. The history of revelation is itself nothing more than the history, guided by God, of the progressive awakening of man's acceptance of God, whose self-giving reaches its (objectively and subjectively) supreme climax in Christ. On this basis man today could come to realise more clearly that Christianity is not one of many competing world religions, but the fulfilment of them all. Only if, in one and the same fundamental theological movement, contemporary man is made aware of all this, will he be psychologically and existentially able, in the concrete reality of his thinking, to accept the "proof" that God revealed himself absolutely in Jesus Christ and not in the other higher religions, however important these may be.

This is perhaps a good place to clarify my attempt at describing one of the essential characteristics of faith today or at any rate to present it in another perspective. In our own life of faith, in our prayers, meditations and sermons, we often fail to see the wood for the trees, as far as the content of faith is concerned. For this reason, our knowledge of the really decisive, fundamental experiences of Christian life is neither precise nor profound. To find deeper existential roots for our faith in the real foundations of our existence must necessarily mean a simplification and concentration of the content of faith, not through rejecting or discarding particular propositions, but through gaining a new perspective on them, unifying them and establishing priorities valid for our Christian life.

It is, for example, not easy to know what prayer is and how it happens. To overcome a feeling of existential disorientation, the feeling that prayer is nothing but auto-suggestion; to believe it is meaningful for a miserable creature to talk into the endless desert of God's silence; to grasp that the word "father" is not the projection into the infinite of childish, subjective concepts which aim at a prerational domination of his existence, but is authorised by a God who, working in everything, liberated his creatures to his own freedom and love; to do more than understand all this theoretically, to realise it existentially both before and after prayer, along with the renewal of all the natural prerequisites of meditation, the evocation of the deepest levels of our humanity—to achieve all this necessitates innumerable efforts, experiences, and new beginnings.

Yet instead of concentrating, in our own and other's lives, on these fundamental, extremely simple aspects of Christian existence, on the simple objective realities, all-important in the world of faith, which are an essential part of these aspects, we rush into explicit forms of dogmatic development, on which modern man is quite incapable of basing his faith.

Sensibilities must be spared, and I must, therefore, refrain from comparing the complications of modern theology with the simplicity of the Christianity it is ultimately talking about. Let me illustrate what I mean by an example. Suppose a priest was given the task of explaining to a layman—not a nun or a pious old lady, but a realist or positivist, an engineer or a professor of science, for example—that he, this engineer or professor, had already experienced supernatural grace, that he necessarily continues to experience it, and that this mysticism is one of the normal and natural things in Christian experience which no one can avoid, even if he overlooks it or cannot understand it or sets it aside as something he does not want to think about. I should be prepared to bet that the majority of the clergy would give up the task even before starting, indeed before they had even faced up to the obviously open question of how far such an attempt could in fact have any success with the engineer or professor. I would almost be prepared to bet that many of the clergy, if they were honest with themselves, would have to admit that they themselves had never had such an experience, that the world of faith was something that had been taught to them from "outside," full of concepts bearing no relation to reality. By this admission, these members of the clergy would prove, not that they had in fact never had such an experience (God forbid!), but that the religious life of grace as the foundation of existence is as much a mystery and puzzle to them as it is to the majority of laymen. For most laymen a Christianity which is extrinsic and conceptually pluralistic, which is present as grace at the very foundation of their existence but of which they are not fully aware, can scarcely be anything more than a system that has been learned, a weak ideology which disintegrates in the cold and brutal realities of everyday life, unless it is propped up from outside by tradition or sociological structures and continues a superficial existence. And even for us priests, if you will pardon my frankness, such a faith would merely eke out an existence, sustained simply by the psychological and sociological conditions of our clerical vocation, which are no different from those of a non-Christian priest.

If the objection is raised that behind this institutional Christianity and its purely conceptual teachings which survive in spite of everything, we can discern the all-powerful grace of God supporting the faithful and their priests—then I can only ask that this obviously right answer be logically followed up. For this grace will then be seen to be the grace which, even unconsciously, we truly experience, that grace which through God's universal saving power is always and everywhere at work, the grace of ineffable, silent access to the mystery of God communicating himself in love and forgiveness. And this experience of grace, this indefinable "mysticism" of everyday life, will be seen to be the essence of Christianity and therefore one of the starting points of fundamental theology. If this experience is deliberately and consciously invoked, our conceptual and institutional Christianity, which of course is and remains something essential, will for the first time be realised in its true simplicity and unity.

6 · The Certainty of Faith

For the moment we do not want to get involved in the difficult episte-mological question of how the truth and certainty of a conviction have to be distinguished and yet are closely connected. The only thing we are in-terested in here is the realisation that there are certainties which can be doubted and that a person simply cannot live without them, and also that such (doubted) certainties are always supported by a personal decision in favour of them, but that this is no argument against the real certainty and truth of the beliefs concerned. That, for example, selfless love makes sense, can only be discovered in choosing it. This does not mean that the meaningfulness of such love is a subjective invention which one can just as well do without.

In the realm of existence there are realities which can be discovered to be real, "true" and "certain" only in being chosen. As long as somebody refuses this free agreement to this reality and can only talk theoretically about it, he or she will be blind to it. It can be proved, however, that there necessarily exist realities which can only show themselves as they really are when we entrust ourselves to them. We therefore cannot say that this or that is non-existent or that its existence is doubtful, because it does not impose its existence on us against our reluctance. The believer and the unbeliever must not demand a certainty of faith, which would be independent of such a free surrender to the reality of faith. There is, of course, no such faith. It canot exist, because the reality which it offers does not really mean a particular item of reality, but the whole of reality in general and of human existence; and this whole naturally cannot be aimed at and defined from a point outside of itself.

Regarding the certainty of faith, which derives from the nature of faith as a trusting and open relationship to the whole of reality, as subjec-tive does not make faith and unbelief equally valid possibilities between which we can just choose. A free rejection of a positive attitude of trust in reality is in general the result of a secret acceptance which is prior to freedom, and so the unbeliever (in this general sense of an ultimate basic attitude) is caught in an insoluble contradiction with himself.

For the moment, it is only important to accept that freedom and cer-tainty in matters of faith do not contradict each other, provided that the believer understands that no certainty can be expected which would be independent of such a decision of freedom. Where freedom admits coura-geously the whole of reality even in its incomprehensibility it has the light of its certainty in itself, even though it cannot take it to the further point of making this preliminary act of trust in an ultimate and all-embracing meaning of reality. The question can be at most, how to bring persons who think they are living without hope in such sceptical doubt to such an affirmation of ultimate trust. Of course, such a free certainty cannot be taught. It can only be pointed out to people that their sceptical reserve, because everything seems to lack ultimate certainty, still lives in its secret depths by an implicit acceptance which has to be appropriated in freedom. Even such sceptical reserve still comes from an implicit assumption of a distinction between truth and error, good and bad, above and below. If this were not so, there would be no possibility of an explanation of sceptical neutrality.

The statement that no clear distinction is possible is again the statement that things do not simply merge arbitrarily. It is an expression of pain at an inability, which would be completely inconceivable if indeterminacy and uncertainty had the last word. Darkness can only be perceived by an eye which was created for light. The believer's essential optimism will make him or her say that in the life of every human being a particular situation will always arise which forces him or her to make a choice for a radical acceptance or a radical rejection, and in doing so emerge from this featureless greyness in which he or she thinks and lives.

Believers will even have the quiet hope that the result will in fact be an acceptance, because they cannot imagine a freedom, created by God, with all the inexorable radicality of a choice between two possibilities, in which an acceptance by freedom did not have a much greater chance than a rejection. In the end there is no neutrality, and an acceptance of reality comes more directly from God than a rejection. In reflecting on certainty in faith we have worked—and we have no wish to conceal this —with a concept of "faith" according to which faith is nothing other than the positive and unconditional acceptance of one's own existence as meaningful and open to a final fulfilment, which we call God. It must, of course, be shown later in more detail that such a belief is already the original seed of the Christian faith and, vice versa, that Christian faith is nothing but the pure and healthy development of this very seed.

However, since the second enquiry casts doubt on faith by means of a general and diffuse doubt of any certainty in any propositions of whatever kind, we must stress here that such a general scepticism which seems to be prior to any specific act of faith is really already unbelief, and that its opposite, the courage to accept absolutely that existence has meaning, is already faith.

7 · Baptism

Baptism is sacramental entry into the Church and thereby into full Christian life. Hence we really only understand baptism to the extent that we understand Christianity and Church. And so if we would explain baptism, strictly speaking we should have to speak of Christianity and the Church. But what it means to be a Christian in the Church cannot be adequately examined in a brief space, and so what we are about to say here on the subject of baptism will necessarily be fragmentary and but a rather arbitrary selection of things that properly should be said.

According to Christian teaching, as attested in the New Testatment and onward, baptism is the sacrament of faith and justification. Hence it mediates that life which God, through his self-communication (or indwelling, or sealing with the Holy Spirit of God), bestows upon human beings in order to render them suited for eternal life in immediate union and community with God. In order to explain what baptism is, therefore, one would actually have to speak of God, his eternal life, and his self-communication to human beings through the gift of the Holy Spirit. This, however, would no longer be simply the doctrine of one particular sacrament (as efficacious sign of grace), but the doctrine of the Christian person as a whole.

Let us, then, take our considerations in another direction—one in which, for that matter, we shall perhaps deal better and more comprehensibly with the major difficulty about baptism that disturbs so many people in the Church today. People ask: What is the purpose of baptism, especially infant baptism, when we know, or may at least hope, that God leads every person of good will to eternal salvation—hence the non-baptized, the "pagans," and, yes, even atheists if they are true to their conscience? In order to make our way through this difficulty, we must entertain certain preliminary considerations.

The human being is a single and yet multiple entity. His or her unity is the unity of a plurality of elements, which, while distinct from one another, yet form a single unity—and form it in such a way that the differences in this oneness mutually condition one another. None comes to its proper perfection and completion without the others. This is a very abstract way of putting it, but what is meant is something we constantly observe in human affairs. The love of one person for another, for example, is, as inner intentionality, distinct from a look, a gesture, an expression of tenderness, and so on; and yet in certain circumstances this inner sentiment and disposition of love can only attain its own adequate reality when it is expressed and "embodied" in just such a physical gesture or deed. Inward solidarity among human beings is a matter of intentionality, a thing of the mind and heart; and yet in some circumstances it is fully and completely itself only when these human beings sit down at table and take a meal together. In such instances and countless others, we notice that there is a "within" and a "without" to the human being— which are different and yet which go together. The "within" attains total and unequivocal completeness and fulfillment only when "epiphanized," brought to manifestation and embodied, in the "without." The "within" can conceivably be present by prevarication, to be sure, as in the kiss of Judas: the "within" which should be being actualized and brought to light, brought to evidence, by the "without" may not actually be present. But when a human being "executes" the "without" sincerely and willingly, the "without" can actually bring the "within" into being. How many people, for example, have inwardly understood what is meant by prayer by actually falling on their knees? Love itself, love as utterly inward reality, can actually increase and grow through loving behavior on the part of one person toward another. Let us presuppose a ready grasp of these brief considerations, then, and ask what all of this can mean for an understanding of baptism.

Let us begin simply and confidently with the datum that God loves each and every human being, has called him or her by name, and has bestowed himself upon this person, with all his reality, both as inmost strength and as goal, in free love, from the first moment of his calling this person into being. God always offers himself as end, and simultaneously as moving force and thrust toward this end, to each human being and his or her freedom, even though this human freedom has the capacity to shut itself off from this ever-present offer, this offer impossible to be rid of—somewhat as a human being has the freedom bestially to contradict his or her inescapable nature as a spiritual, personal being, but cannot refuse to *be* such a being.

This ever-present tender of the divine life is available to the human being, then, always and everywhere from God's side (whether or not the human being knows this), because God has willed to cast, to impose, the totality of humanity upon the God-Man. Global humanity has been taken up and accepted by God in the one Jesus who was crucified and who rose again. From this point of view, this altogether inward offer of grace on God's part, from which offer no human being is ever excepted, is essentially "Christian." But this altogether inward condition of being the object of grace, which is true of every human being, seeks to become embodied, seeks to come to manifestation, in all the dimensions of this human being, as divine and "Christian" reality—as a reality which intends the individual as irreplaceably this individual and a member of global humanity as well.

To be sure, this inner bestowal of grace upon the human being also obtains without the outward embodiment and manifestation demanded by its own inner dynamic. Christian faith has always known this and speaks, for example, of a "baptism of desire," which "justifies" a person—bestows the divine life—even before the baptism of water. It speaks of "perfect contrition," by which a human being accepts, in freedom, the divine life, which has never ceased to be present as an offer, even before reception of the sacrament of penance. But this is not to say that this embodiment, this coming-to-evidence, of the divine grace through the sacraments of baptism or penance is something lying within the area of the human being's free choice. This divine life in the grace of the Holy Spirit seeks, for its own part, to express itself in an embodiment and to come to manifestation in the societal realm of the community of the faithful—called Church. Anyone freely and culpably repudiating this tendency on the part of the divine life to win embodiment and emerge in societal manifestation renounces not only this embodiment process as such but the very offer of God's grace lying at its heart. It is as if I were to say that I do indeed love so-and-so in my heart but were to refuse him a specific service of which he stands in need, a service in which this inward love ought to be expressed—giving as my excuse that, "after all, that's different from inward love." No, one who denies the service also denies the inner love, even though the service and the inner love are not the same.

Thus it is with baptism. In anyone who does not know of baptism or cannot receive it, the divine life lives nonetheless, in the inmost heart of his or her being, as an offer, an overture—or indeed as actually received and accepted in freedom, if he or she in some fashion (perhaps not at all in an expressly reflective fashion) accepts this divine overture in what we call faith, hope, and love. (These theological virtues can subsist in an altogether unreflective way—in an unselfish love of neighbor and in other decisions in which one enters into, abandons oneself to, this divine love.) But when a person lives in a situation in which the embodying and societal manifestation of this divine life called baptism is possible, then he or she may not say that he or she indeed wishes the divine life and simultaneously decline its "evidentiation," its emergence to manifestation. It would be as if someone refused to perform a concrete deed of love and yet maintained that he or she does love. It would be as if a person did not wish to mature as a human being on the grounds that, after all, he or she was already a human being even as an embryo, and therefore now renounces any further development of his or her concrete humanity.

Baptism is the evidentiation, the emergence to manifestation, of the divine life inasmuch as it is always Christian life and life in the Church. In the measure, then, that this embodiment of the divine life is an ecclesial reality, it does not lie within the free choice of the individual how he or she would happen to like to shape this embodiment of the divine life of grace in himself or herself. He or she must will and execute it in the mode prescribed by the ecclesial community. And this mode is precisely baptism by water, accompanied by the invocation of the Trinitarian God. Anyone who wishes to execute a legally effective will, so as to be able to bequeath his or her estate to a freely chosen heir, must do so precisely in a testament that is valid according to prevailing societal norms.

Now, however, two further matters await our attention. These are two questions that arise in the form of objections to what we have been saying. The first objection might be stated as follows. In seeing baptism as manifestation, hence as sign, of the inward divine tender of grace, the *sacramental causality* of baptism with regard to grace would seem more difficult to maintain than if the sacramental action were simply to be considered as the cause of the grace of baptism. The second difficulty regards infant baptism.

Thus far we have been examining baptism as the historical and social manifestation of the divine grace in which God personally bestows himself upon the human being, in the latter's inmost center, offering himself to that human being's freedom as energy of faith in, hope in, and love for God. In this view, baptism would seem to be but the proclamation, the announcement, of a reality which actually subsists independently of that proclamation or announcement. But Church teaching speaks of an "efficient causality" of the sacraments, hence of baptism, with respect to grace. Are not these two propositions mutually inconsistent? Or, on the contrary, is it meaningful to say that the formality of baptism as proclamatory sign of grace and its efficient causality of that grace actually condition each other mutually, so that baptism is the cause of grace *because* it is its sign? Evidently, one may not introduce an arbitrary concept of "cause" into this discussion; rather one must entertain a defensible and reasonable conception of the causality in question here. Scholastic theology itself heeds this same point when it says that in baptism God himself is the proper and sole creative cause of divine grace, and that baptism may only be thought of as an "instrumental cause," whereupon theologians propose the most diverse theories to explain how this instrumental causality of the sacraments is precisely to be conceptualized.

That our point of departure for an understanding of baptism through its character as a sign may not be dismissed *a priori* is evident from the following consideration. When an adult comes to baptism, in order to be able to receive the sacrament worthily he or she must already have faith, hope, and love and this love must emphatically, at least ordinarily, be conceived of as love of God himself for his own sake—"perfect love," then, as distinguished from "reverential love." Now this being the case, the adult in question, according to the common doctrine of the Church and its theologians, must be reckoned as coming to baptism already "justified" —that is, as having already accepted the divine life that has been offered. He or she must be accounted as approaching baptism as a holy child of God through the indwelling of the Holy Spirit. At least in this case, then, the candidate for baptism already possesses what baptism is supposed to bestow by way of causality: the grace of justification.

Theologians attempt to solve this difficulty by arguing that the baptism of this already justified person causally augments the grace that he or she already possesses, as well as adding something that this justified baptismal candidate does not yet possess (for example, sociojuridical incorporation into the visible Church—the "baptismal character"). Surely this elucidation seems somewhat forced, but we cannot stop to examine it here.

Let us proceed, returning to a consideration that we proposed at the very beginning of our discussion. Let us consider what occurs when one person already loves another person with all his or her heart, but then—however difficult it may be, for one reason or another, to do so—declares to that other person the whole force of this love in actual words. The words will now be the expression and manifestation of the subject's love, of course— but at the same time, his or her love will also come to actualization, in all its intensity and definitiveness, via these words. The love would not be completely the same were it not to be expressed in this, its declaration. These words, then, are not only the sign of this love but surely its cause, as well. For this love has been actualized through its declaration, however distinct the two may be in themselves.

Now let us apply this reflection to the baptism of our already justified candidate. He or she brings to baptism the divine gift of grace already received and accepted. But this grace is precisely something which seeks to declare itself in this baptismal action—historically (by embodiment in space and time) and socially (in the Church)—and in so declaring itself, come into its own full being, become actually present in the dimensions of the candidate's "embodiment" and "sociality" as well. Baptism is the effect of grace in the sense that this grace fully realizes, fully actualizes itself through baptism. And in this same measure, baptism is also the cause of grace. (Thus the elucidation above, that the baptism of an already justified candidate "increases his or her sanctifying grace," is so far correct; only it conceives of this increase as a quasi-quantitative one, an addition, and fails to grasp that the "increase" is the realization, the self-actualization, attained by the single grace through the act of positing itself in its full reality through its sacramental sign.) If we view the matter in this fashion, we can understand the proposition that the sacrament is the cause of grace precisely *as* sign. In the sacraments, the note of sign and the note of cause, correctly understood, do not constitute a parallelism, but a compenetration.

Finally, we must consider certain questions pertaining to *infant baptism*. Infant baptism, which was a matter of course in the Church for centuries, is now disparaged as (allegedly) having no foundation in the New Testament and running counter to the personal character of conversion, of becoming a Christian. The Catholic Church, however, holds unrelentingly to the basic defensibility and meaningfulness of infant baptism, even if today that baptism can no longer be maintained as obligatory with the same degree of clarity and certitude as formerly. On what basis, then, can we say that infant baptism is altogether meaningful, and hence ought not to be declined by parents on grounds that conversion to Christ and incorporation into the Church ought to be left to the child's free decision, and therefore that he or she should not be baptized before coming of age?

In the first place, what baptism embodies and declares in a social context is in no way subject to the human being's free choice and determination. God's love, in which God himself becomes the innermost dynamism of the human being and his and her history, is always antecedent to the human being and his or her decision-in-freedom—the decision which asks itself precisely whether it will accept the challenge of God's love or whether it will not—whether it wills to become this human being's salvation or condemnation through his or her free decision. Like it or not, we are asked the question; how we answer is another matter altogether. And it is baptism that publishes this inexorable condition of being addressed, being questioned by the holy love of God. Born into the world, we can of course accept our humanity or hate it. But we cannot dismiss it from the face of the earth. It is a given. Human freedom is always and inescapably a reaction to an external initiative. It never simply posits an originary act in a vacuum. What comes to manifestation in baptism is what the human being inexorably and inevitably is: the creature loved by God and destined for the reception of the divine life. Baptism is thus not an infringement on human freedom, for that freedom is always a responding freedom, an answer to God and the world, a freedom that never has the first word.

At this point the following objection might be raised. The human being's inescapable God-relatedness is not the only thing that is brought to expression in baptism. Membership in the visible Church is bestowed as well—and in this respect, surely a person ought to retain freedom of decision.

Here we would answer: The Church understands itself in its proper being as the historical and societal manifestation of *all* human beings' condition as called by God—and therefore views and experiences Church membership simply as the unquestionably appropriate coming-to-manifestation of this condition of each human being as addressed by God. It may well be—we cannot take up the question in these pages—that in former times the Church drew conclusions from the Church membership of the baptized that are problematic. For example, it concluded that it had a right to apply coercive measures in the case of the baptized that it understood it did not have with respect to the unbaptized. But such conclusions are no longer drawn by the Church. Today the Church recognizes the same freedom of conscience for the baptized as for the unbaptized. This difficulty, then, no longer arises from Church membership. Baptism is merely the self-evident manifestation of every human being's orientation to the Church, and thus involves no preemption of a decision that of course must be taken only in freedom.

There is one more thing to be considered, however, concerning infant baptism. It is something which, in our regions of the world, is obscured by the circumstance that we celebrate infant baptism very frequently and adult baptism very infrequently. Since baptism is the efficacious coming-to-evidence of a divine love that communicates God himself to the human being and not some created good—it follows that baptism of its very nature, of its very being, will be a call to the human being to accept this love. One can therefore say with confidence that infant baptism attains to its proper meaning and full realization only when the human being actually accepts—in faith, hope, and love—this love, God's love, thus proffered.

We may say, then, that infant baptism attains its full meaning and end only in the *adult*. Whether the adult accepts God's self-offering made to him or her as a child simply through an ordinary Christian life in love and fidelity, or repeatedly as an adult ratifies his or her infant baptism expressly as well, is ultimately of no decisive account. In either case the ultimate and decisive acceptance of one's baptism in personal freedom obviously occurs throughout the totality of a human and Christian life in all its length and breadth. But of course it is surely a good and wholesome thing expressly to hark back, in faith and trust, to the baptism one has received as one's life was just beginning. The liturgy of the Paschal Vigil affords us an opportunity to do this by renewing our baptismal vows. But the same thing can be done in a Christian's life independently of official liturgy. He or she will simply look back over his or her life, knowing that this life has been accompanied and borne up by God's power and love from its beginning, and that God in his loving providence has so disposed that this love for him be testified to corporeally and expressly in baptism at the beginning of life. Thus the Christian can render the event of his or her baptism present and endorse it again and again. The Second Letter to

Timothy (1:6-7) says: "I remind you to stir into flame the gift of God bestowed when my hands were laid on you. The Spirit God has given us is no cowardly spirit, but rather one that makes us strong, loving, and wise" (1:6-7). These words were written concerning the conferral of an ecclesiastical office. But surely every Christian may understand them as referring to his or her baptism as well. After all, in that baptism each Christian has received the assignment of keeping this divine fire alive in his or her heart. One ought therefore to celebrate a baptismal renewal from time to time in one's own "chamber," as the Gospel says.

8 · Confirmation

The problem posed for the history of dogma by the relationship between the sacraments of baptism and confirmation need not be broached here. A careful and candid examination of this problem would lead us into the question of the authority of the post-apostolic Church with respect to the sacraments. This examination cannot be undertaken here. Nor would it have a great deal of importance for the concrete spirituality of a contemporary Catholic. However, we may certainly say, simply from the history of the sacraments and the teaching of the Church, that these two sacraments are very intimately bound up with each other, notwithstanding the considerable time generally lapsing between the conferral of these two sacraments in the Western Church. Accordingly, Christian piety, in its search for the sacramental roots of the Christian life, may confidently consider them as a unit: Baptism is the sacrament of the foundational communication of the Spirit, and confirmation is the perfecting of baptism.

The liturgy of the Easter Vigil shows that the spirituality of the Church is quite familiar with a so-called baptismal renewal, in which a believing, hoping, and loving human being accepts anew, that is, once more reduces to concrete actuality, the fact that the eternal, holy God has bestowed himself not only in the hidden recesses of human existence but also in actual historical and societal—ecclesial—palpability, transparency, and irrevocability, both as the human being's goal and as his or her power to reach that goal. The confirmed Christian surely can and should incorporate the sacrament of confirmation, as well, into such a baptismal renewal, even without reflecting upon any differences there may be in the effects of the two sacraments expressly or in detail. After all, God gives his Holy Spirit as the remission of guilt and as justification in baptism itself. Baptism, then, is truly the sacrament of the communication, the conferral, of the Spirit; and confirmation is properly and strictly the sacrament of the "sealing" with the Holy Spirit.

To be sure, in order to confer some degree of intelligibility on the distinction between these two sacraments, theological tradition is at pains to identify effects of confirmation that are not predicated of baptism with the same degree of explicitation. This is entirely justifiable. But it does not imply that these different series of effects, however legitimately distinguished, may be thought of as separate and divided and in no way overlapping or coinciding. No, all such mutually distinguishable effects correspond to differentiations in the one single divine bestowal of grace upon the human being in function of the multidimensionality of his or her nature and tasks. Hence, on the one hand, they are all basically given together in baptism, and on the other hand they come to clear expression, come to more differentiated manifestation, in the other sacraments. This is the basis on which we can correctly and confidently speak in one breath of a "renewal of our baptism and confirmation," and yet can cite specific effects of confirmation. When we give prominence to specific effects of confirmation, we are always explicitating something having its roots in baptism.

Theology sees the specific meaning of confirmation primarily in the ecclesio-societal dimension. Through confirmation, the Christian is enabled and obligated, in a special degree, to bear witness in ecclesial and secular public life to his or her faith in Jesus Christ as the eternal God's irrevocable self-bestowal. Acts 1:8 can certainly be applied to confirmation in a meaningful way: "You will receive power when the Holy Spirit comes down on you; then you are to be my witnesses in Jerusalem, throughout Judea and Samaria, yes, even to the ends of the earth." The grace of confirmation imparts a share in the messianic mission of Christ and in the permanent prophetic and charismatic gift of Pentecost to the Church. Confirmation, we say, strengthens a person for the spiritual combat that he or she must wage, not only interiorly but also in arduous opposition to the godlessness of the world in which he or she must live. Thus confirmation, in a special way, is the sacrament of the royal priesthood of all Christians, through which all Christians are enabled and obligated to extend Christ's mission to the world.

All of this should be taken into account in a "confirmation renewal." Confirmation makes explicit the fact that each of us is co-responsible for our neighbor, even our furthest neighbor. Each of us is the servant and minister of other people's salvation. One can refuse to carry out this mission and task, but one cannot do away with it. The "indelible mark" stamped upon us in confirmation, as in baptism, comports an irrevocable mission to testify to others of God's salvific grace. This testimony to faith in no way primarily implies missionary work consisting in the formal proclamation of the Word or other official Church activity. First of all, a Christian must bear witness in his or her Christian life not by words, but by deeds of unselfishness, fidelity, and love—but all in such a way that it may be transparent from these deeds, to the honest observer, that this Christian activity simply could not be accomplished, as far as its ultimate intelligibility is concerned, except it be supported and borne up by that nameless incomprehensibility we call God and his grace.

Again and again a Christian will be in a situation in which he or she will be called upon to show unselfish loyalty and love such as one only manages when one abandons oneself unconditionally to the God who has irrevocably abandoned himself to us in Jesus Christ crucified and risen. (Whether our Christian accomplishes this deed of abandonment expressly or implicitly is another question.) In such deeds, then, the Christian should, as he or she is enabled and obligated to do through confirmation, first of all bear witness to the eternal promise to which we have fallen heir.

A human being always shares a common life with his or her neighbor not only through deed but through communication as well. Always and inescapably, human life is conducted by words. Even antecedent to any official proclamation by the Church through those having an official charge to this effect, a testimonial to God and his grace through the deeds of one's life will always contain an element of verbal testimony. A Christian life that sought to seal itself up in an absolutely hidden interiority would necessarily smother to death and is, when all is said and done, impossible. Consequently, the testimony to God's claim on the human being that is supported by the grace of confirmation is evidently a testimony that must be proclaimed by all Christians through word as well as work —always in accordance with each person's particular life situation, always in accordance with each person's particular capabilities. But a Christianity that is simply silent, a Christianity consisting in simple, mute interiority, does not exist.

In our confirmation renewal, then, we ought to ask ourselves, again and again, whether we are bearing witness to him whom we seek ever and again to receive and accept in faith, hope, and love as our eternal life. We hear today of something called "political theology." This is a good name for a theology that seeks to explicitate and clarify the social dimension of all the realities of faith. The grace of confirmation is the strength to take cognizance of a Christian's responsibility for Church and society. Truly, then, confirmation is expressly ordered to the "political" responsibility of the Christian as Christian. Recalling our confirmation means reminding ourselves that a Christian may not treat his or her Christianity simply as a "privatistic" matter of personal interiority.

9 · Institutional Piety

Every existing form of piety presented to my choice, as it were, from outside, may be considered under the aspect of the externally inflicted law. It matters comparatively little whether this is strictly a commandment of God or the Church, or only a custom, a tradition or suchlike. All these things agree in this that they confront me with something which is already there, that they at least appear to limit my spirituality which is obviously the most intimate realization of my freedom. Now if personal freedom is basically a unique gift of God, what we call spirituality must have an inner connection with it. Hence the institutional norms of the Church and the freedom which is realized most decisively in the spiritual life cannot be in complete mutual harmony from the beginning.

Freedom Related to the Situation

First of all it must be stated that in Catholicism there is certainly something like a will to the law, even within the sphere of piety. However, as a social being man lives necessarily in community, and though he is the subject of radical freedom, he is yet not its abstract subject, confronted, as it were, with the variety of its indifferent possibilities. Even where we act in our innermost being, claiming the ultimate freedom of committing ourselves we act always within a pre-existing sphere. We are given a certain time which is not of our choice, we have inherited a certain psychological make-up, or we are placed within a definite historical situation. Hence freedom cannot ultimately consist in retiring into a sphere not affected by all these given conditions, nor can it be realized in mere opposition to them. I can only protest against what exists, not for example, against the government of a Herod III or Herod IV. In other words, whether we protest or revolt—and even revolution can be necessary, indeed it can be the sacred duty of a Christian in certain circumstances—we are always still imprisoned within our own concrete situation. The essence of freedom, therefore, may also consist in accepting given conditions in order slowly to change them. Thus—however the philosophers of history from the Stoics to Nietzsche may explain it—there must be such a thing as *amor fati* in its proper sense in which freedom finds its innermost essence. This may also be rightly applied to the social and historical ecclesial conditions of Christian piety insofar as this is realized in freedom.

The Norm as Freedom's Way to Itself

Moreover, we are not simply free but must become so. That truth which is mine and which comes wholly from within is not yet simply what I have only accepted in the formal freedom of Yes or No. I am only on the way to this my actual truth and it is the work of a lifetime to find and accept myself in freedom. For I suppress much of my actual truth, I do not want to admit it; I am perhaps in an ulitmate attitude of protest without noticing it; despite all my talk about the love of one's neighbour I may even be the greatest egoist without realizing it. All I am meant to become may perhaps appear to me as rigid legalism. I can therefore achieve my true freedom only by a change in my given personality which delivers it from the selfishness in which it is imprisoned. And this may be applied also to the piety which appears as legalistic. Hence even in the realm of piety there must be a will to the law.

All those fastings laws, religious customs, devotions (which I may perhaps hate) and whatever else belongs to parish life and hits me as "law" is not necessarily wrong only because I reject it in a protest which is very problematical. Perhaps I may not even have understood some of these things, perhaps they are simply demanded by love for the others, for the Church, which means a certain member of the Church at a certain point of time.

What we should like to emphasize is this: There is a right institutional and legal piety which rightly makes demands on us in the ecclesiastical regulations about the liturgy, fasting, Sunday Mass, etc. It is by no means clear that only that form of the Mass is most marvellous and personally most authentic which disregards all the precepts of the Church including those of the Second Vatican Council. This is no vindication of Christian freedom, however strongly some people may believe it to be.

Christian Spirituality as Permanently Dependent on Its Own History

The whole heritage of the Christian tradition of spirituality belongs, of course, also to this institutional material which is offered as a possibility or even as a demand. Why should we replace a two-thousand-year-old Christian practice of meditation and asceticism by what we have read somewhere about Zen Buddhism and Yoga? It is certainly a rewarding task to synthesize Eastern and Christian piety and ascetism. But it is surely naive to esteem *a priori* psychotherapy and the practices of Yoga more highly than the traditional Christian devotions. If a person does not understand or like the rosary, for example, he is perfectly free, as a Christian, not to say it; yet for me it is a very wonderful thing, and it is my own private experience that it is said also by people of whom one would not believe it. There are, of course, also many literary treasures of spirituality, for example even today we may well recommend reading St. Augustine, St. John of the Cross, Teresa of Avila or any well-edited selection of mystical texts.

Certainly, modern critical exegesis is necessary and valuable. But the light of God and the Holy Spirit were active in the Church long before biblical criticism. A true theologian ought to prove his education also by planning within five or ten years to acquire an idea of the history of spirituality by reading Gregory of Nyssa, Augustine, the great medieval mystics, Francis de Sales or Bérulle and Charles de Foucauld, to mention only a few names. A true piety which respects the "law" might well be occupied also in this way.

The Free Acceptance of a Spiritual Order

We must, moreover, consider what I should like to call self-appointed institutional piety. Spirituality is impossible without a certain order, and this applies to lay people as well as to nuns and Jesuits brought up on the Ignatian Exercises. True spirituality does not consist in pious feelings, because we are perhaps just now in love or have some sorrow. This is at best a foretaste of the real thing, which must bear fruit in a truly personal decision affecting the whole life. This means, to use a provocative expression, that there must be a certain system in the spiritual life. It may be quite modest, corresponding to the daily life of the individual, and can be very different for the parish priest or the layman from what it is in a religious house. It may also be quite different from the spiritual system of the third orders or the Marian congregations. The details do not matter, what is important is that there can be no vigorous spirituality without discipline, without a certain hardness against oneself, without a plan, without making demands on oneself also in the religious sphere and if one does not feel like it at the moment. Every Buddhist monk would laugh at us if we thought these things were unnecessary for the serious practice of spirituality. It would be the same as if somebody wanted to become a professional pianist without practising ten hours each day for six or eight years. How far we shall advance depends on God and our own life. But even though we may have to endure a spiritual odyssey and may meet many unexpected obstacles, we ought to make a little more progress than those who have merely been indoctrinated with a little external Christianity which expressed itself merely in a bored attendance at Sunday Mass, perhaps an Easter confession and the receiving of the last sacraments.

Evidently intellectuals are no better only because they are educated; this shows itself especially in the case of theologians, no matter whether they are priests or laymen, who have chosen theology and spirituality as their profession or even as their intellectual hobby. Surely, even outside the sphere of theoretical reflection we ought to achieve a little more than a Christian life that is content with observing the rules. But actually we intellectuals, too, have not progressed much further in our faith. Indeed, we are perhaps in greater danger, because we think that our theorizing is the same as a true Christian life of prayer, faith, self-denial and humility. Moreover, we may be less truly Christian than the so-called "simple Catholics" of the Christian "people," if only because the intellectual is normally better off than they and can therefore avoid more easily the difficulties and hardships of life. Take, for example, a mother of seven who must work hard to bring up her family. I am less worried that she might miss the true meaning of Christianity than I am in my own case.

If we remain mere amateurs in the actual Christian life, if we have not in some way accepted to obey a law within the context of Christian freedom and self-restraint, then we are no more than miserable bunglers even if we do not carry too much real ballast of historical piety.

10 · Experiencing Transcendence

The essential characteristic of the experience of transcendence is that man's knowledge and liberty always reach out beyond the individual object of inner and outward experience; that this anticipation is the condition that makes objective knowledge and the free act possible, since it is absolutely unlimited, going beyond every declarable object, because every conceivable limitation in the act of being thought of is already exceeded. In so far as the experience of man's transcendental nature really establishes itself, experiences itself as being sustained by the direction in which it tends, and knows that Nothingness is nothing —this goal towards which transcendence tends can only be thought of as the infinite, unlimited reality which remains at root a mystery: that is to say, God. This goal as incomprehensible mystery is—though not as object in the sense of ontologism—really the beginning of the movement of transcendence.

Of course this experience of transcendence, which has God as its direction and its goal, cannot be grasped, in its concrete, specific originality, in the abstract terms we have used to describe it here. A mystagogic pointer to this experience must therefore remember that the person who is not himself trained in philosophy has this experience as a matter of course, but in quite definite shapes and forms. We are not concerned here with the transcendental in absolute and diffuse form, for that is always a given element in the implementation of knowledge and freedom; it is a matter of more intensive realisations which force this experience of transcendence more clearly on the reflective consciousness as well. In this way these realisations make it possible for the "ordinary" person to reflect upon his experience of transcendence with the help of an explicitly verbal thematic treatment of the subject of God, which is already to be found in the sociological environment.

In the nature of things, these primal experiences always arise where the movement of transcendence allows the finite character of the specific object as such to be experienced. Through them, the finite character of specific objects, as something that can neither be overcome nor fulfilled, can become the express subject of reflection, just as much as the affirmation of a fulfilment no longer finite, which still nonetheless exists even in a "negative" experience of this kind. Preeminent experiences of transcendence may be experience of the fear that threatens everything, and experience of surpassing joy; experience of an absolute responsibility, faithfulness or love, which are no longer adequately justified specifically; and experience of the absolute logic which substantiates the individual object but cannot be substantiated by the object itself. We must of course distinguish between forms which coalesce through a free acceptance, and those which come into being in the radical disintegration between the transcendentally necessary affirmation of God, which is not the express subject of reflection, and rejection of God made in an act of human liberty, whether this be the express subject of reflection or not. For one and the same subject experiences himself, knowingly and freely, as being exposed to several experiences of transcendental necessity; and this subject, in his own unity, feels that these have to be reconciled with one another— though the subject himself can never reconcile them.

But wherever someone still unconditionally hopes beyond all empirical hopelessness; wherever a particular joy is experienced as the promise of a joy that is limitless; wherever a person loves with unconditional faithfulness and resolve, although the frailty of such love on both sides cannot possibly legitimise this unconditional determination; wherever radical responsibility towards a moral obligation is maintained, even when it seemingly leads only to disaster; wherever the relentlessness of truth is experienced and unconditionally accepted and grasped; wherever the unsurmountable discrepancy between what is individual and what is social in the plurality of man's different destinies is endured in a seemingly unjustified resolve of hope for the meaning and blessedness which reconciles everything—a resolve which cannot even be given objective form—in all these situations God, as the condition which makes all this possible, is already experienced and accepted, even if this is not expressly and objectively formulated. This is true even if the word "God" is never heard and is never used as the term for the direction and goal of the transcendental experiences known in this way.

Experiences of transcendence of this kind are not just sporadic. They are more widespread than that, and may occur in any given event of human knowledge and freedom, without so much as the beginnings of an express and objective formulation. As the condition that makes knowledge and freedom in everyday life possible, this transcendental experience of God is experienced in its necessity and inescapability, so that the person is faced with the question whether he will also make this inescapability the centre of his existence, in free, primal trust; or whether he will suppress it by escaping to the surveyable individual realities in his life which he can control.

But this does not mean any depreciation of the explicit doctrine of God, or of objectifying reflection about this experience. Man is not merely a transcendental creature; he is also a creature of history and reflection. The fundamentally highest stage is reached when he reflects on the transcendental conditions of objective knowledge and of historical experience—when, that is to say, he reflects about the trend and goal of man's transcendence in whose framework history is pursued. But the individual cannot legitimately escape from the common awareness of mankind. He must explicitly want to have to do with God. On the other hand, the conscious verbal and social formulation of the primal experience of God in history and society means for the individual a radical possibility of reflecting on his own transcendental experience of God and of entering into the history of this reflection as purely and completely as possible.

All that we have said up to now is inevitably abstract and very general. Of course it must be translated into different language if it is to be effective in religious education or catechetical instruction or missionary work. But people must be warned against demanding today the pure and simple "concrete," graphically descriptive language that was possible once. The reason why religious language that sounded much more concrete used to be possible was that people felt able to localise God's workings at particular points in the world and history far more unreservedly; and from these points they could talk about God specifically, so to speak. We cannot go into the question here of whether and in what sense a more or less specific experience of God of this kind is still possible today. At all events, in a radical sense, for us God is only conceivable at all as the final ground and ultimate goal of reality; he is experienced within the sensory world at most indirectly. In view of this, contemporary language cannot, ultimately speaking, avoid being abstract to some extent. This abstractness does not need to frighten us, because man is becoming increasingly aware that language which helps him practically to understand and deal with his material environment is also becoming more abstract. This defence of abstract talk about religion is, of course, not meant to suggest that the language used here is the only one possible, if we want to talk about God.

People must be warned against appealing too quickly and without closer inspection to particular religious, more or less "mystical" experiences, in order to demonstrate that an experience of God is possible. Mystical experiences are either very intensive cases of an experience of God which is basically open to all; or they rouse the suspicion that they are psychological phenomena which can be explained by particular psychical causes. The grace of a transcendental experience of God that is given essentially radical form by his elevating grace is open to everyone, at least in the sense of an offer which a person can freely accept or reject. That is merely a translation of the binding Catholic doctrine about the universal and efficacious divine will to salvation. It is probably true that not everyone has the grace of free acceptance and love at every moment in his life. But we can hope—even though we cannot know with certainty— that the history of every person ends in perfected salvation, and that therefore the effective grace freely to accept the transcendental experience of God will be given at some time or other.

But the grace of acceptance is something which in everyone cannot be reflected on with certainty. Proper reflection on the transcendental experience of God in a knowledge about God which is consciously formulated is certainly again grace, which experience teaches us is not given to everyone. According to the conviction of Vatican II, it does not even have to be given as offered and sufficient grace to every person in every social and historical situation. But this only means that the particular person, in his own psychological and social situtation, is not actually in a situation when he can sufficiently reflect on his existing transcendental experience of God, and recognise it again in what is said to him about God from outside. This basically happens, however, even when an intelligent person in his own particular situation finds it impossible to understand calculus, for example, even when it is explained to him by a mathematician. The claim that the grace of experiencing God has not been given must not assume a mystical-psychological misunderstanding of this grace; nor does it dispense us from a continually renewed attempt to help others to a reflective understanding of their own transcendental experience of God, and thus to make theists of them, even in the dimension of objectifying awareness and of religious society.

A definite mystagogy in the individual's reflection on his personal transcendental experience of God would admittedly have to be slowly developed, in a better way than hitherto. We do not have to think that the word "God" has to stand at the beginning here. In a situation in which religious language no longer enjoys undisputed rule in society, the word "God" will be more likely to come at the end. But this allows a concept of God to be formed which will not later produce a highly dangerous crisis of religious consciousness because of its infantile nature. This mystagogy in the self-realisation of the transcendental experience of God must of course link up with experiences which the consciousness declares are clearly and existentially important and which bear in themselves the transcendental experience of God in such a way that they compel the person to a conscious formulation of this experience. These experiences are always embedded in the whole of existential human experience. Where this perhaps more or less miscarries in early childhood—because the experience of love, faithfulness and security between people, and so forth, is not adequately attained— conscious formulation of the primal experience of God is of course very difficult too. Only where life is freely accepted in general as having a sheltering significance, in an ultimate primal trust, will man in his freedom be also prepared to carry out the conscious formulation of this primal trust in the direction of God. The awakening of this primal trust does not take place effectively merely through words. It comes about through participation in the life of another person who, in his serenity and love, may be able to provide a fruitful model for this primal trust.

From this standpoint we can also acquire an understanding of the connection between the experience of God and man's relatedness to Jesus Christ. Christ is the "fruitful model" *per se* for a committed reliance on the mystery of our existence, which we call God. The believer calls the absolutely radical form of our transcendental relatedness to God, the Spirit of Jesus Christ. It is in looking at the history of Jesus that the Christian finds the historical legitimisation for committed reliance on God, whom Jesus called his Father. Transcendental experience of God and the historical experience of Jesus come together in a mutually conditioning relationship; Spirit and history are a unity in which God is at once man's origin and his end.

It is of course also conceivable for someone to have been indoctrinated about God by the religious society, without himself being able to enter very clearly into this expository process in the light of his own personal transcendent experience of God. He too can of course let the philosophical and theological dynamic that is also part of this objectified concept of God work on him, so arriving at an ever more purified and more subtle concept of God. On the other hand, he does not need to be pestered with the difficult expository process at all, unless his individual or social situation makes such an attempt necessary. In people with a sound philosophical training, this expository process is not necessarily always facilitated by their education; it can actually be made more difficult as well, so that in certain circumstances they stop short at a "troubled atheism" in the reflective dimension, where the horror of being without God is seen, admitted and suffered, and yet this state cannot be specifically overcome on the level of knowledge about which they can reflect.

11 · Experiencing God

When we think of God, abstract and difficult as it perhaps must be for human reflexion, we are asking ourselves where and how the right concept of God is really to be found.

You all know that the transcendental relatedness of man's whole intellectual existence in knowing and loving, in the experience of dread and fear in face of death and so on, is one of the most essential basic features of human existence. We do not begin to have something to do with God only when we explicitly name him, when our knowledge of God acquires a conceptual and thematic structure. This latter is necessary and salutary; it is God's grace. It is then that we speak of God, form a concept and mould this concept, that we fill out this one concept with a thousand names and statements: all this is necessary, good and right. And even now, when we talk about God, we can do so only by forming words about him, by working out ideas, by being conscious of the reality of God in thematic form. But presumably you are aware that this is the secondary —but not, for that reason, unimportant—mode of the original relationship to God, and that this secondary relationship of thematic conceptuality to God is sustained and remains sustained by a previous, unthematic, transcendental relatedness of our whole intellectuality to the incomprehensible Infinite.

In the light of all this it is clear that the genuine, concretely (and existentially) realised relationship to God ought not merely to bring out and fulfil more precisely the objective-conceptual themes about God, but ought also previously and simultaneously to deepen, invigorate and bring to the fore this primal—in the most profound and necessary sense, "subjective"—ontological and transendental relationship to God.

This, however, does not at all mean indulging in clever talk about these sublime things. For this again would simply not be the primal, transcendental relationship to God himself, but something secondary—in fact, merely talk about this relationship. But how then can we bring out this primal relationship to God? How must we really make it active so that we feel ourselves sustained and encompassed by God so to speak from behind and from the very depths of being? When we think of God, when we fill out our concepts of God, make them more complex, enrich their content, how do we really manage to observe that we are again living on a more primitive relationship to God and on its realisation? How do we see that we remain encompassed by God, that all these concepts are in fact merely a pointer to that primal relationship to God, which of course is always dependent also on this thematic objectivation? All this in fact remains obscure. We have to admit that we theologians and we Catholics of today, in spite of all our talk about God, possess and practise really very little hermeneutic and maieutic for this more primitive experience of God given in the very roots of existence.

If what philosophy has said about this original structure of man in his intellectuality is true, then evidently such experiences must occur. Be still for once. Don't try to think of so many complex and varied things. Give these deeper realities of the spirit a chance now to rise to the surface: silence, fear, the ineffable longing for truth, for love, for fellowship, for God. Face loneliness, fear, imminent death! Allow such ultimate, basic human experiences to come first. Don't go talking about them, making up theories about them, but simply endure these basic experiences. Then in fact something like a primitive awareness of God can emerge. Then perhaps we cannot say much about it; then what we "grasp" first of all about God appears to be nothing, to be the absent, the nameless, absorbing and suppresssing all that can be expressed and conceived.

If we do not learn slowly in this way to enter more and more into the company of God and to be open to him, if we do not constantly attempt to reflect in life primitive experiences of this kind—not deliberately intended or deliberately undertaken—and from that point onwards to realise them more explicitly in the religious act of meditation and prayer, of solitude and the endurance of ourselves, if we do not develop such experiences, then our religious life is and remains really of a secondary character and its conceptual-thematic expression is false; then we talk of God as if we had already slapped him on the shoulder—so to speak—and, in regard to men, we feel that we are God's supervisors and more or less his equals: the result is that, for all our preaching, we ultimately lack credibility for the men of today and for those who really count. Whenever piety is directed only by an ingenious, complicated intellectuality and conceptuality, with highly complicated theological tenets, it is really a pseudo-piety, however profound it seems to be.

Once again, however, consider for example the situations in which man is brought back to this basic experience of God. Somewhere, someone seems to be weeping hopelessly. Someone "packs it in" and knows—if he is now silent, if he is now patient, if he now gives in—that there is nothing more that he could seize on, on which he could set his hopes, that this attitude is worthwhile. Someone enters into a final solitude where no one accompanies him. Someone has the basic experience of being stripped even of his very self. A man as spirit in his love for truth reaches—so to

speak—the frontier of the absolute, about which he has no longer anything to say, which sustains and is not sustained: that absolute which is
there even though we cannot reach out and touch it, which—if we talk
about it—is again concealed behind our talk as its ground. Someone experiences joy, not knowing where it begins and ceases, for which there
appears to be no solid reason, which even seems to have no object. Someone does not really seize on, but is seized by, a final loyalty. There is a
time when object, ground and horizon, and all that we see in these,
merge—so to speak—into one another. Wherever these things happen,
God is really already present and available to man.

All that man has then to say of this God can never be more than a
pointer to this primitive experience of God. If someone says that this is
mysticism, then it is in fact mysticism and then this very factor of mysticism belongs to God. But it is not mysticism in the specific sense: it is the
obviousness of being encompassed absolutely by God at the moment of a
man's whole awakening to mental existence. These things remain banal
for us; this primitive, nameless and themeless experience is apparently
wholly repressed and buried by our daily routine, by all that we otherwise have to do with men and things. This primal religious relationship to
God can be buried again even through our theological, ascetic and pious
chatter. All this proves indeed how much we must constantly struggle in a
more genuine, more religious life to set free and constantly dig out this
primal relationship to God; but it proves precisely how primitive and
deeply rooted is man's relationship to God and proves how much this primal relationship really matters.

Up to a point we ought to be able to show an atheist that the very fact of
denying God is itself an affirmation of his existence and that this is not
merely a question of formal logic, but a veritable realisation of a man's
genuine, vital, concrete existence. This much has to be presupposed if what
we still want to say about God is to make sense at all. What remains to be
said really brings us back every time to what we have just touched on. It
should only encourage us to awaken in ourselves this primitive experience
of God, the experience of course of God as the ineffable and incomprehensible.

12 · The Hiddenness of God

The perfect beatitude granted to man by God consists in immediate access to God, i.e., God is himself the fulfilment of man. All communication in the created order, in so far as this can be conceived or is to be

found in traditional theology (*lumen gloriae*), must be understood in relation to the direct access to God as communication with his immediate presence. It cannot be a question here in any sense of a created reality originating in God which merely represents God and only makes him indirectly present to man as the cause of the fulfilment which is properly ours. Of course this theological assertion can be taken as an interpretation of the experience of faith which can be directly grasped in Scripture. The proposition as defined by Benedict XII (Denz. 1000–1001), which counts as dogma for Catholic theology, cannot be anything else than the expression of a *radical* human hope in the Spirit of God, despite all the other possible formulations of this proposition. God himself in his own very being wills to be the beatitude of man. This fulfilment of the *capax infiniti* through the *infinitum* may not be weakened by an appeal to other modes of communication which are of a more finite and intelligible nature. This "metaphysic" need involve no more than the assertion that God himself and nothing else is our eternal life, however he may be understood by us here and now. This theological proposition forms the basis of all the reflections which are contained in this essay. However philosophical and speculative the line of thinking may appear, its only purpose is to make the primary theological statement intelligible and to prevent it being weakened or undervalued.

"*The* Truth" occurs in the basic experience of the mystery itself. Such knowledge is not in origin a defective mode of real knowledge, in the usual sense of the term. For such knowledge is directed to what can be comprehended and penetrated and only fails in this endeavour in a particular instance, without the object which is partially perceived becoming something totally unknown. What is called knowledge according to the common usage originating in the western tradition of philosophy, i.e., comprehension and mastery, consists in the ordering of data in a horizon of understanding and system of coordinates which is evident to us as the object which we possess identically with ourselves. But it is this which is a defective form of the true knowledge in which the mystery itself unfolds. If knowledge in the ordinary sense is regarded as a secondary and defective form of the real nature of knowledge, then it is of no importance whether ordinary knowledge is understood in the sense of the creation of functional connections between the primary data of an original experience, or treated as the vision in which what is seen is comprehended. For the essence of knowledge lies in the mystery which is the object of primary experience and is alone self-evident.

The unlimited and transcendent nature of man, the openness to the mystery itself which is given radical depth by grace, does not turn man into the event of the absolute spirit in the way envisaged by German idealism or similar philosophies; it directs him rather to the incomprehensible mystery, in relation to which the openness of transcendence is experienced. Man as transcendent subject is not the shepherd of being but the one protected by the mystery. In the primary realisation of his being (*dasein*) and in the philosophical reflection derived from it, man comes to be himself and here he does not experience himself as the dominant, absolute subject, but as the one whose being is bestowed upon him by the mystery.

This is the reason why, in forming any concept, he understands himself as the one who reaches out beyond the conceptual into the nameless and the incomprehensible. Transcendence grasped in its unlimited breadth is the a priori condition of objective and reflective knowledge and evaluation. It is the very condition of its possibility, even though it is ordered to the inexpressible. It is also the precondition for the freedom which is historically expressed and objectified. Thus the experience of the nameless mystery as both origin and goal is the a priori condition of all categorial knowledge and of all historical activity; it is not merely a marginal phenomenon at the end of the road. Otherwise it would merely be a matter of a journey into the bright light of categorial and ultimately scientific understanding, a journey on which a man grows weary in the pursuit of knowledge, leaves what is still unknown to itself and gives the name of mystery to this unmastered realm of the intelligible. In contrast knowledge in the primary sense is the presence of the mystery itself. It is being addressed by what no longer has a name, and it is relying on a reality which is not mastered but is itself the master. It is the speech of the being without a name, about which clear statements are impossible; it is the last moment before the dumbness which is needed if the silence is to be heard, and God is to be worshipped in love.

If one insists that knowing in the basic sense consists in a piece of clear and ordinary understanding and in the science based upon it, then what we have said would have to be formulated in a different way. The manner of formulation is ultimately of no special consequence. The origin and goal of knowledge in the mystery is one of its constituent elements. In an unthematic way this is experienced in day-to-day knowledge and may be called "primary" in the sense of the *a priori* condition of possibility of all knowing, even though it only becomes thematic in a secondary sense through subsequent reflection upon its own a priori presuppositions. There may be many truths. They can be clear and can guarantee control over reality. But they all stem from the unfolding of the mystery itself, from the *one* truth. This is not merely a later collection of truths but precedes them as the condition of their possibility.

The presence of the one truth is of course unthematic, since it exists in the first instance as the condition of possibility of spatio-temporal and categorial-historical experience. It can therefore be overlooked and suppressed; its silent presence can be ignored in the face of immediate phenomena which in their variety and particularity can fill the space of life and consciousness. Where, too, this one truth is expressed in word in the ultimate courage of existence and, almost against its own nature, finds objective form, it can be confused with other objective expressions and so lack truth and credibility. But this does not alter the fact that the one truth is the primary event of the spirit; it is the mystery which endures and unfolds and establishes the essential human capacity for truth.

In other words the *deus absconditus* is the source of truth for man, which is freely bestowed upon him and determines his identity. Man always stands before the *deus absconditus*, even when he tries to look away and refuses to accept the truth that clear knowledge of the reality of the world, which gives him mastery over the world, comes from this *deus absconditus*. Knowledge is primarily the experience of the overwhelming mystery of this *deus absconditus*.

Divine revelation is not the unveiling of something previously hidden, which through this illumination leads to an awareness similar to that found in ordinary knowledge of the world. Rather it means that the *deus absconditus* becomes radically present as the abiding mystery. This mystery presents itself through revelation as the source of forgiveness, salvation and an eternal home. Revelation does not mean that the mystery is overcome by gnosis bestowed by God, even in the direct vision of God; on the contrary, it is the history of the deepening perception of God *as* the mystery. This continues in the direct presence of God afforded by what we call the beatific vision and can only be sustained in the loving surrender to the enduring mystery. It is the lost and not the blessed soul who perceives everything as infinite variety and so perceives nothing at all. The blessed abandons himself unconditionally to the direct self-communication of the mystery of the *deus absconditus* from which come love and salvation. If the theoretical intellect is understood as the capacity for conceptual mastery and comprehension, then beatitude means that the theoretical intellect is set free to love the mystery, which lays total hold of us by its direct presence.

The history of revelation, then, consists in the growing awareness that we are involved with the permanent mystery and that our involvement becomes ever more intense and exclusive. If revelation is seen in this perspective, there is certainly a great deal more to say about it than we usually find in discussions of revelation. But if the climax of revelation, the communication of the Spirit of God himself, takes place when a man loses everything in death except God, and *in this way* achieves blessedness, then the history of revelation can well be written in the manner proposed here. In any history nothing can ultimately be explained without reference to the ending. In our case the ending is the advent of God who is the enduring mystery and is accepted in love. In that history, therefore, the mystery is not removed by a slow process of attrition; rather all the provisional realities are dismantled which can lead to the belief that we can only achieve a relationship to God through what we believe we know about him. But such knowledge only offers figures and images, either good or bad, which represent and shape him to our needs. This process only lasts until we finally let go of everything in the assurance that God, the one who fundamentally cannot be shaped to our needs, becomes through his self-gift the being who alone is fitted to us. For through his own very being God has granted to us that the measure of our knowledge, desire and activity need not be ourselves but is the immeasurability of God himself. The fulfilment of the created order consists in the fact that God, who is our absolute future, is the incomprehensible mystery. This incomprehensibility is not to be taken as the limit of fulfilment but rather signifies its limitlessness which is loved and experienced as such.

Of course this doctrine represents a danger for man. If he derives enjoyment from its theoretical and objective expression and turns it into a secret idol, then the highest fulfilment is distorted into a terrifying disorder. Only if the incomprehensible mystery is itself the object of love, if knowledge goes beyond the self and knowledge and love penetrate the mystery through such ecstasy, no longer returning to the self, only then is the final and greatest danger removed, the danger, that is, of turning the doctrine into a sublime gnosis in which once again a man replaces God with self. One cannot escape this danger by refusing really to accept that it is the will of God to be *himself* the absolute future of man and to be his proper fulfilment. He desires to be the beatitude of man in his incomprehensibility and not despite it, and this is the key to man's own self-understanding. The incomprehensibility of God as the blessed fulfilment of man, if one wished to develop the metaphysical line of thought any further, is the same reality as the incomprehensibility of God in his own being and in the free gift of the mystery to man in his individual concrete history. This is realised in the single "free decree" of God, which is at root beyond understanding since once again it is identical with God himself, who is the fulfilment of man and his reconciliation and forgiveness. This applies to the sinner as well as the justified, for the sinner is resolved in himself to reject God, because he wishes to escape from the incomprehensibility of God and seek refuge in the intelligibility of his own knowledge and action.

13 · Everyday Mysticism

Christianity refuses to recognize a systematic and more or less technically developed "mystical" experience of transcendence as the sole and necessary way to man's perfection; and, on the other hand, Christian theology, at least in Catholicism, will not cease to regard such mystical experience of transcendence at least as a possible *stage* on the way to perfection and as a paradigmatic elucidation of what happens in faith, hope, and love on the Christian path to the perfection of salvation wherever salvation in the Christian sense is attained.

This thesis must be further elucidated in its two aspects.

On the first part of the thesis, Christian teaching and the practice of authentic Christianity cannot admit that the "mystic" (whatever may be the exact meaning of this term, of the phenomena of immersion, of the formless experience of the absolute, etc.) is the only one who has gone or goes on that path to perfection of which the last stage directly and alone borders on man's perfection (however the term "perfection" is to be more precisely interpreted). The teaching of the New Testament that the fulfillment of God's commandments in the conscientious observance of routine duties in faith, hope, and love for God and men bring the person through death immediately to perfection and unite him finally with God, the description of the last judgment in the eschatalogical discourses of Jesus (for instance, in Matthew 25), and many other things in the teaching and practice of Christianity that need not be mentioned here: all this forbids us to regard mysticism and particularly its more or less technically and explicitly developed form exclusively as the necessary and final stretch of the way before attaining perfect salvation or all ordinary practice of the Christian life merely as the *preparatory* phase of the way of salvation which leads to perfection only when it ends up on the higher path of contemplative mysticism. Christianity rejects such an elitist interpretation of life, which can see man's perfection as attained only in the trained mystic. This is particularly important, since Christianity rejects the theory of the transmigration of souls and cannot localize such an explicitly mystical phase for the individual in a subsequent life. This in brief is the content of the first part of our first thesis.

This however does *not* mean simply that mystical experience as such could be or ought to be regarded merely as a single and rare exceptional case in individual human beings and Christians which is granted to the latter either by psycho-technical effort or by a special grace of God as a rare privilege or by both together, without really having any constitutive importance for the actual way to perfect salvation.

In the Christian theology of mysticism up to the present time views have been maintained which denied to mysticism in *any* way a constitutive importance for the process of salvation or conceded something of this kind at most in cases where it is a question of a special "heroic" heightening of perfection, of "holiness," of gaining a particularly high degree of final glory (which, despite its finality, can, according to textbook theology, have varying degrees). But the first part of our thesis does not necessitate such an interpretation of the really crucial phenomena of mysticism, an interpretation of this mysticism in which the latter has absolutely no constitutive importance in any respect for the event and achievement of final perfection. It seems to me (from the nature of the case we shall return to this point) to be the task of Christian theology as a whole and the Christian theology of mysticism in particular to show and to render intelligible the fact that the real basic phenomenon of mystical experience of transcendence is present as innermost sustaining ground (even though unnoticed) in the simple act itself of Christian living in faith, hope, and love, that such (as we may say) implicit transcendence into the nameless mystery known as God is present by grace in this very believing, hoping, and loving; it seems to us that mysticism in its explicit sense and as expressly practised may signify a higher degree of the Christian ascent to perfection from the standpoint of an objectively reflecting psychology, but not from a properly theological standpoint, and that mysticism in an explicit experience has therefore (conversely) a paradigmatic character, an exemplary function, to make clear to the Christian what really happens and is meant when his faith tells him that God's self-communication is given to him in grace and accepted in freedom whenever he believes, hopes, and loves. The proof of such a *perichoresis* between the normal and routine practice of the Christian life and an ultimate and absolutely radical experience of transcendence into the mystery of God cannot of course be produced here and now in this first thesis. Otherwise a whole theology of the Holy Spirit, of possession by the Spirit, of experience of the Spirit by grace, of the theological virtues (as event of immediacy to God as distinct from the intramundane moral virtues), would have to be developed (which of course is not possible at this point).

14 · The Theology of Mysticism

There is no generally received theology of mysticism within the body of Christian theology. There are great mystics who furnish us with the testimony of their experiences; and among these, especially in classic Spanish mysticism, there are a number who have sought to confer upon their experience, upon the unfolding of their mystical path, a certain theological systematization. This systematic reflection on mystical experience is always shaped in large measure by the conceptualizations of a particular mystic's faith and theology, which he or she will inevitably invoke in attempting to describe, indeed sometimes actually to systematize, his or her basic, primordial experience, and bring it within the system of coordinates of his or her other philosophical and theological convictions and opinions. The result—even within classic Spanish mysticism—is an extraordinary variety of descriptions and systematizations of mystical experiences, propounded by writers the genuineness of whose mystical experience we would not wish to deny.

Besides this literature, there is another body of spiritual literature, which one may by no means ignore, in which the mystical element thrusts through to expression, time and again, as the ultimate source of this literature's authenticity and vitality, even though here we have only occasional effective testimony to the authors' mystical experience, and, again, no generally received theology of mysticism. Moreover, a developed and received theology of mysticism would require a description and systematization of the relationship between Christian and non-Christian mysticism; but despite every imaginable thesis to this effect, we have neither in any degree of adequacy.

The same will have to be said of the relationship between mystical and parapsychological phenomena. There have been attempts at a systematic theology of mysticism at least as far back as the times of classic Spanish mysticism and continuing to our own day (although it must also be observed, regrettably, that interest seems to be waning today). But these theologies of mysticism, where the *ultimate* foundational questions are concerned, are too brief and simplistic. They merely more or less repeat, piece by piece, the descriptions offered by Spanish mysticism of mystical experiences and the mystical way, rather levelling them out and blurring some far-reaching distinctions. They engage in rather superficial polemics over the question of whether "infused contemplation" or other "mystical graces" belong to the ordinary path of Christian striving after perfection or are a "special grace," bestowed relatively infrequently and likely enough to be missing even in the presence of "heroic virtues" in the "saints." There also prevails, in such theologies of mysticism, a rather too naive and unreflecting "extrinsicist" model of God's "intervention" where mystical phenomena are concerned. Some of contemporary theology's considerations regarding the relationship and unity of grace and "nature" are scarcely even broached.

A *first* basic problem that must be handled in a theology of mysticism will be a more precise conceptualization of the *mystic's relationship to what he or she experiences as in "absolute and utter nearness."* In the mystical experience, the "mystical" subject undergoes an "immediate" experience, transcending mediation by categorical objects of the everyday, not only of himself or herself but of very "Mystery"—sheer, quintessential Reality, God, or whatever else this object of experience (which is not *a priori* identical with the mystical subject) might be called. Otherwise there is no question of religious mysticism at all. The question necessarily arises, then, whether in such mystical experiences the subject and object of the experience are indeed experienced as purely and simply one, or whether, even here and precisely here, the radical distinction between God and creature, even in the latter's most sublime elevation by grace, not only abides but actually emerges as datum. In the abstract one could imagine that, for the most heterogeneous reasons, this abiding distinction, which a correct metaphysics and a Christian theology must posit as presupposed, is "overlooked" or "bracketed" in the mystical event. Or perhaps one could conceive of a "mystical" experience of oneness between subject and *world* as such, which the subject might thereupon precipitantly identify with a oneness of the mystical subject with *God* himself. Or perhaps, in the mystical experience of a radical love for this God who communicates himself, a selfishly particular "individuation" or isolation falls away and disappears, and then this phenomenon, in subsequent reflection, is mistaken for a plain and simple suspension of the finite subject. But all these possibilities constitute so many reasons why it is of the highest interest to hear the mystic on the subject of his or her mystical experience and its interpretation, so that not only the metaphysician who holds to the absolute transcendentality of the human spirit and the theologian who maintains the distinction between God and creature may have their say in this matter but also the one who most clearly and unmistakably experiences the relationship between the human subject and the Reality we call God.

A *second* basic problem for mystical theology will bear on the relationship between the mystical experience and grace/faith. Traditional mystical theology is constantly in difficulties here. It calls these mystical experiences "grace"—but this grace is "grace" for mystical theology primarily because it is thought of as a gratuitous, unowed intervention on the part of God at some particular point in time and space, where the inaccessible God communicates himself in a special manner. But how such a "grace" is related to the grace that Christianity proclaims as proffered by God to *all* human beings does not really emerge very clearly, even when these mystical graces are indeed basically seen as the flowering of supernatural potentialities in the justified human being as such. This ambiguity is most annoying when we inquire into the relationship between the mystical experience and that *experience* (the word is correct and important!) to which we Christians give the name of "faith," holding it to be the fruit of the Spirit of God.

Mystical illumination and unification is most often represented as an occurrence in which God communicates himself so "immediately" that it is really no longer very clear how faith is not being simply outstripped, overtaken, by this mystical light, at least for the duration of the mystical occurrence itself. An authentically Christian theology of grace, of faith, of the possession of the Spirit, and of God's indwelling (realities which, after all, it is not legitimate to misunderstand, neo-Molinistically, as purely factual data beyond the reach of consciousness) can by no means admit that it would be possible to drive a wedge between faith and the experience of grace, on the one hand, and the face-to-face vision of God, on the other, in the form of some *tertium quid* that would be theologically and essentially distinct from them both—some middle ground, then, properly and specifically transcending the Christian's graced condition (this too is always an *experience* of grace) in a way that is meaningful for salvation, on the one hand, and yet, on the other hand, is not an actual, however transitory, partaking of the vision of God (which we must reserve, despite so many conceptualizations in the mystical theologies, to those who by their death have simply and in an unqualified manner entered into their ultimate reality). The human being's divinization, the possession of the divine uncreated Grace (realities which Christianity recognizes as attaching to all the justified), cannot properly be surpassed by anything short of the vision of glory, the immediate vision of God, which is reserved for the human being's final and actual consummation and completion. It cannot be admitted that mystical experience outstrips the domain of faith, outstrips the experience of the Spirit of God basically already given in faith, through an experience that would no longer be faith. Mysticism must be conceived of as falling within the framework of ordinary grace and faith. Mystical *theology*, wherever it has any claim to be more than parapsychology (in the widest sense, including everything not present in ordinary everyday consciousness), must on its own principles be only a part of dogmatic theology.

Two things that this thesis does not exclude—on the contrary, that it includes—are: *First*, we are not saying that the dogmatic theologian as such can or must say anything about mystical experiences insofar as these are *psychologically* distinct from everyday experiences of grace. When and to whatever extent such experiences occur (to the point of enjoying "essential" differences of a *psychological* kind), it is the mystic and the experimental psychologist within whose competency an investigation of these phenomena falls, not that of the dogmatic theologian. The latter need only establish that there can be no *theologically* higher experience on earth than that of faith, in the Spirit of God, and that therefore a genuine mystical experience (as distinguished from natural "altered states of consciousness," and so on) is only to be understood as a "variety" of this experience of grace in faith. And then it will presumably fall to the empirical mystic and the experimental psychologist to explain the origination of this mystical variety of the experience of God.

Consequently, neither our thesis of mystical experience as a "variety" of that experience of the Spirit which is radically offered to every person and every Christian (understanding "mystical experiences" in the strict sense, as distinguished from any natural altered states of consciousness, or parapsychological occurrences in the usual sense of the word, which could per se be acquired or learned) nor our thesis that therefore the theology of mysticism as such is part of dogmatic theology in general—neither thesis, I say, implies that such a theology of mysticism can only be constituted from the same sources and via the same methods as those employed by traditional dogmatic theology (Scripture, the magisterium, Church tradition, and so on).

On the contrary, when and to whatever extent the empirical mystic actually reports his or her mystical experience as such, the specific subject of the report will be that *experience of the Spirit* in grace that is given with faith, hope, and love in God's self-communication to human beings—although of course the specific *manner* in which this experience of the Spirit in grace is undergone contains moments of a "natural" sort, as we shall presently observe in more detail. Empirically descriptive mysticism as such (where it does not simply report natural altered states and the like) can surely be theology of revelation, since the subject of its report is divinizing grace in the proper sense. After all, what we are in the habit of calling revelation in word, and theology of revelation, is nothing but the reflexive objectivization (in history and word) of what occurs in God's self-communication in grace as this self-communication is basically experienced—although of course the pure and authentic objectivization of this divine self-communication has reached its irreversible pinnacle precisely in Jesus Christ and the absolutely certain expression of its truth in the teaching of Christianity. Hence even in an "extra-Christian" mysticism there can be an experience of grace, as well as in an extra-Christian theology of revelation (at least fundamentally)—even though such theology of revelation will always be oriented to that theology that expressly refers to the crucified and risen one, inasmuch as the mystical occurrence of surrender to God, as he is in and for himself, ultimately succeeds only through Jesus' redemptive death as it renders itself historically manifest in this victorious occurrence.

Here we come still more explicitly to a *third* basic problem for mystical theology: the relationship between "nature" and "grace." Here these concepts must both be understood in their strictly theological meaning. Just as mystical experience must not be conceptualized as an occurrence which overtakes and surpasses the supernatural experience of the Spirit in faith as something basically higher than this experience, so also the "specific difference" of this occurrence as contrasted with the Christian's "ordinary" experience of the Spirit must be in the realm of what is "natural" to the human being: a special sort of experience, in itself natural, of transcendence, and of "return" within oneself. This does not contradict what we have just been saying of mysticism as experience of grace. The *psychological* essence of mystical experiences is distinguished from the "ordinary" essence of everyday occurrences in our awareness only in the dimension of "nature," and accordingly is basically something that can be acquired, that can be learned. But such occurrences in the soul, natural in themselves, can, as any other human act of consciousness, freedom, and reflection, be "elevated" by God's self-communication in grace, habitual or actual—that is, these acts can be radicalized by God's personal self-communication, can be rooted in the immediacy of the self-communicating God, just as habitually occurs in the ordinary "supernatural" acts of faith, hope, and love in the "ordinary" Christian life. The special psychological, in se natural, particularity of such acts can contribute, from a point of departure in this particularity, to these supernaturally elevated acts' being existentially more deeply rooted in the inmost center of the person, and to their more extensive stamp and transformation of the total subject.

Whether the (in se natural) greater personal depth of the mystical act and the accompanying greater reflexivity of the (in se natural, but elevated by grace) experience of transcendence are in themselves miraculous (preternatural)—or whether they are naturally attainable, under certain presuppositions, through exercise and practice—or whether both alternatives are possible depending on the intensity of the phenomenon—is a question that cannot be decided by the theology of mysticism as such. If we consider this question to be de facto an open one (at least as far as the capacities of theology itself are concerned), then we must say that, as far as we know, it is conceivable that simply natural altered states of consciousness could be pure experience of transcendence: that is, they could be (totally or partially) disconnected from categorical mediation.

There can be no absolute, basic objection to giving such experience the name "natural mysticism." But it would be preferable to reserve the notion of "mysticism" to those psychologically extraordinary phenomena that are elevated by grace and involved properly supernatural experience of the Spirit, as we have endeavored to do here. The more precise question, then, would continue to be whether such natural phenomena (of altered states and so forth), however crucial they may be existentially, are really *only* natural, or whether, in their very process as in subsequent reflection upon them, they are only grasped as such, while actually always being supernaturally "elevated"—that is, radicalized to the immediacy of God himself by what we call, in Christian terms, "grace." This question pertains to the *theology of grace*. If the supernatural elevation of spiritual/personal human acts of in se unbounded transcendentality are conceptualized only as intermittent, occurring at discrete points in space and time and then only under further conditions, then the answer to the question we have posed will be the first: that is, we shall hold that there are natural altered states of consciousness that are *only* natural. But if another theology of grace were to posit (as it would be legitimate to do) that the transcendentality of the human being is, *a priori*, always and everywhere finalized and radicalized in God's immediacy by his self-communication in grace, regardless of whether, from the viewpoint of human beings' liberty, this hypothesized bestowal of grace upon a human being exists merely in the mode of offer, or in the mode of acceptance, or, finally, in the mode of refusal—then our question would have the second answer: each in se natural act of altered state of consciousness and so on would be always and everywhere elevated by grace, would be an act of mysticism in the proper sense, a salvific event—once again, even when this basic peculiarity of this mystical occurrence does not appear especially clearly, and is overlooked in subsequent reflection or misinterpreted in the sense of a pantheistic "mystique" of a phenomenon of undifferentiated unification.

The writer of these lines elects for the latter alternative. We cannot of course, in the space of this article, set forth the premises and theses of the theology of grace underlying this second option. But this third problem of mystical theology is basically reducible to the thesis that mystical (i.e., borne up by grace, comporting actual experience of God's Spirit) experiences are not distinguished from the experiences of ordinary Christian existence, from the ordinary Christian life of grace and experience of the Spirit, in virtue of their having a higher mode of being *as mystical* experience of the Spirit—but rather will be distinguished from such ordinary experience in virtue of the fact that their natural substrate (altered states, etc.) as such is distinguished from everyday psychological states and occurrences.

Here, perhaps, we have a point of departure for developing a solution to a *fourth* basic problem of mystical theology: the question of whether mystical "experience" is a normal developmental stage on the path to

Christian perfection, or is an extraordinary phenomenon, one not ordinarily coming into play even in Christian life at its most intensive. In dealing with this question we must begin by emphasizing that, as we have already said, the mystical experience, precisely in its formality as the human being's unification with God in grace, precisely as the Christian's experience (in the strict sense of experience) of the Spirit in grace, is not a "higher" stage of the Christian life in grace. Or at most it will be only *indirectly* such, inasmuch as the mystical phenomenon (as cause and effect) may be an index of a Christian's acceptance of the grace of God's self-communication proffered him or her in an existentially very intense degree. But for the rest this fourth basic problem would likewise be a matter for a natural empirical psychology. Presupposing that the latter can indeed say anything in its own right about the human being as the singular and plural subject of a definitive story of freedom, directed, in the sight of God, to final consummation, then if this psychology can make it clear that such a radical self-positing of the subject in an unconditional surrender, embracing the totality of his or her existential being, to the Mystery we call God, is possible *without* such natural altered states of consciousness, then the question would be answered in the negative: not every personal and Christian maturation toward a perfection and completion asymptotically approached in this life implies natural altered states of consciousness, although these could be most helpful; mysticism, then, would not necessarily be a part of every Christian life. On the other hand, were the competent psychology to establish that such in se natural altered states and so forth, even when not furthered by "techniques," and perhaps often practically unreflected upon, necessarily belong to a personal maturation process, then mysticism in the proper sense would indeed be a phenomenon of a normal sort in the process of the complete becoming of a human being and a Christian, regardless of whether, to what extent, and with what good or poor results such a mystical experience were to be made the object of reflection.

15 · Experiencing the Spirit

What if we do not dare to call ourselves mystics, and perhaps for very different reasons cannot take any personal part in charismatic movements and practices? Do we have any experience of the Spirit? Do we merely nod respectfully in the direction of other people's experiences which we ourselves find rather élitist? Do such people merely offer reports of a country that we have never seen and whose existence we are content to accept much as we might credit that of Australia if we have never been there?

We accept, and even confess as Christians supported by the testimony of Scripture, that we can have such an experience of the Spirit, and *must* have it as something offered to us in our essential freedom. That experience *is* given to us, even though we usually overlook it in the pursuit of our everyday lives, and perhaps repress it and do not take it seriously enough.

Experiencing the Nameless Mystery

If I try to bring the reader's attention to such experiences, then I must presuppose what has been said in previous sections on "Experiencing Transcendence" (§ 10) and "Everyday Mysticism" (§ 13).

In the midst of our everyday awareness we are blessed or damned (have it how we will) in regard to that nameless, illimitable eternity. The concepts and words which we use subsequently to talk of this everlastingness to and into which we are constantly referred, are not the original actual mode of being of that experience of nameless mystery that surrounds the island of our everyday awareness, but merely the tiny signs and idols which we erect and have to erect so that they constantly remind us of the original, unthematic, silently offered and proffered, and graciously silent experience of the strangeness of the mystery in which, in spite of all the light offered by the everyday awareness of things, we reside, as if in a dark night and a pathless wilderness. (There we are in darkness and a desert place—but one that reminds us of the abyss in whose depths we are grounded but can never plumb.)

Anyone who wants to can, of course, irritably and as if tried too far, let the matter drop and continually repress it. He can try to ignore the night that alone makes our tiny lights visible and enables them to shine forth. But then a man acts against his own ultimate being, because this experience of his orientation to boundless mystery, if seen for what it really is, is not some extraneous spiritual luxury but *the* condition for the very possibility of everyday knowing and wanting (even though he usually overlooks this and fails to consider it in the to-and-fro of everyday life and the pursuit of knowledge).

If we were to use the term "mysticism" to describe this experience of transcendence in which we always, even in the midst of everyday life, extend beyond ourselves and the specific thing with which we are concerned, we might say that mysticism occurs in the midst of everyday life, but is hidden and undeclared, and that this is the condition of the very possibility of even the most ordinary, sober and secular everyday experience.

God, the Inclusive but Illimitable Ground

In this unnamed and unsignposted expanse of our consciousness there dwells that which we call God. The mystery pure and simple that we call God is not a special, particularly unusual piece of objective reality, something to be added to and included in the other realities of our naming and classifying experience. He is the comprehensive though never comprehended ground and presupposition of our experience and of the objects of that experience. He is experienced in this strange experience of transcendence, even though it may not be possible to arrive at a more exact metaphysical characterization of the unity and variety between the transcendental experience of the spiritual subject in knowledge and freedom, on the one hand, and the experience of God himself which is given in the transcendental experience, on the other hand. This kind of definition is too difficult a philosophical undertaking and unnecessary in the present context.

Nevertheless, the unlimited extent of our spirit in knowledge and freedom, which is ineluctably and unthematically given in every ordinary experience, allows us to experience what is meant by God as the revealing and fulfilling ground of that expanse of the Spirit and its unlimited movement. Transcendental experience, even when and where it is mediated through an actual categorial object, is always divine experience in the midst of everyday life.

The Unrestricted Movement of the Spirit and the Bestowal of Grace

At this point I must add a statement that is both philosophical and theological in a special, reciprocally conditional way. The boundless transcendental movement of the human spirit to God is so radical that this movement does not merely take God as an asymptotic goal that is always at an infinite distance, but as that which itself directly comprises the attainable goal of that movement.

Philosophically speaking, we can conceive and hope in this radical aspect by which God in himself becomes the goal of this movement, at least as a possibility that cannot be excluded. Theologically speaking, we do grasp this possibility as actually given by God; we use the term "grace" for the actually given radical aspect of the transcendental movement to the immediacy of God in himself, right up to future direct perception. This comprises the actual and ultimate essence and nature of what we call grace, the self-communication of God in the Holy Spirit, and of what has its ultimate fulfilment in the direct loving contemplation of God. Existentially speaking, we freely conceive this radical nature of our movement towards God which is supported by the Spirit of God, when we entrust ourselves unreservedly and unconditionally to the movement of the Spirit; as far in fact as it can actually go when in our freedom we set it no bounds but, so to speak, allow it to move right out, in its own boundlessness, and up to the immediacy of God himself.

If grace is understood thus, if it is understood philosophically as possibility, seen theologically as reality and realized existentially in hope (thematically or unthematically), then in the factitious order of reality, transcendental experience which is experience of God is always experience of grace, because the radicality of the experience of transcendence and its dynamic thrust is borne by the self-communication of God which makes all this possible in the innermost midst of our existence. It is borne by God's self-communication as the goal and power of a movement towards him which we call grace or the Holy Spirit (at least as an offer made to human freedom). Transcendental experience that allows God to be present is always (on account of the salvific will of God in regard to all men, by reason of which man is directed to the immediacy of God) experience of the Holy Spirit, irrespective of whether a man can or cannot reflectively interpret in this way his ineradicable experience of the nameless God, and whether theological terms of the kind we have used are available to him.

I must add something to the foregoing: everything that has been said is also true of the average everyday experience of man in knowledge and freedom, but it is always true of circumstances in which spiritual knowledge and freedom are given, in which a man exists as a real subject and enjoys his reference to ultimate validity by way of and beyond himself. This transcendental experience of God in the Holy Spirit is, however, given only unthematically in everyday human experience, where it is overlaid and hidden by concern with actual realities with which we are taken up in our social world and environment. This transcendental experience of God in the Holy Spirit in everyday life remains anonymous, unreflective, and unthematic, like the generally and diffusely extended light of a sun that we do not see as such, turning instead to the individual objects of our sensuous experience as they become visible in the light.

Everyday Experience and the Experience of the Spirit

But even if we ignore the question whether such transcendental experience of God in the Holy Spirit could properly occur in instances of undirected absorption, in a state of consciousness void of objects of any specific kind, and in mystical experience for its own sake, there are in any case actual experiences in our existential history in which this intrinsically given transcendental experience of the Spirit occurs more obviously in our conscious minds: experiences in which (to put it the other way round) the individual objects of knowledge and of freedom with which we are concerned in everyday life, by their very specificity more clearly and insistently reveal the accompanying transcendental spiritual experience, in which by themselves and implicitly they indicate that inconceivable mystery of our existence that always surrounds us and also supports our everyday awareness, and indicate it more clearly than is otherwise usual in our ordinary and banal everyday life. Then everyday reality of itself refers to this transcendental experience of the Spirit which is implicitly and apparently featurelessly there and always there.

This indication, which is always associated with our everyday reality conceived in knowledge and freedom, and more insistently brought to our attention in certain situations, can also be intrinsically given by reason of the positive nature of that categorical reality in which the magnitude and glory, goodness, beauty and illumination of our individual experiential reality promise and point to eternal light and everlasting life. But it is already understandable that such a form of reference is most clearly experienced where the graspable contours of our everyday realities break and dissolve; where failures of such realities are experienced; when lights which illuminate the tiny islands of our everyday life go out, and the question becomes inescapable whether the night surrounding us is the absurd void of death engulfing us, or the blessed holy night which is already illumined from within and gives promise of everlasting day. When therefore I refer in the following primarily to those experiences which in this second way allow transcendental experience of God in the Holy Spirit to go forward, that does not mean that people and Christians are forbidden to let this experience of God occur in the first way, and thus to receive it. Ultimately the *via eminentiae* and the *via negationis* are not two ways or two stations one behind the other on a way, but two aspects of one and the same experience (though, as I have remarked, for the sake of clarity it is quite justifiable to lay special stress on the *via negationis*).

Experiencing the Spirit in Actual Life

I can now refer to the actual life-experiences which, whether we come to know them reflectively or not, are experiences of the Spirit. It is important that we experience them in the right way. In the case of these indications of the actual experience of the Spirit in the midst of banal everyday life, it can no longer be a question of analyzing them individually right down to their ultimate depth—which is the Spirit. And no attempt can be made to make a systematic tabular summary of such experiences. Only arbitrarily and unsystematically selected examples are possible.

Let us take, for instance, someone who is dissatisfied with his life, who cannot make the good will, errors, guilt and fatalities of his life fit together, even when, as often seems impossible, he adds remorse to this accounting. He cannot see how he is to include God as an entry in the accounting, as one that makes the debit and credit, the notional and actual values, come out right. This person surrenders himself to God or—both more imprecisely and more precisely—to the hope of an incalculable ultimate reconciliation of his existence in which he whom we call God dwells; he releases his unresolved and uncalculated existence, he lets go in trust and hope and does not know how this miracle occurs that he cannot himself enjoy and possess as his own self-actuated possession.

Here is someone who discovers that he can forgive though he receives no reward for it, and silent forgiveness from the other side is taken as self-evident.

Here is someone who tries to love God although no response of love seems to come from God's silent inconceivability, although no wave of emotive wonder any longer supports him, although he can no longer confuse himself and his life-force with God; although he thinks he will die from such a love, because it seems like death and absolute denial; because with such a love one appears to call into the void and the completely unheard-of; because this love seems like a ghastly leap into groundless space; because everything seems untenable and apparently meaningless.

Here is someone who does his duty where it can apparently only be done with the terrible feeling that he is denying himself and doing something ludicrous which no one will thank him for.

Here is a person who is really good to someone from whom no echo of understanding and thankfulness is heard in return, whose goodness is not even repaid by the feeling of having been selfless, noble and so on.

Here is someone who is silent although he could defend himself, although he is unjustly treated, who keeps silence without feeling that his silence is his sovereign unimpeachability.

Here is someone who obeys not because he must and would otherwise find it inconvenient to disobey, but purely on account of that mysterious, silent and inconceivable thing that we call God and the will of God.

Here is a person who renounces something without thanks or recognition, and even without a feeling of inner satisfaction.

Here is someone who is absolutely lonely, who finds all the right elements of life pale shadows; for whom all trustworthy handholds take him into the infinite distance, and who does not run away from this loneliness but treats it with ultimate hope.

Here is someone who discovers that his most acute concepts and most intellectually refined operations of the mind do not fit; that the unity of consciousness and that of which one is conscious in the destruction of all systems is now to be found only in pain; that he cannot resolve the im-

measurable multitude of questions, and yet cannot keep to the clearly
known content of individual experience and to the sciences.

Here is someone who suddenly notices how the tiny trickle of his life
wanders through the wilderness of the banality of existence, apparently
without aim and with the heartfelt fear of complete exhaustion. And yet
he hopes, he knows not how, that this trickle will find the infinite expanse
of the ocean, even though it may still be covered by the grey sands which
seem to extend for ever before him.

One could go on like this for ever, perhaps even then without coming to
that experience which for this or that man is the experience of the Spirit,
freedom and grace in his life. For every man makes that experience in accordance with the particular historical and individual situation of his
specific life. Every man! But he has so to speak to dig it out from under
the rubbish of everyday experience, and must not run away from it where
it begins to become legible, as though it were only an undermining and
disturbance of the self-evidence of his everyday life and his scientific
assurance.

Let me repeat, though I must say it in almost the same words: where
the one and entire hope is given beyond all individual hopes, which com-
prehends all impulses in silent promise,

—where a responsibility in freedom is still accepted and borne where it
has no apparent offer of success and advantage,

—where a man experiences and accepts his ultimate freedom which no
earthly compulsions can take away from him,

—where the leap into the darkness of death is accepted as the beginning of everlasting promise,

—where the sum of all accounts of life, which no one can calculate
alone, is understood by an inconceivable Other as good, though it still
cannot be "proven,"

—where the fragmentary experience of love, beauty, and joy is experienced and accepted purely and simply as the promise of love, beauty and
joy, without their being understood in ultimate cynical scepticism as a
cheap form of consolation for some final deception,

—where the bitter, deceptive and vanishing everyday world is with-
stood until the accepted end, and accepted out of a force whose ultimate
source is still unknown to us but can be tapped by us,

—where one dares to pray into a silent darkness and knows that one is
heard, although no answer seems to come back about which one might
argue and rationalize,

—where one lets oneself go unconditionally and experiences this
capitulation as true victory,

—where falling becomes true uprightness,

—where desperation is accepted and is still secretly accepted as trustworthy without cheap trust,

—where a man entrusts all this knowledge and all his questions to the
silent and all-inclusive mystery which is loved more than all our individual
knowledge which makes us such small people,

—where we rehearse our own deaths in everyday life, and try to live in
such a way as we would like to die, peaceful and composed,

—where . . . (as I have said, we could go on and on):

—*there* is God and his liberating grace. There we find what we Christians call the Holy Spirit of God. Then we experience something which is
inescapable (even when suppressed) in life, and which is offered to our
freedom with the question whether we want to accept it or whether we
want to shut ourselves up in a hell of freedom by trying to barricade ourselves against it. There is the mysticism of everyday life, the discovery of
God in all things; there is the sober intoxication of the Spirit, of which the
Fathers and the liturgy speak which we cannot reject or despise, because
it is real. Let us look for that experience in our own lives. Let us seek the
specific experiences in which something like that happens to us. If we
find them we have made the experience of the Spirit which we are talking
about.

16 · Prayer

There are certainly many people today who find prayer difficult even
though they are prepared to confess the unnameable, nameless God as
the one ground of all, as the all-permeating mystery. They are under the
impression that because this nameless God is an, as it were, faceless and
ineffable mystery he cannot be addressed. They think, more or less explicitly and reflexively, that he who bears and embraces all should not be
turned by prayer into an "object" of thought and speech, addressed and
separated from all he bears.

Because he can be correctly thought of only when he is strictly understood as the all-overwhelming and incomprehensible mystery, these people think one cannot name him without turning him into an idol. They
think they may not reach out in prayer to one who has no name, who as
mystery cannot be "clearly" expressed. They prefer to keep silent with
averted face before this God and resignedly make for those regions of existence in which lie before one's mind and heart the individual surveyable
realities with which one can really deal knowing what one is about and
what is to be expected.

There is much to be commended in these sentiments. Prayer can be itself only when it is understood as the last moment of speech before the silence, as the act of self-disposal just before the incomprehensibility of God disposes of one, as the reflexion immediately preceding the act of letting oneself fall, after the last of one's own efforts and full of trust, into the infinite Whole which reflexion can never grasp.

Accepting all this, however, we have also to say that we can and must undertake the ever new venture of addressing this incomprehensible God. Such address does not, of course, take place, as in the interhuman field, on a horizon which supports the exchange and embraces both partners of the dialogue like a third party. *God* is the very possibility of address; he himself brings our prayer about when we pray. But if this is so, he can also be the one addressed. Here we need not raise the question—which we can leave to Christian philosophers and theologians—whether such a possibility of a real address to God, in which although himself the ground of speech God is yet the one spoken to, belongs to man's essence or is made possible only by what in Christian terminology we should call God's self-communication in grace, or Holy Spirit.

We can also leave open the question whether prayer as an address to God is possible only because in his self-communication to the world, called grace or Spirit, God not only carries history but made history his own and gave himself as a partner in it when, in a truly historical revelation, he addressed us in the world with the word which the world is. And the question is also open as to what and how far the rendering possible and meaningfulness of our prayer has to do with Jesus of Nazareth and his prayer to the Father, however important it is for our prayer in the concrete.

Whatever the answers to these subtler questions, man can at all events speak to God, address him and in his address come to him—if he is really praying, that is, and not attempting to subject God to himself with some form of conjuration—in grace as the place of prayer, which is everywhere. It is not easy to render this statement intelligible, because it is the very loftiest thing one can say about man. That the creature can "treat" with his creator, that is, that the creature, radically dependent and caused as he is, the one who in his very being is derived, by turning back on himself, to some extent can "do business" with his Ground, and in that "business" must still know and realize that what he is doing is God's work to the very last, is certainly a statement which finally establishes, in a still more comprehensive theological proposition, that, precisely because of and not merely despite his radical dependence on God, the creature is a genuine, true reality who does not evaporate into essencelessness when he faces God, that God can in sober reality create a free other to stand before him and relate to him.

A product of man's hands does not talk to its creator. God, however, can in his all-powerfulness so posit us that we are really something in his sight and with relation to him. Here dependence and autonomy are two qualities which increase in equal and not inverse proportion. This basic relationship between God and the creature, as Christians understand it, must be clear if we are to understand the possibility of a prayerful address of the creature to God.

All this, however, is only by way of introduction. I must return to something I was saying earlier in my preliminary remarks: prayer exists, and in it God becomes our You, the one addressed of whom we have a fundamental expectation that he can answer, that he has addressed his word to us even before we begin to speak, that our address to God is therefore an answering address. Prayer like this exists. And all questions about the legitimation of prayer as an address to God must start from this fact. The axiom that it is legitimate to argue from reality to possibility is particularly pertinent here.

We pray, mankind prays, therefore we *can* say You to God. We do not need first to devise some essence for man and then, basing ourselves on that pregiven and predevised essence, inquire into whether such an essence can meaningfully address its own incomprehensible, unearthly ground and abyss. We start from the reality of such worshipping address and must then determine man's essence in basing ourselves on that reality: man is the one who can say You to God; his finitude and his dependence are such that they are open in autonomy to God as his partner, to whom of course man in prayer must still surrender as the one who has received everything, including the ability to address God and the address itself, from the one he addresses.

Therefore one must venture and not tire of venturing to speak to this You; ignoring the paradox of it, one must struggle for and suffer a higher naïvety, as the first and provisional naïvety, which conceived of self and God too ingenuously as two realities who could establish a mutual relationship, is, as it were, shrivelled up in the mortal terror at God's incomprehensibility and all-bearing power. When this ability to say You to God is no longer self-evident but experienced as man's highest possibility, given and disclosed by God, when we notice that the word we speak to God in such a way that it can really reach him is worked and spoken by him in us, when (to adopt the sublime language of New Testament theology) we experience that God's Spirit must pray in us and he himself say Abba, Father, as our word if we are to be able to say Father, then our address to God has for the first time found its true essence, has not become impossible, as we might think, but on the contrary has for the first time become what it must be.

When we step outside the circle in which we utter this You in prayer, the possibility of prayer as an address to God films over to the point of disappearing from view. God then becomes a faceless entity, the obscure mystery who almost threatens to rebuff us, who reveals the full extent of our nothingness, and faced with whom the words stick in our throat.

If, however, we find the sudden courage still to speak our You into this darkness in hope and trust, if we do this again and again, if we make no arrogant demand that our call into this silent darkness should receive an immediate, particular answer which simply overwhelms us instead of being the soft and silently saving presence of this mystery, we notice that we can say You to God, trusting and so waiting for the moment when this mystery of our existence will show his face unveiled as everlasting love, which is an eternal You to You.

17 · Petitionary Prayer

There is a tendency in modern theology to ease the difficulty of petitionary prayer by seeing prayer in terms solely of doxology, praise, confession, adoration, honour with regard to God, before whom all petition wholly retires. It is no doubt self-evident, or should be, that petition as merely making known in demand or in appeal to condescension and compliance one's own will is not in itself prayer. We must therefore try and view the matter from a different angle.

Attempts have been made to facilitate an apologia for prayer of petition by saying that one can or should in genuine petitionary *prayer* ask for only "heavenly" things, not earthly things for the satisfaction of needs immersed in the dailiness of life, because, it is said, such earthly things are to be conquered by the struggle of our own efforts: to expect them from God without our own exertions is simply to ask God for marvels, for miraculous interventions in the world's course which do not exist, cannot exist or are reserved for God's very special friends, among whom we should not be too ready to number ourselves.

There is much in all this that is true and to be borne in mind if we are to maintain a clear distinction between the essence of prayer and magical conjuration. However, we should not be in too much of a hurry to try to sublimate and "demythologize" petitionary prayer, because throughout the history of religion men have resorted to genuine and (if one may so call it) "solid" prayer of petition.

The Old Testament Psalms, which Christianity too has regarded as authentic models of prayer, are full of petitions. And we should not forget that Jesus's Our Father is a prayer of petition and not a selfless glorifi- cation of God, and that as well as the heavenly gifts asked for daily bread is mentioned (even in primitive Christianity there was a temptation to in- terpret it as the bread of eternal life).

When we ask whether and why even man today can genuinely and un- affectedly utter a prayer of peition, and that both in and for his earthly needs, then in my opinion we should, at least at the beginning of theolog- ical reflexion on such petitionary prayer, leave aside overprofound and oversubtle theories. These have, incidentally, been dealt with already by traditional theology, as it too, and not only so-called modern man, was familiar with the questions posed by the prayer of petition in particular (apart, that is, from the questions posed by prayer in general). It is rea- sonable to ask how petitionary prayer is reconcilable with God's omni- science, which does not need us to inform it of our needs, with God's providence and its eternal immutable designs, and with the immutability of God and his will which we are powerless to change.

Illuminating solutions to these and similar problems have been of- fered. People have asked whether the "effectiveness" of a prayer of peti- tion for temporal gifts is to be proved empirically, whether, for example, the weather in south Tyrol, with its pious Christian farmers and field processions and blessings of the weather, would be different if Tibetan peasants, who do not practise this kind of prayer, were resettled there. If one were a somewhat rationalistic and sceptical Christian, one could also ask what, without being presumptuous, one is to think of the many tes- timonies of astonishing answers to prayer, from those of places of pil- grimage and the experience of particular pious people and groups to Christian Science. But, as I have said, I shall not properly speak of all this in questioning and defending the prayer of petition.

Only two things must be said to give an understanding of petitionary prayer, and together they seem to me to make the possibility and mean- ing of petitionary prayer sufficiently intelligible. Firstly, prayer of peti- tion is prayer and meaningful before God only if the desire for a deter- mined and even worldly individual good asked for is also at the same time man's absolute surrender to the sovereign decrees of God's will. One can- not come to God in prayer without giving him oneself, one's whole exis- tence, in trustful submission and love, and in acceptance of the incom- prehensible God who is beyond our understanding not only in his essence but also in his free relationship to us and must be accepted as such.

A petitionary prayer which is not thoroughly imbued with Jesus' words before his death: Let your will be done, not mine, is not a petitionary prayer, not a prayer at all, but at most the projection of a vital need into the void, or the attempt to influence God as it were by magic, which is

senseless. Only when and in so far as a person gives himself up unconditionally to God and his incomprehensibility, which of course he can do
only in faith, hope and especially love, are all goods of a temporal nature
for which he petitions properly (= totally) relativized; man acknowledges that the opposite of what is concretely asked for can be salvific too:
if, that is, it is granted by God's incomprehensible freedom and accepted
by man as God's will.

Man's desire for a determined temporal good is not just brushed aside
as of no account, but it is absorbed into that freedom man attains when,
because he has surrendered to God, he is dominated by no individual
force in his existence. Everything—life and death, health and sickness,
power and powerlessness, the past, the present and the future—ceases to
be physically or ideologically absolute for man, unconditionally willed or
rejected, when he steps before God and lovingly surrenders to him. Praying with genuine prayer, man retains his freedom, unique, ultimate and
entire, and also his freedom with regard to what he himself wills with the
particular will to existence which governs him. Only in this way is the petition which one tries to direct to God really prayer certain to reach God.

My second statement must be added here. The person who steps into
God's presence in this way and yields and entrusts himself unconditionally
to his mystery is a concrete person, not an abstract ideal, not a merely religious person who longs for God only. He is a person of daily, profane
and banal needs and anxieties. He must place himself before God in
prayer just as he is, just as he may permissibly know himself to be: willed
by God, in the pressures and needs of his life, which cannot be adequately
illumined or simply sublimated into the religious.

This person does not need to have undergone a transformation so that
he is in pure harmony with God's decrees—which he does not know and
indeed cannot know exactly—before he comes into God's presence. He
may, in the act of surrender called prayer, place himself before God just
as he is, the one who must give himself to God precisely in his concreteness, the one therefore the pressures and needs of whose life concern some
particular thing which seems necessary to him as opposed to something
else, and this the more so in that he cannot know whether, with his desire
for this particular thing, he is not really willed by God in such a way that
this divine willing is willed to be fulfilled in man's concreteness and not
merely as a willing sublimated into single-minded surrender. When,
however, a person places himself before God as one who as a threatened
creature totally submits to God and at the same time wills a particular
thing unquestioningly and legitimately, when he is one delivering himself up in his concreteness to God, then he is uttering a prayer of petition.
And he does not then need to know exactly *how* the precise relationship of

this prayer of petition to God's omniscient and almighty and immutable decree is to be conceived.

It is understandable from this that the prayer of petition is not properly to be thought of as a secondary form of prayer. If it is prayer, it is the loving praise of God (even though not perhaps as explicitly as other forms of prayer specifically couched in doxological terms); if and because it is *petitionary* prayer, it places needy man at his most concrete before God; it is the form of prayer at which man is mindful not only of who *God* is, but also of who *he himself* is. When petitionary prayer is understood in this way, the question of *how* it is granted (if it is granted) is of secondary importance, because a person at prayer should not think he is heard only when his prayer as concrete request is granted in precisely the same way as that in which he had proposed it. Whether one says, referring to the granting of a prayer in the usual sense, that the granting—seen as the granting of *this* prayer—has already been included in the eternal plans of God's providence, or whether one says that it consists in the *salvific* acceptance of the concrete object of prayer, which (at least in the cases where one cannot speak of miracles) in its innerworldly quality as an earthly reality is part of the world's course, which would have proceeded in exactly the same way even without the prayer, these and similar ideas do not seem to me to be so important.

18 · Prayer as Dialogue

Every reader of devotional Christian literature and every listener to sermons on prayer is familiar with the statement that prayer is a "dialogue with God." Proofs of this commonplace of Christian spirituality and the theology of prayer are not usually adduced expressly. Perhaps it will not come entirely amiss, therefore, to offer some reflexions on the question whether and in what sense prayer can be called a dialogue with God, because the word "dialogue" would seem to presume that in prayer it is not only man who speaks, but God who speaks too, addresses us and in addressing us answers our word.

The question I am dealing with here, therefore, is not the wider, general question of whether prayer is possible at all and if so what makes it possible, the question in other words of the personal address which man offers to God (not by any means an easy problem today), but the question of whether and in what sense we can say that prayer includes an address of God to man, so that we can properly call prayer a dialogue between God and man.

It is undoubtedly true that man today has great difficulty in understanding and acknowledging that in prayer he experiences something like a personal address on God's part. If we can discount (justifiably in such a short essay as this) the wider question of a personal experience of God as existent and the relationship between God on the one hand, man and the world on the other, in other words, the wider questions which appear more than sufficiently problematic to man today, the difficulty of experiencing prayer as dialogue lies in the fact that what is usually or frequently interpreted in unsophisticated piety as God's address to us at prayer is primarily experienced as one's own psychical state or activity (this is an undoubtedly accurate statement; it certainly cannot be dismissed impatiently today).

The question is consequently how this should be understood as a particular manifestation of God, as his address. The man of today has the impression of to some extent talking to himself in prayer, consulting with himself, even though this self-communion of his is *about* God and his self-reflexion possibly *before* God. When he experiences sudden, unexpected and intense new insights and impulses, as does happen, the man of today is more than likely to understand them as movements within his own existence, as suggestions thrown up from the deeper psychic layers, as the breaking out of what has hitherto been repressed, as the fortuitous interplay of subconscious constellations, and so forth. He will refer to the fact that the same perhaps extraordinary psychological phenomena also occur where there is no specifically religious context—in artistic intuitions and ideas, which cannot be programmed, or in sudden changes in personality not motivated by explicitly religious factors, and so on.

We need not inquire here whether he is in fact justified in doing this; the fact remains that man today is under the impression he is being asked to accept a miracle or an outdated mythology when, because of its suddenness, urgency and significance, he is asked to take a powerful, unexpected, psychical happening as the result of a momentary spatio-temporal intervention of God in the normal processes of his consciousness.

It strikes him, at least in general, as no less improbable and incredible in the psychic field than in the external field, where he does not reckon with miracles (in the sense of fresh interventions of God in the world "from without"). Even when he acknowledges God's existence, he explains the course of his inner world by innerworldly causes, which themselves remain innerworldly even when they produce less common phenomena in the field of his consciousness.

There are, of course, still many people in the Church today, especially in the many "pentecostal" groups, who interpret particular psychic events—speaking with tongues, baptism of the Spirit, radical conversion, and so on—unashamedly as charismatic interventions of the Holy Spirit "from without," although this to some extent ignores the fact that all such happenings are primarily *theirs* and (at least until such time as cogent proof of the contrary is offered, and so far it has not been, even by parapsychological phenomena) must be explained as effects of their own internal and external condition. Add to this that to outsiders all such enthusiastic phenomena have their parallels in non-Christian religions which clearly display the peculiarities, horizon of consciousness, speech and limitations of all these psychical causes, and one is hard put to it to discover or know where to look for what necessarily derives from a special, miraculous intervention of God. Because of these and similar considerations, man today finds it very difficult to discover anything in his prayerful consciousness which he could interpret as an address by God distinct from his own mental processes. Prayer seems to him to be a monologue or at best a talking to himself, but not a dialogue with God, an event which one could seriously and without too many reservations call a conversation or an exchange.

In such a difficult situation, one might be tempted to interpret prayer as dialogue with God by saying that it is a discussion (in readings, applications, and so on) with the word of God in revelation and holy scripture. God speaks to us in Scripture; in meditating on Scripture, prayer responds to this word; and there thus arises an exchange, a dialogue with God in prayer. Certainly this view makes some sense to the Christian, who sees Scripture as God's word, but it too has its difficulties. It really succeeds only in putting the problem a stage further back, because revelation accepted by man's spirit (if it is not, of course, it is not revelation) and revelation objectified in Scripture raise basically the same question: how can the content of a human consciousness, which in consciousness has become a part of man's subjectivity and suffers from all its limitations, and is ultimately to be interpreted as the effect of this human causality, be heard and understood as the word of God? Even discounting this serious problem (which we cannot pursue further here), there is still another difficulty in this view.

In prayer, a devout Christian believes he is the recipient of an actual address from God calling him in his individuality and individual life's decision. If, however, this Christian has to regard the application of the word of Scripture, which in itself is universal, to himself and the actual situation of his life as his own work undertaken at his own expense and peril, as the application therefore of merely universal norms to a concrete situation of individual decision whose "more" over and above the universal is still precisely that on which it depends, no such dialogue would take place, as however is maintained by one who conceives of prayer as a dialogue. All that remains is a merely human application of a divine word of universal significance to an individual and the concrete, ever-unique questions of his life.

A man at prayer is still only talking to himself, even though he enjoys the assistance of a universal divine word. The passage from universal revelation to the concrete imperative is solely man's work, and even though he thought of it as (in part) the work of divine grace, it is not clear how he could interpret this help from grace in the application of the word of Scripture to himself and the questions of his life as a divine address because of which the concrete imperative (which calls to the man who prays) could be understood as the call of God.

It is true that assistance from such grace in actual decision is understood in theology as "illumination" and "inspiration," but it is still questionable what precisely this statement means, in that there is at least one great school of theology which interprets this illumination and inspiration, in so far as it is the condition of salvific acts, as merely "entitative" and beyond consciousness, and therefore claims that nothing is added to the understanding of an address by God in prayer.

Even if it were said that such a process of prayer, in which a salvific decision is taken, as well as being supported by supernatural grace is accompanied by "medicinal" graces which urge this event to a concluding, salvific decision, I have not advanced any further into my question. That is because this medicinal grace is interpreted as the result of innerworldly causes in itself and therefore also primarily, and the same difficulty from which I started in my question about the possibility of being addressed by God in prayer therefore remains. Even this medicinal grace is part of innerworldly reality in the web of causes and effects, can therefore, like everything else in the world, be understood as God's free creation through which God intends our salvation, but not as God's address any more than anything else in our history.

I suppose that many people make my question easy for themselves by first taking as given the knowledge of the personalness of God, and then promptly concluding that we can address him. Having got so far in the argument, one is under the impression of already standing in a relationship of direct, actualizable dialogue. However, even when one presumes that God is to be thought of as "personal" in and for himself, the other two steps to actual dialogue with God are not justified: that the personal God can be addressed by us remains obscure; and that he answers such an address and is not silent has particularly to be clarified. Even when one says, with regard to the second step, that God has abandoned his silence, spoken to us in his verbal revelation and communicated with us, the same question recurs: why the exchange in prayer is more than a conversation with oneself about the universal revelation of God in his history of revelation, more than mere application of this revelation to one's own situation at one's own expense and peril.

I must try to proceed in another direction. The presupposition, up to now regarded as self-evident, underlying our reflexions on prayer as dialogue with God is that God says "something" to us *in* prayer. The presupposition of my problem was that a particular individual, categorial content of consciousness—one of many—in a special and distinctive way effected directly by God and grasped in this special causality, constituted something like a dialogue with God. This presumption raised the difficulty I have already mentioned. How would it be, however, if we said and were permitted to say that in prayer we experience ourselves as the ones spoken by God, as the ones arising from and decreed by God's sovereign freedom in the concreteness of our existence? If we said that what God primarily says to us is ourselves in our decreed freedom, in our decree-defying future, in the facticity (that can never be totally analyzed and never functionally rationalized) of our past and present?

If we understand my question in this way, it is of course understood that the relationship of "partnership" and "dialogue" between God and us is unique and incomparable and cannot simply be thought of univocally on the model of an interhuman relationship of partnership and dialogue. Consequently the concept of "dialogue" for our question must have a unique and incomparable quality if it is to indicate the distinctiveness of prayer. If we can answer the newly-posed question in the affirmative, we are ourselves (in our transcendentality, which is experienced as such at its origin, as we might say) the utterance and address of God which listens to itself. That, however must not be understood merely as a general statement, but as a statement about present existence in its wholly determined, unique and historical actuality, given up to itself and *therefore* experiencing itself as spoken to itself by God.

God's most original word to us in our free uniqueness is not a word arising momentarily and categorially in addition to or separate from other objects of experience within a wider area of our consciousness, but is we ourselves as integral, total entities and in our reference to the incomprehensible mystery we call God, the word of God which we ourselves are and which as such is spoken to us. As soon as these phrases, which are at first sight of merely existential-ontological significance, are taken in conjunction with the presupposition that this transcendentality is already and everywhere (because of God's universal salvific will) raised and radicalized by virtue of God's immediacy by what we call supernatural grace as God's self-communication, then such phrases are seen to be directly theological.

When a person, in the Spirit and by grace, experiences himself as the one spoken by God to himself and understands this as his true essence to the concreteness of which the gratuitous grace of God's self-communication also belongs, and when he admits this existence and freely accepts it in prayer as the word of God in which God promises himself to man with his Word, his prayer is already (in one sense, to be elaborated later) dialogic, an exchange with God. The person then hears himself as God's address, heavy with God's self-promise, in the grace-filled self-communication of God by faith, hope and love. He does not hear "something" in addition to himself as one already presupposed in his dead facticity, but hears himself as the self-promised word in which God sets up a listener and to which he speaks himself as an answer.

Obviously it cannot be my business here to ground the statements just formulated in a theological and philosophical anthropology. If it could be, care would have to be taken that the statements were not merely uttered and substantiated as affirmations reaching man and given to him only when he thinks and talks about them in subsequent statements. They should rather be understood and proved as transcendental: that is, here, simply as statements whose content is always and everywhere realized and known in and together with man's spiritual and free self-realization as the unthematic conditions of the possibility of all human existence, so that then this transcendentally dialogical existence can be taken up into prayer, partially thematized and accepted in reflexive freedom, and prayer itself understood as a dialogue. As I have said, however, these statements cannot here be either explained more precisely or substantiated more accurately.

However, so far I have named only one aspect—the "transcendental" —of prayer from which prayer as dialogue becomes intelligible in a particular sense. I must add to this a second, from which the usual understanding of prayer as an exchange is given some justification as well as purified of mythological and miraculous misunderstanding. If man unconditionally and unfeignedly accepts his absolute openness to God (which is God's most original word to man), given by God and his freedom, if it is not hidden, distorted and misused by a free predecision of man to wholly determined categorial contents of his consciousness, then (the reader will, I hope, permit this perhaps apparently arbitrary jump in thought) arises what Ignatius of Loyola calls in his *Exercises* "indifference" and (if this indifference is really realized and sustained in radical freedom) "consolation without preceding cause."

If a particular individual object of choice now becomes part of such an ultimate dialogical freedom, without disguising, confusing or restricting, even in the course of further spiritual experience and questioning, this pure openness to God, it is experienced as the means by which this indifferent openness to God in unconditional surrender to him, and therefore (to put it the other way round) in unconditional acceptance of God's word which we ourselves are, is accepted and maintained, and this categorial object of choice (however conditioned and innerworldly in itself) can and may be conceived as a moment of this dialogical relationship between God and man because and in so far as this object is inserted into the conversational dialogue as a whole without jeopardizing or abrogating the latter's unlimited and unconditioned openness. From a purely innerworldly and categorial, objective point of view, such a categorial object of choice on which a man decides in prayer can still be problematic and perhaps later, compared with man's innerworldly needs and structures, be seen to be inadequate, provisional, ephemeral, even harmful; but here and now it is the best mediation of this indifferent, transcendental openness in which man experiences himself as God's word in promise, and therefore is God's salvific will.

In such a logic of existential knowledge and freedom, prayer becomes dialogical even in its categorial character as a succession of individual contents. That which enters our consciousness with rich sentimental feeling or with a suddenness and unexpectedness that leaves us breathless, is not so alone in being considered the effect of the Spirit and so as God's address that it has to be enthusiastically defended against a hardheaded and sceptical psychology. Rather, where the particular, consciously appropriated reality on which one decides can serve as a positive mediation of a permanent and unconditional openness to God (we could also say: of an unconditioned critical freedom), such a particular object may be understood as spoken to us by God in and with that fundamental address of God to ourselves which we ourselves are and which we perceive and accept in prayer.

It is not maintained here that the two aspects of prayer I have just tried briefly to indicate adequately constitute the dialogical character of prayer. I should be happy if the reader agreed I had at least clarified it a little further. And of course I cannot now clarify the consequences of such an understanding of prayer as exchange. It is possible that it now seems even harder than one usually thinks to understand prayer seriously and soberly as a conversation with God, and especially to experience it in practice as a conversation now that it has been "demythologized." If this is so, I am not saying that the normal believer should have reflexively before his mind in unreflected everyday life all the considerations I have put forward. After following such reflexions and feeling disillusioned, he may experience prayer as a dialogue with God —because that is what it is—in a new sort of naïvety.

19 · Community Prayer

Praying with others does not generally come easy today, not even to a believing Christian. He or she understands, to be sure, that there is and must be an official liturgy of the Church, where many people pray together, hear the word of God together, praise God together, profess their common faith, and celebrate together the memory of Jesus' death and resurrection. But even those who gladly come together with others to perform this official act of Church worship, as if it quite went without saying that they should, and who are glad to take part in a well-planned liturgy, often experience that liturgy as something altogether different from the prayer that rises to God from the inmost depths of a heart full of gratitude or need. It is not the same as the prayer an individual makes when he or she kneels, alone, before God in adoration, praise, thanksgiving, petition, or even desperate plaint.

But may we not pray together in this way as well? Not to depreciate the great and holy liturgy of the Church, with its solemnity and sacred dignity—but can we not find, midway between this liturgy of the people of God as such and the prayer of one alone and lonely, or alone and withdrawn in mystical dialogue into the stillness of God, another prayer, between the two extremes? After all, two persons who love—love each other in genuine trustfulness and familiarity—can be one with each other in such a way as to be able to spill out their hearts and declare their painful need to a third person, so that their plaintive approach to this person becomes really efficacious, and they receive relief and consolation from the third party. Then why should it not be possible for such persons to pray with each other as well and experience this capacity for "community prayer" as genuine fulfillment of their humanity and "inter-humanity"?

This prayer, too, can have the most varied forms. It can be the plain, sober prayer of a family, short and obvious, as if it went without saying that one says one's prayers. It can be the Our Father prayed together by husband and wife as they once again expressly entrust their love to one another, along with the burden that they are for one another, in the peace of an evening. And it can be the heartfelt, not purely ceremonial prayer for the enlightenment of the Holy Spirit, uttered in a little "basic Christian community" before the Scripture reading, or in a parish council meeting before the deliberations. In earlier times, at any rate, it was still felt to be the obvious thing to do to pray together in the classroom at the beginning of a lesson, or to invoke the Holy Spirit before a lecture in theology. In olden times in the Austrian Tirol, at the sound of the Angelus bell, the innkeeper would go to the parlor and join with all his guests in praying "The Angel of the Lord. . . ." Even today, at a funeral, Christians still pray the Our Father in common for the eternal rest of the departed, and surely they feel this less as official liturgy than as personal prayer.

This is not to say that there is anything in such a vital prayer, personal yet common, that must not also be present in the official liturgy if the latter is not to be simply a routine ritual but true prayer, worship in truth (John 4:24). We are only saying that, even apart from official Church liturgy, there can be really genuine, personal prayer in community, and that this prayer will be a manifestation and fulfillment of what stamps the Christian life everywhere and always: that we are ever carried forward in the accomplishment of our salvation, through Christ, yes, but also by all the members of the one Body of Christ in which we live and exist. In such prayer, realized in a free community of prayer, the Christian performs a basic deed of his or her Christian existence: after all, love for God and neighbor form an indissoluble unity, and ultimate nearness to God, regardless of whether this is reflected upon or not, creates ultimate nearness to one's neighbor, and vice versa.

As with all prayer, prayer in common must become ingrained, it must be learned. It may not be allowed simply to be the product of a mood of the moment or of sudden improvisation. Prayer in common must be learned today anew; it must gather experience, so as to be able to overcome barriers and open closed doors, and really be the common dialogue of human beings with God, in which each person hears and says, together with others, the same word as the others dare to say to their God. We must not expect this common prayer always to succeed equally well. Especially in the beginning, we may well have to feel it as something laborious and clumsy. There is nothing amiss in its being felt, in the beginning or indeed even later, as a dry exercise of one's duty. This is of no importance. The great common prayer welling up from the midst of many hearts in the storm of the Holy Spirit can very well be the reward of laborious prayer in little communities, just as an orchestra's grand performance is the fruit of a great many toilsome hours of practicing together. But what a blessed marvel—and yet one we should prepare for— if human beings, bound together in inward love, were to praise God, thank God, and weep before God together in common prayer, and thereby be enabled to experience that the one, eternal God loves each of them, altogether personally and uniquely, as a member of the holy society of all the redeemed!

Ought we not consider it our grave and sacred task to learn such community prayer? Lovers are not ashamed in each other's presence. They allow each other into the inmost mystery of their life and being. Then why should they be embarrassed to pray together? One must make the attempt and be willing to take on the task of common prayer as a grave, yet happy duty of Christian piety.

20 · Reading the Bible

Some of the Desert Fathers, in their radical renunciation of creatures, actually gave up Holy Scripture. We need not find fault with them. Surely we can assume that the Spirit of God had so filled them, the whole of Scripture had become so interior to them, that they no longer had need of its words and letters. After all, when we come to die, we shall no longer be able to read and so shall have to have what we now read written and printed in the Word of God already written on the tablets of our hearts. But for the ordinary Christian life of a person who knows how to read, Bible reading belongs necessarily to the spiritual life.

To be sure, such converse with Holy Scripture can be of very different sorts in the Christian life. Some will find a scientific, exegetical familiarity with Holy Scripture useful, perhaps even necessary, merely for their Christian lives. For others, a single word of Scripture may strike so deep into their heart that their whole life is transformed by it and delivered over to God's grace, and now this single word will never again cease to resound in their life, so that they really need not read much more in Scripture—where, after all, everything we read is ultimately calculated to arouse the same response in us in any case. And between these two extremes in the way a person might do his or her spiritual reading in Scripture, for the edification of the inward human being and the upbuilding of his or her love for God and neighbor, there are the most diversified manners and ways in which converse with the word of God can be maintained.

It is likewise altogether understandable and legitimate that Christians should relate differently to the individual writings of the Old and New Testaments, each according to his or her own individuality and call. When all is said and done, it is the same Spirit of God that breathes forth from all the writings of the Bible, not only from those of the New Testament but from those of the Old as well, if we read these individual writings within the totality of revelation and from our basic orientation to Jesus Christ in the Church. On the other hand it is also understandable and justifiable that a simple Christian might leave certain books of the Old Testament, for example, pretty much out of account, even picking and choosing among the Psalms, for instance—and then read the Gospels and gain nearness to Jesus in these rather than wrestling his or her way through Saint Paul's theology, which can sometimes be difficult.

But some familiarity with the sacred writings of the Old and New Testaments is a basic of the Christian life. We in our part of the world have, after all, learned to read newspapers and magazines. We read day in and day out. We may even have quite a collection of books of our own— perhaps even our own little library. How, then, could we dispense ourselves from a continual reading of Holy Scripture? After all, it is part of the content of our faith that the Holy Scriptures, written under the inspiration of the Holy Spirit, have God himself as their principal author. The human authors too, of course, were truly authors of Holy Scripture, not just stenographers taking divine dictation, and they bring their whole personal human history and particularity to these writings. The precise relationship between the divine Author and these human authors may be rather nebulous and cause ongoing difficulties for simple readers of the Bible. But this does not gainsay the fact that when we read the Scriptures as they should be read we read the word of God himself in them. That is, when the process of this reading is genuinely supported by the vehicle of the inward grace of God, by the Holy Spirit who is given to us and who has inspired these Scriptures, then we hear in Holy Scripture not just discourse about God but God's actual word to us. Hence a Christian ought repeatedly to ask whether faith in Scripture as God's word is a reality in his or her life or merely part of a theoretical faith-conviction.

One may of course read other spiritual writings, too, writings which are not "God's word to us" in the same sense that Holy Scripture is. This literature, too, can surely be useful to us in our spiritual life, especially when—again, in any number of very different ways—they are interpretations or explanations of Scripture itself. But a Christian should not nurse such foolish modesty as to think that he or she cannot reap crucial encouragement for his or her own life directly from God through his own word, and must rest content with the "derived discourse" of preachers and spiritual writers. Not that we need spurn this discourse—it is the echo and acceptance of what Scripture itself tells, and we certainly must not lapse into a spiritual solipsism that condemns what our brothers and sisters have learned from Scripture through the assistance of the divine Spirit. But average Christians, too, have the right and the duty to venture to approach the Bible personally. If they read it humbly and self-critically, ever docilely grafting their own understanding onto the understanding of Scripture enjoyed by the Church at large and its magisterium, Scripture's guardian and interpreter, then they can actually hear, from the Bible itself, God's word for themselves and their lives, that word of his upon which they depend in life and in death.

We must really let Scripture speak, of course, in stillness and solitude—and perhaps too where its inexorable summons comes softly to us, yet in such a way as not to be able to be missed amid the hubbub of our daily lives. We must, to be sure, enjoin silence upon the clamor of our everyday superficialities when we are reading Scripture. And yet we must also bring our own lives, with all the darks and lights of their variegated texture, to that Scripture reading. Long ago, in the year 1734, J. A. Bengel said: "Apply yourself wholly to the passage, and apply the passage wholly to yourself." We must read Scripture again and again, even when it seems to mean we must wander through wastelands. For then, time after time, our own life situation and a passage from Scripture will collide with and illumine each other. The illumination will be mutual—because, while we should really let God's word speak to us, still we should remember that the Spirit who fills this word is the selfsame Spirit who is hidden as well in the interior of our own life situation.

Holy Scripture is not just another book. Generally we can read a book through once and lay it aside when we have finished. But Holy Scripture is more than the testimony of a religious experience of humanity, ever transcending the experience of an individual human being. It is the word of God himself, the word of the God who condescended in his own infinity and incomprehensibility to communicate and share himself in these human words. This is why we can never "finish" the Bible and put it aside. If the Bible were nothing but human words, conceptually finite and historically conditioned (of course, it is this, too), if it did not contain the marvel of God's own condescension occurring within our narrow confines and "becoming event" ever anew as it is read—then of course we could "finish" Scripture. But as it is, Scripture is the inexhaustible source and wellspring of our spiritual lives. We must "practice" reading Scripture. We must learn to use all the tools we have available for reading the Bible, each of us according to his or her own capabilities. We must vanquish sloth and tedium again and again. We can try reading Scripture in company with others—and thus experience, to our own blessing and profit, how the word of Holy Writ "comes alive" for and in others, how it bears its fruit in them. We cannot have the blessing of humble, patient reading of Scripture inculcated in us from without. We must seek to hear Scripture, time after time, by actually reading it ourselves. Then shall we experience its strength and power, and shall come to appreciate that its attentive reading is an irreplaceable part of the spiritual life.

21 · The Mission of Every Christian

The Church in its totality, in all its members, has a missionary task. Love of God and love of neighbor are one. Grace and salvation are incarnational-historical. In virtue of Christ's express commission, in virtue of his summons to all peoples to come to the Church and to a salvation that no longer knows any national boundaries, in virtue of the life of faith in its capacity as testimony—on the strength of all these things, not even Christian existence at its barest can be "realized," reduced to actuality and practice, without being in some degree "missionary."

No member of the Mystical Body of Christ is alive for himself or herself alone. Each has a function of service to perform for the others, even for those members who are still merely "potential"—since these too have a true, and in a way already actual, relationship, through the Incarnation and the universal salvific will of God, to those who are members of the Church in all the dimensions of their life and in all the dimensions of the Church. Thus the primary subject of full missionary authority and initiative, and of the missionary task, is the Christian as Christian.

To be sure, the missionary function of most Christians in the concrete will perhaps have no directly palpable relationship to the missionary work of the Church in the proper, direct sense—other than precisely in their contribution, as living members of the one Church, to the life and activity of that Church, which does directly and concretely carry forward a missionary activity. But this in no way militates against the fact of a basic orientation of every Christian to the missionary task of the Church. Only, this basic orientation can be even more concretely actualized in function of each person's concrete life situations, in function of his or her direct call through the official Church, and in function of his or her individual, inner summons of grace. This concrete actualization will still be that of the (genuinely supernatural) moral obligation to reduce the Christian life to concrete practice, whether by explicit (private and liturgical) prayer for the missions, by concrete material deeds done for them, by accepting a personal vocation actually to live in the missions (for example, even in a contemplative community in the missions), or by direct activity as a lay person, deacon, or priest (whether this activity be officially commissioned by the Church or undertaken privately), for example in a religious community or secular institute.

22 · Penance and Confession

1. According to the Gospel and the teaching of the Church, penance in the sense not so much of an isolated, intermittently posited activity as of a basic attitude determining the whole of Christian existence, in the sense therefore of a basic *metanoia* (conversion to God through faith and contrition) continually renewed, is a grace from God and a charge on man as an individual and on the Church as a whole. It has to be asked whether this permanent *metanoia* in the individual, which means basically *both* change of mind *and* change of external behaviour together with the institutions, has not been narrowed down to too individualistic an assurance of salvation, and whether this permanent *metanoia* in the Church as a whole has been misinterpreted as an *aggiornamento* which is certainly necessary but which never matches the radicality of ecclesial *metanoia* as it should be experienced.

2. This situation in the life of the individual Christian and of the Church today is made worse by the fact that the understanding of the Christian significance of sin and forgiveness of sin must be re-acquired and re-expressed so that modern man's temptation to unfetter his relationship to God as a sinner by appealing to his genetic, psychological and social conditioning and finitude can be met in the right place and in the right way. This is because these attempts at unshackling the relationship are in themselves justified, but do not erase the more radical basic experience of being referred to God's grace as a sinner.

The Church, however, must recognize that it is faced here with a new challenge to which so far in its preaching, catechesis and initiation into basic religious experience it has not sufficiently adverted.

3. The dogmatic theologian must clearly emphasize (as also when dealing with public worship) that he would be stunting theology and the Christian understanding of existence to an unacceptable degree if he maintained that, to the extent that the process of penance (as *metanoia*) in the life of the Christian impinges on the ecclesial sphere or even in general, it is limited to the reception of the sacrament of penance in the sense of individual confession. The following can be just as much salvific events of metanoia, provided that they are recognized (more or less thematically) as God's work and are experienced (again, more or less thematically) as God-given, as the grace of forgiveness and the bestowal of life: genuine acts of self-criticism, of "revision of life," of the avowal of guilt, of the plea for pardon (where it has not degenerated into a cheap process of self-exoneration or a social stunt), of the rejection of social conventionalisms and institutionalisms with which one has up to now identified oneself to

one's own advantage; the admission of a social self-manifesting "movement" which one has up to then tried to obstruct out of indolence or egoism; a readiness to confront the harsh truths in one's own existence—which the keener gaze of psychology and depth psychology today reveal —about one's own poverty in relationships, one's egoism, one's false introversion, pseudo-forms of the religious, false taboos of the sexual and so on; and many other partial manifestations of conversion and breakthrough in human maturity and of the assumption of one's own interhuman and social responsibility. To this extent the (individual and collective) elimination of cliché-ridden and stagnant forms of what is really meant by penance is to be regarded as a legitimate process which is itself a part of *metanoia*.

4. Even the sacrament of penance itself can escape a purely legalistic or even ultimately magical misinterpretation only if it is understood, administered and received as a particular concretization of this *metanoia* in the context of the Church. The clearer and more convincing this concretization of *all* the dimensions of penance, and the less attempt made simply to dispose of a single sinful occurrence in the past, the more prospect there is for the sacrament to be appreciated and made use of today.

5. Discerning and realizing at their roots the ecclesiological aspects of sin and forgiveness of sin reflects not only the necessary understanding of man's social dimension today but the teaching of the second Vatican council. It must not be undertaken as merely theoretical ideology on the occasion of the reception of the sacrament, but must be clear in the actual structure of the sacrament in general. There must be an inner unity, not just competition, between penitential services and particular receptions of the sacrament.

6. The interpretation, theologically unanimous since Thomas Aquinas, of the yearly duty of confession universally laid down by the fourteenth Lateran council nearly 750 years ago has also been prominent in catechism classes and popular religious instruction. It states that the Easter duty is properly a commandment of the Church's human law only when there are sins not yet submitted sacramentally to God's forgiveness which, both objectively *and subjectively*, are such as, in biblical language (Gal. 5:21; 1 Cor. 6:9; etc.), to exclude from the kingdom of God. Of course the duty to submit such grave sins to the sacramental consolation of the Church's pardon, because of the nature of sin, of the Church and of the sacrament of penance, refers to "grave sins" thus understood, even independently of the humanly issued commandment of the Church, in so far as God's forgiveness of these sins must be salvation-historically, salvifically, sacramentally and ecclesially manifested at some time or other in the life of the sinner through the act of the Church. The determined period of time in which this fundamental duty is to be fulfilled is of

human law in the Church; in principle it could be abrogated and certainly must, like every other human law, be so construed and applied in the Church that it serves man's salvation and not his ruin.

7. Contrary to a trend in moral theology over the centuries (from perhaps as early as the Irish, Anglo-Saxon and Merovingian books of penance), there is no reason, in either dogma or religious and popular education, either with regard to the extent of the objective grave matter or with regard to the presumption of the extent of the sins committed subjectively as grave, to follow the rigorism which at least since the post-Tridentine period has predominated in moral theology and the practice of the sacrament of penance until today. Such rigorism, both in determining the extent of the *materia gravis* and in presuming that an infringement of the law in a *materia objective gravis* more or less always involves a subjectively grave guilt in the normal Christian, cannot be theologically substantiated. The presumption that there are sins which are subjectively very grave and therefore liable to the strict duty of confession in Christians who are living a life of basic church-Christian practice is also a position that is open to severe doubt. Consequently the frequency of grave sins which must necessarily be submitted to the forgiveness of sacramental confession has to be judged within a church of people who seriously desire to live a Christian life.

Now, as the experience of the Church in patristic and early medieval times shows, if the only sins submitted in confession are grave ones, the confession of such sins, at least in the form of the sacrament customary today, becomes psychologically very difficult if not in practice impossible, except perhaps on one's death-bed. Hence (leaving out of account here other psychological and similar reasons) an unnuanced and indiscreet propaganda for the opinion that only sins which absolutely need sacramental confession should in fact be included in particular confession is to be rejected. The reception of the sacrament of penance in particular confession retains its justification and its usefulness today (given the necessary reservations to be clarified below) even when sins that absolutely speaking do not need to be confessed are in fact confessed.

Precisely when one feels, for reasons which cannot be enlarged on here, that a too clear-cut distinction between grave and venial sins, as is customary in the average moral theology and church practice, is too facile and legalistic (even though such a distinction is sometimes correct and indispensable), then one has no proper grounds (unless one is going to deny the sacrament of penance itself) for canvassing the view that only grave sins, even where subjectively certain, should be submitted in particular confession. Nevertheless, *avoiding* such propaganda does not depend on acting as if every Christian were under a strict duty in church law to go to confession at least once a year even though he is aware of no serious sins.

8. It seems to me to be still certain today that according to the teaching of the Council of Trent the duty of receiving the sacrament of penance for objectively and subjectively really serious sins refers to particular confession, which in this case cannot be replaced by a penitential service of a general nature, even when that service is intended to be sacramental and so structured, and even though such a sacramental absolution with no more than a general confession may eventually, with or without alteration in the Church's positive command, be legitimately substituted for an actual particular confession.

If the real extent of objectively and subjectively grave sins is not arbitrarily enlarged with a thoughtless rigorism, in a form of the sacrament of penance which respects human and liturgical norms, the Tridentine specification of particular confession (and with it the commandment of the Church as laid down in Lateran IV) is still humanly, religiously, liturgically and pastorally justifiable today. Only, however, on these premises. If these premises are not fulfilled, then of course one can foresee a drop in the use of particular confession which would exceed the limits of the dogmatically binding and what is Christianly, humanly and pastorally correct. That is not to deny that there is also a drop in the frequency of particular confession due to the conditions of the period in which we live and based on a certain change in the relationship of the Christian to the sacraments in general, on the complexity of human life for which advice in the confessional is less easily given than before, on a change in the relationship between pastor and Christian, and similar factors into which I cannot enter here.

9. A general penitential service should not be regarded as a substitute for particular confession, which makes forgiveness more equitable and technically more manageable. Where it is valued in the religious feeling of the average Christian *solely* as just such a substitute, it need only lose the attraction of novelty and it has both weakened the habit of particular confession and become itself but seldom practised. Penitential services can still be an independent form of penance in the Church because of the nature of sin, the social conditionality and effect of sin, and the nature of the *Ecclesia semper poenitens*. Sometimes, too, it can be a much greater help to personal *metanoia* for the individual than particular confession, which, because of the number of penitents, the pressures on today's clergy, and one's psychological, psychotherapeutic (and not seldom also religiously weak) experience, has less genuinely religious significance for an initiation into true *metanoia*.

If other necessary conditions are observed, and with the above-mentioned proviso with relation to the duty to confess sins which are both objectively *and* subjectively grave, a priestly absolution can have sacramental significance for the individual even in a general community confession. I do not really believe that this sacramental quality can be absent if the priest, who pronounces God's forgiveness as the representative of the Church, sincerely means what he says. Such a sacramental quality seems to me to be present even when the priest leading the penitential service and pronouncing pardon over the community does not expressly reflect on the sacramentality of what he is doing or even perhaps thinks he can exclude it. An explicit declaration of the service's sacramental nature because the service is conducted by the official Church would be desirable, but it does not seem to me to be a necessary condition for the penitential service to be sacramental.

10. These services of penance should not, however, or at least not merely, be, almost in the style of a sensitivity group or the Salvation Army or any pentecostal movement, the common cultivation of a conversion and purification event still ultimately experienced as an individual event, but must take up and embrace in a Christian way the secular ethos of an increasingly effective responsibility of the individual within a society as such. In this way they could really become the actual manifestation of the self-realization of the Church as the body called to true and constant *metanoia* and to a self-realization in which, more clearly than Thomas Aquinas could envisage, the Church as the concrete, even though officially structured, community also becomes the sacramental bearer of the manifestation of man's conversion and God's forgiveness, and ecclesial penance really becomes the penance of the Church itself. The question then immediately arises: what sort of community must it be to be the real, genuine bearer of this realization of *metanoia*?

23 · Sin, Guilt, and Fundamental Option

In our spiritual life we are always in danger of using an enormous, complicated equipment of terminology, of stereotyped formulas and concepts, of ascetic and moral motives, which distract us from taking a cool look at reality. We talk so much about virtues and sins and all the rest and at the same time we have from the very beginning a definite idea of what these things are, of what they look like, so that we perceive only with difficulty their real meaning.

Before we can consider sin in our life, we ought to make a meditation on our life unemotionally and realistically, and at the same time avoid giving it any moral stamp from the very beginning, so that we can come face to face with our reality.

Don't let us ask: Am I humble or arrogant? Do I love God or not? Am I someone who is ready to sacrifice all for the love of Christ or am I not? But let us ask: What am I really making of my life? What am I doing? What kind of person emerges when I am described for once in the matter of fact terminology of an unbeliever, of a psychologist, of someone who can test my reactions?

Let us look at the people around us, not to judge or condemn them, but in order in this way to produce more easily a technique for self-criticism. Don't we find there—whether among priests or laity—many people of whom we are bound to admit that they certainly want to obey God's commandments and do on the whole obey them and yet we have the impression that a great deal in their lives is terribly wrong. It is no use saying therefore that there is no question at all here of sin, but only of dispositions, peculiarities, of incapacity in one respect or another, that all this is prior to any moral reaction and judgement. This person is in fact like this: he does not get away from himself; perhaps he does not realise at all how out of touch he is, how he underestimates or overestimates himself. He does not grasp the fact that he is seeking his effects in a field where they cannot be achieved; he does not notice that he is taking things very easily; he does not feel that there is any moral problem about settling down in comfort, leading a mediocre life, about what a modern psychologist would make of his thousand substitutes for action—certainly morally unquestionable—in which he comes to terms in his solitude with his failure in a scarcely commendable, evil way.

We have only indicated a few of the many things that happen in this way. That is—once again—the life of a particular individual, seen from a human and realistic standpoint, in the light of his mastery of life, and even (we say this quite soberly and seriously) in the light of his success in life, leaves a very great deal to be desired; and yet the person concerned thinks that his moral status is perfectly in order.

Of course it is clear that such a realistic meditation, coming to grips with life, looking to a person's success, his inward composure, his joy in life, his contact with other people—in a word, to the way he masters life on this earth—and a meditation asking how such a person stands with God cannot really be made to coincide. It is even obvious that we would be greatly mistaken in attempting to consider the two ways simply as two different ways of expressing one and the same absolutely identical reality. To do so would not only be incorrect, but it would mean also that we were not bringing a genuine, radically Christian mentality to our understanding of life. In other words: there are obviously human inadequacies, twisted outlooks, meannesses, blindnesses, abnormal reactions in regard to coping with life, which really have nothing to do with what a person is morally, in God's judgment.

In the normal, average, religious life, however, these two ways of meditation lie too far apart. Theoretically also they are too far apart. For it does in fact remain true in terms of dogmatic and moral theology, and of philosophy, that what is right, pertinent, in accordance with human nature, whatever consists in harmony with reality and is therefore also in harmony with God, that this too is moral. From a dogmatic standpoint, it remains absolutely correct that those objective twists of character, the stupid opinions, bad habits, limitations of talent, which are perhaps beyond the control of human freedom, are also in fact the very thing that ought not to be.

If I see that someone is fundamentally lazy, does not exploit his talents, fails to set about his tasks as forcefully, radically and energetically as another person applies himself to his secular calling in order to achieve something and to earn a living, I don't solve the problem by saying: The poor fellow doesn't understand his situation, he doesn't know about it, he means well, somewhere at least he is in touch with reality, but he is objectively blind to the possibilities and opportunities in his life. This does in fact raise the question whether this blindness in regard to life's real opportunities is inculpable. The person concerned may claim to have a good conscience, but perhaps it is only apparently good: he has perhaps heaped up on his innermost personal conviction so much rubbish by way of pretexts, surrenders in his life, of cowardice and cheap excuses, that he now thinks everything is in order.

Before saying that we are sinners, we would have to examine our lives calmly in the light of standards that are applied today. The weakness of touch, the introversion, the unease, the traumata, which we fail to transcend: these and a thousand other aspects would first have had to be observed in an appropriate consideration of our own person before we could ask: What have these to do with sin? Only then could we ask: At what points do we find the basically sinful roots of our condition which we have just examined so realistically?

The same holds for the danger of wrecking our life. If we say *a priori* that we are human and capable of sin, then again there is a danger of overlooking the real sins. Let us raise now the moral question: Where, at what point, through what causes, can my life with its tasks, with its possibilities, break down? (It is all the same whether anything or nothing could be done about it—this is another problem.) We would first have to discover prior to any moral judgment where the danger of such a breakdown lies. Does it arise from health, from my stupidity, from an innate difficulty in measuring up to what I ought to achieve? Are there any other things that could ruin my life, moral or immoral, or having nothing to do with morality? Am I in danger of a spectacular catastrophe?

The danger of a spectacular breakdown does exist. But at least equally serious is the danger that our whole life will slowly but surely fade into oblivion: the danger of mediocrity, of no longer really believing in a personal achievement, of giving up everything.

There is of course one capitulation that is imposed on everyone: we grow old, sick, tired, face the approach of death. There is also real breakdown, a hopeless situation, which is the proper achievement of our lives, perhaps imposed on us and required of us by God. Why should this not be the case? Someone could be called to a position in the Church for which he was not really suited, where even with the best will and with heroic efforts, from a purely human, intramundane standpoint, he cannot make much of his situation.

Such things do happen and we are right, but perhaps overhasty, to speak of them as our share in the cross of Christ. Before we think of these things, maintaining our sober, realistic view of life, we might ask: Before we pass any moral judgment, where is the danger of failing in regard to our positive, genuine, possible, attainable task in life? Such a failure must not be described at once as a sin. The question is not so much whether it is a sin or not, but how this sort of thing can be avoided. Not much is gained merely by stating the moral requirement in regard to this task: Do this.

Let us be honest. We preach and listen to others preaching too many moral imperatives and axioms and we far too rarely present ourselves and others with the question: How do I set about fulfilling what is required of me and how do I avoid what has to be avoided? It is an old-fashioned, but absurd view that a person knows without more ado how he has to set about doing something and that the only problem is whether he wills to do so or not.

Of course, each man in his original, spiritual, personal freedom is also faced with decisions whether he will or not: Will you respect this norm of God or not? Will you risk the leap or will you nervously stick to your present position and refuse to accept this task? But when my confessor tells me to fight against distractions at meditation, he has not told me how to set about it.

An example of this kind shows that the way in which in the concrete we have to satisfy a moral demand that life imposes is a question to itself and very much a question of content, and it must be distinguished from the question of what moral requirements are imposed on me. This "how" or "in what way" has no direct connection with strenuous moral effort or anything of that kind, but relates to a practical way—one might say, a skill—and to a rational, practical knowledge of how something must be done.

It is useless to advise someone who is out of touch to interest himself in his fellow-men, to have a heart full of love for all. It is of little use to tell someone who is nervous to be bold and take a risk. What is required is a calm consideration of the situation in a perspective, in categories and terms, which to a certain extent ascetically demythologise one's life and then really permit things to be seen as they are. Then you may ask: "How do I come to terms with these things?"

When we have ascetically demythologised our life, we can ask the further question: Where are our sins to be found? Or, more cautiously: Where are the dangers of sin lurking? Then we can and must say: Sin, in the theological sense, is a reality in my life. It is a fact, it is a permanent possibility, it is always a danger, it is always something which in the last resort I cannot judge or measure, in face of which I always flee to God's mercy. Sin is a reality in my life, for "if we say that we have no sin, we deceive ourselves" (1 John 1:8). And the Council of Trent teaches (DS 1573) that it is false to say that "without a special privilege from God, it is possible to avoid all sins, even venial, for a whole life-time." But when we assert that it is not possible to avoid all venial sins in the course of a whole lifetime, aren't we turning this terrible fact into something trivial and dangerously simple by claiming that it is a question merely of venial sins, of surreptitious sins?

Even assuming that it is a question only of venial sins, we don't want to conceal the fact that venial sin too can sometimes be a dreadful handicap to our apostolate, perhaps more so than a grave sin. Indolence, love of comfort, uncharitableness, arrogance—in a word, the sort of thing that gets on the nerves of laypeople when they see it in clerics—are often only venial sins, but how damaging they are to aid for souls, to our apostolate, to the reputation of the Church. But in connection with the statement that not all venial sins can be avoided throughout a whole lifetime, there is another fact to which we should pay more attention.

Are we so sure that manifestations of the basis of our human existence, rightly or at least with probablity described as venial sins, do not emerge from a primal source of our spiritual personality that is itself in a state of grave sin? There is a "fundamental option," there is a basic, human decision which remains anonymous, which cannot be grasped concretely in its material detail, cannot be judged and arrested, and yet nevertheless exists. When we consider our venial sins, we must therefore ask ourselves if they are really so harmless in this respect. Is the proposition that all men, without special aid from God, commit venial sins likewise innocuous? There is a final infidelity, a final cowardice, a final refusal to give our-

selves to God, a final want of love, a final egoism, which render it completely unnecessary to admit to ourselves that final rejection of God
which comes from the depth of our soul: we can in fact refuse to see that
our trivial faults and imperfections are a cover for a final basic attitude
which is truly mortal sin.

Are there not people of whom we are inclined to say that they have in
fact committed some grave sin and perhaps not yet got out of it, but in the
last resort are loving, selfless, inwardly looking to God, more than some
others who nervously avoid introducing any kind of disorder into the tidy
pattern of their lives? One of those beatified as martyrs at the time of the
Boxer rebellion had been a hopeless opium addict and always said that his
only chance lay in martyrdom, although in other respects he was a devout
Christian. His parish priest—rightly, it might seem—refused absolution
for years. Yet, if this man longed for martyrdom, really knew and admitted before God how miserable and wretched he was and asked God to
free him from his self-imposed imprisonment, may we not ask if, even
before his martyrdom, his life was not really rooted and founded in the
love of God—more perhaps than that of the parish priest who rightly
refused absolution?

If we say then in theological terms that sin is a reality and always an
immediate possibility in our lives, we should not make light of this proposition. The more or less indefinable character of venial sin, which we
really commit (as Christians we cannot deny this), does in fact make our
situation endurable only if we get away from ourselves and flee to God
alone, loving and trusting in his mercy. Understood in this way, anyone
can make a meditation on his own sins, even if he is quite sure from the
standpoint of moral theology—that is, as far as his duty of confession is
concerned—that he plainly and clearly has not committed any grave sin.
The person is not for that reason justified before God. For even if he were
justified, he has always to remember that this is due to the more radical
salvation through grace on God's side and not to his own merits.

If, however, our theological consideration of sin leads to the conclusion
that sin is a reality in my past, in my present, and a radically menacing
possibility in my future, then we may and must also. conclude that it is
reality encompassed by God's grace. God's grace, God's love, God's will
to salvation in Jesus Christ is really greater than our sin. We can never say
that we are certainly justified, predestined to eternal life. As true Christians therefore, who have understood what Christ, the incarnation, the
cross and redemption, really mean, we may not preach Christianity as a
commandment of God and as offering a possibility on which we decide
only in an ultimate sovereignty which is not encompassed by God. We
would then have to preach to Christians that God has given certain com-

mandments and, in what we call grace, the possibility of keeping these commandments.

This is important and right and must always be preached. But the question remains whether this way of preaching Christianity is adequate, whether we cannot ourselves make more of it. The answer must be that we can. I cannot of course claim to be certainly predestined to eternal life; but I must to some extent open the ears of faith and the heart of hope, not in order to produce a theoretical proposition about my predestination and God's salvific will, but to listen to God's word telling me: I love you in a way which in fact includes your freedom, and by loving you (we call this efficacious grace), I give you what you have to do.

Of course we cannot indulge in theories about this, we cannot turn it into a theoretical proposition about the "restoration of all things." It must never become a weapon against God, an excuse for taking things easily, a dispensation for ourselves. But if we strive with all that we have and are to get away from ourselves and run to God, if and in as much as we do this, in the dimension of Christian hope, in spite of the sins which are real enough in our life, we have the right to accept from God the assurance: I love you, you who are a sinner, and my grace is more powerful, more loving, and embraces all that you are, even your sin.

In the light of all this, the Christian's meditation is a meditation on where he comes from, not on where he is going; it is a meditation on what he would be of himself and not a meditation on what he is by the grace of God. Such a meditation on sin therefore, if it is truly Christian—that is, if it sees the human, true, responsible freedom, which a man cannot throw on to anyone else, as nevertheless encompassed, sustained, redeemed by the grace of God—is a meditation on our own sin which is an expression of the gratitude of redeemed love, which from this source has the courage to transcend its own limitations, to sacrifice what it cannot sacrifice by its own strength, to set about doing what it could not do from its own resources. Think of Augustine, who knew what he had to do and thought he could find no strength in himself. He looked—so to speak—into the empty jar of his own finiteness and asked how he could accomplish what he ought to do.

Whenever it is a question of real decisions against sin and for God, it is impossible to feel and enjoy first of all the capacity for these things and then to act accordingly. Nevertheless, we can always act in virtue of our powerlessness, jump while absolutely dreading the leap, because God is with us, because—without our being able to observe and as it were enjoy it in advance—our impotence, our weakness, and our cowardice, are always surpassed by God's power and mercy, by his grace: grace which frees us for action and is not merely the means as a sort of autonomous—

and what Augustine might call emancipated—freedom. Understood in this way, Molinism would not be Molinism, but theological nonsense and an appalling, existentially false attitude for a Christian. We are those who, in the gratitude of redeemed love, find the courage to say "Yes" to God and his demand.

24 · Indulgence

We can entreat God that he may, as far as possible, grant us favourable circumstances in his guidance of our lives, such as will as quickly and as beneficently as possible shape this process by which our whole sin-damaged being is transformed once the basic decision of conversion and repentance has been taken. Who has not actually uttered this prayer if he is a Christian (even if he has never hitherto regarded that which he prayed for from this point of view)? Who has not already entertained the idea: "If I could only die one death, the 'true death' in which my entire being with all that it has become throughout my entire life was made over to God in faith and love in an act of radical self-surrender down to the last fibre of my being, so that nothing was held back, nothing denied, but death was the total act of a totally committed faith!" No theologian will deny that through so intense a degree of love for God we would be liberated from all "temporal punishments due to sin" as well if this grace was bestowed in its entirety upon the individual. Nor can anyone deny that one instance at least of a blotting out of the temporal punishments due to sin does exist, that namely which we regard not as *an* instance but as *the* definitive instance of this process.

We can, therefore, ask God to grant us the greatest and most favourable chance possible of achieving the maturity of the Christian man as a whole. Such a prayer need not for one moment spring from egoistical promptings or from the impulse to escape from these punishments as "cheaply and painlessly" as possible. Nor need it involve any denial of the truth that for Christian living too there is a genuine attitude of "standing by one's past" and "bearing the consequences," so that to flee from this would be cowardly, un-Christian and ultimately speaking futile. Time is, in fact, not only God's gift, through which the most important factor, namely salvation, must be achieved; it is also the restriction which ensures that that which must be achieved shall be achieved only gradually. Otherwise we could never in fact pray for the coming of the Lord by saying: "Come soon." The attainment of maturity can take place in various ways: in circumstances of anguish, toil and frustration or in the midst of a

tempest which we nevertheless feel as blessed; in an attitude of freedom
and enthusiasm in which we experience as the blessing bestowed by a
powerful love that which seems to another the anguish of a weary process
of "dying." Thus we can ask God that he may bestow upon us the possibility of a swift and happy maturing process. But we cannot ask him to
allow us to share in God's own holiness and beatitude when we are only
half ready and immature. Surely we can in all reason ask God to work out
the destiny of those who are to be made perfect by him soon and by the
more joyful way. And what we can reasonably ask for ourselves that too
we can ask—one might almost say still more readily and more selflessly—
for others.

This is a prayer to which the Church can lend her support. As a source
of truth and a means of grace she has never merely been the external controlling organisation. She is the one Body of Christ in which all the members live for one another, suffer for one another and are brought to perfection for one another. When God regards an individual he always sees
him in his place in the whole, as one with Christ the head and as one with
all the brethren of this one Christ. No one lives to himself alone, no one
dies to himself alone. Each one is beloved by God by the very fact that
God regards his Christ and his Cross—beloved as part of a single reality
which God creates in the midst of mankind, destined as they are to be
brought to perfection. Through her prayers, therefore, the Church can
give her support to this entreaty for the remission of the temporal punishments due to sin. And when she does this then she does it as that which she
is, as the one great union of those who have been sanctified and redeemed, as the Bride of the Lamb, as Head and Body, the one Christ.
When God hears her then he regards that which she is as she prays. She is
the Church of the saints, the Church of the one Christ. He grants her a
hearing for her prayer in virtue of that which he has bestowed upon her
prior to any prayer, namely in virtue of the grace of Christ which has
been made powerful and victorious in the Church. Indeed the Lord himself says with regard to the hearing of the prayers of the disciples: "The
Father loves you *because* you have loved me and have believed that I
have come from the Father" (John 16:27). This is what is meant when we
speak of an indulgence as coming from the "treasury of the Church."

The "treasury of the Church" is God's own will to save—ultimately
speaking, therefore, God himself—to the extent that this is present in the
world with the force of an irrevocable victory in *that* Christ (as head)
who has been decreed by God from all eternity, precisely *as* "the firstborn
among many brethren," in other words in union with his "Body" which is
the Church. Rightly conceived of, therefore, the significance of this idea
of the "treasury of the Church" is precisely not that some part of its con-

tents is paid out as from some public fund which can be doled out in limited quantities and by instalments, something which otherwise the individual would have had to pay out of his own resources. And the fact that this is not the case means that the question of whether the treasury of the Church could ever be exhausted, seeing that so much is spent and paid out "from" it, is utterly ruled out from the outset and therefore does not need to be solved by any subtle explanations. For the same reason it is also clear that God is not compelled to grant such a prayer for the remission of the temporal punishments due to sin *precisely on the grounds that* he can no longer demand that which he has already received (namely *out of* the treasury of the Church.) He looks to the working of his own grace. This is the reason why he guides one to his perfection by this way and another by that. It is done according to his own free and incalculable measure, and in an order proper to him and decreed by him. But because in and through this sovereign power of divine grace there is a truly effective prayer—indeed, according to Christ's words an infallibly effective prayer—and because this prayer can be that of the entire Church, above all because it can and should be applied to the swift and happy attainment of the perfection of the whole man—for these reasons the Church can give her support as intercessor to the prayer of the individual for the remission of the "temporal punishment due to his sins." Where she does this in God's grace, where she does it well—for she must always perform such things through her members—where the individual is worthy of having his prayer heard through God's grace, there God hearkens too to the prayer of the Church of his own Son. It hardly needs to be specially emphasised once more that this takes place through the grace of God, who supplies the seed and the final flowering of this prayer and this worthiness according to the unfathomable decrees of his own good pleasure which is in no sense conditioned by any act on man's part.

With these provisos we can say that God gives the individual that which the Church implores on his behalf for his salvation. Thus the Church has always prayed for the sinner, who even as a penitent still bears the burden of his guilt. In the penitential practice of the early Church her intercession during and at the end of the period of penance belongs to the indispensable elements of ecclesiastical penance. She does not merely reconcile the sinner in that, by restoring him to harmony with herself, she imparts to him once more her own Holy Spirit which is the remission of sins; more than this, she actually prays with the repentant sinner for the forgiveness of the whole of his guilt with all its further effects. In view of the fact that it is, in fact, a *repentant* sinner that is being treated of, this applies in practice primarily (if we adopt the theological distinction and terminology current today) to the remission of the temporal punishments due to sin, to the total overcoming of the guilt. Even today this prayer is constantly being made. It is true that except for a small remnant it has vanished from the penitential liturgy used in the sacrament of penance itself because for practical reasons the accusation, considered as the initiating act of the penitential process, and sacramental forgiveness by the Church have been brought together in a single process, and the result of this is that the period of penance, the full overcoming of sin with all its consequences within man, is left almost exclusively to the Christian penitent who receives the sacrament. Yet for this reason the Church still continues constantly to be she who prays for the blotting out of the sins of her members and the punishment due to these sins, in the prayer of the Our Father, in the sacrifice of Mass, in the penances performed by her saints and of all upon whom the guilt of the age weighs as the Cross of Christ and who bear this Cross in faith and love, in the explicit prayers of intercession which are constantly being made in the most varied forms on behalf of sinners. It is to be hoped that in the projected renewal of the liturgical forms of penance these aspects will be brought out still more clearly.

From such a prayer as this no one can be excluded from the outset unless he has himself renounced his share in it by separating himself from the Church so that he can no longer be named in the liturgical intercessions in the manner in which the children of the Church have the privilege of being named (cf. 1 John 5:16). But in a special way we can include anyone in this prayer of the Church, and God's help can be extended to him in particular by means of an explicit and solemn intercession. Those who believe in the meaning of prayer, and who know what is meant by the Church, can be seized with awe at the following idea: the holy community of the redeemed, the Bride of Christ, stands at the throne of grace on my behalf! From her heart which is unceasingly and inalienably filled with the wordless sighings of the Spirit of God, prayer rises up on my behalf! It is *she* who says to me "May Almighty God have mercy upon you, forgive you your sins. . . ." It is *she* who promises this prayer to me, and she does this not merely in general terms or implicitly, but explicitly and as pledged by an act of her supreme authority to pray on my behalf.

Such prayer remits, "bestows" not simply in an authoritative remission of the punishments due to sin as though it were a simple "amnesty" of a punishment to be imposed in purely external terms that was in question, as though this punishment served *only* as a manifestation of the majesty of the law. In fact, as the Council of Trent explicitly declares, the Church does not ascribe to herself any power precisely of *this* kind, of granting an "amnesty" from a punishment imposed in the sacrament of penance in a purely external ("vindictive") sense, even though precisely in this she is still exercising her power of binding and loosing as defined in Matthew 16 and 18 (Denz. 1667 ff.). Even less, therefore, can she intend to use any such power outside the sacrament, especially since in fact the theologians commonly derive her power to grant indulgences from the same power of binding and loosing as spoken of in the gospels. But the holy Church which—as Tertullian has already said in a similar context—is always hearkened to, can assure the sinner in a special and explicit act, of a prayer of intercession such that it draws down a remission of the punishments due to sin. Now provided that we understand this *special* prayer in the right way and in the way in which we have attempted to interpret it, we can say: This is precisely what takes place in what we call an indulgence.

In earlier times the Church combined an assurance of prayer of this kind with the remission of a specific ecclesiastical penance which she had, of her own power, previously imposed upon the penitent in the sacrament of penance. But in a certain sense she replaced the effects of the performance of this penance by the penitent with her own intercession. And because of these facts she still gives expression, even today, to the intensity and urgency of this assurance of prayer in the form of sentences of the old canonical penances which in earlier times she remitted for the penitent in such a case. Because the Church prays, because she prays for salvation (and not for earthly things)—on these grounds she knows that she is "always heard." But because from the side of him for whom the prayer is offered the effectiveness of this prayer is always dependent upon his prior subjective dispositions (which themselves in turn fall under the powerful and also incalculable dispositions of the grace of God)—because of this we never know in the particular case when and how this prayer attains its goal. In the light of this we already see that the remission has not, and cannot have, the function of either diminishing or replacing the personal penance of the individual concerned. Of its nature the remission can only be aimed at securing that through the help of God that may really take place swiftly and easily which penance itself is also designed to achieve: the total cleansing and total maturing of the individual throughout his entire being, in which his initial endowment with grace is the heart and centre of the whole process. This remission, therefore, can only achieve its due effect where the individual genuinely has the dispositions necessary for penance. For without this there can be no question even of true repentance. Now if this is not the case even a forgiveness of the actual sins themselves is not possible, and therefore neither is it possible to obtain a pardon or remission of the temporal punishments due to sin.

We are presupposing that the process by which the individual is brought to full maturity, a process which is not merely psychological but in a true sense religious also, is not always and necessarily simply completed with death. This is not so even in the case of those individuals who, under the grace of God, have made their orientation towards God definitive and final in their lives and through their deaths. Even from the purely empirical point of view we cannot have the impression that a final and complete integration, in which the individual's basic decision pervades the whole of his being at all of its levels, coincides in every case with his death. Certainly according to Christian doctrine death is the end of that period in which an eternal destiny is worked out. What comes "afterwards" is not a prolongation of the period or its continuation in an endless series of new ages, but rather the definitive fixing and the eternal validity of what has come to be in time. But unless we wish to regard man as simply "coming to an end," so that we can then go on to say that he undergoes a "resurrection" of the flesh, thereby becoming something absolutely new (which, however, would be tantamount to a radical denial of his continuing identity and of eternity as the fruit of time), then, precisely upon a Christian conception of the history man as an individual, we must recognise the existence of a further period of time between death and the final consummation of all things, during which the acts performed in freedom during man's time on earth are brought to their maturity. For this history of man precisely as human only attains its ultimate end and consummation in the resurrection of the flesh, in the transfiguration of all that is real in man taken as a whole, and not merely in a sort of Platonist history of the individual spirit. We cannot picture to ourselves what takes place in it, but this is no reason for denying such a possibility. Every attempt at describing this possibility serves in its result to show how impossible it is to deny that the possibility itself does exist. But even while renouncing any such attempt we can still say this much: supposing that the *history* of the individual as such is not simply terminated with death; supposing that with death considered as the outcome of a specific and determinate stage in this history belonging to the dimension of space and time man enters still more into an open relationship to the totality of the world (though he does not become "liberated from the body" in the sense of a negative and empty separation from the cosmos); supposing all this is true, then he experiences the contradiction between the divinely ordained nature of his own being or that of the world on the one hand, and that which he still is through the still surviving effects of his own acts, in which his guilt has been objectified. He experiences these as the painful and punitive consequences of his sin. Now the painful process by which this contradiction is overcome is his purgatory. But just as in this life, so too even after death this process can be slower or quicker, more or less painful or happy, according to the particular circumstances and the prior conditions which determine this in each individual case. That the "poor souls" may be granted a swifter and more happy maturing process—that is what we pray for when we pray for them, and that is the object of that intercessory prayer of the Church which is promised to us in an indulgence which we gain "for the holy souls."

An indulgence, then, implies that the Church agrees to offer her official intercession on behalf of the repentant sinner. And it is expressed in the form of a remission of some (hypothetically imposed) canonical penance (when it is a case of indulgences for the living). The necessary prior condition for this to be achieved is that the individual gaining the indulgence must perform some good work which is specifically prescribed. In earlier times, in which the indulgence properly so-called emerged, this good work constituted primarily some part of the canonical penance which had been imposed or else some other penance, generally easier, which had to be performed in place of the original one. Today the conditions laid down by the Church for gaining an indulgence consist only of some very small task, almost symbolical in its effect. This should not lead us to the point of no longer taking indulgences seriously, as though they were "cheap" and to be had in great quantities. Many indulgences are offered. Whether many are also "gained" in *reality* is another question. An indulgence is only gained in the definitive sense when the intercessory prayer of the Church achieves its goal. But in the last analysis this can only take place in a heart that is disposed to penance, in an individual who, working from a basis of faith and grace, strives through his actions and sufferings to ensure that he may become more and more a new creature fashioned after the image of Christ in all the dimensions of his being. It is in order that this may be achieved that the holy Church assures the Christian, by granting him an indulgence, of her help and intercession.

25 · The Ignatian Exercises

1. Even today the *Spiritual Exercises* of St. Ignatius of Loyola must still be (although this does not exhaust their specific essence) a time of solitude and prayer because a time of personal encounter with God. They are intended to foster *decision and choice*. The material content of choice can ripen in an "encounter with the world" and extend to political decisions, but this alters nothing in the decision's formal (generic) character as "lonely" decision, as loneliness and prayer.

This is philosophically and Christianly justified because an individual person is never just a mere function of a community, not even of the Church. That does not prejudge the question of how far a discreetly appointed meeting with others (apart from the master of the *Exercises*) can, or even must (today), be used as a particular means during this solitary period. The *Exercises* demand only that their user take and accept himself in his ultimate permanent solitude before God, and they must therefore expose flight into the masses (even ecclesial), not encourage it.

2. The *Exercises* are exercises in choice and decision *before God, to God, in* Christ and his grace, otherwise they are not exercises. They therefore presuppose and existentially *put into practice* the fundamental substance of Christianity: that the living, incomprehensible God exists, that we have a personal relationship with him in freedom and by grace, a relationship which despite all mediation (through and in Christ, and from Christ through the whole width of worldly existence) is immediate (*on both sides*), that this relationship to God in prayer and decision can and must become thematic and is not just the unthematic, hidden ground of a relationship to the world. The *Exercises* presuppose that there is an existential decision through an individual call of God to the actual person. To be credible today, therefore, the logic of the existential decision ("discernment of spirits") and the concept of a revelation of God by means of a personal, individual address (and incidentally the concept of revelation in general) must be "demythologized," and the exercitand (or person practising the *Exercises*) brought to experience such a divine address in a way that is both sober and genuinely acceptable today. It must therefore be made clear to the exercitand that the *Exercises* are not the abstract indoctrination of a theoretical doctrinal system with all its "practical" consequences (to which point of view Jesuit intellectualism and anti-Ignatian juridicism have inclined in centuries past), but an initiation into man's religious experience and sanctification from within.

From this it follows that a commentary on the *Exercises* must include not only a developed theology of the dogmatic, objective statements of the *Exercises*, but offer a (formal) theology of the existential experience of grace and of the "psychological" (what a misleading word that can be) instructions to facilitate a more lucid and more explicitly accepted experience. There need be no fear of infringing the nature of this experience as grace, provided only that it is understood that this grace is *always* offered, that it can take on the *most disparate* forms of experience, that a nondecision (a "silence of God") can also be a grace-given experience, and so on. It follows from this that the *Exercises* are *essentially* exercises for *individuals*. Group exercises can to some extent avail themselves of the name only if they are so constructed that they provide a serious context for the growth of an individual religious history.

3. The perception and acceptance of a divine call in decision (in "choice") always has—corresponding to the nature of man and Chris-

tianity—two unified, mutually conditioned aspects: one "transcendental" and one "categorial," the aspect of radical decision for God (as its aim) *and* the mediating realization of this decision in a concrete demand and mission of historical life: *metanoia*, or conversion to God, in faith, hope and love on the one hand *and* the concreteness of this *metanoia* in a particular real situation as demand for a particular act (the shaping of life, the choice of vocation, love of one's neighbour, the endurance of life's distasteful dailiness with its pressures, and so on) on the other. These aspects cannot be separated; but their reciprocal relationship is not static and cannot be theoretically tabulated, but has a history of an individual and epochal nature and must therefore be again and again determined in historical decision (of the Church in a given period, of the individual in his life).

4. Several points follow logically from this.

(*a*) The fundamental relationship of immediacy to God (the transcendental aspect of every decision and the choice realized and deepened in this or that particular choice, in other words the ever new *metanoia* as such) cannot *today* be simply presumed as given either theoretically (as the self-evident givenness of an institutionally powerful Christianity with its indisputable public opinion) or existentially (as the uncontested inner faith of the individual), as if the *Exercises* had to deal solely with the concrete choice under its categorial aspect ("What does God's will, which is self-evident, hold for me here and now?"). In this respect, the situation of the *Exercises* is essentially different from that of Ignatius' time, even in so-called believing and "practising" Catholics who very often brush aside and do not really master the fact that their belief is contested.

The *Exercises* today must consequently take this situation much more lucidly and deliberately into consideration, under every aspect: in the choice and composition of their thematic material with the help of which the choice is to be made, in their consideration of the religious situation of the exercitand today, which blocks the religious experience and threatens him precisely when he does not thematically (consciously) accept it or brushes it to one side (as, for example, many of an older generation of religious orders did), and in their language. This does not mean that the *Exercises* should be turned into a course in theoretical problematic on the essence of Christianity and its credibility today.

The *Exercises* master, however, must bear all this in mind in his initiation into the basic religious experience and its believing, radical acceptance in the course of the exercitand's confrontation with his real concrete question of life (usually to be discovered for the first time) which calls him to a decision. In consequence, especially the question of the structure and articulation of the thematic of the considerations proposed in the *Exercises* must be posed in a radically new way. The question can perhaps be solved by a bold differentiation and contradistinction in the order of the *Exercises* as proposed by Ignatius. It could also be, however, that (at least for certain exercitands) radical changes in the thematic itself are necessary and justified. Today a longer and more explicit *introduction* to the point at which Ignatius allows the exercitand to begin the *Exercises* is probably nearly always necessary.

(*b*) Despite (because of) what was said under (*a*), the *Exercises* are and remain choice and decision in a concrete life situation and not a mere theoretical initiation into the essence of Christianity. This is not only because they have been so understood historically, but particularly because the basic, total *metanoia* (fundamental option), which is not just a theoretical—and not concretely possible only as theoretical—cultivation of Christianity, is possible only in the concrete life situation and that situation's origin in decision. (What has today become) the *Exercises'* obligation mentioned under (*a*) above does not, therefore, contradict the old object of the *Exercises*. On the contrary, man will come to know what is really meant by God, sin, grace, forgiveness, Christ, discipleship of Christ, cross, only in a question of actual existence posed concretely, faced squarely and not brushed aside, and accepted in free responsibility.

Therefore, if an initiation into existentially accepted Christianity in faith, hope and love for God is not to remain abstract indoctrination (whatever its depth of theological insight), if it is to try and extract this concrete situation as one of decision from the shrouded, marginal position it at present occupies in the exercitand's consciousness, it must be able to awaken both Christianity as a whole *and* a personal decision grounded on it.

Again the question arises of the theology and intitation technique ("psychology") of such a confrontation of the exercitand with his life's question which demands to be answered here and now and which very often lies somewhere other than he himself at first suspects. For Ignatius (as the giver of the *Exercises*, not so much for himself, in his own decision and choice, as his "memoirs" show) the genuine objects of choice were usually given openly (as the various vocations pregiven and preformed by the Church and society). Today they have first to be found, and given the complexity of man today lie much more deeply hidden than previously.

5. Any commentary on the text of the *Exercises* must devote itself equally explicitly to the content of the affirmations and to the methodological instructions. The apparently merely methodological-psychological instructions of the text raise more than psychological problems: they often imply a whole theology; commenting them therefore is *also* a properly theological undertaking. The commentary should not be an edifying paraphrase of the text, as we have been used to in our *Exercises*.

There must be some rigorous questioning: What does this mean? Does that exist? Can a man of today really understand the other? Where will he find by his own devices an intellectual access to all that is expressed here in an almost archaic and apparently mythological way? What are the presuppositions underlying the text, which we today can no longer presume to be self-evident, but have to set out explicitly to recapture? And so on. All this applies equally to the theological content of the text's affirmations and its methodological instructions and rules.

26 · Faith and the Stages of Life

Faith Initiation of Children

Except where parental instruction is concerned, religious education is generally based on a catechism or children's Bible. The question spontaneously arises whether a catechism is really an appropriate basis for the religious initiation of a child. After all, in the final analysis, a catechism —however "childlike" its language—is still a summary of dogmatic theology for adults. Where is it written that in every stage of development, even the earliest, a person must explicitly confront the whole of the doctrine of the faith, each and every individual element of it? Content selection in religious education should be much more radical. When religious education is conducted in such a way that ten to twelve-year-old children have already heard everything once, what they can actually assimilate existentially has not been presented in adequate depth and vitality, nor with the promise of anything *new* still to come in their faith experience or in religious instruction in later stages of development. It is scarcely any wonder, then, if this age marks the beginning of a period of decline in a knowledge of the faith. That knowledge has reached its apex now, and it should scarcely be cause for surprise if from now on it is regarded with increasing disinterest and a blasé attitude. When we make children into miniature adults in the area of religion, simply for fear of not being able to reach them later, they will no longer wish to become really adult later, in the religious area, by acquiring *new* religious knowledge and experience.

Further, it is true, of course, that children think in graphic, dramatic images. But this is no proof that, for example, the Bible "stories" about the Garden of Paradise, the fall of Adam, and so on are appropriate material as children's stories, or that they do not do more harm than good to the faith later on, having been understood childishly in the first place. Perhaps much of this material belongs in a later stage of instruction when the poetic-mythical character of these narratives can be rightly grasped from the start—when the content of a 'statement can be distinguished from its form. There may well be enough other, less dangerous "models" for religious concepts to be planted in the soil of the child's soul, into his or her still fanciful life, than revelation's own "official" ones—to which it is hard to arouse a critical, and yet faith-filled, relationship when they have been employed too early.

Similar dangers, of which we ought at least to be cognizant, lurk in certain religious customs with which it is very easy to get the child intensely involved, and which surely enjoy great potential for religio-social formation. But—just to take one example—when serving Mass (or singing in the choir, and so on) is perceived as a specifically *children's* activity, later harm may outweigh early advantages. Today, when the adult adopts such a distracted attitude toward the whole area of religious usage in any case, perhaps it would be better for the child to perceive these activities as the sacred privilege of the adult, for which a child must gradually become "old enough," as it is with other privileges. The case is the same with other religious usages. Eventually they endanger the faith, rather than foster it, when they appear as a "privilege" of children, later to be laid aside—too often right along with what it has concretized: religion itself.

The Puberty Crisis and the Faith of the Adolescent

The puberty crisis is mainly a sexual and social one. It is dangerous, therefore, to seek to control it too directly, massively, and immediately from a point of departure in the religious area. The reasons for this are not only that this crisis (especially the discovery of a new relationship to one's milieu, and puberty in the strict sense) must be controlled from an inward experience of reality itself (after all, we are dealing with the law of *nature!*) and not simply via external moral norms—nor only that insight into what is meaningful in reality is something which must be acquired—but above all that such crises, with their conflicts and temporary setbacks, must be prevented from being too nakedly experienced as a questioning or destruction of religious piety, which is still "young" and tender even without such an added threat. A simple, human, confident, patient, tolerant (in the good sense of the word) attitude toward children in their puberty crisis will in the long run be more successful than seeking to help them directly through methods involving a massive array of explicitly religious motivations. Otherwise the actual religious decision, which comes later, will be anticipated—experienced too early—and run the risk of being vitiated.

This should afford the pastoral counsellor no pretext for "taking the easy way out" and encouraging the tendency, so often present in youth in any case, to make the sexual area the all but exclusive battleground of the *religious* decision. This is particularly important in view of the fact that physical maturity frequently comes earlier today, and spiritual maturity later, than in times past. As a result, the new experience of a rich charge of the "concupiscent" in life's reality can often simply not be morally and personally assimilated during this "awkward age" between the two maturations, as pastoral counselling would like it to. This is why pastoral counselling so often exaggerates its demands and instills in youth the notion that non-fulfillment of these demands implies a final decision against a religious interpretation of life.

Faith Dialogue with Adults

The faith decision that indelibly marks the average person's life would seem to occur typically some time between the ages of twenty and twenty-five. In earlier generations it may have come sooner—maturation occurs later today, and there is good reason why it should. The quantity of "material" to be assimilated in this integration process by the individual, in free possession of himself or herself, is incomparably greater than it was in times gone by. Furthermore, social ties which formerly accelerated this maturation process (or even simply substituted for it and replaced it) no longer enjoy the same currency.

Hence this time of life is in itself the most important time, the privileged time, for the help and support that the Church must offer a person in his or her faith. And yet, de facto, this same time of life is unfavorable in many respects, so that the educator in the faith must have a great deal of perseverance, patience, tact, and confidence, for there are going to be a good many disappointments. He or she must stalwartly resist the temptation to transfer the main field of activity to times of life (childhood, old age) that are "easier to work with." Young men and women in the early stages of adulthood can find their inward independence as mature persons only by enjoying a certain distance from the environmental influences that have been stamping them up until this time. And yet, in this, their critical period, they require a partner with whom to enter into dialogue. And so this time is precisely the time when instruction in the faith should take the nature of a *dialogue*. Hence the religious educator can enter into such a relationship of dialogue with clients at this stage without fear of hypocrisy, since, after all, he or she must be convinced that the impending faith decision ought to be the act of the young person's own responsible freedom, and of course such an act is possible only where room for it is honestly afforded—room to make a decision that the religious educator may have to qualify as objectively mistaken, but perhaps also as subjectively innocent.

Now the possibility of a subjectively innocent, yet objectively mistaken decision has become very considerably enhanced in today's global spiritual atmosphere by comparison with earlier times, and this is something that the religious educator, with unprejudiced patience and trust in the God who can write straight with crooked lines, must bear with and take into account in his or her own conduct. During this stage, the young person must find the God of his or her own understanding—God in an image which will be a function of this person's particular time of life as well as of his or her whole particular being. The religious educator can be helpful in this quest. God will not be so much the protecting, sheltering—but also supervising—"Father," but rather the "God for us" who opens the doors on infinite space for the human deed and the adventure of living, who enjoins responsiblity, and who encourages human beings to make their own decisions.

In this developmental stage, this age of life, furthermore, "commandment" as *external* regimentation, as regulation on the part of a higher authority, should be transformed in a person's understanding into the *intrinsic* appropriateness of what is commanded for the persons and things it concerns, which is precisely where the sovereignty of the divine will comes to evidence. This transformation of the understanding of law, too, calls for a relationship of dialogue between the religious educator and the man or woman of this age of life.

This is also the time when a person's employment or profession leaves its decisive stamp. For the life of faith, it is important first of all that there be a positive relationship between one's profession, its ideals and realities, on the one hand, and a life lived in faith on the other. But the young person should also be helped to assimilate a critical view of the dangers his or her profession may occasion in the form of a partial blindness to human realities which fail to surface in the "subject matter" and methodology of a given profession. The many professions of our day having their origin in the natural sciences are of special concern here. Their ideal of "exact" knowledge and experimental demonstrability may easily result in the atrophy of the cognitive power used in faith. The members of such professions must be repeatedly reminded and helped to understand that they cannot adequately cope with the totality of their lives, for which they are responsible, by the methods and results of the natural sciences alone. They must be shown again and again that a skeptical attitude toward other forms of knowledge, including faith, is itself an option and actually has less solid grounds in intellectual honesty than the decision for faith and the realities of faith—which alone furnish a point of departure for a meaningful understanding and adequate assimilation of the totality of human life.

The Mature Years

By contrast with "youthful idealism"—which can masquerade as a snobbish hedonism and rebellion against the older generation, and yet still be there—the developmental stage in which men and women live their lives in family, trade or profession, and participation in public life in the secular world leads them to the direct execution of concrete tasks and the direct attainment of concrete goals in the here and now. Consequently, this time of life is often characterized by a diminished openness to "metaphysical questions" and religious realities. This is a situation calling for tact, caution, and self-confident modesty on the part of the religious educator. Religious educators must not create the impression that a Christian of this age is not quite authentic, not quite right as a Christian, or is "written off" by the Church, just because he or she does not measure up to a certain standard of religious or Church involvement and practice (often enough quite arbitrarily determined by clergy). Religious educators should strive to make it clear to people of this time of life that the "world of faith" is not an ideological superstructure, adventitious to so-called reality. Nor indeed must they too quickly and superficially maintain that "you can't get along without religion." This is true, of course, if correctly understood. But it can also be understood too hastily and superficially, and it is not as easily grasped empirically by today's men and women as many apologists of the faith seem to think. This is the time of life, then, that stands in need of religious educators who will, first, emphasize that the honest, sober performance of the tasks and responsibilities of ordinary everyday life of itself constitutes a substantial part of Christian existence (and hence has no concrete relationship whatever to any merely "natural virtues")—however it may be that the daily need to "grunt and sweat under a weary life" is less than the substance of divine revelation itself. Second, however, religious educators will also have to make a constant effort to keep it well before their clients' minds that what Christianity means, explicitly states, and seeks to make the explicit motivation of daily conduct is finally nothing else but the last radical depths of the very same reality the human being experiences in his and her daily round of activities (understanding human experience here as *global* human experience, of course). Christians in their mature years will have to be reminded that they may have implicitly accepted and assimilated Christianity merely by their totally responsible conduct, their obedience to life's seemingly blind demands, and their openness to the mystery of existence in genuine, unselfish love of neighbor and so on. Religious formation at this stage of development should therefore primarily take the form of in-depth answers to the questions that men and women face as an outgrowth of their trade or profession, their family life, and their activity in public life.

The Faith Context of Old Age

Ministry to the elderly is one of today's new necessities, arising out of our longer average life expectancy, which results in an increasingly large proportion of the population falling into the category of the "aged."

There are new tasks, burdens, and positive opportunities in life today for the elderly—the "fourth generation." These are the result of a longer life expectancy, retirement, smaller families (which find it difficult to have the older generation living with them), and so on. These new factors, which can be either positive or negative, create a new religious situation, as well, and present the religious educator with new opportunities, as well as new dangers, for his or her work of animation and formation to faith.

Questions like the meaning of loneliness, the meaning of one's disappointment with so much in life that has only been failure, so much that has marred and spoiled that life, the impending encounter with death, and so on now form the background of the religious question—in both a positive and a negative way, for there is always the danger of falling victim to a bitter skepticism. Now is the time to impart to people the understanding and the courage they will need to cope with their new religious situation. They should be helped to see that the mere fact that their earlier developmental stages have not been especially distinguished by religious elements and interests should not give rise to the suspicion that their new religious attitude is nothing but a sign of senile anxiety about life and a cowardly need for security. Such suspicions arise, unfortunately, in the elderly themselves. No, the elderly should be brought to see that it is "normal" to be "more religious" in old age, and that the authenticity of their piety is not suspect merely because it was not altogether clearly present before. Each developmental stage provides its own context, its own opportunities and particularities, and challenges us to embrace these particularities in openhearted fashion and with resolve, and not to fight to hang on to the mentality of the stage that has gone before.

Again and again we observe cases in which a Church ministry has originally been undertaken primarily for relatively extrinsic, social reasons only to see its subject gradually grow into the properly religious meaning of the activity involved. Hence one should not restrict the assignment of ministerial tasks to those who are already "very devout."

Old age, then, can be a time of new religious interest and fruitfulness. But this does not mean that the minister should seek to control the specific problems of the elderly *only* from an activation and deepening of the religious life. No, he or she should also encourage other ways in which persons may fashion for themselves a full, "cheerful" old age, making every effort to see to it that it be still a time replete with human contacts—

an old age that its subject can affirm and endorse. The religious educator should involve that "devout" elderly in these same efforts. Finally, as the Second Vatican Council (*Gaudium et Spes*, no 66) admonishes us, we should take care that the elderly have "work opportunities"—surely in the broadest sense, to include all meaningful activity—as a warranty for their dignity as human beings.

L·O·V·E

27 · Love

Love is not an achievement which can be exactly defined; it is what every man becomes when he realizes his unique essence, something that is known only when it is done. This is not to say that there is no general notion of love, according to the general statement that man is obliged to love God and that this is the fulfilment of the whole divine law and all the commandments. For this principal commandment obliges man precisely to love God with his whole heart. And this heart, this innermost centre of his person and thus of whatever else belongs to the individual, is something unique; and what is risked and given in this love is only known afterwards, when man has found himself and truly knows what and who he actually is. In this love, also, man is concerned with the adventure of his own, at first concealed, reality. He cannot estimate beforehand what is demanded of him; for he himself is demanded, he is risked in his concrete heart and life which are still before him as the unknown future and which reveal only afterwards what this heart is that had to be risked and spent in this life. In all other cases one can know what is demanded, one can estimate, compare and ask whether the risk is worth the gain. One can justify what has been done by the result which turns out to make sense. In the case of love this is impossible. For it justifies itself, but it is only truly itself when it has been perfectly achieved with all one's heart.

Fundamentally the Christian ethos is not the respect for the objective norms with which God has endowed reality. For all these are truly moral norms only where they express the structure of the person. All other structures of things are below man. He may change and transform them as much as he can, he is their master, not their servant. The only ultimate structure of the person which adequately expresses it is the basic power of love, and this is without measure. Therefore man, too, is without measure. Fundamentally all sin is only the refusal to entrust oneself to this measurelessness, it is the lesser love which, because it refuses to become greater, is no longer love. In order to know what is meant by this man needs, of course, the multiplicity of objective commandments. But whatever appears in this multiplicity is a partial beginning of love which itself has no norm by which it might be measured. One may speak of this "commandment" of love if one does not forget that this "law" does not commandsomething, but asks of man to be himself, that is the possibility of love by receiving God's love in which God does not give something else, but himself.

But despite, no, because of his absoluteness God is no impersonal It, no unmoved receptacle of the transcendence and love of the spiritual person; he is the living God, and all human activity is essentially response to his call, which is the ultimate basis of its historicity. This historicity of man is taken seriously only when he knows himself to be essentially, not only accidentally, something that cannot be disposed of, but is integrated into the sovereign freedom of God. This is actually only the anthropological expression of the fact that every creature depends permanently on God. In the case of man this means that he remains dependent on God in his understanding of himself which is characteristic of his humanity, that he can never integrate God as an element into this understanding. It belongs to man's creatureliness that he experiences and affirms the mystery of God and his freedom. He therefore accepts the creaturely dependence which is proper to him if he does not imagine that he may finally dispose of himself, for example as "pure nature," but that he must wait for an historical interpretation by God himself.

What had been said above of the interrelation between the transcendental and categorial exercise of freedom is realized in this historical interpretation. Human freedom is always freedom with regard to a categorial object and an inner-wordly Thou, even when it begins to be directly freedom before God. For even such an act of a direct Yes or No to God does not envisage immediately and solely the God of original transcendental experience and his presence as revealed in this, but first the God of thematic categorial reflection, the notional God.

If the word of God can be spoken in this world at all it can only be spoken as a finite word of man. And, conversely, the direct relation to God is necessarily mediated by inner-worldly communication. The transcendental message needs a categorial object, a support, as it were, in order not to lose itself in the void; it needs an inner-worldly Thou. The original relation to God is the love of neighbour. If man becomes himself only through the love of God and must achieve this by a categorial action then, in the order of grace, the act of neighbourly love is the only categorial and original act in which man reaches the whole categorially given reality and thus experiences God directly, transcendentally and through grace.

28 · Love for God and Human Beings

The essence of the love of God is already almost inevitably misunderstood when that love is thought of as the observance of an individual, particular commandment—one commandment among others. No, just as God is not rightly understood when he is thought of simply as a particular reality, a partial reality in the sum total of all realities, so also the love of God may not be degraded to the status of a particular achievement among a plurality of things to be achieved in human existence. The love of God is the totality of the free fulfillment of human existence. It is not, in the last analysis, the content of an individual commandment, but is at once the basis and the goal of all individual commandments. And it is what it must be only when God is loved for his own sake—when love for him is produced and experienced not with a view to human self-assertion and interior self-fulfillment, in the accomplishment of certain individual exploits which people require of themselves, but when human beings, ultimately without self-seeking, go out of themselves, forget themselves because of God, and really lose themselves in the ineffable mystery to which they willingly surrender.

The human being attains his or her fulfillment in one single, total act of his or her existence: in the love of God for his own sake. But this fulfillment is, precisely, only reached when not it but God is sought. Inasmuch as such love is the whole of the fulfillment of human existence, there is nothing more self-evident than it, since only a whole, and not a part, is self-explanatory—only a whole can be understood in itself. At the same time, however, inasmuch as this love is surrender to God, a surrender to the never-to-be-comprehended, a surrender to that which remains mystery for all eternity—this self-evident love is at the same time incomprehensible in itself. That is, it is not resolvable into elements that are better understood in separation. When love of God is lauded from the pulpit as the condition of salvation, it is not a particular achievement on the part of human beings that is meant, but the one total self-fulfillment of the human being, at once self-evident and incomprehensible, in which the human being dispossesses himself or herself in self-abandonment to God.

When we consider all this—and yet at the same time experience this curved-in-on-itself subjectivity of ours that ever seeks itself as its end and goal—then such a love of God for his own sake, this eruption, this breaking out of the locked-up narrowness of our own existence, necessarily appears to us as a miracle, which ultimately only God himself can bestow upon us. When we hope for the salvation of all humankind, what we are hoping for is this unspeakable wonder of the love of God for us, which itself bestows upon us the very thing that is the sole salvific deed of our lives. This love is to be hoped for against and despite all manifestations of a hugely sinful (or most sublime) selfishness on the part of the human being.

It is this real love for God that must be kept in view, as we now proceed to ask ourselves about the relationship between love for God and love for neighbor. It is this true, genuine love of God that we shall be speaking of, and not some individual, particular moral exploit.

The relationship of the love of God to a love of neighbor is not merely in virtue of the fact that a love of neighbor is commanded by it and functions somehow as a practical test case for it. The relationship is much more intimate than that. Love of God and love of neighbor stand in a relationship of mutual conditioning. Love of neighbor is not only a love that is demanded by the love of God, an achievement flowing from it; it is also in a certain sense its antecedent condition.

This relationship of mutual conditioning, of mutual inclusion, must not of course be understood in the sense of a secular humanism, as if love for God were only an old-fashioned, mythological expression for love of neighbor—so that, when all is said and done, one could simply skip over it today if one could still maintain an inexorable, unselfish love for human beings without it. No, God is more than a human being—infinitely more. He is the loving God to whom the human being reaches out in adoration across all human reality. And yet a mutual relationship does obtain between love of God and love of neighbor, in their real mutual conditioning. There is no love for God that is not, in itself, already a love for neighbor; and love for God only comes to its own identity through its fulfillment in a love for neighbor. Only one who loves his or her neighbor can know who God actually is. And only one who ultimately loves God (whether he or she is reflectively aware of this or not is another matter) can manage unconditionally to abandon himself or herself to another person, and not make that person the means of his or her own self-assertion.

29 · Love for Jesus

First, it seems to me, one must come to grips with the fact that human beings necessarily commit themselves, entrust themselves, to others, and that indeed they must do so. This self-opening of one's own personhood to another, this handing-over of oneself to someone else, admits of the greatest variation in intensity and form. One form it can take, perhaps the clearest, is that of marital love. Here, unconditionally (at least in a certain sense), a human being confides himself or herself to another person. Only if one thus abandons oneself, and lovingly sinks into the other, does one succeed in finding oneself. Otherwise, a person languishes in the prison of his or her own selfishness.

Now, there is a very important aspect in this basic, factual occurrence of human existence that calls for our special attention. And it is this: A reasonable, responsible self-abandonment requires grounds upon which one feels called to abandon oneself to another, and thereupon justified in doing so. But these grounds, always and necessarily, are more tenuous and more problematic than the act of abandonment itself, the act of self-commitment in its absoluteness. Or, to put it the other way about: The act of self-commitment to the other has a radical, absolute, unconditional quality by no means adequately founded or based on the antecedent grounds for that act. This is the fact, and a human being can see, in his or her human existence, that it can scarcely be otherwise. One must have reasonable grounds for abandoning oneself to another—for committing, for entrusting oneself to another. And yet, in this self-abandonment, once all antecedent considerations, verifications and demands of reasonableness and legitimation are posited—one ventures more, and *must* venture more, than these grounds seem to justify.

Every trusting, loving relationship to another human being has an uncancellable "plus" on the resolution-and-decision side of the balance sheet—as over against the reflective side, the side that tallies up the justifiability and reasonableness of such risk and venture. Here we can draw our first conclusion with regard to the subject under consideration: a genuine love relationship to Jesus.

One can pursue exegesis and biblical theology, one can launch a thousand investigations into the historical figure of Jesus—one can seek to bring to light just what Jesus said, how he said it and how he meant it, what happened to him, how his environment reacted to him, and how he understood himself. One can research what we term his miracles with all precision and all exactitude. One can attempt a more exacting psychological analysis of why and how his first disciples, after his death, came to the conviction that he had risen again. All these considerations and investigations are good and necessary (to be sure, according to each person's opportunity for perception and verification, in the thousand different ways in which this sort of legitimation of a human conviction can be undertaken). But always there remains that "plus" on the side of the freedom to take a risk—on the side of love, precisely—in a truly Christian relationship to Jesus; for this relationship is above and beyond all these historical, exegetical and critical sciences (and of course also above and beyond the historical witness of tradition and the Church concerning Jesus). Only when Jesus himself is accepted and loved in himself, over and above one's own knowledge about him—Jesus himself, and not our mere idea of Christ, nor our mere willingness to brook the lucubrations of historical science—only then does a true relationship to him, the relationship of an absolute self-abandonment to him, begin.

Before we attempt to portray our peculiar, unique, and radical relationship to the unique person that is Jesus of Nazareth, in an absolute commitment and an unconditional love, there is still one preparatory consideration calling for our attention. As we have already said, our relationship to Jesus must involve more than an abstract idea of Christ— otherwise we should be simply hypnotized by our own idea of him and riveted to that, instead of loving a concrete, actual human being.

But after all—or so it seems at first—the concrete Jesus is cut off from us, is he not, by geographical space, by the distance of history and culture, and by the span of two thousand years. Can one love a person in earnest when that person is that far away? When one seeks to do so, does one not necessarily fall back into an enthusiasm for an *idea* of Christ, for one's own self-invented ideal of the selfless human being?

The normal Christian, not considering all these questions quite so precisely, will at first simply reply: But this Jesus is alive today. He is risen. We can find him with God. And therefore a loving, radically immediate, unique relationship to him holds no insuperable difficulties.

This is all very important, of course. In fact, it is basic to our Christian understanding of a relationship to Jesus. Were he not the Resurrected One, the Saved One who abides with God, the one returned to God and there achieving his definitive survival and being, precisely in the incomprehensible infinity and ineffability of God—then our love would surely be no more than the quest (ultimately, a meaningless quest) of an ideal in history's past. Indeed, were it to be taken as adequate by itself alone, the rather too hasty answer we have just heard would present us with a brand-new difficulty of its own: The blessed in heaven, whom we believe to be saved and in God, appear to us to be just as removed—at an infinite distance—as if they had disappeared into the incomprehensibility of God himself, and were no longer distinguishable from him.

We cannot delve more deeply into this difficulty here. Rather we must simply recall that God is "a God of the *living*," as Jesus himself tells us he is, and that the departed are everlastingly current, and so can be, and are, really near to us in their silent love. But is this nearness not, once again, precisely the nearness of the God who saves them and keeps them, but also hides them? And does not this same thing then apply to Jesus?

Many men and women lovingly seek to reconstruct within themselves, as it were, extraordinary personalities of history. There are people who observe a cult of Napoleon. There are people who honor Goethe in such fashion that he has great importance and significance for their lives. Such people seem to have succeeded in bridging the historical distance between themselves and their heroic idol of the past. Such phenomena should by no means be undervalued. One could certainly say that a person who had simply let none of the heroes of history into his or her life, who practiced no hero worship whatever in any sense, who had no capacity for dialogue with the figures of the past, would somehow be stunted, diminished, in his or her own humanity.

But evidently it will not be enough for us to say that we bridge the historical, cultural and temporal distance to Jesus simply and solely in this way. There must be something more to it than that. Were we *only* to say that Jesus now lives with God, that he still exists, that we can still call on him, as Stephen did before his death—"I see the heavens opened, and the Son of man standing at the right hand of God" (Acts 7:56)—then, as we have said, we would have a basic prerequisite for an immediate relationship to Jesus, a prerequisite that is absolutely necessary and important. But then there would still be the question whether, with this "eternal Lord of all," as Ignatius Loyola calls him, his bygone, now past history actually still has a meaning for us—or whether we are really just falling back once more into a cult of an abstract Christ-idea.

If we cast a backward glance over our own religious history we cannot exclude such a danger *a priori*. When a Teilhard de Chardin speaks of Christ as the Omega of world history, the question arises at once whether this Teilhardian Christ-All as goal and ground of all evolutionary history can still seriously have anything to do with Jesus of Nazareth. But how— without simply appealing to an ancient and approved hero cult, but nothing more than that, and yet without watering this Jesus down into an idea of some sort—how can we make this relationship to Jesus comprehensible for today and tomorrow?

Actually, we notice we have the same problem with respect to the cultus of the saints (which has an altogether official place in the Catholic Church and may not be allowed to be dismantled by cries for reform). When I honor Francis of Assisi, I not only strike a relationship with his. exemplary life of long ago. Nor do I simply cultivate a Franciscan idea of the person who loves God and the world unselfishly. I also pray to Francis of Assisi. I call to him in the definitive redeemedness of his existence. This reflection shows us that the problem of an immediate, genuine relationship to another person who is seemingly far removed from us historically is a more general one than merely one of our relationship to Jesus. This circumstance permits us to examine things the other way about and apply this general Christian attitude and deportment to the special question of our relationship to Jesus.

Human beings seek nearness to one another. When they are in one another's direct physical presence and seek to love one another in these circumstances, they seek to exist not only in a physiological contact of flesh on flesh, but to render such contact, when it is to be meaningful, the expression of a really total, personal, fully mutual and reciprocal exchange of love between them. Here we have a mystery that we cannot hope to solve at this point in our discussion—if indeed it can be solved at all.

What happens, then, when two human beings love? What happens when, despite their diversity, two persons succeed in existing in such mutual exchange of themselves, such mutual communication and sharing, that it can be said that their love makes them *one*? Is there really such a thing as this uniting, unifying love—a love that genuinely surmounts all the seemingly insurmountable barriers, that spans all the gulfs of separation thrown across its path by the physical, material (and existential, too) diversity of two distinct subjects?

This is yet another question that cannot be answered in detail here. But one thing is altogether clear. When we observe human love, we see that this same basic diversity between two people, this basic division separating them, obtains even when they are very near one another, even when they actually seek to unite themselves bodily. They are different, they are distinct. Their respective existence is not given *a priori* as if it sprang from one source and origin. With all their physical and physiological proximity, the two remain diverse, distinct. They fall back, or at least they seem to fall back, into separation again, even when, in the act of supreme love, they seem to have achieved a unity, a oneness. But (and now we come to the point) even though this basic diversity obtains between two lovers, indeed abides in the very basis of their love, and yet does *not* cause their love not to be—difficult as it may be to explain the coexistence of diversity and unity in love speculatively—then neither can a seemingly great distance in space and time between two persons who seek to love, and actually do love, betoken an impossibility for love. After all, even before its encounter with this spatial and temporal difficulty, love must face a much more radical difference—and experience shows it is perfectly capable of doing so. For this earlier, greater difference is given in the very ground, the root, of this love. Indeed, their difference is actually to be reaffirmed in this love—for the lover loves and affirms the other precisely *as* other, certainly not seeking simply to absorb the beloved into his or her own peculiar way of being.

Now if such love, always and in all situations, in its very roots, is beset with this difficulty—a difficulty that constitutes precisely one of the tasks of love—then it cannot mean death for this love if it has to come to grips with an at least apparently great spatial and temporal separation. Lovers naturally seek the greatest possible nearness and palpable bonds of affection—at once the alleviation and the expression of their love's intensity. But they love each other across time and space. Such a love knows that it is yet but on the way to the goal of definitive union in love—that it must bridge, in fidelity, the chasm still provisionally sundering the lovers. But to say that love must founder, or no longer be, when a like distance in time or space separates lovers would be to vacate the true and genuine essence of love.

Hence we must say: One can love Jesus, love him in himself, in true, genuine, immediate love. To be sure, we can and must unhesitatingly stipulate, in this case, that the one who is loved is really alive with God. To be sure, we may stipulate and grasp by faith that it is this Jesus, on his own initiative, out of the depths of the divinity that is his and that preserves him in life, who seizes the initiative of his love for us, and through what we call grace—the divine gift of love for God and Jesus—makes this love for him possible for us.

Under these two conditions and stipulations of ours, however, it is really possible to love Jesus, across all space and time. We read his biography. It is not the biography just of someone's past. This biography has taken on definitiveness in his resurrection. We read Holy Scripture in the way two lovers gaze at one another in the living of their daily life together. We feel and experience in the depths of our own existence, what this concrete human being—who has not simply sunk away in the shadowy anonymity of God after all—has concretely to say to us. We allow ourselves really to be told something by him that otherwise we should not have known for our life. We find ourselves face to face with a synthesis, and indissoluble one, between norms that are ever valid and Jesus as their unique model. This synthesis forms the basis of a consequence for our lives that is something more than an acknowledgment of the exemplar of a self-evident norm. The imitation of this person by no means implies his demotion to the status of mere exemplar of principles we have already adopted. Jesus becomes, in this love of ours for him, the concrete Absolute, in whom the abstractness of norms, and the insignificance of the purely contingent individual, are transcended and overcome.

A little story may help show what I mean. Once I was having a conversation with a modern Protestant theologian, whose theories, to a normal Catholic Christian like me, necessarily seemed rather rationalistic—very much an existential "Jesuanity" and no longer really having a great deal to do with the Jesus of the normal Christian faith. At one point I put in with,

"Yes, you see, you're actually only really dealing with Jesus when you throw your arms around him and realize right down to the bottom of your being that this is something you can still do today." And my theologian replied, "Yes, you're right, of course—if you don't mean it too pietistically."

I think one can and must love Jesus, in all immediacy and concretion, with a love that transcends space and time, in virtue of the nature of love in general and by the power of the Holy Spirit of God.

At this point in our considerations we have only sought to make it in some measure clear that the spatial, cultural, and temporal distance between Jesus and us need present no insuperable obstacle to our really loving him—loving Jesus himself, the concrete person who, only through his seeming disappearance into the incomprehensibility of God, can come right up close to us as the concrete, historical person he is—on condition that we *want* to love him, that we have the courage to throw our arms around him.

There are still two observations to be made about this loving relationship of ours to Jesus. First, the experience of true love for "third parties" is in no way constricted or diminished by our love for Jesus. This "ordinary love for neighbor" is precisely a prerequisite of our love for Jesus. Here we may safely paraphrase what we read in John: How can we love Jesus, whom we cannot see, if we do not love our neighbor whom we do see? And the other way about: This love for neighbor can and should actually grow through a love for Jesus, for it is only in a loving relationship with Jesus that we conceive the possibilities of love for neighbor that otherwise we should simply not hold to be feasible, but which present themselves nonetheless wherever we subsume our neighbor in our love for Jesus because he or she is Jesus' brother or sister. Further: It happens that this immediate love for Jesus, as it is meant in these pages, is not simply present from the start. It must grow and ripen. The tender interiority of this love, to which it need not be afraid to admit, is the fruit of patience, prayer, and an ever renewed immersion in Scripture. It is the gift of God's Spirit. We cannot commandeer it, we cannot seize it violently and without discretion. But we may always know that the very aspiration to such love is already its beginning, and that we have a promise of its fulfillment.

30 · Following the Crucified

In the exegesis and in the theory of Christian spirituality it is pointed out that "following" and "imitation" (despite the iridescent expression "imitation of Christ" as used in traditional Christian spirituality) are not absolutely synonymous terms, that we must start out from the New Testament idea of following, even though Paul is aware also of the idea of imitation. Certainly we are not really expected to copy and reproduce the life of Jesus as such. We live in historical situations different from those in which Jesus himself lived, we have a different and always unique task which is not the same as that which confronted him in his own historically conditioned and restricted existence; he and we together form the one Christ of the one and unique total history of salvation, in which, for all our crucial dependence on him and on his historical existence in life and death, we do not reproduce him, but (as Paul says) complete his historical individual reality, to become the one Christ in head and members, who is identical with all redeemed humanity, hidden in God and belonging to God himself. In the light of all this, rightly understood, we could say that Christians are followers and not imitators of the Crucified. And yet this is still not the whole truth.

If we were to consider and realize only what has just been said, there would be a danger of turning the imperative of following Jesus in practice into abstract moral principles, perfectly clear in themselves, and reducing Jesus, his life, and his death, to a merely illustrative example of a moral precept which could exist independently of him. But following Jesus, his life, and him as crucified, is in the last resort something different from the realization of a universal ideal, perhaps realized particularly explicitly and purely in Jesus, but in fact simply as an "instance" of a universal idea that in principle is independent of him. In his life and in his death there must be something that is unique and as such the content and norm of our following of Jesus, so that this following is itself authenticated as such by him and not because his life and death are in their turn authenticated by an ideal, a norm, claiming validity in themselves and independently of him.

If we keep this in mind and do not explain this unique following solely as being driven by his "Spirit," regarded also as a suprahistorical factor, it becomes understandable and in principle legitimate that the whole history of Christian piety should have brought an element of imitation of the concrete Jesus into his following, should have been oriented to his stay in the wilderness, his fasting, his nightly prayer, his concrete poverty, his renunciation of concrete power and so on, although it cannot be proved or can be proved only with difficulty that following Jesus, seen theoretically and practically, is not possible without these concrete ways of imitating him. This must be remembered when we are talking of the following of Jesus; this following must not *a priori* be absolutely opposed to the imitation of his concrete life, difficult as it may be to say and obscure as it may be in the meantime what exactly can and should be present concretely in the life of Jesus for this imitative following, which can be found in him alone and by which alone this imitative following can be authenticated. If in this question we were to appeal immediately and solely to a *disposition* in which we follow him and thus attempt to evade all questions about a concrete content of this imitative following, then the question would promptly have to be raised about what this disposition really consists in and why it cannot be made intelligible also without direct recourse to Jesus.

We are thus faced with an obscure problem, the difficulty of which becomes apparent in the whole history of Christian piety. In the earliest Christian times the devout person sought to imitate Jesus by following the example of the first witness, by martyrdom. But when martyrdom ceased to be possible, people imitated him in the wilderness, in nightly prayer, in poverty, in renunciation of marriage, but then became somewhat embarrassed when faced with the question of how *those* Christians were to follow Jesus who could not adopt these particular ways of following him, how this following is possible without having to appeal merely to a "disposition," a following in the "Spirit."

Today we might perhaps think that we can and must follow Jesus concretely by a solidarity with the poor and oppressed, by a critical attitude to institutionalizations asserted by power in society and Church, by courage for conflict with the powerful. In principle it is certainly possible in this way for what is up to a point a new form of imitative following of Jesus to enter into the Church's sense of faith and from that standpoint also to resist any retreat to a purely internal and private disposition in the following of Jesus. And, since we certainly ought to follow Jesus not only in death but also in life, the emergence of such a new way of following him is certainly of the greatest importance, particularly since the established forms of this concrete following have hitherto been more or less identical with the ways of life of the religious orders, while the "laity" found such a life-style alien and had no desire to regard themselves as belonging to the following of Jesus only insofar as they remotely or closely imitated the style and mentality of the religious life. But, even if all this is evident and must be regarded as important, the real question that faced us with reference to an imitative following, not to be reduced to a mere disposition, does not yet seem to be solved.

The preference which Jesus showed and lived out for the poor and oppressed in society and which certainly cannot be deduced from an abstract and universal morality, not even from Christian love of neighbour alone, does not present any style of following for the poor and oppressed themselves in society, unless it is to suggest that these poor and oppressed are to follow Jesus by bearing their lot patiently. This is a conclusion drawn only too often and too recklessly in the course of the history of Christianity; but it seems to make religion the opium of the people, it is highly problematic and fails to grasp the difference between voluntarily showing solidarity with the poor and oppressed as a supremely personal act and being caught up in poverty and distress in a way that simply cannot be completely transformed by concrete freedom alone. Moreover, the question will have to be left as it stands, without an absolutely positive answer, whether the preferential treatment of the poor and oppressed on the part of Jesus must be a crucial principle for the style of following on the part of *every* individual Christian or whether this must be said or perhaps desired seriously at most of the community of believers, of the Church as a whole.

This brings us to the question whether there cannot be a particular, concrete, in a sense imitative following of Jesus which must be neither attributed to an internal disposition alone nor merely regarded as taking individual forms and as changing at different periods of Christian history. If we are not to take refuge in an abstract moral idealism, it seems to us that this question can be answered only with the proposition: *the Christian, every Christian at all times, follows Jesus by dying* with him; following Jesus has its ultimate truth and reality and universality in the following of the Crucified. It cannot, I think be proved that there is any other concrete substance of that following which could hold for *all* Christians taken together and which remains concrete. Our reflections up to now on the following of Jesus thus lead naturally to the reflections on the following of Jesus precisely as crucified.

In what exactly does the following of the Crucified as participation in his death consist and why is this equality of fate, the solidarity of death, something in which we not only resemble him but depend on him in the proper sense of the term? At first, the very opposite seems to be the case. Despite its extraordinary concrete peculiarities as a violent death, Jesus in his death shares the lot of all of us; in his death he seems to be following in the way of a dying humanity and not humanity following in his way. There is no need to insist at length that our following of Jesus in dying refers to death as such and not to an historically individual peculiarity of his death, which (at least normally) we cannot share at all. But in this respect is he not following us more than we follow him?

We may safely and must ask about the equality of his death and ours, before we raise more explicitly the question why we are dependent on him in this respect—follow him, that is, in the proper sense—and why we and he thus do not simply share as equals the same lot that is assigned to all of us. If we ask first of all only about the equality of our death and his, the question is also of course but by no means solely about death as a physiological event. But we are certainly asking too about this physiological event of a medical exitus, since man not only has a body, but also is body, the entire breadth and depth of human existence up to the most sublime actualizations of that existence is realized corporeally, in a true sense: that is, it is not the body that dies, but the person in his body. But this means that death in a human and Christian sense is thus essentially more than a mere medical exitus, in which the heart stops and the electrical brain currents cease. Death rightly understood is an event involving the whole person and might take place at that crucial point where the act of freedom is finalized, not by any means necessarily in the chronological moment of the medical exitus (even though this is a real factor in the finalization of man's history of freedom), but occurs in a true sense throughout the whole of life and reaches a climax at that moment not ascertainable by our reflection in which man's temporally extended history of freedom reaches its finality. But what does the person do when he thus brings his history of freedom to its finality and irreversibility in death, in what way ultimately and at the hidden core of existence does the one decision of freedom become irreversible, the decision which, although temporally extended, is achieved in the one life of man? We cannot answer the question here by developing precisely and at length an existential ontology and theology of death. It is possible to answer this question only briefly.

It is true that the individual decisions of freedom, which are integrated into the one life's decision, occur on the basis of the categorial individual material of our life presented to us from our milieu and environment. But these individual decisions are elements of the one life's decision only insofar as (over and above their finite and particular content, even though by their mediation) there occurs in them an assent or a refusal to that infinite horizon and objective of freedom which alone makes possible freedom in the proper sense in regard to the subject and its individual objects and in the final understanding is known as God. If and insofar as the decision of freedom in regard to an individual categorial object of an intramundane character is also a transcending of this object, leaving it behind and in a sense renouncing it, and in this respect and in this way the infinite objective of freedom (called God) is recognized as such and thus as dissociated from the individual object, such a decision is right, affirms God himself as such, although this does not of course require the innermost structure of the true act of freedom to be present as such explicitly and objectified and verbalized. This innermost structure of every real decision of freedom, insofar as it is an internal factor in human death as an existential act, makes itself clearly felt in what we experience empirically as death. In death, empirically seen, the world withdraws from the subject of freedom, and even the latter is lost to itself. Everything perishes; it is, as Scripture says, the night in which no one can work.

How does the subject of freedom encounter this decline, in which it can cling to nothing individual and not even to itself in its explicit factuality? There are two ways in which the subject of a freedom can accept this decline. Either the subject in the last resort culpably refuses to accept any freely bestowed love from another person, regarding itself as condemned to an absolute autonomy and autarchy as to absolute futility, against which only a radical protest is possible; or it accepts with resignation and hope this eclipse of all particular realities as the dawn and approach of that silent infinity into which each particular act of freedom has hitherto always risen above its individual object, in order in a sense to be lost into this merely apparently empty infinity. In the first case death is the event of final perdition, in the second the beginning of redeemed finality in God.

It is impossible to explain more precisely here how and why this self-surrender to the loving incomprehensibility of God, in the decline of all particular objects of freedom occurring in death, involves what we describe in Christian terminology as the one triplicity of faith, hope, and love, which justifies us and brings us to final salvation, assuming of course (and this has to be assumed as a datum) that this self-surrender of the subject of freedom to the loving incomprehensibility of God, leaving behind and transcending everything individual, is sustained in the present and only real order of salvation by a self-communication of God (described as grace) always and everywhere forestalling our freedom, by which God himself radicalizes our self-surrender toward his immediacy and gives himself as response to it.

Perhaps we can now say a little more clearly in what the common feature in Jesus' death and ours consists, what we do when we follow him in his dying, even though this does not yet explain why in the death that we have in common he is the imperative, productive model, why our dying in the proper sense *depends* on his dying and is thus really a following of the Crucified. According to Scripture we may safely say that Jesus in his life was the *believer* (notwithstanding the traditional teaching that at the innermost centre of his existence he had an immediacy to God such as is given to us only in eternal life) and that he was consequently the one who hopes absolutely and in regard to God and men obviously the one who loves absolutely. In the unity of this triplicity of faith, hope, and love, Jesus surrendered himself in his death unconditionally to the absolute mystery that he called his Father, into whose hands he committed his existence, when in the night of his death and God-forsakenness he was deprived of everything that is otherwise regarded as the content of a human existence: life, honour, acceptance in earthly and religious fellowship, and so on. In the concreteness of his death it becomes only too clear that everything fell away from him, even the perceptible security of the closeness of God's love, and in this trackless dark there prevailed silently only the mystery that in itself and in its freedom has no name and to which he nevertheless calmly surrendered himself as to eternal love and not to the hell of futility. In that sense his death is the same as ours, even though the concrete circumstance of dying vary between a gruesome stake at which the cruel madness of human beings tortures another human being to death and a deathbed in a modern hospital where white uniformed doctors do everything possible to prevent the dying person from noticing the state he has reached. Whether we die in one way or another can make a vast difference in many respects, so that we may rightly wish for an easy and gentle death. But in the last resort what happens in death is the same for all: we are deprived of everything, even of ourselves; we all fall, each of us alone, into the dark abyss where there are no further ways. And this death—which in the first place is simply ours—Jesus died; he who came out of God's glory did not merely descend into our human life, but also fell into the abyss of our death, and his dying began when he began to live and came to an end on the cross when he bowed his head and died.

Jesus died as we die. When we say this and visualize up to a point the content of the statement, what we see is Jesus following in our way and not ourselves in his. If and insofar as we continue always to see him as the eternal Word of God, who assumed our human reality, our life, and our death, as his own reality, the statement that Jesus died as we die can of course give ineffable dignity and eternal consolation for our own death. If we believe that our own human reality has been assumed by God, this is true also of course of our death. Since the eternal Logos of the Father suffered it as his own death, this death must be redeemed, sanctified, emptied of final despair and futility, filled with the eternal life of God himself. This can and must be said, if we assume what Christian faith professes about Jesus Christ as the only begotten Son of the Father himself and if in the light of this faith we say that he died as we die, even though we shall not go on from this point to develop its implications for our own death as redeemed.

Can we now say however that we have answered the second question above-mentioned, the question of whether and in what sense we really *follow* in our dying the dying Jesus on the cross, so that Jesus' death truly becomes the productive model of our death, that our death is different from what it would be if we did not die precisely as following him. It would certainly be possible to work out an answer to this question by continuing from the point now reached in our reflections. It could be shown more explicitly how the assumption of our death by the eternal Logos as his own does not merely assimilate him to us but also transforms our death. But we want to try to answer this second question in the light of a somewhat different consideration, since this makes it more simple and more tangible.

Jesus died into his resurrection, his death is the event of gaining the finality of his human reality in the life of God himself. Jesus' resurrection is not merely an event that could not be expected, attached in a singular way to his death. It is the consequence of his death itself as such, if it is seen at the same time as the death of him in whom the eternal God imparts his own life to the world as its gracious endowment and as the event in which this Jesus accepts finally and irrevocably this self-communication of God through death. However the "three days" between Jesus' death and the awareness of his resurrection are to be more precisely theologically interpreted, the idea of this temporal interval must not be allowed to obstruct our view of the intrinsic unity of the death and resurrection of Jesus. In his resurrection the very thing that happened in his death is completed and made effective: the incomprehensible God finally accepted this human reality as redeemed, precisely because the latter was surrendered unsupported and unreservedly into the incomprehensibility of God himself. We can really say that (in the sense of an indissoluble essential connection) his death is his resurrection and vice versa, since he entered into definitive life precisely in death and in no other way.

But since this is true in the first place only of the only-begotten Son of the Father and in the radical sinlessness of his faith, hope, and love, as distinct from us sinners, his death, despite all its similarity to ours, is in itself quite different from the death that we for our own part and independently of following him can die and must die. If then his death is to become a real determinant of our own death and in that very peculiarity which as such distinguishes his death as death into resurrection from our death as penalty of sin, he must give us a share of his death.

But this again implies two things: on the one hand his death must take place for us; he must die in a community of fate and in solidarity with us, and the Spirit of God, in whom he accepted his death purely and simply as the dawn of life, must be offered to us as the opportunity of a death with him. On the other hand, for our part, this opportunity of dying with him as a beginning of life must be accepted in freedom. Since both preconditions exist or can be realized in freedom, it is possible to die with him; the determinant of unity with the resurrection, essential to his death, can also as grace become a determinant of our death, and this death of ours then has a peculiarity which is not merely (like the other determinants of death) common to his death and ours, but belongs to our death only in virtue of his, so that there is present that peculiarity by which a mere similarity between us and Jesus is turned into a real following. In faith in him and his grace our death is transformed from a manifestation of sinful God-forsakenness or an open question that is involved in the mysterious incomprehensibility by God into a death leading to the loving acceptance of our existence of God into his own life, a death into resurrection. There is still something explicitly to be added however to this consideration of the way in which the similarity of death with Jesus and with us becomes a real following of the Crucified in dying.

Our death and Jesus' death, even and more especially as resurrection, occur as a passing into the silent incomprehensibility and unavailability of God. It is for this reason that death is the supreme and most radical act of faith. The following of the Crucified as such is in itself a supreme act of faith, a surrender in hope and love to the incomprehensibility of God which completely takes away from us who are here the result of this act of death, as into a total extinction. We must say this in the first place about our death as following of the Crucified, but that is not all that is to be said about this singular unity of Jesus' death and our death.

It is true that Jesus by his resurrection vanishes from us into the unavailability of God. But his resurrection is at the same time the event of salvation history which, even if grasped only by faith, is part of the history of this world and this humanity and is grasped and acknowledged precisely by faith as such an historical event that truly changes the world. His resurrection took place in this world, even though it is the event that raises this historical world of becoming into the eternity of God. The resurrection has an absolutely peculiar and unique but nevertheless real tangibility in history. This must be remembered also in regard to his death as entry into this resurrection. If in his following we die with him, the question whether we die into the life of God or into sheer annihilation is not answered in a way that is empirically verifiable in regard to our death as such; there is certainly no tangible assurance of a death leading to a resurrection, since (at least normally) we cannot for our own part make any unambiguous judgment about the final destiny of a dying person. But from the clarity of Jesus's death as the way to his resurrection, from the historicity of Jesus' resurrection, a light is thrown on the ambivalence of our own death and this light, too, is part of our dying with Christ. In this manner the situation is the same as in world history in general.

In the history of the world itself as distinct from God's eternal plans, *before* the resurrection of Jesus, the victorious irreversibility of God's self-communication to the world was not firmly established or tangible, the final outcome of world history was not perceptible as salvation in history itself. The drama of world history as a whole was also still unfinished and ambivalent. Things are different after the resurrection: there the peripe-teia of the drama of world history to good, to eternal salvation, has al-ready taken place. It is true that we cannot deduce from this any un-equivocal conclusion for the individual and his individual destiny of salvation; but even for the individual the situation of hope is different from what it was before Jesus' resurrection. From the one reality already existing the success of other possibilities can be presumed. This is true particularly when an historically and sociologically explicit relationship to Jesus' resurrection is present as promise to the world as a whole. What has been said here in general about the relationship of world history to Jesus' death and resurrection is therefore true also of the relationship of our dying to Jesus' dying, particularly when this relationship is explicitly realized in faith. Our dying admittedly retains an openness and ambiva-lence, but it is encompassed by the promise that exists for us in the victori-ous death of Jesus into his resurrection. Paul says: "Here is a saying you can rely on: if we have died with him, then we shall live with him" (2 Tim. 2:11).

We said earlier that death in a theological sense does not in the last resort coincide chronologically with the medical exitus, but occurs throughout the whole of life and reaches its completion only at the end. Hence, from the nature of the case, it was legitimate for Christian piety in its entire history to seek to realize the following of the *Crucified* in Christian *life*, in the acceptance of everything that Christian usage even up to the present time described as the "cross": the experiences of human frailty, of sick-ness, of disappointments, of the nonfulfillment of our expectations, and so on. What occurs in all this is part of man's dying, of the destruction of life's tangible goods. In all these brief moments of dying in installments we are faced with the question of how we are to cope with them: whether we merely protest, merely despair (even for brief moments), become cynical and cling all the more desperately and absolutely to what has not yet been taken from us, *or* whether we abandon with resignation what is taken from us, accept twilight as promise of an eternal Christmas full of light, regard light breakdowns as events of grace. If in this second way (which cannot by any means be so easily distinguished from the first) we take the cross on ourselves daily, we are accomplishing part of the follow-ing of the Crucified, we are practising faith and loving hope in which death is accepted as the advent of eternal life and the following of Jesus, the Crucified, reaches its completion.

31 · The Saints

The Church professes herself to be the holy Church. This profession is not left to her own choice. She cannot refrain from making this profession, as it were out of modesty or in view of the sinfulness of her members. It is her duty, because she must profess God's grace. But when she does this, she must not merely praise God's salvific will by grace which is "in itself" equipped to forgive and to sanctify. She must praise the grace which has had powerful effects, which has conquered, which has become real and manifest to us. Hence she must say: God really *has* redeemed, he really *has* poured out his Spirit, he really *has* done mighty things for sinners, he *has* let his light shine in the darkness. His light shines, it is visible, and there is a tangible assembly of those whom he has called out of the kingdom of darkness and whom he has brought into the kingdom of the Son of his love.

Because the Church must praise *God's grace*, she must also profess herself to be the holy Church. This profession humbles her; for she always testifies anew by this against what she is of herself: the flock of the poor, the stubborn, the sinful, of those who of themselves are very obviously lost. Yet she may not on this account omit this profession. She must sing: "You have loved us, O Lord, and redeemed us by your blood; you have made us to be a kingdom and made us priests to God your father" (Rev. 1:5–6). She must not declare this merely as a *possibility* provided by God; she is no Pelagian for whom man's choice from mere, God-given possibilities would have to be the last word, and so she must testify to this as an event which has actually taken place. She must not behave as if it were in the last analysis still questionable or at least still a completely incomprehensible and hidden fact that God with his word of mercy has had the last word in the dialogue between himself and the creature, as if one could merely "presume" that God has poured out his Spirit without giving any evidence at all of his mighty wind and his tongues of fire.

Eschatological Testimony of Faith

This hymn of praise to the grace of God in the profession made by the holy Church, a profession belonging to the innermost core of the Christian Credo, must now be clarified in its theological traits, and this from several points of view. This profession made by the holy Church is a profession of the *visible* Church. It is, of course, a profession of *faith*. Certainly, what is professed is *actually* seen, and acknowledged as seen, by the grace of God and in the light of faith (without thereby questioning the apologetic, faith-testifying function of the holiness of the Church as a mark of the true Church of Christ). But this holiness of the Church is not by this fact something which is present merely as something absolutely beyond experience, as something merely believed to be present in a completely hidden way in the Church and contrary to all history and experience, merely believed to lie under the sole outward impression of the Church's hopelessly sinful state and failure, and yet believed by a despairingly paradoxical "nevertheless." This holiness makes the Church a *signum elevatum in nationes* (Denz. 1794); one meets her if one looks for her and wants to see her with a humble and open mind; she shines out, she proclaims herself in a real way, one can meet her. God's deed in giving his grace to man is witnessed in her works which are such that we can praise the Father on account of them (Matt. 5:16); it is witnessed in its fruits which are love, joy, peace, patience, tenderness, goodness, faith, modesty, continence (Gal. 5:22f.).

This manifested, "proclaimed" holiness of the Church is not merely a pure "facticity" which can be observed subsequently here and there and contrary to all expectations. It can be seen to be rather something which is ordained by God in his decrees. It is indeed always an act of man's free love and of the free obedience of his faith. But precisely this act is determined and given gratuitously by God; precisely this act is borne and guaranteed by the greater power of the grace of God, God who of himself no more allows the Church as a whole to break out of his love than out of his truth, not because man could not do so but because God grants the grace to the Church really to do freely what he wants of her; not merely her word and her objective preparations for salvation (preaching and the sacraments), but also her "existential" being is intended to proclaim the final victory of grace, since in Christ on the Cross God has the last word in the dialogue between himself and the human race, and this word is the effective word of mercy. Hence the Church *must* in *all* ages proclaim—even though in a sense ashamedly, yet quite clearly—that she is the holy Church. She knows what she thus affirms of herself, not merely by her past experience of herself by God's mighty deed which has been promised to her by God's word before she had any—otherwise very problematical—experience, and which goes beyond and anticipates this experience. The proclamation of her own holiness is an eschatological statement of faith and not merely a kind judgment of history which condescends not to overlook the good which "after all also exists" over and above everything ugly.

Yet precisely in this way, this statement must be a concrete one. If the Church were simply to say that she is the holy one and mean by this simply that this has to be said in general—as it were, at random and without indicating anything absolutely definite, but simply because it is not very likely that God's word and grace should nowhere gain a real and final victory—then she would really have proclaimed grace and its holy law merely as a possibility and as a challenge, but not grace as the victorious power and the law as fulfilled by grace. In this case, she would after all be preaching a merely abstract "idealism"; she herself would be an ideal and a postulate but not the God-given fulfilment which has already surpassed everything merely morally demanded, everything which merely ought to be. She would after all be merely the law and not the *pneuma* which is poured out. She herself would be on the side of the law which is the goad of sin; she would be merely on the side of those to be redeemed and not the tangible expression of the grace of redemption. If this were so, then the more the Church would speak about holiness—the clearer and more forcibly she would proclaim the mere demand for holiness—the more she would be the Old Testament synagogue of the law. Yet she is after all distinguished from the latter precisely by the fact that she does not proclaim the law as a demand (although she must do this also, since we, her listeners, are always in transition from the servitude of the flesh to the freedom of the Holy Spirit); rather, she proclaims the fulfilment of the law which has been accomplished in us by the grace of God. Hence, she must be able to state her holiness in the concrete. She must have a "cloud of witnesses" whom she can indicate by name. She cannot merely maintain that there is a history of salvation (without it being known exactly where it takes place with real, final success), but she must *really relate* that very eschatological history of salvation which she is herself. The prize of her actual saints belongs to her innermost being and is not merely something which she "also" achieves "on the side," something which has been inspired by a purely human need for hero worship.

Creators of New Christian Modes of Life

Having reached this point, it can now be seen more clearly what is the exact function of the saints in the Church. They are of vital importance for her constitution, not merely as successful products of the Church in her role as an institutional establishment of salvation, products who—brought to maturity by instruction and education, direction and means of grace—are, as it were, handed over as the completed end-result to the "triumphant" Church. They belong, precisely as saints here on earth, to the very essence of the Church; if she lacked her saints, she herself would not be what she must be. The Church is not merely a saving institution and thus the teacher of truth and administrator of the means of grace, directed—as if to mere objects—towards those who do not administer this institution in an official capacity. If the Church were holy merely in her objective institutions, then she would be the Synagogue and there would be the danger (and, in the long run, the insurmountable danger) that the unholy sinners might turn the holy institutions into a weapon against God himself and that they might destroy these institutions together with the "synagogue." These baptized, sanctified men—who believe and love—*are* the Church (a platitude which, alas, is still not really understood and lived by the people of the Church today). This Church, understood as the people of God to which belong all those who are baptized and who have the true faith—this Church understood as the Body of Christ whose members are not confined to the office-bearers—must be holy, must represent in a historically tangible manner the victory of God's grace.

It is certainly true that this happens already through all the "saints" in the *biblical* sense, i.e., through all those who have been justified by faith, love and baptism, and who thus live a truly Christian life, since all "saints" who have been called by God, who have come into his holy nearness and who have been claimed by him as his property, form the assembled congregation of Christ, the holy Church. Those whom we in present-day usage call saints have in fact no special advantage in this respect over all those "saints" in the biblical sense, i.e., in regard to formation of the holy Church as the historical witness of the holy and sanctifying God and his grace which has already and finally begun its reign. We can indeed say that these saints in the modern, liturgical and canonical sense tower over all the other "saints"—in other words, over us ordinary Christians—by their "heroic" virtue, but that this virtue is something extraordinary and that therefore these saints have an extraordinary task to perform as representatives of the holy Church. This is quite correct, but it is surely not enough. For where the Christian reality is present by the power of grace (which signifies an absolutely new beginning), everything which follows from this and grows out of it cannot signify anything more than a difference in degree as compared with the absolutely new being in relation to the one who has not been justified.

The heroic nature of the virtues of the (canonized) saints cannot *alone* explain their special task in the Church. But they undoubtedly have such a special task. For why otherwise can the Church exercise in their regard alone that authority and power of decision by which she reaches into the ultimate secrets of conscience and into the very depths of eternity, an authority and power of decision which she cannot exercise in regard to everyone who has passed over, signed by faith and who now rests in the sleep of peace? This surely cannot be explained simply by the fact that such a procedure would be too awkward and that it really does not benefit Christian existence—which must work out its salvation in "fear and trembling"—if every Christian who has died a good death were to be "canonized." No doubt it is also not explained by saying simply that the Church would ultimately no longer be the believing, merely hoping Church who is still a pilgrim, if it were known with certainty of all those who have belonged to her right up to death that they have finally attained salvation. For it is, of course, true that—even if the general separation were to take place merely at the boundary of death, and thus in a way clearly recognizable for all others here on earth—then the Church would no longer be both the Church of saints *and* sinners, the threshing floor covered with chaff and wheat, the net filled with good and bad fishes, and this in such a way that the division between the two is known by God and his angels alone. All this is true but does not itself explain why only a few ("heroic") Saints among the "saints" in the biblical sense can and may be canonized. These must have a more particular task than merely being "especially excellent" cases from among the ordinary (average) "saints."

But in what does the specific importance of (canonized or canonizable) saints for the constitution of the holy Church consist? To make any headway here, it will be necessary to note the following: we must not conceive the holiness of the Church and of the saints merely as the complete fulfilment of an always equal and static, supernaturally moral debit which floats as an unchangeable ideal over the history of the Church and which is realized ever anew by new generations of the Church under her direction.

The Church has a genuine history, a unique history of salvation and hence also of holiness. Even though the "essence" of Christian holiness remains always the same, it does not simply always "happen" in the "same way" in each saint. The differences between saints (which no one would deny) are not merely sublime accidents of a merely temporal kind, which are of no consequence for the holiness itself which they realize. No, precisely these unique accidents of history, the "individual factor," the "physiognomic element" of the saints enters into eternity with them, into that eternity which is not something purely abstract but the genuine and permanent, individual product of history. Otherwise there would be a *"cultus sanctitatis"* in the Church but no *"cultus sanctorum,"* and one would have to recommend moral theology books for reading and not the lives of the saints. Just as there is a real development of dogmas, i.e., a history of the appropriation of truth, so there is also a history of holiness, i.e., the always unique, unrepeatable history of the appropriation of God's grace and of the partaking of God's holiness.

Hence, the true nature of Christian holiness cannot be clearly and solely deciphered from a Christian theology of essences or, even less, from a "natural law" (with a supernatural goal), no matter how necessary and indispensable such philosophical and theological ethics may be. The nature of Christian holiness appears from the life of Christ and of his saints; and what appears there cannot be translated absolutely into a general theory but must be experienced in the encounter with the historical which takes place from one individual case to the other. The history of Christian holiness (of what, in other words, is the business of every Christian, since everyone is sanctified and called to holiness) is in its totality a unique history and not the eternal return of the same. Hence this history has its always new, unique phases; hence it must always be discovered anew (even though always in the imitation of Christ who remains the inexhaustible model), and this by all Christians.

Herein lies the special task which the canonized saints have to fulfil for the Church. They are the initiators and the creative models of the holiness which happens to be right for, and is the task of, their particular age. They create a new style; they prove that a certain form of life and activity is a really genuine possibility; they show experimentally that one can be a Christian even in "this" way; they make such a type of person believable as a Christian type. Their significance begins therefore not merely after they are dead. Their death is rather the seal put on their task of being creative models, a task which they had in the Church during their lifetime, and their living-on means that the example they have given remains in the Church as a permanent form.

Anyone who really understands what is meant by the history of the spirit and by the fact that the history of the Church (and of her holiness) is a unique and connected history will not object against what has been said that in this case the "old" saints are no longer topical. For the history of the spiritual means precisely that something *becomes* real in order to *remain*, not in order to disappear again, so that this permanence does not militate against the real becoming of what precisely was not always there already, and the becoming is the event of what is eternally valid and not of what is swallowed up again. The creative, first appearance of a historical form (and thus also, for instance, of holiness) just does not mean that the past of a spiritual history becomes thereby simply outmoded. (Plato has not ceased to be important for us simply because we can no longer philosophize with him as if there had never been a Kant.) At most, the only truth in this objection would be the fact that even the creative models of our holiness have still a further history in the Church after their death, through the always new historical realizations of the holy in the Church. (Thus, for instance, even a dutiful son of St. Francis can today no longer prescind "romantically" from the fact that since the time of St. Francis there has been an Ignatius; and even the sons of St. Ignatius are not the guardians of "final truth," for "final truth" is not to be found in the history of holiness, i.e., in the historical validity of the life of Christ, since he too *lives* on even to the end of history.)

The Adventure of the Saints

When the Church canonizes, she says: this life which has been lived is genuine and full Christianity, although—no, because—the way in which such a saint has lived is not at all self-evident: in the desert and quite "unecclesiastically"; as an intellectually daring scholar; in humdrum conditions and within pitiful horizons; as a perfectly normal Central European, as a very "egocentric" beggar (almost like any typical down-and-out); and in a thousand other ways which one never recognizes as Christian possibilities until afterwards, until after they have been lived in a holy way. For the most part, such things are recorded afterwards in the "lives of the saints" as at best merely proofs of the virtue of the saints. For the rest, however, they are rendered harmless, or are deftly touched up, as if it were immediately evident that one can be a Christian, and even a saintly one, in *such* conditions. Yet in reality the way the saint lived his life was an adventure, and an adventure whose "rule" it was impossible to discover simply in any theoretical moral rule or in the rule of a religious order (alone), even though the saint himself, in his humility and simple fidelity to the inner inspirations of the Holy Spirit, often was unaware how "original" (in the truest sense of the word) and how unique he was (at least in this or that aspect of his Christian existence).

How many Christians today realize clearly that Francis of Assisi managed to achieve what the Waldensians had in mind and what in their case was rejected (and quite rightly, since it was distorted) as unecclesiastical idealism? The clashes of St. Ignatius with the Spanish Inquisition and his later fights for the characteristic ideal of his Order (even Pius V was still trying to impose the communal choral Office on the Jesuits), the persecution—to the point of his ignominious and bitter confinement to the monastery—which a St. John of the Cross had to endure, the inquisitorial process together with monastic confinement inflicted on Mary Ward, the very real danger of being put on the Index which threatened the holy Doctor of the Church, Robert Bellarmine (at the hands of Sixtus V, because he did not seem "papal" enough) . . . such and many similar facts show that the style of Christian existence lived by the saints and sanctioned by their holiness was not by any means self-evident to their contemporaries. Only someone who *from the outset* has tacitly lowered Christianity, with its exorbitant demands, to the level of the standards of the "decent citizen" who is "practising" can think that it is really quite obvious how a Christian should love and that consequently there is no need for the successful risk —a risk canonized by the Church precisely because it was successful—as the ones taken by the saints who are our examples. Only someone who underestimates the ever new character of situations of history can imagine that he can be satisfied with Christ and imitation of him, arguing that all the saints in their lives can express only a very small aspect of the one Word become flesh. "Be imitators of me as I am of Christ" (1 Cor. 11:1), say the saints together with St. Paul. The Church, by canonization, confirms their word, not so much or even principally in order to honour the saints but because she thus finds her own task, her own nature, in so far as it has to be realized precisely here and now and then continuously maintained as thus realized.

32 · Devotion to Mary

It might be maintained that when faith is in question, nothing can be said except about God the most high, the thrice holy, the inexpressibly mysterious, God who alone constitutes our salvation and our eternity. It might be held that there is no room for anything else in preaching and theology. One might consider that everything else must recede into profound silence, however praiseworthy it might otherwise be, or deserving of reflection. One might think it only permissible to speak there of God, his grace and his redemption, and consequently of his Incarnate Word. It might be held that nothing more could be said about anything else in preaching and theology, than is said, for example, about Pilate, who also figures in the creed. Just as there are human beings who are named as it were in the margin of the creed, simply because in the history of the Word made flesh, they represent humanity's refusal of faith, so also, one might say, there may be persons mentioned in passing in marginal notes about the faith. They are named, to be sure, but are not an object of faith, of what it affirms, or of theology.

Consequently we must first answer the question: Is there any such thing as a theology of man? Only when we have answered this question can we boldly, confidently and joyfully enter the domain of faith and theology, in order—if it is possible to say anything at all about man—to say something about that human being who is the holiest, most authentic, and happiest human being, to say something of her who is blessed among women.

There is in fact a theology of man, a preaching of the faith and a theology that praises and glorifies God, by saying something about man. How is this? God is indeed really all in all. There is nothing beside him worthy of mention for its own sake, when faith is preached and theology pursued. In this holy house of God one cannot really speak of anything, praise anything, mention anything except the eternal God and him alone. Before him everything else sinks into the abyss of its absolute insignificance.

There is not, in theology and in faith, God and then everything else imaginable as well, there is only the incomprehensible triune adorable God. When mind and heart are raised to him confessing their belief, all else must fall silent and be passed over in silence. Then there remains nothing for a man but to adore and praise that Godhead. For the life of faith and the endeavor of theology are of course one day to blossom into that one life whose entire content is the loving contemplation of God face to face, the eternal praise of his grace alone.

And yet there is a theology of man himself, a confession of faith that says something about man himself, not in the margin of the profession of faith in the one eternal God, but comprised in it. How is this? Because God himself, in the life of the blessed Trinity, in his ineffable glory, in his eternal life, has taken us into this eternal life that is his. We do not need to be dead, as a poet of our day wrote, for God to live. He has not only given us something that he created out of nothing, something finite. Beyond all that, he has given us himself. He called us from nothingness, that we might truly be, he gave us freedom, that we might be able really and truly to be his partners, in his presence. He has made a covenant with us. He has not only willed to deal with us through the creation, where everything we meet with is always merely finite, a sign only, and a mere pointer to the God who ever remains beyond. He has willed to act directly with us himself, so that what happens, and what he does, what he shows and what he gives, is ultimately, in reality, himself, even if as yet only in the promise that he will one day reveal himself to us face to face, with nothing to stand between him and us any more. Further,—it is the most adorable mystery of faith—he has himself become man in the person of his Word.

Since that is so, and since it belongs to the mystery of our God that he is not only the God of the philosophers, but the God of Abraham, Isaac and Jacob, and what is more, the Father of our Lord Jesus Christ, who has become man, and our brother, it follows that for us Christians there is no acknowledgment in faith of the eternal God, unless we praise him for having given himself to us so totally, that we can proclaim with truth about one who is a man: he sitteth at the right hand of God the eternal. Consequently no doctrine of God is possible any more without a doctrine of man, no theology without anthropology. It is no longer possible to say who God is in the full truth and reality of his actual life as he lives it, without saying that his eternal Word, in whom he utters and expresses himself, is man to all eternity. It is impossible now, here in Christendom, *post Christum natum*, now that Christ is born, to say anything true, genuine and concrete about God, unless one acknowledges him as Emmanuel, God with us, the God of our flesh, of our human nature, the God of our human sacramental signs, the God of our altars, the God who was born of the Virgin Mary and consequently God and man in one person, a human being among us. Since this is the true, real living God it is clear why the countenance of a man is seen within the sphere of divine faith and theology. For the same reason such a genuine theology necessarily, not merely accessorily, as part of its essential function, glorifies man, and can only praise God by so doing. That is ultimately why a mariology is possible, a teaching of the faith concerning the blessed virgin mother of our Lord. That is why mariology is not merely a piece of the private life-story of Jesus of Nazareth, of no real ultimate significance for our salvation, but an affirmation of faith itself concerning a reality of the faith, without which there is no salvation.

There is a further consideration. We human beings are important for one another. We mean something to one another, not only in the every-day things of life, not only because (since we exist) we have parents, not only because, in the biological sphere, in the external life of the civil community, of art and learning, we are always dependent on a great human community. That is not the only reason for our importance for one another. Even in our salvation we are also similarly dependent on other human beings. That goes without saying, as a matter of course, yet it is difficult to grasp. One might think we were only important to one another for this life, for external things, or at most in the domain of the spirit here on earth. Or one might think that when it is a question of how God stands to me and I to God, of the ultimate decision about my eternity, of how I shall fare one day, when through the inexorable loneliness of my death, I stand utterly alone before the face of God, that then, in all that, I am absolutely alone and isolated. Then, surely, there is only the one God, and myself, his love and mercy, and my irreplaceable freedom in guilt and grace. Yet it is not so, for all that. All that has been said is true, but it is not the whole truth. For we still belong to one another, even then. Each has his own, inalienable, unique freedom, from which he cannot escape, which he cannot shuffle off on to someone else. But for all that, it is not a lonely isolated freedom, not even when it is deciding the eternal destiny of a human being, or making the fundamental choice of a human life. For the eternal Son, the eternal Word of the Father, was made flesh, born of the Virgin Mary. In our family, out of our race that stretches from the first human being, Adam, to the last, the Word of the Father was made flesh.

There is, therefore, a community in nature and in grace which takes effect in a community of sin and guilt, of the mercy of God and his grace, a community of origin and goal. But guilt and grace, origin and end, are God's concerns. Consequently the community of mankind extends into the domain of man's eternal salvation with God. It is a community in eternal welfare or loss, a vast community which acts out as a whole, and not only in individual human beings, the great drama of history before the eyes of God, and which brings to light what God's thought about mankind was. Only all these thousand and one varieties of men who, in cooperation or in conflict, form the one course of world history, together bring to realization what was really intended when God said in the beginning: "Let us make man to our image and likeness."

Since we belong to one another, not only in everyday life, in politics and secular history, but in the unfolding course of salvation, there is, then, a history of grace and salvation, in which we all belong to one another, and so none is without importance for the others, and all are important for each individual. Each must bear the load of guilt and grace, not only for himself, but also for all the rest. What one suffers, prays, weeps over, endures, and finds blessedness in, is of decisive importance for everyone, for the innumerable host of men and women who live that history. We belong together. But then, since it is God who is occupied with us in that history of grace, since our faith and theology must speak of him as the Lord of that one single history of humanity's eternal gain and loss, it again follows that man will have to be included in what faith has to preach and theology to state, for they are an account of God's saving work for us. And he has so disposed his dealings with mankind, that one human being is important for another there. He has simply willed that his redemptive work in us shall be effected by him through human beings. That is way the Blessed Virgin Mary must be included in what faith and theology have to say about those who are important in the divine plan of redemption. For she is the mother of him on whom salvation is entirely built, because he is God and man in one person. And Mary is also of decisive importance for our salvation's being found in Jesus Christ, inasmuch as this was given to her in God's unfathomable salvific will itself. She must have a place in theology. A doctrine of God involves a doctrine of man, and as part of it, a doctrine of Mary. In the midst of the praise faith gives to the one God of salvation, of the Incarnation, of grace, and of the one divine plan of redemption, what concerns Mary must be spoken.

What does all this signify for us? First and foremost, it means that Christian theology has something to say about man, that is, about ourselves. If we want to use for once that fashionable word, we can have an existential theology. Nowadays there is a lot of talk about men. Even in philosophy, man is made the key to the interpretation of being and reality in general. Well, it is quite possible to say that when we are engaged in our May devotions, we are engaged in a Christian understanding of the human situation. It is God's word concerning us that we are there concerned with, a blessed and holy understanding of our own life. For there we are not seeing man merely as an ambiguous being, placed between two abysses of nothingness, nothing but anguish and distress. There we are speaking of Mary. We are praising her as blessed and holy, and by doing so, we are also, ultimately, saying something about ourselves. When we celebrate May devotions, we call nature to our aid to praise man as the image of God, to proclaim that he is redeemed, called by God into his own holy and blessed life. We are celebrating and proclaiming the Christian idea of man. In fact we are very up-to-date (if indeed we have any mind to be so), when we expound the old sacred truths we acknowledge every time we kneel and pray: And the Word was made flesh . . . born of the Virgin Mary.

Our reflections show us, furthermore, that we all belong together. We all share the burden and the blessedness, the danger and the salvation of all the rest. That of course is why we meet in this sacred congregation. A congregation praying, singing, and listening to the word of God, is not only an assembly of lonely, solitary people, not only a number of isolated individuals, who, impelled by concern for their eternal salvation, gather here for merely practical convenience, in order to try to work out their own private salvation for themselves alone. We are a holy community praising God by praising the glory of the Blessed Virgin precisely because in our very salvation we are dependent on this virgin mother of God. We are a holy community, truly belonging together and therefore meeting together, truly experiencing in unity the grace of him whom God gave us by the obedience and the body of the Blessed Virgin. We are those who have been called away from the loneliness and isolation of the individual into the unity of the love and grace of God.

So we must be in the everyday world too. We cannot pray here together if outside we cannot get on together in love and mutual trust, associate in mutual forbearance. Consequently, devotion to Mary is something that, by the very root from which it springs, has something to do with love of one's neighbour. For no doctrine concerning Mary could have importance and significance for us, if it were not true that each of us is responsible for the salvation of his brethren, and can and must intercede for them with prayer and sacrifice and aid. That is why Mary is not only the mother of our Lord, but our mother too. And so we have come here together to praise Mary once more at this time in the joy of our hearts. Such praise is ultimately praise of the eternal God himself, who in the person of the Incarnate Word has drawn near to us, when the Word was made flesh, born of the Virgin Mary.

33 · The Parish

If and insofar as the Church as one and whole is itself a reality of faith and not merely a secular sociological organization (even though the latter would serve a supernatural purpose, comprehensible only in faith) and if, however, this Church as itself a reality of faith has inevitably a spatial character, then it must also be said that a territorial parish within this Church likewise participates in the peculiarity of the one Church as a reality of faith. In the Catholic understanding of faith the Church as a whole is indeed one Church, but an episcopally (that is, spatially, territorially) constituted Church. This territorial structure of the Church is obviously in the first place an empirical and secular reality, but this very reality is nevertheless taken up into the mystery of the Church as the unity of human beings in the Holy Spirit and in the profession of faith in Jesus Christ as Son of God, crucified and risen, the historically palpable, irreversible self-promise of God as salvation of the world.

This mystery of the Church as sacrament of the world's salvation becomes effective territorially, it becomes effective in space and time. The nature of the Church does not consist merely in the ubiquity of the Spirit of God, who is poured out equally on all flesh as innermost dynamism of humanity and its history. The nature of the Church consists even more in the fact that this undeniable although hidden ubiquity of the Spirit is manifested historically, sacramentally, sociologically, and incarnationally and that this incarnational and sacramental manifestation makes the ubiquity of the Spirit of God (unconfused and undivided) irreversibly and historically palpable in the world. Thus the Church as sacrament of the world's salvation (as seen from above) has an unquestionably territorial character and this territorial character of the Church as sociological factor (as seen from below) shares in its quality as mystery (as, for instance, the water of baptism is earthly water and yet in baptism becomes the actual and effective manifestation of man's sanctification by grace).

The parish, too, as a territorial factor participates in this quality which is part of the territorial organization of the Church. This becomes even clearer when we remember that the most effective and radical sacramental self-realization of the Church as the redeeming unity of human beings together in God occurs in the eucharist. Here the Church is present in its completeness and here it is unquestionably in place, in the local community, which is not absolutely necessarily but preferably and normally the parish community. It is understandable, therefore, that the New Testament, especially Paul, sees the Church first of all as the local Church, as (we may say without prejudice) the Parish Church, at a time when there was still no difference between an episcopal and a parochial community Church. There can indeed be communities for the eucharistic celebration which are not parishes in the modern legal sense: personal parishes which do not have a directly perceptible territorial character, eucharistic communities which are not directly supported and authorized by the parish, monastic communities, etc. But when the eucharist is celebrated, people must always meet together in some place; if the eucharist is to be celebrated legitimately in this way at a chosen place, there must always be a relatedness to a local bishop or at least the explicit or tacit reference to the pope, who is not everywhere but resides in Rome. Hence it is clear that the Church's territorial character, particularly in its supreme realization, can nowhere be eliminated. And it is precisely this territorial character which is most simply and normally present in the parish community, *the* community, which is based on a primordial human reality that can never be wholly eliminated, on a group of people living together in a particular area. Precisely because this primordial human phenomenon, despite all opportunities for people to form a community or society for other reasons, can never be excluded from human existence and because it enters into the eucharistic celebration (as the matter of the sacramental sign enters into the sacrament in its unity with sacramental grace), the parish community participates in the territorial structure of the Church, which belongs to the latter's substance, since it is part of the Church's sociological, historical, and incarnational nature. A parish is not merely a secular concern belonging to a religious society as a police district belongs to the state, but a spiritual reality in which a person learns or can and should learn that not only his temporal existence but also his cosmic-spatial existence is sanctified and encompassed by the grace of the holy God of which it is the incarnation.

Of course, this theological thesis of the spiritual potentiality of human beings living together is not merely an indicative, but also an imperative. As the person who baptizes is required to provide water, the Church must provide a local group of neighbours in order to be able to celebrate the eucharist and thus fully realize itself historically and sociologically as sacrament of the world's salvation. This sort of local gathering of neighbours, of course, is not to be understood merely as a physical and geographical reality, but as a truly human factor of a genuinely neighbourly fellowship in righteousness and love, such that this human reality can enter into the eucharistic celebration. And it is to this human reality that the imperative resulting from our theological thesis on the spiritual quality of the territorial parish refers. This imperative, of course, must be fulfilled in the first place through all the other functions which belong directly to the parish as such, even though this does not mean that these other tasks of a parish as such are merely means to the end of forming this territorial community which is to be the human substratum of the eucharistic community. But all the rest of the functions of the parish as such (religious education, religious courses for adults, welfare work, etc.) also contribute to the formation of such local neighbourliness in the full human sense of the term, even to the formation of a spiritual community as such, and may and must therefore be appreciated and promoted also from this standpoint.

This imperative for the formation of local neighbourliness can and should relate, as far as it is possible and necessary, to more than is directly envisaged or implied by the specific tasks and functions of the parish. As far as it is possible and necessary, the work of the parish and the pastor may and should relate to the secular reality of local neighbourliness as such. Let us assume that parish and pastor, when necessary, make the greatest possible effort to see that a spatial agglomeration of human beings becomes even in the secular sphere a genuinely human fellowship, a truly human fraternity living together in mutual knowledge of one another, in sticking together, in trust, and providing mutual help. By this very fact they are contributing to the conditions in which a real spiritual community in common praise of God, in a common acknowledgment of expectation of the coming Lord, in unity in the Holy Spirit, can be realized in the eucharistic celebration; in this way the eucharistic celebration is not merely a casual external assemblage of individuals looking for the satisfaction of their personal needs as they might look for this in a department store. If a country-parish priest, in a place where it is possible and humanly appropriate, meets the farmers and farmhands after mass for a meal in the local inn, this, too, can be a consequence of this spiritual imperative established by the above-mentioned theological thesis.

If, as hitherto, we tried to envisage the theological quality of the Christian local community, of the territorial parish, in the light of the eucharistic celebration, this does not mean that the theological character of the parish is solely based on the act of worship; all that was intended was to make clear as simply as possible the fact that the territorial parish has a theological quality. Insofar as the rest of the functions of a parish have, on the one hand, an independent theological significance and are not merely means to the end of the eucharistic community, but have, on the other hand, more or less necessarily a local basis, even in the light of these other functions of the parish there emerges a peculiar theological, spiritual quality; it is not merely an unavoidable secular reality, but is assumed in its human spatiality into the mystery of the Church.

34 · Basic Christian Community

The notion of a "basic Christian community" is of course one that ought to be taken for granted in the sense that any parish should be more than a mere administrative district of a regional Church office. Any parish should be a genuine community in faith, hope, and love, a people truly abroad together on a common pilgrimage.

At the same time, this concept has obvious difficulties, and considerable ones, for parts of the world like ours. In the first place, we cannot simply adopt the structure, style, and procedures of the basic Christian communities of Latin America, where they are the hope of the Church and of Christianity itself. The words "basic community" offer a challenge to our Christian hearts and minds, but the expression is, after all, by and large a "Latin American import," and the temptation will have to be resisted to expect these communities to be able to operate among us here as they operate in Latin America, especially in Brazil. There, thousands upon thousands of living, vital, basic communities seem to have been built up from the "grassroots," not in competition with the official Church of the bishops, but out of a consciousness that where Christians truly live in faith in Jesus Christ and in hope, and where they unflaggingly join together in a true community of this faith and assume responsibility for secular society, here there will have to be basic Christian communities. This is particularly legitimate in places in Latin America where a great dearth of priests prevails, and where obviously not every parish can have its own pastor, as still used to be taken for granted in our own countries and regions thirty or forty years ago, when even the smallest village had a church and pastor of its own.

The great vitality and numerical growth of the basic Christian communities in Latin America can be a lesson for us, a stimulus and a spur to form a vital sort of basic community in our own lands, especially since we too have a shortage of priests. But the *concrete form* these basic communities of ours ought to take cannot be simply and directly transported from Latin America. The reason for this is twofold. First, our parishes, in the number and organization in which we still have them today, cannot simply be ignored. Much of what they have to offer is simply not offered by parishes in Latin America. This is why the basic communities there are much less in competition with traditional parish structure than this same form of basic community would be in our northern lands. To be sure, we too may sometimes be in need of small basic communities, not identical with the parish. When a particular pastor shows little religious interest and creativity, then, in certain circumstances and under certain conditions, Christians most surely have the clear right, despite all their ultimate ties with the sacramental Church, to come together, help one another, read Holy Scripture together, and pray in common, even when their endeavors are met with little support and understanding on the part of a particular pastor, someone, perhaps, who is no more than an ordinary office worker in his church. Still, in our countries, a basic community should live as far as possible in such a way as to help and encourage the *parish itself* to become a basic community of creative, spontaneous, living Christianity, with its responsibility accepted and carried out from the ground up.

In other words, when basic Christian communities are formed in our lands they have a greater, more urgent, direct responsibility to establish contact and ultimate unity with the corresponding parishes and pastors. We neither can nor ought act as if we could or should build, in our context, with the help of basic communities, a Church which would simply leave the sometimes rather grossly bureaucratic Church of the parishes, dioceses, and other Church structures already in place out of the picture altogether. Efforts of this kind could lead to nothing but little sectarian outcroppings that would quickly die out again.

In certain circumstances—when no priest is had and none can be found, or no priest whose thinking and acting is to any decent extent a living, Christian one—Christians may by all means form a little Christian cell, a basic Christian community. But in our lands we must be especially careful that such genuine, praiseworthy efforts are not corrupted into sectarian splinter groups, holding themselves aloof from the presbyterial Church, the lawful administration of the sacraments, and episcopal governance and administration. This may not be a problem in other countries, at least not for the time being, but it would be a problem for us, and therefore our basic communities cannot simply be carbon copies of those in Central and South America.

Furthermore, in a Latin American society, where there are not a great many secular social substructures, a genuine Christian community necessarily has tasks and responsibilities, which it has the duty and right to carry out, which do *not* exist in precisely the same form in the case of our own Christian communities. After all, in our society many social tasks whose performance is necessary for people to be able to live lives worthy of human beings are performed by secular society itself. Consequently, there is no immediate place for the discharge of these responsibilities by a Christian community as such. In the South American rain forests, when a woman falls ill and the nearest hospital is a couple of hundred miles away, obviously her neighbor will nurse her and look after her children. Certainly in a society where people are hungry, perhaps starving, and the organisms of secular society fail to look after them, Christian love of neighbor will have to step in and see to it that these people do not starve. But in a society where there is unemployment compensation, social security, and the like, many functions are taken in hand by secular society—functions which for that matter cannot be performed by the basic Christian community.

And so, basic communities in our regions and countries face a serious dilemma. In their quest to be communities of concrete, practical vitality, can they and should they be more than simply communities of religious activity in the strictest sense? Or will they find no other areas of activity whatever, so that they will simply have to be communities of prayer, proclamation of the Gospel, and dispensing of the sacraments? The solution to this dilemma must emphatically be in favor of basic communities that are more than mere vehicles of prayer, worship, and a theoretical proclamation of the Gospel. I am of the opinion that a basic community can only be a basic community if, over and above the abstractly religious, the purely religious, it molds an actual community of human beings who really feel that they belong to one another, who are in some true sense a family, a Church community, a confederation of love, a union of genuine Christian believers. Such a community should be a unit in which living Christian love is not only theoretically proclaimed but concretely practiced. Otherwise there will actually be no "basic community" at all, and this group will fall back into a parish style such as we are seeking precisely to get beyond with our basic communities. This is the real problem of basic communities in our regions and lands.

Are there tasks and activities that transcend the sphere, strictly speaking, of the abstractly, the theoretically religious, and yet are not already "taken" by secular societies, their organs, and their structures? I hold that this question can and should be answered in the affirmative. To be sure, such a basic community need not and ought not seek to be sufficient unto itself with respect to each and every desire, striving, and life accomplishment of men and women today. A basic Christian community need not sponsor a concert, for example. One can just as well go to a concert put on by someone else. There are a thousand things in today's adult education that need not be offered, ghetto-style, by a basic community. A basic community must clearly distinguish itself from a sectarian community in these matters.

A sect is a religious structure that not only holds itself aloof from major religious organizations, on some grounds or other, but seeks as it were to offer its members everything, in complete self-sufficiency. Here one is with one's fellow sectarians at all moments and in all the activities of human existence. One fears the baneful draft of secular life. One basically seeks an ideal that until a few decades ago was a strong characteristic of the life of the Church itself and its devout faithful. When my grandmother wanted to read a novel, she did not go to a city library or to a secular bookstore, but to the Borromeo Society Library. The books she gave as Christmas gifts were books from the Borromeo Society catalogue. I have nothing against parish libraries. Why should they not exist if they are conducted in a reasonable way and perhaps indeed meet genuine religious needs that a secular library today does not meet? But the ideal of a single sectarian community for all areas and activities of life is not something that a basic Christian community of today or tomorrow should strive to achieve. That would be misdirected.

What human needs are there, then, which are not religious in the strict sense and yet are genuinely human, and which are not met by other, secular associations and societies, so that they might call for the intervention of a genuine basic Christian community?

Surely a genuine basic community should be a community of common *prayer*, the common reading and study of *Sacred Scripture*, and a common *love of neighbor*. Still, such a basic community in our countries should be more than simply a group of Christians who, along with their secular life, also have religious needs and seek to perform some religious activity. Here then is the place for creativity and imagination in discovering and actualizing this sort of potential in our basic communities today. Everywhere we hear the lament that, in spite of all their social security and all their social networks, human beings feel isolated. They find no genuine, living contact, no relationships of confidence and trust, no real opportunities for genuine mutual reliance. There must, then, be tasks in abundance waiting to be discovered by a basic community that seeks to be something more than simply an association of prayer in the narrowest sense.

Of course, it is not unthinkable that a Christian might find the sorts of things a basic community can do, can achieve in its creativity—what it has to offer an individual—outside such a community. One can readily imagine a rather individualistically inclined Christian who attends church on Sunday, receives the sacraments, reads the Holy Scriptures in private, and otherwise evinces an occasional interest in things religious when the proper circumstances arise, and who nevertheless copes with life quite well enough without having to belong to a basic community in the strict sense. But there are surely many people as well who feel a religious dereliction, a loneliness, and coldness, who feel more intensely than most others that they want to praise and adore God together with their Christian brothers and sisters, and open their hearts to religious questions and problems in some degree of mutual relatedness to their fellows. There are surely men and women who rightly feel that they are personally unable to concretize true, unselfish love of neighbor without approaching that neighbor and sharing his or her burdens in a Christian community in the more narrow sense—in a basic community, then.

Surely there are many people who feel, justifiably, that they are far from having discharged their human and Christian duties of unselfish love merely by complying with the obligations imposed on them by today's secular society—by paying their taxes, making contributions of money in response to solicitations by the Red Cross or other such praiseworthy undertakings, and so on. Now without each Christian having to feel re-obligated to all these things "from above," in a spirit of legalism, why should there not be genuine basic Christian communities where human beings band together, in the bond of love that is the Holy Spirit and not secular humanism, not only to praise God in this union of theirs, but also to help one another cope with their lives wherever this may be meaningful and needful. Such basic communities, surely, have their tasks today. One has only to look for them with love's eyes, and seek to discharge them in the power of the Spirit.

35 · A Worshiping Community in the Home

There are a good many preliminary considerations to be undertaken before one can address the question of the possibility and forms of a community of worship in the home.

Men and women today find it fundamentally difficult to express their personal religious experiences in the presence of others or undertake them in common with others. Where this originates—to what extent it is conditioned by the general climate of our current stage in spiritual history when the question of transcendence, indeed the whole question of God, is no longer answered by all in the same way—or to what extent there are completely different inhibitions operating here and forming the basis of this "religious shyness"—these are questions which we shall have to leave out of consideration here. At all events we do know that these inhibitions exist, and hence it is scarcely cause for astonishment that a common religious service in the home, even just for the family, is more difficult for many people today than simple participation in a public worship service in which the individual can to a certain extent still hide in the anonymous throng. There one need not express oneself, need not confess one's inner religious emotions or lack of them. There, even today, it is still the pastor who, by and large, does what is to be done, vicariously, for all the others.

The case would be different, surely, if a husband and wife were to pray together, or if parents were to pray with their children (in more than a mere exercise in religious training, such as a mother might undertake with a very young child). I think a basic difficulty arises where worship in the home is concerned.

Now of course one might point out, quite correctly, that there are countercurrents as well in society today. It may be that the younger generation enjoys greater spontaneity in these matters. Nowadays we have workshops that are built around mutual dialogue and deal quite openly with the inner experiences and personal relationships of the participants. One could also cite certain religious groups and sects and their activity as evidence that the direction our youth may be taking is not necessarily a one-way street to a more and more hidden interiority and "privacy" where religious matters are concerned. Obviously it need not be. One might also recall that at least in a marriage between Christians one can surely assume the religious element to be present in both partners, and that that element will therefore not necessarily be something that these partners will have to conceal from each other. Forty years ago, a woman of my acquaintance, a lady of high station, told me that all of her children had actually been conceived in a religious atmosphere, more or less in prayer or with prayer. I would certainly not recommend anything like this today, but I will say that the sphere of personal intimacy could surely absorb the religious dimension in an appropriate, meaningful, spontaneous, unconstrained way, and so, once more, build a basis on which marriage partners could pray together —and then, when they have children, incorporate their children into this common religious activity of theirs.

In earlier times, but not too long ago for me to remember, the members of a religious community cultivated "spiritual conversation" to a certain extent—without constraint and yet rather explicitly. Today this is no longer so likely to be the case. On the other hand, it is certainly not a priori impossible. Why, then, should members of an alert, energetic family not also discuss their religious questions and problems, which they certainly must have, and overcome many of the inhibitions one seems to have when it comes to such things—and still not become indiscreet, or talk such delicate things to death? Then, once there is religious conversation in a family, this could serve as the prelude to that family's common prayer.

I recall how as children we prayed the rosary together with our mother for the repose of the soul of a great-aunt who had died. Or, for another example from my own experience, Psalm 130, the *De Profundis*— "Out of the depths I have cried to thee, O Lord"—is still engraved in my memory from those childhood years. When I was a teenager—and we children and adults were probably more forward than reticent when it came to expressing religious reflections and observations—we once had a Family Consecration. In those days it was to the Heart of Jesus, and it took place before an image of the Sacred Heart. Things like that—the blessing of a home, for instance—were anything but unusual events in our lives. In a word, then, the basis of a home community of prayer was more ready to hand than it is today. It was a matter of course for us. Surely it could be re-activated today. Surely it could be made to come alive again.

The notion that religious expression can be genuine only when it occurs in absolute spontaneity, without special times and forms, is in the last analysis a piece of nonsense. Musicians have to practice, do they not, precisely in order to be able truly to express themselves, in their innermost spontaneity, in the great moments of their musical lives. And so it is, too, with things religious: planning, practice, thinking things out beforehand —in a sense, organizing—very definitely has a place. Nor is this contrary to the essence of religion. Hence, in certain circumstances, a home community can very definitely possess a piety fostered in common, and yes, organized to a degree, and so be something like a home religious community. Surely this is difficult to put into practice today. Everyone knows that. When is the whole family together nowadays? When is everyone even home at the same time? How often does the contemporary family still spend its Sundays together? All these difficulties, characteristic of society in general today, make themselves felt in the religious praxis of a home community.

One can take advantage, for example, of a birthday or a wedding anniversary or the like, to invite a particular priest—one not too overwhelmed either in actual fact or in his own mind with parish duties—to celebrate a home Eucharist. The occasion will of course be quite suited for having a few friends over as well. It may even be that this little touch of the "official" will make it easier for individuals to participate without feeling ill at ease. And if this particular priest does not proceed in too legalistic a fashion, but exercises a certain creative imagination, and does a modicum of on-the-spot improvising, those present may be able to manage, without undue embarrassment, a common religious action that actually possesses a certain outward thrust.

For example, the priest may be able to get a dialogue homily going in which the participants, without becoming indiscreet or "heavy," will be able to join, "opening up" and finding the courage to express themselves personally. Such a worship service, then, could get beyond certain inhibitions associated with common religious experience, and yet at the same time not present an obstacle to active common participation on the part of the home community—which of course is the tendency in an official worship service in church.

A home community can and should, however, also gather when no official representative of the Church is present. This is what the old farm families of the Tirol did, for example. For them, regular recitation of the rosary together in the evening was simply a matter of course (perhaps too much a matter of course). It was part of the life ritual of their farm communities. There was no priest in attendance, nor was it necessary to have one—the father of the family, perhaps, or the mother, felt it his or her obvious responsibility to see to it that the children not "play hookey" and so on. With a bit of imagination, communities or little home groups that like to play music together, or sing, for example, could be the point of departure for some religious expression or other—if someone among them were to find the courage to strike up some religious music some evening.

Of course, prayer in common at home need not be practically restricted to old-fashioned sorts of things. The new, too, should gradually be introduced. This will require a certain amount of conscious resolve and determination. For instance, when a couple marry, why should they not expressly agree not only to go to Mass together on Sundays but to pray the Our Father together in the evening? It is easy to see how meaningful this could be. This, or something like it, could be agreed upon, then, and room made for it as a kind of routine—and then, even if it were broken off from time to time, there would be no cause for surprise when one or the other partner gave it new impetus. When people understand one another really well, it is often only the beginnings that are hard, and after that an exercise like this becomes pretty much a matter of course.

Surely there are many people today who, again, feel a kind of relief at being able to participate in a religious action of this kind—who feel that it is easier for them to cooperate in something like this than to pray to the Father in heaven all alone in the New Testament's "private chamber." If they can easily do it alone, more power to them. But I believe that, strange as this may sound, there is a considerable number of people, who, while they would never think of missing church, nevertheless find it very hard to make church the occasion for personal prayer—or who attend Mass on Christmas or Easter pretty much as a matter of course, but are never seen in church on an ordinary Sunday, and who likewise find it hard to make church the occasion for personal prayer. People like this would presumably be happy to assist from time to time in the kind of religious activity we are describing, something of a more or less casual, "easy-going" kind. One could make religious activity on their part easier by furnishing such an atmosphere, and they might even be grateful, whether or not they expressly thought of it as a matter for gratitude. When the mother of a family takes the initiative, the father may be glad to join in, even when he makes no special effort on his own.

We hear a great deal today about "giving witness." And there can be no doubt that the Christian has a basic duty to bear witness to the faith, in his or her own human, existential situation, wherever it is appropriate, feasible, and meaningful to do so. But here again we encounter the same old difficulty: Where is there anyone today willing to talk about how he or she really believes in God, prays to him, and experiences an inner freedom and security in a personal relationship with him? Where is there anyone today who tells another that he or she looks at Christ on the cross and feels that this says something to him or her?

There must surely be such a thing. But here again we have the same difficulty. People often feel in need of help in order to be able to articulate the religious. They may have difficulty finding situations in which they have the impression that any religious "testimony" of theirs actually reaches anyone. It is remarkable, though, how sects and their members, or peoples in cultures other than our own, feel no embarrassment at all, in fact easily find the courage to express themselves religiously—while we have such difficulty with it.

36 · The Eucharist

In the Last Supper, the Lord gives the apostles his body and his blood as food and drink for life everlasting. He wanted this sign of his love—a sign that actually contains him—to remain as the expression of unity with him. Some time before, when he promised the Eucharist on the shore of the Lake of Galilee, he said:"Whoever eats my flesh and drinks my blood abides in me and I in Him" (John 6:56). "To be in Christ Jesus" is the heart of Christian existence. It demands that everyone called by the Lord to participate in his sacrifice must accept in his own being this sacrifice and the life that it entails. Whoever receives the sacrament of Jesus' heart without preparing his own heart has missed Jesus completely. Such a person has misunderstood the meaning of *opus operatum*, and has degraded the Eucharist and the sacraments to mere magic. The sacraments have not been given to us to take the place of our own personal effort, or to make our effort easier! We can only approach the sacrament of the heart of Jesus Christ with an open heart. We can only receive the grace of the Eucharist insofar as we personally also realize the sacrifice contained in it.

The constant switch back and forth in John 6, where Jesus promises the

Eucharist, between the acceptance of Christ in faith and the reception of him in the tangibility of the sacrament as food and drink, also brings this point out. Therefore, preparation and thanksgiving, which are a personal association with the Christ who comes to us under the appearance of bread and wine, are also a part of the true reception of the sacrament —notwithstanding his presence to us that is fully independent of us. (Naturally, this should not be taken to mean that the preparation and thanksgiving for the Eucharist should take on one definite form. Our attitude toward the Eucharist can certainly be, depending on the circumstances, a tormenting silence of a persevering inner emptiness, an uneasiness toward God.)

Since everything in Jesus' previous life is ordered to his death on the cross as the high point and the culmination of his life, the Eucharist has a special meaning for us as the participation in his death. "Whenever you eat this bread and drink of this cup, you are proclaiming the death of the Lord until He comes again" (1 Cor. 11:26). Is that not something really colossal? What is well known by men and likewise fiercely repressed, what is common and still very strange, what is mentioned only in hushed tones, what is truly a senseless catastrophe—this is the death of one man—and we make it into the central theme of the great liturgical feast that fills God's house with its grandeur. Through the remembrance of the death of a crucified criminal, we profess belief in joyful hope and victorious life. With all the pomp of the liturgy, we announce this death, the killing separation of flesh and blood, as the decisive event of world history which must be proclaimed and celebrated over and over again. We do not do this because we make little of death or because we try to pretend that basically everything is not so bad after all. Instead, we do it in order to understand that the destiny of our miserable human existence, which is to sink deeper into death as our life goes on—that this destiny is the merciful, eternal call of God's love. This is a love that redeems and fills our being because it is an absorption into the death of Christ.

In the Eucharistic celebration, therefore, we announce not only the death of Christ, but also our own death. Thus, we see that death is not just the last moment of life—it was not so for Christ and it cannot be so for us. Death is the final, fulfilling act that is always present in life and is born from life. Death is present when we make our first entrance into existence, and it reveals itself in its ultimate form in what we usually designate as "dying."

If we daily celebrate the death of our Lord in the Eucharist, then we should consider how Christ the Lord accepted death. First of all, the death that we must endure is something imposed on us without our consent. If Christ is really the Son of Man and our brother, than this also applies to him—and it applies to him in a special way because he did not deserve death. But the Lord obediently accepted this fate as the incomprehensible disposition of the Father. Obedient throughout his agony! The main thing to practice in this retreat is imitating him in this. In spite of all restraint and reserve, and in spite of all our distractions, the meditation on the Eucharist should bring us to the point that we say to Christ: "I want to love you in your crucifixion; I want to practice right now the readiness that you will one day inexorably demand of me—how, I know not—so that I will not have to suffer my soul to be torn away from me in the despair of the Adamitic sinner; I want to give you my life with a final, silent, actively indifferent faith and love. This is the only way to endure your death." Still, all talk of willingness to love the cross would only be empty bombast, would only be the lifeless idol of a visionary, unless it came from the power of Jesus Christ himself. Since the Eucharist immerses us in the death of the Lord, it is also a participation in his power on the cross. In order to be able to die our death in such a way that we can truly endure it as our salvation, or, in other words, in order to discover the death of Jesus Christ in our death, we receive the body that he offered for us and we drink the blood that flowed from his heart so that he might always be with us.

The Eucharist, certainly, means more to us than just a participation in the cross of the Lord! It would be false to consider it only as a sign of his bitter suffering, or to think of it as the continuation of his weakness. Ultimately, it is a sign of his powerful sacrifice. And the Eucharist is really the sacrament of Christ's glory. In accordance with the words of the liturgy, it is truly a "pledge of future glory" for us. Ignatius of Antioch calls it the "medicine of immortality." It is precisely through suffering, through being used up, that the priestly mission and power achieve their highest realization in this sacrament. Since Christ does not release us from his fate, let us hope that we will discover in our association with the sacrament of his heart what we will be and what we really are. Only from this association can we draw what we need, in order to become what God demands of us: priests who overcome the world in Christ, and win it over for God with their faith, hope, and love.

Our unity with Christ finds its historical tangibility in the unity of the Church. Therefore, the Eucharist should be spoken of as the sacrament of our ecclesiality, of our incorporation into the mission and fate of the Church. As often as we receive the Eucharist we affirm anew our attachment to the Church and her claim on us. Just as we identify ourselves with the crucified and glorified Lord, so also we are identified with his Mystical Body and its appearance in the Church. Our incorporation into the Church, which is the "elevated sign" of his Mystical Body, is increased by the sacramental reception of the body of Christ. The idea of the unity of the Mystical Body through the Eucharist is hardly known by the Eucharistic piety of our private devotions. We should try to make this truth of faith something living for ourselves and the people to whom we are sent. St. Paul writes in 1 Corinthians 10:17: "The very fact that we all share *one* bread makes us all *one* body."

When we receive the body and the blood of Jesus, it is really we who are received and incorporated. This is the Eucharistic teaching of the Didache and the apostolic Fathers! For whoever is received into Christ finds it even more difficult to remain alone than is normally possible for man. Augustine calls the Eucharist the "bond of love," and the Council of Trent clearly brings out that the Eucharist is the sacrament of the Church. This is not something vague and of little importance for the great community of the entire Church. It applies with concrete urgency to the men who are gathered together here and now in the name of Jesus Christ. Large Church organizations are illusions if they are not first fully realized in definite individuals.

As the sacrament of the heart of Christ, the Eucharist is the source of our love for our brothers and sisters, but it is also the judge of this love. The meaning of 1 Corinthians 11:29 will always remain true: By sins against the love of neighbor, we eat and drink judgment for ourselves in the Lord's Supper. If there is and should be *one* Church in *one* body of the Lord, which is bound together with the bond of true love, then that must be especially true for those who approach the same altar.

For the priest, this sacrament of charity for men and of responsibility for their salvation contains a specific mission to them. In his priestly existence, he is perpetually bound to the men God has committed to his care. The Eucharist is the most fundamental sacramental expression of the service he is to render to his fellow men.

Through our priestly existence, we are sent out to others. The primary character of our life is simply that we are sent—just as the Word is sent by his Father. That which is most intimate in our lives is the fact that we are related to our brothers and sisters in the name of the Lord. Ours is a pressing vocation that does not proceed from our own inclinations or from our own life-situation. Our vocation far surpasses whatever is required of other Christians! The lay Christian must try to bring others to supernatural salvation when the circumstances of his daily life bring him in contact with them. We who are priests put our seal on the special nature of our calling, and on our closer connection to our brothers and sisters by means of the eucharistic celebration. It is right here that we declare our special responsibility for their salvation, because Christ has ordained us to stand at his altar in front of the community and as its mediator. He wants us to be the spokesmen and the representatives of the community; he wants us to offer up the people of God to God when we utter the most holy words in his name and in the name of the Church: "This is My body!" and "This is the chalice of My blood...."

37 · The Sunday Precept

In order to say something intelligent about Sunday and to cover somehow all the problems involved, we ought *first* to ask about the exact meaning in the Old Testament of the Sabbath precept, of sanctifying the Sabbath. Undoubtedly there were religious and social reasons for it. The precept was meant for all in Israel: slaves, as far as there were any, normal and ordinary people, the better off, and even the beasts. But I do not want to say more here about this Sabbath precept.

Second, something ought to be said about the historical and theological aspects of the adoption of this precept in the Church of Jesus Christ. Here of course (and this has primarily and directly nothing to do with Israel) should be mentioned the peculiarity that the Church continually celebrates afresh in the weekly liturgical sequence the resurrection of Jesus as a unique historical and fundamental salvation event. A theological content is thus available which was not present in the Old Testament celebration of the Sabbath, even though behind all these celebrations there is a basic human datum: the fact that man can celebrate and should celebrate in a temporal sequence the anamnesis (memory) of events that occurred once and for all in salvation history. Admittedly, this is a theological problem for its own sake and extends to these solemnities as a whole. I do not know exactly what the situation was in the Old Testament or in later Jewish times, if and in what sense the Sabbath observance had anything to do with the exodus from Egypt. It might be said anyway that the Sabbath precept in Israel, too, had an anamnestic (commemorative) dimension in terms of salvation history and was related at least to God's rest on the seventh day of creation. In a word and in any case, in the Christian celebration of Sunday there is a reference to a quite definite event of salvation history, so that the question arises as to how, why, and for what existential-ontological reasons man is the being that can celebrate historical events which are apparently simply past. And what is the meaning of such an anamnesis? Is it merely historicist reflection, inspired by a certain historical curiosity, on a past event which nevertheless cannot in this way really be brought up again out of the depths of the past? Is it possible with the aid of this kind of recollection to make something like this present in the proper sense of the term or, so to speak, continually to repeat it? But also I will not discuss here this second point on the Christian adoption of the Sabbath precept as a way of recalling the death and resurrection of Jesus.

Third, however, I want to say something quite different. Although somewhat disguised in the ordinary course of preaching, according to the Church's universal teaching, there is no Old Testament precept which, as such, is still binding on Christians. And among these abrogated precepts is that of the Sabbath observance. If a Christian preacher insists on the Church's Sunday precept by recalling the thunder and lightning of God's holy covenant on Sinai, he is telling lies, he is asserting something that simply does not make sense. We must say, then, that the Sunday precept properly speaking is not a divine precept, either in the light of man's permanent nature (as preternaturally or supernaturally elevated) or in the light of the Old Testament: it is and remains a precept of the Church. That the Church has a right to issue a precept of this kind and that this right and the fulfillment of the precept by the individual Christian have also deeper, more universal foundations and grounds, this again is a different question. That a human person is a worshiping being, that the Christian in his religious existence must necessarily relate again and again to the death and resurrection of Jesus, that, consequently, he must (to express it somewhat prosaically in terms of moral theology) from time to time take part in the eucharistic memorial celebration of this death and resurrection of Jesus, all these are deeper reasons justifying the Church's Sunday precept; but the requirement of attending mass on Sundays and, as we used to say, abstaining from servile work is a precept of the Church and basically no more than that. That the concrete form of this precept, its interpretation, the strictness or elasticity of the interpretation, are conditioned historically is something we have certainly experienced in recent decades.

Fourth, if we recognize soberly, honestly, and without dissimulation, that it is a question here of a positive precept of the Church, then (independently now of the question of a conceivable or not conceivable, a desirable or not desirable, further development of the concrete shape of this precept) it is in any case clear that the precept is open to all the restrictions and interpretations appropriate to a human precept, which simply does not directly involve man's eternal nature nor, consequently, his permanent supernatural determination by grace as such. Obviously, a positive precept of the Church is open to many more possible interpretations and can more easily cease to bind in the concrete individual case as a result of excusing causes or other reasons than a properly divine precept of natural law or a divine precept of the supernatural order as such. It can really be taken for granted also today that an individual can consider himself dispensed in the concrete from the Sunday precept of participation at mass, not only because of sickness, but for other sound reasons. There is no need here to go into the casuistry of how there can be reasons for dispensation from the obligation of Sunday mass, or what these are. That is a different question, with which other people can amuse themselves. In any case, on the one hand we should take this Sunday precept seriously (even though it is no more than a precept of the Church) and, on the other hand, we have the Christian's liberty to interpret and apply these human statutes and precepts with a certain magnanimity and inner freedom. I do not know if this could be a practical rule of thumb (that is something for the moralists to consider), but I would say that whenever and in whatever cases the inner existential and supernatural justification of the Sunday precept is not conclusive for the individual case, the Church's precept as such is not to be regarded in that individual case as binding under pain of grave sin.

We might presumably attempt to justify this proposition from various aspects. It might even be said that the Church can by no means impose an obligation, as we say, under pain of grave sin, unless it is also required for deeper reasons by natural law or supernaturally by law or morality. But we may also perhaps leave aside a universal justification of this kind and face the situation at the present time. There now exists in the Church a mentality (which is not opposed by the institutional Church) which regards the Church's precept (even though it amounts to more than this in its formal implications and authority) as not really binding under pain of grave sin, unless participation in the eucharistic sacrifice is seriously required as a result of an existential and mental-spiritual necessity. What exactly do I mean by this?

From the very nature of the case and in the light of his faith, a normal Christian is obviously aware that he must frequently take part in the celebration of the eucharist, whether there is a precept of the Church to that effect or not. An obligation of this kind, which arises, so to speak, from the nature of things and which already or again exists as an institutional arrangement quite independently of the properly official precept of the Church, can certainly not be proved to be binding in the concrete every Sunday. But a Christain should have the good sense to admit that he would certainly be basically, if not perhaps also expressly, denying his inner, fundamental, essential relatedness (conferred by baptism) to the incarnational structure of the death of the Lord (that is, to his sacramental presence in the eucharist) if he simply did not bother about mass over a long period. This is an obligation that can, of course, become concrete, even if it is impossible to demonstrate mathematically exactly when and where. It is like living in the same house with my mother: Who is to say when I have to talk to her? And if she lives elsewhere, it is impossible to demonstrate on what day I must visit her or for how long. Nevertheless, as a human being and as her child, I have a serious moral obligation toward this woman to realize my personal relatedness to her in the concrete by visiting her. How often that should be cannot be calculated mathematically. Attendance at mass likewise may depend on all kinds of circumstances: on the state of my religious development, on my opportunities or difficulties of being present, on my entire subjective, particular character, etc. One person will perhaps commit a serious offence against love for his mother if he is living in the same town and does not visit her for months. For another, a quarterly visit may be quite sufficient.

It is rather similar with the mass. I would say that a Christian ought to know (precept of the Church or not) that he has an obligatory relationship to the Church's eucharistic celebration as the memorial of Jesus' death and resurrection by which he is redeemed. And where an obligation of this kind seems in the light of a reasonable, serious, and scarcely disputable human judgment to find concrete expression, so to speak, and to be concentrated in an actual celebration of mass on a particular Sunday, the Church's precept becomes one that we normally describe as a morally grave obligation. It becomes binding under pain of grave sin.

Where this is not the case, the Christian ought to take part in the eucharistic celebration at least every Sunday, if only because he really should occasionally do something Christian, the omission of which does not bring him at once into serious conflict with God. But apart from that radical obligation, I would claim that the Church's precept is not concretely binding here and now under pain of grave sin. Like the speed limit on the motorway, it is a standard which we must observe in a spirit of both Christian freedom and seriousness. At the same time, the question remains completely open as to when and where in a normal human life there can be an absolute dilemma between the fulfillment of a precept and grave sin (which would lead to eternal perdition). This is not to be tried out in regard to the Sunday precept in particular, since this is not an appropriate test case.

Fifth, we must have regard for a number of consequences of the development of modern industrial society. These include the five-day work week, the varying work periods, the fact that it is very difficult to impose the Sunday precept and participation in the eucharist as binding on people in certain occupations (bus conductors, for example, and the service sector as a whole); the fact that in some places the obligation can be fulfilled by attendance at Saturday evening mass, which, despite biblical analogies, really amounts to a departure from the Sunday precept; the present-day opportunity of other evening masses which in a religious sense and existentially may be more appropriate and convenient for modern people on a weekday than a Sunday mass in particular; the fact that the weekend of Saturday to Sunday or even merely Sunday is rightly seized on by people in the large industrial centres as an opportunity to escape from the concrete cage of the metropolis, to enjoy a longer period of recreation, etc. These and similar facts raise for the Church the question of the situation in principle and generally today in regard to what is know as the Sunday precept.

Briefly, it might be said that this Sunday precept as such, being a positive precept of the Church and not directly a commandment of God, is subject to the Church's discretionary decision and consequently could be abolished. That is not to say that the Church could dispense itself from the task of continually reminding Christians of their relatedness, to be concretely realized, to the sacramental celebration of mass and not merely to the death of the Lord as such. Nevertheless, the Church could abolish the Sunday precept properly so-called and, for example, leave it to individual Christians to decide how to realize this essential relatedness to the eucharistic celebration in their concrete life, likewise how often they would do this and on what days, etc. This is a real possibility.

At the same time, however, it must be pointed out that it is difficult to say whether the Church *ought* to make its pastoral decision (which cannot be simply arbitrary) on these lines, or could even be *permitted* concretely from a pastoral and human standpoint to do so. In the first place, even at the present time in our modern industrial society, the individual days are not absolutely reduced to a secular level. Monday to Friday amounts in fact to something different from Saturday and Sunday. It might even be said that the two days of the weekend have acquired, as a result of secular cultural and civilisatory developments, more clearly and firmly a special position in regard to the other days. They are freer than they could be formerly. If the farmer's wife nowadays gets her milking machine working comparatively quickly on Sunday, she has in any case more leisure than she had even twenty or thirty years ago, when each cow had to be milked separately. And there is ample evidence that the weekend in secular terms possesses more clearly that civilisatory and cultural status which makes it suitable for a special and even religious demarcation of Saturday and Sunday, or simply of Sunday. Allowing for the greatest magnanimity in detail and in regard to particular groups of people, these and similar reasons could quite appropriately move the Church to keep to the *joint* celebration of the eucharist and the death of the Lord on a particular day.

Of course, many other reasons could be mentioned. Even in a modern society of people supposed to have come of age, the stability of a general practice is something wholly appropriate and useful. It might be said that, even in regard to religious matters, it is unreasonable to leave people too much to their own initiative as isolated individuals. We might point to the fact that even at the present time there are also secular celebrations of important historical events, commemorated in a joint service on a particular day. Whether these are national feast days or youth initiations is immaterial. In any case, while admitting the Church's freedom in principle, as emphasized above, to abolish the Sunday precept (if it seemed better to do so), it might nevertheless be asked if the Church today could and should uphold the precept if it is rightly understood. For whatever cannot be proved conclusively to be necessary in the light of man's nature must not be regarded on that account as superfluous.

It must be remembered that man lives and can live not only from those things whose metaphysical and transcendental necessity can be proved. It must be remembered that a person cannot expect whatever he does or ought to do or what is perhaps even required of him to be proved to be irrevocably necessary. It is impossible to prove transcendentally that we ought to shake hands when we meet or part from someone. Nevertheless, it is reasonable to do so and anyone who denies this in principle, maintaining that theoretically we might just as well rub noises, is an idiot who is determined from the very outset not to admit the undemonstrable and yet factual and meaningful realities of human life which must be respected if life is to go on. Of course, the Church can appropriately keep to the Sunday precept, as we said, justifying this by a reasonable explanation, interpretation and eventually the application of casuistry to the precept. In my opinion, if the Sunday precept is maintained and interpreted with Christian freedom, it will not involve any unsurmountable pastoral difficulties, not even in the present-day society.

There is a further consideration. It is basically true that the cultural and civilisatory development of modern society, with its faceless masses, its flexible working hours, etc., has brought with it a situation which is not particularly favourable to the Church's Sunday precept. But we can at least raise the question of whether the Church must look on, so to speak, indifferently or passively at these secular developments and then introduce slight changes in present arrangements in order to give effect to the pastoral conclusions from secular reality as it is and otherwise to do nothing. We could certainly ask why the Church (for good reasons and without claiming a predominance over the secularized, profane society) should not intervene to influence directly the trend of development in that society. After the Russians, at the beginning of the Bolshevist regime, had introduced an absolutely flexible working week which inevitably made no distinction between Sunday and any other day, they apparently gradually came to see that their plan humanly and reasonably was not particularly wonderful or glorious and, if I am correctly informed, returned to a common rest day. The opportunity could arise for the Church to contribute, perhaps even with merely secular and human arguments, to the further development of secular society in a direction more favourable to the Sunday rest, the Sunday precept, the Sunday celebration, more than the trend seems to have been up to now. It would indeed be a good thing if on one day the noise in the streets were to cease more or less entirely, if there were one day no lorries were traveling, etc. All these and similar things are quite possible. It is not by chance that, in West Germany at least, league football matches are played on Saturdays.

All I wanted to do here was to suggest briefly that there are circumstances in which the Church has not only the abstract right but also the concrete opportunity, without offending non-Christians, positively to steer the development of secular society to a point at which the Sunday precept and the Sunday celebration would fit more conveniently into the total framework of civil life.

38 · Priestly Spirituality

We begin with a very simple thesis: priestly spirituality is first of all simply Christian spirituality, Christian life in faith, hope, and love. Priestly spirituality is not (at least, not primarily) a kind of extra to a normal Christian life, but (while, of course, determined by the concrete life task of the priest as distinct from other Christians) the spiritual, Christian life of a Christian purely and simply. Today this is really obvious in the light of the practice and nature of the priesthood. It is obvious in the light of *practice*, for, exactly like other people, we have to live in a secularized milieu, we are impugned and called in question by a world of secularized values with its rationalism, with its technocracy, with its crowds, etc. One way or another, like other Christians today, we are living in a diaspora; neither for them nor for us are faith and Christian life and the hope of eternity to be taken for granted as something that we could pass over, so to speak, as unimportant for us and then find greater scope to develop a sublime spirituality as our special job or as a kind of hobby. We are poor, tormented, frightened, threatened by the world as a whole, by politics and industry; just like the others, we are caught up into the whirlpool of secularization; faith in God, in an eternal life, the persuasion that our freedom is to be exercised responsibly before God, all these things create exactly as many difficulties for us as they do for other people. If this were not the case, it would not be an advantage, but a sign that we are living out of touch not only with our time, but also with our office and our own life, since we cannot really live this office and this life otherwise than in a genuine confrontation with our time and situation, society, culture, and lack of culture.

Priestly spirituality, then, is first of all Christian spirituality which, as such, is required of every Christian if he wants to be a true Christian and not merely a conventional or folkloristic Christian. But if we say this, the question will inevitably be raised as to what exactly this Christian spirituality is. We can, of course, say that it is life out of faith, hope, and love, it is life from the Holy Spirit; we can say that it is life from the Spirit of Christ, life from the Gospel; we can say that it is life from the following of Christ; we can say that it is life from the hope of eternal life, out of an ultimate responsibility in which we are aware that, whether we want it or not, we are living our life to the very end in freedom for or against God. We can say that Christian spirituality is life oriented to God's judgment, it means coping with sin that cannot be eliminated by referring to social or psychological constraints, etc. We can say all that; it is all true, and here and now there is really nothing more that I can say; to say anything more precise would require at least an eight-day retreat.

Simply to provide a spur, a question that is meant to be disturbing, I would like to add the following in regard to this Christian spirituality which is basically identical with priestly spirituality. When we speak of "spirituality" (whether the term is a good one, very understandable, or pastorally useful is another question) we mean "life from the Spirit." But then the question arises as to just what this is supposed to mean. And the crucial point for us personally and in our pastoral work today is whether we not only succeed in getting this "pneumatic," spiritual dimension of our existence into our own heads or the heads of other people by an abstract, conceptual indoctrination (which today will be more or less ineffective), but whether we can discover this Spirit as what we really experience in ourselves. And this is extraordinarily difficult today in the age of sociological criticism of ideologies, in the age of natural science, in the age of Freud, in the age of depth psychology and of the psychological corruption of human beings. Is there in fact anything of this kind? Have you ever really experienced the Spirit of God? Suppose you say: "Yes, I was once touched, or I was at one time devout, or I had the impression that there is some sort of God who is good, who quite likes me, although he allows children in Vietnam to be killed by napalm bombs." In that case you ought to unleash on this claim of yours to have discovered the Spirit in yourself all the corrupting elements of psychology, of sociological criticism of ideologies, of rational psychology, technology, etc., and then ask if anything remains or if all that is left are merely words like "God of love, grace, Holy Spirit, God's indwelling," etc., to which we cling because of some sort of feeling that in the long run we cannot do without this sort of thing. Are these words not all mere husks, long ago deprived of meaning in a long historical process from the time of the Enlightenment?

I said earlier that I cannot answer this question now. The reason why I raise it at all is in order to make clear what are the innermost structures that a Christian, and consequently a priestly, spirituality must have in order really to cope with these problems.

At most I can add only a few words which seem to be even more abstract and merely refer to the matter under discussion without getting to the root of it. In the last resort spirituality is man's absolute transcendence, beyond any categorial reality in him or outside him, into the absolute mystery that we call God; it is ultimately a transcendentality dying, crucified, becoming torn apart with Christ, not as a theory but as what happens in us in our concrete existence when we confront this life with its ultimate dependence on the incomprehensible mystery of God and achieve the acceptance, the endurance, of this life concretely with Christ through all categorial breakdowns, through all death, through all disappointment. Of course, such an experience of our own absolute transcendentality, crucified with Jesus into the absolute mystery, has a history in us. This is something that comes into existence slowly, we reach these things only gradually; perhaps there will be some people who never notice it or do not consider and cannot express in words what has taken place in them. At the present time, I think, at least the priest (we shall come to practical matters later) should slowly come to see that something of this kind exists.

For the moment that must suffice to mark out the problems involved in the first statement that I wanted to make, to the effect that priestly spirituality today more than ever is simply Christian spirituality and not an addition to the Christian life. In this sense spirituality is understood as truly Christian life emerging from the innermost centre of our own existence and not merely as a fulfillment of religious conventions prevailing in Christianity and in the Church. Spirituality, Christian spirituality, is the active participation in the death of Jesus and, since he is risen, in that death as successful and as assumed into that ineffable, incomprehensible, not controllable, not manoeuvrable ultimate mystery *quod omnes* (as Aquinas would say) *vocant Deum*.

39 · Priestly Office and Priestly Life

In the priesthood of the New Testament, liturgical functions and kerygmatic preaching are always inseparably united. A limitation of the priesthood to the liturgical service would not be in accord with Scripture. The priesthood of the New Law is not designated in Scripture from the liturgical function—the New Testament reserves this for Christ. The naming of priests and bishops is based on a missionary and directive function with regard to the community. Naturally, this is not meant to deny that the priests of the New Testament in a very true sense stand before God in the name of the community as official cult figures. Since our priesthood is the essential continuation of the high priestly office of the Incarnate Word of God, both elements—liturgical worship of God and speaking in his name—must form an inner unity. Our liturgical, strictly sacramental function can only have its validity from God's mystery that has been spoken to us; it is this mystery that ushers our cult into the depths of the divinity. And our prophetic kerygma is ultimately nothing but a repetition of the word of God that came into our world, bringing grace along with it. The teaching office of the New-Testament priesthood gets its inner power from the possession of the sacramental words. The living word, which gives a definite spatio-temporal reality to the transcendent grace of God, is spoken by the New-Testament minister of the divine worship primarily at the altar as a sacramental word. But since this "graced" word necessarily reaches out into the whole world, and since it only makes sense inasmuch as it is directed to all men, the priest of the New Testament must bring the word of grace to man by his preaching and teaching.

Despite their inseparability, liturgical worship and prophetic sending are two different functions of the priesthood of the New Testament. Depending on the concrete call of each individual, either the one or the other can be predominant. There are and should be priests who spend most of their time with the liturgy. Others are primarily involved in preaching or in doing acts of charity. A long time ago, St. Paul said that he did very little baptizing, since his mission was to preach the word. But no matter where the emphasis is placed, the liturgy and the sacraments should never be neglected, nor should the drive be abandoned to bring God to men and men to God. It takes a sending of this kind—in our own view, at least—for the priesthood of the New Testament to achieve the existential determination that distinguishes it from the other modes of Christian existence, that is, from the lay state or the life of a monk.

Corresponding to the nature of the New Testament priesthood, the

Western Church demands as a minimum that, in living a priestly life, the official and the personal mutually determine each other. Actually, many official powers as, for example, jurisdiction, the authoritative word, and sacramental power, are independent of the personal holiness and the pneumatic gifts of the office holder. This is true at least insofar as validity is concerned, and the matter in question does not represent the whole Church. Instances such as these can even be very frequent. But even so, the official and the personal cannot be totally separated in the Church! Fundamentally, the Church represents the historical tangibility of the victorious grace of God. She can never degenerate into a mere "salvation club" in an external, legal sense. Despite the fact that she is really a Church of sinners, she still always remains *the holy Church* to the very end. Through her existentially lived witness, she must announce that the grace of Jesus Christ cannot be destroyed, and that through him the world has already achieved its blessed finality. This, of course, does not exclude the possibility that individuals can live in such a way as to lose the grace of Christ.

The Church as a whole could never say: I announce God's truth and I administer his sacraments, but the private lives of my office holders really have nothing to do with this. Were God to permit a separation of official acts from personal attitudes such as this, then the Church would no longer be the continuing Body of Christ in the power of the Holy Spirit, and thus the abiding epiphany of God in the world, but she would be instead a shocking lie and a horrible advent of the final defeat of God. For God did not enter into this world just to shake it up for a time and perhaps tear this or that "soul" from it—he made it into his own holy home by means of his own enfleshment. If the Church were to become a basic denial of the change of the world into the Kingdom of God, then she would be degrading herself into the Synagogue. For the grace of God could actually be separated from the liturgy of the Synagogue, and as a matter of fact the Synagogue abolished itself because of this divergence. The holiness that belongs to the Church by reason of the grace that has been given to her must be the obligation of the lives of all her members, and especially of her priestly representatives. This means that each one of us must personally ratify his priestly state. *I* must bring my life into my priesthood to the best of my ability, and *I* must bring my priesthood completely into my personal life. In other words, I must be a holy priest. This is not a question of what is fitting. It is an obligation flowing from the essence of the New Testament priesthood.

Like the Church as a whole, I must guarantee through my whole person the truth of my preaching and the validity of sacramental efficacy. Even if it is true, in spite of Donatism, that I possess priestly powers which remain effective in the face of pesonal sinfulness, still that only remains true because the holy Church is standing behind me, and I can only act in her name. Therefore, even my most non-holy official act will always appeal to the Church's holiness and be informed by it.

Our office gives us no guarantee that we will successfully integrate it with our priestly life. Therefore, we cannot take pride in ourselves before God because we have an official position. Rather, we should hold onto it with fear and trembling lest we be lost after preaching to others and bringing them the grace of God.

In this connection, we priests can consider further how personal holiness should interiorly permeate our priestly existence, and how the latter should shape the former. We can consider how the personal holiness of the priest must be different from the holiness of lay Christians, because his mission, his responsibility for the salvation of others, his familiarity with the word of God, and his performance of Christ's sacrifice put a special stamp on his holiness. We can also ask ourselves whether or not we have been infected by certain false forms of priestly existence. Under these we would mention religious functionalism, clerical fanaticism, religious sterility, resignation, and clerical skepticism.

We should also consider in this meditation the relationship between the priesthood of the New Testament and celibacy. It is very important for us to apply what we have said so far to this specific sacrifice that the Western Church demands as a prerequisite from candidates to the priesthood. If what we said above about the relationship between the priesthood and its realization in personal holiness is true, then the celibacy of the priest of the New Testament, even if he has not made a vow of chastity, should not just be something that he must tolerate. Rather, it should be the heart and soul of his priesthood—a personal commitment that makes his priesthood alive and fruitful.

If the priest of the new law continues the mission of the Incarnate Word, if he is supposed to speak the words of eternal life and bring men the message of God's love, if he must preach this God as triune and as giving himself to us—and preach it in such a way that, as the go-between and chosen one, he must live out in the world the generation and Incarnation of the Word plus the resultant generation of men to true supernatural childhood, then the sacrifice of his sexual love is no mere suitable or becoming way of life. No. This renunciation is fundamentally an efficacious sign of that which God himself has implanted in us, and which surpasses all earthly life-communication: that is, his own life as the life of the new and eternal covenant!

We should consider what Jesus thought about the priesthood, how he trained the first priests of his new law, and what type of men he chose.

Call to mind the words he uttered about the priesthood to his chosen ones and also to us. Finally, we should ask the Lord, who has called us to follow him in the priesthood, to give us the grace to follow this call honorably, to love him, to remain true to him with all our hearts, to make every effort to accept the great gift of himself worthily so that God's grace, which is always given to us—we who cannot be worthy of it and who are only made worthy by it, may not descend on priests who have become unworthy of their calling.

40 · New Offices and Ministries in the Church

In one of our new Good Friday General Intercessions, we pray not only for the pope, the bishop, the community of bishops, priests, and deacons but also "for all who hold a ministry in the Church," and these are distinguished from the "whole people of the redeemed." At least that is the way it is in the German [and North American] version of this second Intercession, while the Latin text speaks only of "all the clergy." The German text, then [like the North American], implies that, alongside the three classic ministerial offices (of bishop, priest, and deacon), there are other ministries in the Church as well, which are identical neither with these three classic offices, nor with the tasks that fall to a Christian simply as a member of the Church.

But, it will be objected, this is self-evident. There have always been sacristans and a whole host of other persons appointed by the bishops and priests to discharge particular, limited services for the Church—catechists, other religion teachers, non-priest staff persons in the chancery, and so on. Yes, this is correct. But this has nothing to do with the question we are raising here. Let us put it in another way: whether the person who cleans the church cleans precisely the church or another building instead is ultimately of no importance for his or her function. Thus there are of course a great number of tasks and functions in the Church which are necessary or useful, and which the Church must indeed have, but which do not properly partake of the essence of the Church as instrument of grace, and hence do not particularly set their functionaries apart from the rest of Christians—as bishops, priests, and deacons, at least from a certain point of view, are elevated above other Christians.

This distinction, this discrimination, which pertains absolutely to the Catholic understanding of Church, must of course be interpreted very carefully. The three classic offices in the Church denote a task and authority not attaching to the other members of the Church in the social structure of Church orders. But by this very token, these subjects of the several degrees of priesthood are, after all, in a position similar to that of the functionaries of a professional chess club: their function cannot be discharged by the individual players, but, at the same time, their function ultimately serves one end only—that excellent chess be played. Just so, the priestly office, precisely through the authority exclusively reserved to it, has as its sole end that the priesthood of the faithful, the priesthood of those who believe and who love—that faith, hope, and love in all Christians—continue to be living and vital, and indeed increase. Thus when the priestly office, with all the authority exclusively attaching to it, is seen in the Church "functionally" as a ministry for the Christian being of all Christians, this in no way implies that the ordained priest is not to be understood as having been sent by Christ himself, is not to be perceived as coming to the rest of human beings from Christ. But he has this status precisely in virtue of his participation in the relationship of the global Church (in which he has a specific function) to the individual human being. This functional understanding of the priestly office does not preclude —on the contrary, it positively implies—that the ordained priest's own life will be stamped by his office. It implies that he will have the obligation of actualizing "Christian being" in his life most intensively, as a testimonial to his official mission—somewhat as it would be desirable that the officers of a chess club be good chess players themselves, in order to be able to do real justice to the particular task committed to them.

We are indicating all this here only in order to exclude misunderstandings and anticlerical feelings from the start, since we are distinguishing the office, with the person holding it, from the mission of each Christian, and Christians as such. The question that must be posed—and it is a question of spiritual importance—is whether the three classic offices exhaust the list of official ministerial offices in the Church, or whether other functions as well—of course in a gradation which we might qualify as "essential," if you will—exist or are conceivable in the Church, functions similar or analogous to those of the priestly office in the three degrees of sacramental orders. Here, of course, we cannot take up the question, so difficult for the history of dogma, as indeed for dogma itself, as to what authority the Church has, or perhaps had in its originary stage as primitive Church, to form and distinguish the necessary office within it into distinct offices.

However this thorny question may be resolved (which will also determine how we are to understand the origin of the ministries with Jesus— his personal "founding," his "establishing" of these ministries), at all events we can say that the de facto ecclesiality of the Church adequately demonstrates that, besides the three classic offices in the Church, there are also other ministries, which in the last analysis do not constitute mere secular support services for the office of the priesthood, but which, in at least analogous fashion to the latter, actually share in the mission and task of sacred office in the Church as ultimately one single office. A Christian who has taken up the profession of a teacher of religion, and allows it to permeate all of his or her activity and actual life, is surely not simply a lay person in the Church in the same way as an attorney might be; nor does he or she have the same function in the Church as the person who keeps the church clean for the pastor. No, he or she shares, in his or her own particular way, in the official mission of the Church vis-à-vis the Christian people. He or she is a teacher in the Church, an associate in the mission and responsibility that accompanies the divine and official proclamation of the Gospel. This and similar offices in the Church there surely are, or can be created in response to the concrete situations in which the Church must carry out its task. The boundaries of these further offices and functions alongside the classic priesthood of orders can of course be fluid vis-à-vis the mission and task (including the missionary task) of all Christians. Indeed one need not hesitate to ask whether such offices may not in some fashion participate in the sacramentality of the classic offices. Such a participation would not militate against the unity of priestly orders, since there are differentiations and degrees within the latter in any case. And there definitely has been sacramentality in the Church without the faith consciousness of the Church having as yet been reflected upon it: Thomas Aquinas, along with most medieval theologians, denied the sacramentality of episcopal consecration, and yet this sacramentality of course existed even in those days, and not only since the last Council expressly taught it.

From this point of departure it would be altogether possible to develop in detail a spirituality proper to such new (or old) offices in the Church, alongside the classic priesthood. A married theology teacher, who has received from the Church the task of forming those who are to be the heralds of divine revelation, should not resolutely insist, "I am a lay person and want to be a lay person," but should make the particularity of his or her office the shaping principle of his or her Christian spirituality.

Still other new (or old, but anonymous) offices in the Church, with their particular spirituality, await creation or discovery. When we know more clearly who we are and what we are doing, this being and this doing can become better, purer, and more fully real.

41 · Office and Free Charism

In this article we shall address the fundamental, divinely instituted distinction in the Church of the bearers or carriers of the Church's self-actualization, in their unity and distinction. That is, we shall address the distinction between office and free charism, and between the office-holders (the hierarchy) and the subjects of free charism. But before we can examine this distinction, we must first underscore the essential coherence and community of all these distinct gifts and distinct carriers of the manifold functions in the Church. In entering upon this latter consideration, we shall prescind from the fact that the Spirit of God can also distribute such gifts to men and women who indeed do not belong to the historically tangible society of the Church (for example, because they are not baptized), and yet whose gift and mission, bestowed and aroused by the Spirit, can nevertheless be meaningful for that Church.

The Church is the quasi-sacramental unity of spirit and historical tangibility, in function of the general incarnational principle of salvation history. This being the case, and in proportion as this is the case, all the functions of the Church are determined by this structure of this Church. The free charisms, while not subject to institutional administration, are always those of such men and women as are baptized, profess the one common faith within the one Church (in the dimension of human convergence in society, then, and not just privately), and are inserted into the one, socially structured life of the Church, so that they place even their freest and most personal charisms at the service of that concrete Church. And, conversely, basically no authority of office in the Church is authority of office *over* the Church but is authority of office *in* the Church. Such authority necessarily rests upon that same Christian existence that the occupier of an office has in common with all members of the Church. In spite of its origination in a commission from above, authority of office in the Church is such that it can be exercised only within a Church which is vitalized in its totality by the Spirit of God; and only thus, and through the efficacity of free charisms bestowed thereby, is this authority of office the apt subject for reception of the execution of such authority.

Furthermore, the individual officeholder himself can execute the authority of his office in concrete reality only when he possesses a certain measure of free charism. Even the authoritative instances that operate sacramentally, *ex opere operato*, can have this real mode of efficacity of theirs only if they are exercised de facto freely by their subjects and exercised in favor of a suitable addressee, a properly disposed recipient of the sacrament. But both of these presuppositions of this concrete sacramental event depend ultimately upon free charisms, understanding charisms in the broad, comprehensive sense of that operation of God's grace which is always free and never subject to institutional administration as far as lies with human beings. After all, the nature of the Church as eschatological community of salvation, in contradistinction to the Synagogue and other pre-Christian historical modes of the manifestation of the divine salvation, consists precisely in this, that the unity obtaining between divine grace and its historical (categorical) tangibility can now no longer be altogether dissolved.

On this basis, then, we perceive that an ultimate, basic unity of all divine salvific activity attaches to and resides in the Church, and that this unity embraces all legitimate and essential distinctions among the various charisms and their personal vehicles. In Christ's dispensation there can be no operation of God's grace that would be purely and simply non-ecclesial. The institutional element in the Church in its entirety has fallen heir to the eschatological promise that it can never be definitively deprived of the Spirit. Surely, reciprocation between office and free charism is not perfectly fluid. A clear line of demarcation within the societal dimension of the Church as such (in the dimension of sacramental sign, then, in the dimension of official word and law binding the community as such) is altogether possible, indeed inevitable. Still, office and free charism in the Church belong so intimately together that neither can exist without the other, and each, despite the distinction between them, abides in permanent orientation to its counterpart.

These, then, are the presuppositions and reservations with which we may now undertake to examine and clarify the difference between office and free charism. It is only under these presuppositions and reservations that the peculiarity, difference, and communality of all Christians as vessels of the Church's self-realization can be understood. We say *"free charism"* from the outset—since, both biblically and factually, instances of authority of office in the Church are gifts of God's grace, not only because they are given through God's free, unmeritable donation, but also because authority of office in the Church tends, of its very nature, to the sanctification of the members of the Church, and signifies a demand and pledge of the officeholder's own sanctification, even in the case where it is (validly and efficaciously) exercised by a sinner.

The fact of a like distinction is indisputable from the standpoint of a Catholic understanding of Church. On the one hand, there is office in the Church as permanent (permanent in principle) commission, originating with Christ, for determinate functions in the Church—and as commission that is unambiguously discernible in the dimension of the historical and the juridical (laying-on of hands and apostolic succession), so that the coming-to-efficacy of this function is recognizable from the legitimacy of the commission, and not simply conversely (the validity of the commission recognizable from the factual coming-to-efficacy of the function). But on the other hand there are, in the Church of God, influences of God's Spirit on individual faithful which are neither subject to constraint on the part of human beings nor foreseeable and "administrable" by official organs, nor yet attainable via the positing of sacraments alone—and yet which make their appearance in the Church in the widest variety of forms and degrees of intensity. Inasmuch as the abiding existence of a hierarchy of divine institution, endowed with instances of authority which do not fall under the disposition merely of every baptized person, is defined dogma (*DS* 944, 1610, 1767 ff., etc.)—and inasmuch as it can surely be regarded as the unequivocal and altogether certain teaching of the ordinary magisterium of the Church that there are effects of grace, not only *in* the Church (for the salvation of the individual) but also *for* the Church, which are not identical with these instances of authority of office and their exercise—therefore the fact of this distinction is not open to doubt. But then, inasmuch as both of these elements are among the constitutive elements of the Church, a practical theology having as its object the apposite and felicitous self-realization of the Church may not conduct itself as if its task were restricted to directives for the proper conduct of office alone.

Evident as is the fact of such a distinction, however, the proper basis of this distinction, and thus also the nature of office and of free charism, stand in need of further clarification, and this clarification is available. We do not come to an adequate grasp of the peculiarity of office in the Church, in its distinction from the free charisms and at the same time in the intimate communality of these two gifts, if we proceed simply from a model of the legitimate distribution of determinate instances of authority by those in original and self-evident possession of this power. This inadequacy obtains even if we conceptualize the possession of these instances as permanent and ongoing, and view their mediate concretization as translation into inalterably determinate, societally recognizable, and hence juridically identifiable forms. That this model is insufficient, indispensable as it may be for the concept of office in the Church, is clear from a twofold consideration. First, this model would fail to account for the peculiarity of office in the Church in contradistinction to office in the Synagogue, or to the authority of a divinely authorized office in a profane society. Hence we must make a further distinction between office in the Church and other divinely authorized office—in their material content, however, and not in the formal structure of office as such. Second, this model by itself fails to account for the existence of free charisms in the

Church itself, since after all one could readily imagine that the gamut of functions in the Church could rest upon a commission of offices alone, if these offices were simply to be constituted by this formal commission having a determinate function in and for ecclesial society. These offices would of course be ultimately constituted by the mission and commission of determinate individuals by God and Christ, who would lend these individuals determinate instances of authority, and hence rights, vis-à-vis other human beings. But the peculiarity of office in the Church derives from the fact that it is an office *in the Church*, and that it receives its peculiar note from the nature of the Church.

We perceive this peculiarity most clearly when we observe office in its highest, that is, in its indefectible, perfections—that is, when we observe it as infallible magisterium and mission of the sacraments *ex opere operato* —and ask ourselves *why* there is *such* office. In pre-Christian salvation history there was no such office. After all, there were no sacraments, in this sense, nor any magisterial *office*, as distinguished from a non-institutionalized prophetism—although, at least in the lawful religion of the Old Testament there were the royal and priestly offices, holding their authorization from God. Now, it is evident that the peculiarity of New Testament office derives from the eschatological peculiarity of the Church. The Church, in the New Testament sense—that is, as distinguished from a legitimate religious institution before Christ—is the abiding presence of Christ (both as fruit and as mediation of Christ's salvation). But in Christ, and only in Christ, resides the incarnational unity, incarnational in its kind, of God and the human being, of grace and historical tangibility. Thanks to this unity without confusion, yet without possibility of division, of the divine and the human in Christ, we have this unity as well in that presence of Christ that is the Church: we have the indefectibility of the Church wherever, and only where, this same presence of Christ in the Church is unconditionally engaged—we have indefectible office in magisterium, conferral of grace, and all other elements of the Church's self-actualization. We have office as such in the Church in the measure that this office is characteristic precisely of the Church as such.

That is to say, because the Church is a *society*, it necessarily has office. But because this society is the *eschatological presence of Christ's salvation*, it has an office which, under certain preconditions, in virtue of the special assistance of the Holy Spirit, is in many instances indefectible. Were office in the Church only of that type that must be at hand in any legitimate society, any society in conformity with God's will, then it could be established "from below," and yet would have, in its capacity as comprising legitimate human instances of authority in a profane but "God-willed" society, divine authorization standing behind it. Still, in its concrete form and actualization, it would be surpassable and defectible. But office in the Church is established by God for the reason, and in the measure, that he constitutes the indefectible Church as the definitive instance of representation of the incarnational truth and grace of Christ. To the extent that office arises in this way, it is indefectible in its nature —or, conversely, office is never *juris divini* except where and to the extent that it represents this indefectible presence of Christ as such and unconditionally engages it in its activity. Where this is not verified, there is simply no office of divine right, but either office of human right, as freely determined authorization from below (ultimately, then, free charism), institutionalized in ever provisional and varying ways in function of practical considerations, or indeed free charism itself. This is not to say that the execution of office *juris divini* obtains *in indivisibili* in every case —that office is always and everywhere performed indefectibly or not at all. After all, the individual instances of performance of office form, in view of the plural constitution of the human being and of the Church, a unity of moments whose individual moments need not actually and wholly contain the nature of this unity (just as, for example, human freedom, of its nature, is the human being's total disposition of himself or herself, utterly and definitively, and yet the nature of this freedom is not engaged in each and every free act—not in a venial sin, for instance). Thus where there is office *simpliciter* in the Church—that is, office corresponding to the eschatological nature of the Church—this is office *juris divini*, office in itself indefectible, total self-engagement on the part of the Church. But where it is not a matter of such office, then we are dealing basically with free charisms, which are institutionalized after the fact and secondarily if at all, and to the extent it may be possible to do so.

Now it is clear why office in this sense cannot be the sole vehicle of the self-realization of the Church as a whole, and therefore (since, after all, we are dealing with the self-actualization of the Church as such) why free charisms and their personal vehicles are also required. No historical and temporal being can realize itself simply through acts in which it posits itself utterly, in a total engagement, in each act. Anything of the kind would contradict the temporality, or historicity, and the plurality of such self-actualization. Now, the Church is precisely the pilgrim Church—en route, merely, to its consummation, possessing indeed its own indefectible nature (as God's eschatological self-communication to humanity in Christ), but precisely in faith and hope, and not in vision. Were the Church always, simply, and in every act to behave indefectibly, then (understanding this indefectibility not only as a negative limit, but as absolute fullness of this self-actualization) it would no longer be the temporal, historical Church on a pilgrim journey: it would be the presence of the definitive Kingdom of God itself. Not that the self-actualizing of the Church is simply an accidental unity, a conglomeration of indefectible and defectible acts of this self-realization. In all its acts, both its eschatological indefectibility as well as its pilgrim existence must unfold. Within such acts, the relationship of these two facets need not and cannot always be the same—but neither moment can be missing, in any of them. The event of the freest charism is thus specifically Christian charism, co-determined in its peculiarity by the nature of the indefectible Church, inasmuch as this charism is experienced and received in specifically Christian faith and hope, and is a coming-to-efficacity of the grace irrevocably bestowed on the world in Christ and the Church in such a way that this "remorselessness" of grace is made manifest in the historical Church. And, conversely, the most official *opus operatum* and the most infallible magisterial pronouncement of the Church repose firmly upon what they properly intend: free charism, charism not subject to official administration, inasmuch as the infallible bestowal of grace in the sacraments is only efficacious where non-sacramental grace effects the acceptance of the sacramental grace through the former's gift of "disposition," while the infallible magisterial pronouncement, in like manner, can only be understood really aright and salvifically where it is heard in the no longer officially administrable grace of faith and the understanding of the faith.

Consequently we may say that the vehicle of the Church's self-actualization is the free charism of all the members of the Church, inasmuch as it is the whole self-actualizing of *faith, hope,* and *love* which transpires here; but the grace of these cannot be adequately "administered" by an office, and this charismatically "vehicled" self-actualization of the Church will thus have its *official* vehicle: in office, as it both generates that office and presupposes it, just where this historically and societally tangible self-actualization so engages the Church as a whole that the latter would cease to be the eschatologically definitive presence of Christ in the world and in history were this, its tangible and historical act, not to be what it claims to be. We are not implying, by these observations, that the concrete office, and the concrete determinations of the self-actualizing of office (in an indefectible or defectible manner), could be deduced from these abstract principles when this concrete office and its concrete actualizing were not known beforehand. We only imply that the inmost, metaphysical nature of such office comes in contact with concrete office and its concrete determinations because, and in the measure that, it is experienced in its concrete actuality. And once its nature is reflexively known, ˙induced a posteriori from the experience of this office, from Scripture, and from the teaching and practice of the Church, then it is indeed entirely possible to reverse direction and deduce a practical norm for this office, in cases in which, in practice up to a given point in time, it has not been altogether clearly possible to do so.

42 · The Religious Life

The Second Vatican Council, in its great and momentous Dogmatic Constitution on the Church, *Lumen Gentium*, declares that the religious life, life in an order or community officially approved by the Church, belongs and must belong to that Church—not in the same manner as office, surely, but in another, just as crucial way. But the religious life does not belong to the Church because religious claim to be the better or the real Christians. Those who love the most, believe the most, and hope the most, are the best, the most excellent Christians. Where this "best" Christiantity occurs, God alone knows, but it occurs in all the conditions and callings of Christianity.

But what Christianity *ought to be* should, according to the challenge of the Second Vatican Council, be vital and alive in the religious life and come to manifestation there. And what Christianity should be is ultimately *faith, hope,* and *love*—faith in eternal life, hope in the absolute future that is God himself, and a love that is love of God and neighbor in absolute unity.

What, then, is the essence of Christianity? First of all, we may say simply: hope—hope that the terrible, seemingly desperate darkness that pervades life nevertheless is scheduled for a happy and blessed issue. Christianity is hope. Christianity is love for neighbor, and indeed a love for neighbor that wins its final strength from a faith-filled gaze at the Crucified and Risen One. It is through all these experiences that we finally know what is meant when we say "God." Only the one who hopes, through all life's darkness, for a final, happy meaning and outcome to life, who "makes contact" with Jesus, the Crucified and Risen One, finally knows who is meant by the word "God." Otherwise we imagine something strange and curious under that name, or else the name is only an empty wrapper, and one uses it without knowing what is meant by it.

This, Christianity's essential element, must not be allowed to remain pure theory, in heads and Sunday sermons. It must become concrete, immediate, sober, ordinary life, in the midst of the so-called profane, secular, daily round. Here is where hope, faith, love, and loyalty to neighbor must be lived. These demands perhaps likewise actualize other demands, perhaps even exemplarily. None of these things are privileges that we religious may arrogate to ourselves. But we have made profession of this ultimate meaning of life, and precisely because these highest ideals must become palpable in the midst of our lives, we seek in some measure to organize and institutionalize them, altogether concretely, in the midst of the daily round of those lives. We seek to render them praxis in a Church in which there are human beings who give testimony that they hope, that they live the life of love, human beings who without despair take their stand where life is absorbed into the intangibility of the lot of the Crucified One. These human beings form the Church and bring it about that this Church is a sign of hope, a symbol of love, a call to responsibility for neighbor. These are precisely the human beings—the ones who seek to bear witness, concretely and simply, practically, without empty talk, in life's deeds—among whom we religious ought to be found. We should, as the Second Vatican Council says, be a "sign" of what the Church ought to be for the world—a proclamation, an ever renewed confirmation and attestation that, when all is said and done, the world lies cupped in the hand of God, in God's power, in God's love, in God's faithfulness, in God's mercy, in God's blessed future.

It goes without saying that we are not arrogating to ourselves the exclusive privilege of being a sign of the Church. A husband who does his duty faithfully and unselfishly in the midst of a busy life, a mother who sacrifices herself for her children, a patient who must stare death in the face without hope of recovery and yet has given over and abandoned himself or herself into the hands of the incomprehensible God—all these, as people of the Church who profess that they are Jesus Christ's, are, in all these things, witnesses of what the Church should be. They are vessels of the function of the Church, signals of hope for the world's salvation in the midst of a world that seems so dark despite all the grand achievements of which it boasts today. We claim no privilege here. We feel no exclusive call here.

But why should we religious not say: We seek, in our way, as God has given it to us, as it is needful, full of blessing, and useful for the world— though the world may need other blessings too—we seek to serve our neighbor, in word, in deed, in love, in fidelity, in care, in unselfishness, in prayer? Others may do it in other ways—God gives his grace, his gifts, as he wills—and God be with them. But we claim the right to do it our way. And it is of course not really so, that the world cares nothing for this deed, this witness. At the very least, the world would scarcely be happy to do without those who serve the sick and the dying, the poor and the little ones. For here is where the world can still best be shown that there is something within it other than disguised selfishness, something besides the struggle for survival—that there really is, and can be, such a thing as love, as faith, as hope of eternal life.

43 · Vocation

When the subject of vocation is broached, and a particular trade or profession, in the ordinary civil meaning of "vocation," is to be selected, many people have the impression that they must somehow feel a clearly palpable inspiration. This is true of those who decide in favor of a spiritual calling—the priesthood or the religious life—and it is true for others who decide for an apparently profane calling, but who ascribe a value to conformity to God's will and guidance. They think that where their concrete calling is concerned, the will of God is not sufficiently contained in general principles and norms, but that God must make known to them what calling they should choose in a private revelation of sorts, a kind of heavenly inspiration. When they think they feel no such inspiration, they conclude that they have no real vocation to this calling. This is a false notion, to which the word "calling," or "vocation," seems to lead again and again. This is particularly the case where there is a question of a vocation to a religious calling.

At the beginning of this century, this issue was a much mooted one in the Catholic Church where religious vocations were concerned and was expressly discussed. A French theologian named Lahitton had come out with the thesis that, for the genuineness of a spiritual vocation—for the certitude that God had a given person in mind for this calling—nothing more was required than, first, a genuine aptitude for this calling, and second, one's free choice based on motives appropriate for that calling. If both these conditions were present, the vocation was genuine. And indeed Pope Pius X, without issuing any especially solemn pronouncement or definition, declared this interpretation to be a legitimate one, and a norm which prospective candidates, confessors, and spiritual directors and counselors might quite justifiably follow, indeed should follow.

It may be that this decision rested rather too much on a conceptualization of the human being as composed of intellectual understanding and free will and nothing else. Perhaps it was overlooked that a concrete human being, with his or her subconscious, with his or her predispositions, with his or her unchangeable past history, and so on, is a very much more complicated being than just a rationalistically interpreted aptitude plus a legitimately motivated free decision. But since all these other things, which must also be at hand for a reasonable choice of vocation, can and must quite meaningfully be reckoned as *aptitude* in a person, modern psychology and anthropology will have no really fundamental objections to raise to Lahitton's theory—even if the question, how one can more precisely recognize this required aptitude, and this legitimacy and purity of motives, is perhaps more difficult than a Church rationalism and stoicism (if we may so call them) thought it to be back in those days, at the beginning of the twentieth century.

And so, if we take the basic idea of this theory as legitimate, then we can confidently tell a person facing a decision as to a vocation: Don't look for mystical illumination and inspiration from on high. Soberly examine all your inclinations, experiences, drives, and internal and external relationships, in the light of this calling, to see whether you are suitable for it. Perhaps seek the aid of psychologists and other counselors. Examine whether you have the right motives—for instance, whether you want to be a priest not in order to seek preferment, but in order to serve human beings. And if your examination points to an affirmative answer, then you can confidently and calmly say, I have a vocation to this or that calling, and I need not anxiously seek out any other, additional experiences in a religious mysticism as evidence of my aptitude or of my free, rightly motivated decision, in order to be able to say, "Here I see I have a vocation that God has given me." God gives a vocation precisely by giving the aptitude for it, and sees to it in his providence that correct motivations for such a decision are present.

A further difficulty attending the question of a vocation, especially a religious vocation, in young people today arises from the fact that such a vocation, by its nature as well as in the interpretation of the Church entails a permanent obligation. Today young people ask: How do I know that, five, ten, or thirty years from now, I shall still be the person who is able to fulfill this permanent obligation?

Fear of making a lifelong commitment to something for which, for one's own part, one has insufficient certitude that one will really be able to fulfill its lifelong obligations, is very common today. One sees that the structure and mentality of a society change much more rapidly today than in times past. The external props and stays of a public consensus concerning a religious vocation are no longer available as once upon a time. Rapid changes in group mentality, which then influence the individual, can be observed with regard to marriage as well. Marriages are entered into as a lifelong commitment and then are often broken off very quickly. These and similar things cause great insecurity and anxiety today when it comes to choosing a religious vocation. One does not trust oneself to take on such a lifelong obligation.

What is to be said to this? Many things. *First,* we must notice that this problem exists always and everywhere. There are, in human life quite generally, a great many decisions that can be taken and then in one way or another "taken back." One can decide today to live in Vienna from now on, and two years later decide to move to Innsbruck. One can buy this necktie today and another tomorrow. There are surely a great many decisions in life that are subject to revision. But when we look closely, we see that, inescapably, human life again and again confronts other decisions that are not subject to revision. Even if one rejected the indissolubility of marriage, one would still have to admit that for someone, for example, who obtains a divorce after ten years of marriage, the decision taken for those ten years, at least, can no longer be reversed. We have only one life to live, and once we have lived it, the opportunities of the past are gone forever.

This is what a young person today should say to himself or herself: Life is such that, ineluctably, we have to make decisons that, like it or no, we can never truly and properly revoke. And since we cannot revoke them, we have to have the courage to dive into the water, even if we cannot make out the farther shore very well, and are not one-hundred-percent certain that we have the strength to swim to that shore. *The courage for irreversible decisions is something that belongs necessarily to the essence of the true and valiant human being.*

Second, to be sure, this alone does not solve the problem. One can of course say: There are such decisions. They are demanded by life. We are, as Sartre would say, "condemned to freedom"—and to a freedom that can go forward, but that can never again retrace its steps along its chosen path.

But one could say that with a religious vocation the case is rather more difficult. Again, we must admit from the outset that another vocational choice is in a certain sense easier to change, easier to revise. And yet, even in secular life there are vocational decisons which in practice can often no longer be revoked. A person who has gone through six years of medical school and then a three-year residency can perhaps decide to become an artist or a mechanic instead. In many cases this may be possible. But the direction taken in a prior vocation-decision of this sort, the time spent on it, the disadvantages entailed in changing it even from the point of view of society at large—and the social situation in which one lives—are no longer to be done away with.

The same is true, of course, at least in the teaching of Jesus and the Christian Church, regarding divorce from a particular marriage partner. You can climb aboard, but the train does not stop. Divorce may be an easy and common thing today, but in most cases it is obvious that "getting off the train" has human, existential consequences that are anything but easy and gratifying.

And so one at least has to say: A religious calling is entered into with the consciousness that it comprises an irrevocable decision, and therefore that one must have the vocation corresponding to it. But this is basically a human problem which, difficult as it may be in certain circumstances, and bound up with so many burdens, does come up elsewhere, and not just with religious vocations.

Third, besides all this, the following must be observed. Young people will very often say, with regard to religious vocations: I have the good will here and now to take on this duty and these obligations—for instance those of the priestly vocation and office—but how can I guarantee how things will look in ten, twenty, or thirty years?

In my opinion, one may altogether calmly and legitimately tell such a person: How and what you are going to be thirty years from now need be of absolutely no concern to you here and now—provided, first, that you have settled that you have an honest will at the moment to be a priest and honestly and rightly to carry out the duties of your priestly office and the other obligations with which the Church has bound up the priestly calling; and, second, that, as far as it depends on you, as far as it lies in any way within the field of your freedom, you live today in such a way that you will be able to carry out this priestly office and its obligations tomorrow as well. In a sense, you need not make decisions and dispositions now for when you are forty. But you can live and act now in such a way that, as far as lies within your freedom, you will still be able to be an honest and enthusiastic priest when you are forty. *If,* and to the extent that it is *without fault of yours,* owing to circumstances beyond your free disposition over your life, your further individual history were to take such a form that you could no longer be equal to your priesthood, then you can and should unashamedly apply to the Church for release for your priestly obligations. And you will receive it.

That someone should direct his individual history, through his own fault, in such a way that the office of the priesthood could no longer be performed by him later is of course perhaps a case that frequently occurs. And in practice there can even be combinations of both types. But this does not enter into our present considerations.

Life is such that one is constantly making decisions with a hope that offers no rational certitude that things will continue to go meaningfully and well. If you build a house, you must reckon with the possibility that lightning may strike and burn the house down. But of course you will surely not decide not to build the house for all that. You will put a good lightning rod on the roof. Then prospects will be such that you will have good reason to hope, as far as human discretion can judge, that the house will last. This is much the way in which a young person should think: I am starting out on the road to the priesthood. I am trying, as far as it depends on my good will, to direct my own inner development—which, after all, is not just coincidence or blind fate—in such a way as always to be able to be a priest. Then for the rest, this young person can say, I trust God and my life, even though the latter depends to a large extent on circumstances beyond my free control. Then my life will take a meaningful course in one way or another.

All of us, of course, have a certain *Lebensangst*, a certain existential anxiety and fear. Both within and without we are ever threatened; our lives are not utterly guaranteed to be automatically happy and blessed. But there is no overcoming this *Lebensangst* through flight from a courageous decision. One must, as Ignatius Loyola says, leap into one's determination with both feet. If a sensible self-examination, and the assessment of reasonably wise and prudent spiritual counselors, indicates an aptitude for a religious calling, and a person can seriously and honestly tell himself or herself, "In this religious vocation, I want to serve the Church, and in the Church, people, and in people, God and Jesus Christ, and I am trying to see to it that other motives, which of course can come into play, not gain the upper hand"—such a person, in trust in God's direction and governance, should be really confident that he or she has a vocation to the priestly or religious state, in faith and hope. A free decision for a meaningful life-calling, which one truly can follow and wishes to follow, already means that the vocation for it is at hand.

44 · A Spirituality of Calling

"Calling" is a biblical word, originally, with a theological content, although today it is used to denote any function in a society that is necessary or useful for that society and has a certain duration. In other words, it denotes a trade or profession. For the spiritual life of a Christian today it is very important to be able to endorse one's "secular" calling as a task for one's spiritual life having a meaningful content. That is, it is important that a person's secular calling be a divine vocation as well, a calling in the biblical sense too. There is great danger of regarding and cultivating the spiritual life today as something lying out beyond the confines of the work of one's worldly calling.

The spiritual being of a Christian and his or her professional earthly task are all too often felt as two discrete areas of life, having little or nothing to do with each other. An earnest human being will of course still see, even today, that there are moral demands accompanying his or her earthly calling—"professional obligations," like honesty, loyalty, industry. But this is not sufficient when it really comes to integrating an earthly profession into one's spiritual life as such, integrating it as an essential moment of that spiritual life. When the spiritual moment of one's "calling" is seen as limited to this single moral aspect, Christians generally see their spiritual life only where they experience their married life as supported by God's grace, or where they cope with life's ultimate bitterness and disappointment, and finally with their death, in calm and hope.

The duties of one's calling are not often seen today as part of one's heavenly calling by God in Jesus Christ. They are not often seen as task and adventure in the Holy Spirit. And yet it would be altogether possible to look upon them in this way. Not that the staid sobriety and hardship of daily service in one's trade or profession should be unduly glorified. Calm and patient coping with the daily banality and "ordinariness" of the average professional or work life, without heavy ideologizing, itself belongs to one's calling as a divine vocation in Jesus Christ. But the Christian should nonetheless be able to understand his or her earthly calling as a heavenly vocation. This is not as easy in some trades as in others. A like understanding of one's profession is certainly more easily accessible to a gifted educator and teacher than to someone who has to earn his bread swinging a sledgehammer, and who is happy when the day is over and he can forget his work. But in principle the understanding of one's calling as a divine vocation is possible in any trade or profession. An artist, a researcher, a teacher and educator, someone in government, or people of similar "ideal" professions, will certainly find it easier to do so, however hard it may be to "put one's nose to the grindstone" and forge ahead to success in such a calling. But this is no reason why it should be impossible to see, in a hard trade as well—one in which a man or woman is forced to engage by social and economic circumstances in order to earn a living—a heavenly vocation.

To what is every Christian called by God? All divine vocations, however they may be thought of, are summonses, vocations, to complement the descent of the eternal God into flesh. They are always vocations to earthly ordinariness and death, vocations to believe in the light shining in the darkness, to actualize love that seems to go unrewarded and unrequited, to enter into solidarity with the poor and the "shortchanged"—the brothers and sisters of Jesus Christ who are anything but the elite, and seem rather to belong to some sort of hideous, mass-produced humanity. Only through the performance of this task as a mission to "those below" does the Christian really accomplish his or her radical surrender to God's incomprehensibility as a beatifying surrender through faith, hope, and love. Otherwise he or she remains locked up in the prison of his or her own selfishness. After all, the path of the spiritual life is a path that cannot bypass the cross of Jesus Christ. All earthly fulfillment, however surely and legitimately it may be looked upon, accepted, and enjoyed as God's good gift, is still but the beginning of God's eternal salvation—although this beginning it surely is when it is made over, in hope and trust, to the incomprehensible disposition of God in the death of Jesus, and thereby in our own death.

We only invoke this construct of the Christian life, and apply it to the earthly calling, in order to show that an earthly calling can be a heavenly vocation. It should not be used to imply that ordinary earthly trades and professions must be understood as vocation to the discipleship of the Crucified One only when they are hard jobs people work at in order to earn a living. No, in the case of these kinds of employment as well, a human being and Christian has the right and obligation to seek to render them more humane, easier, and more enjoyable. One may rightfully do one's very best to "find a better job." One can always see, even in the humblest and most toilsome trade, a positive contribution to society—one without which that society can by no means manage for its life and happiness as a whole. One should make an effort to discover the positive facet of even the humblest calling, and only the resentful, embittered person will not be able to see this facet. But the Christian has no grounds to idealize and glorify an ordinary trade or profession, as those must do who have no eternal hope, and hence who exalt the toilsome calling that others, usually, must bear with—and so keep the lowly patient and content.

Even in the humblest and hardest calling, the Christian should soberly and honestly recognize the mission to participate in Jesus' lot—the destiny of the cross—and accept it in sober patience and in hope against hope. Not only the pleasant and "fulfilling" aspects of a trade or profession, which, when all is said and done, can be found in any and every calling, are meaningful for the Christian life—but the hard things, too: the frustration, the boredom, the banality of an ordinary trade (things not spared even the most ideal professions, by the way). These things as such are tasks and actualizations of the spiritual life itself, if only we understand them aright. Not only a legitimate struggle with the frustration of one's calling—not only escape from the wearisome toil of one's calling by what one does with one's free time, by tourism, and in the other things of one's private life, are Christian opportunities—but all these other elements as well, terrible as they are, the hard things about an ordinary trade or profession, can themselves be understood as heavenly vocations. To be sure, they nail a person to the cross of a life that so disappoints him or her. Nor is this person taken down from the cross by the mere fact that he or she is calling for a blessed existence on this earth for coming generations. But the Christian who prays, the Christian who experiences the incomprehensible nearness of God in the void of his or her existence, can recognize, can bear, can hold up under the frustration of his or her calling, for the short course of this life, as a participation in the death of Christ, who has definitively found God's eternal light in the darkness. The light and the darkness of any calling can lead to the discipleship, the following of Christ, and be a heavenly vocation.

45 · Marriage

Two baptised individuals voluntarily bind themselves in marriage. In this something takes place in the Church too. Here we do not need to adopt the approach of canon law, or to ask what precise conditions are required by the divine or human law upheld by the Church and from the nature of the case in order that such a bond of marriage (let us not call it a "contract"!) may take place precisely *in* the Church and in the context of her life as a "visible society." But at basis all this is already given in virtue of the fact that it is two baptised individuals that are involved, and a marriage between them, something which always has a social relevance. Because married love has the character of a pointer and a sign, marriage itself is never a mere "worldly affair." For this love itself is no worldly affair, but rather the event of grace and love which unites God and men. When a marriage of *this* kind, therefore, takes place in the Church, it is an element in the process by which the Church fulfils her own nature as such, one which is brought into being by two baptised Christians who, through their baptism, have been empowered to play an active part in this self-realisation. As baptised, therefore, they act in a manner which is precisely proper to the Church herself. They make manifest the sign of love in which *that* love is visibly expressed which unites God and men.

Now when the Church achieves the fulness of her own nature in this way precisely at this *essential* level, making it effective in the concrete and decisive living situation of a human individual, there we have a sacrament. In that case there is no need for this purpose of any *explicit* words of institution uttered by Jesus (we could never establish as a matter of historical fact that he ever uttered such words, nor is it even probable that he did so), such as for instance are to be found in the case of the Eucharist. The "word of institution" in this case consists in two factors: on the one hand in the fact that the religious relevance of marriage is acknowledged and that it is recognised that this too is something that is achieved through the word and the deed of Jesus himself. It also consists in the fact that marriage has been instituted by the Church as an eschatological sign of salvation for the kingdom of God (considered as the absolute proximity of God to man) until the end of time. On the other hand marriage itself and of itself carries with it its own profoundly significant theological dimension.

Those theologians who invoke the support of Ephesians 5 for the sacramental nature of marriage were unable to perceive this point clearly. And because of this there has always been a certain embarrassment about this theology which, ultimately speaking, proves to be utterly unnecessary. For the saying from Genesis 2:24 which is quoted in Ephesians 5 appeared to raise marriage *in general*—not merely that between Christians—to a sign of the unity between Christ and the Church, and it was believed that this could not be conceded without difficulty. In reality this is perfectly possible if we think out exactly the full implications of what we have said with regard to the character of marriage as a sign referring to married love and the special theological dimensions belonging to this. In Christian theology, in fact, we certainly do not have to maintain that a sacramental marriage is related to a non-sacramental marriage as a sacrament to a purely secular human activity. On the contrary both are related to one another as the *opus operatum* to an *opus operantis*, and this latter too is wholly an event of grace. The order in which the one stands to the other here is similar, for instance, to that relationship which a sacramental forgiveness of sins bears to a non-sacramental one achieved merely though repentance. For this too takes place as the outcome of grace and in grace. Marriage does not become an *event of grace* only at that stage at which it acquires the status of a "sacrament." On the contrary the event of grace in marriage becomes a *sacramental* event of grace as *opus operatum* in those cases in which it takes place between two baptised individuals in the Church. The case here is exactly as with the faith which justifies of itself even *prior to* baptism, and which then becomes *opus operatum* in baptism. Up to the present, if I am not mistaken, there has been a strange naiveté among theologians in their approach to marriage in that distinction and unity which is familiar to every theologian in the case of faith—baptism, penance/sacrament of penance—has not consciously been worked out and applied here. In the two former cases the grace-given event of justification is initiated not merely at the moment when the sacrament as such is conferred, but already prior to this at the stage of faith and repentance. *On the other hand* in the dimension of historical manifestation as such this sign only acquires the character of an *unconditional* pledge of grace from God, in other words that of an *opus operatum* and so of a "sacrament," when it takes place in the Church and takes its place in the concrete in the context in which such a pledge acquires its historical manifestation. This is the Church herself considered as basic sacrament. When a marriage takes place between baptised people in the Church it constitutes an element in the Church's role as basic sacrament, so that the parties actively share in and contribute to the Church's role as basic sacrament, for both give manifest expression to the unifying love of the grace of God, and a marriage of this kind between them achieves this precisely *as* an element in the social unity of the Church herself. Now because of this the marriage as an event of grace gives rise to a "sacramental" event of grace in which this sign actively contributes to the irrevocable manifestation of God's pledge of grace to mankind, that pledge which is constantly in force and of which God himself never repents. And this manifestation is nothing else than the Church herself.

On the basis of this conception of the "institution" of this sacrament we can now proceed more freely to evaluate the findings of dogmatic tradition with regard to the doctrine of marriage as a sacrament. We do not need to force the evidence here so as either to postulate or to construct for ourselves any explicit doctrine hypothetically supposed to have existed right from the outset, in which marriage would always have been considered as a "sacrament" and as such subsumed under a general concept of sacrament. The less we make use of any such idea—so long as we still understand and experience the "sacramental" nature of a sign of salvation in the Church—the better it will be. When, therefore, we find this also confirmed by the dogmatic tradition we should regard this as neither surprising nor shocking.

What has been said, however, still needs clarification to some extent in terms of what is familiar to us from the catechism as a formal statement of what constitutes marriage as a sacrament. It is customarily said that marriage is an image of the unity of Christ and the Church, and that it is a sacrament in virtue of this. On an initial reading of Ephesians 5:22–33 we may, perhaps, receive the impression that the vital common basis for the similarity between the relationship which Christ bears to the Church on the one hand and that involved in marriage on the other consists in the fact that the husband represents Christ while the wife represents the Church. In that case the unity of marriage as such would itself be a relatively secondary reflection of the unity between Christ and the Church, which in turn would be based on a reflection in which the married partners were regarded as separate from one another precisely in respect of the different roles they play. But surely we would still have to say that even for Paul himself this way of viewing the matter is secondary, conditioned perhaps by the parenetic context and more or less conditioned too by the sociological factors prevailing at the time. On this showing, then, it would not simply be the text quoted as a whole which would constitute a statement of central theological importance, but rather the particular passage of 5:29–33 that would have primary importance in it, for these particular verses bear upon the unity of love as such, as constituted in *one* flesh and body. The relationship of leadership and subordination as expressed in the love of solicitude and help on the one hand, and in obedience, submissiveness and "fear" on the other, is not the objective factor that is decisive in this parallel. If for our present purposes we can take this as established, then all that needs to be clarified here is where, in more precise terms, Christ is to be fitted in in the basic conception put forward in this study. First in the case of Paul it is clear that he regards the order of creation depicted in Genesis 2 as belonging to the order of grace and redemption, so that right from the outset that order of creation, and so too of the marriage of Adam, had the significance of pointing forwards to this order of grace. In our terms this is implicitly asserted—albeit on quite different theological principles—when we emphasise that every moral attitude on man's part (and this includes also what is presupposed to such an attitude) is everywhere and in all cases sustained and subsumed by the bestowal of grace by God upon the creature. "Covenant" is the more sublime and more ultimate factor which, by comparison with the creation considered as the positing of a creature still not determined in a specific direction, has in turn the character of unmerited grace. But precisely because of this "covenant" is the goal and the all-embracing factor which sustains and subsumes creation as the positing of the condition which makes covenant possible, since it provides the potential covenant partner. This means that objectively speaking everything that takes place in terms of human morality has a hidden relationship to Christ, in whose being and work precisely this imparting of grace finds its eschatological culmination and manifestation. Because he is the goal of it all he provides the basis for the whole dynamism of human history as imparted to it through grace, impelling it towards the immediacy of God.

We are speaking, then, of a unity in love between two human individuals. They are united in a love which consists not merely in the fact that both are aiming at a single common goal in this earthly dimension. This unity, rather, refers to the persons themselves in so far as their orientation to the last end has an eternal validity. And where the unity of love in this sense is achieved, there we have the operation and manifestation of that grace which constitutes the unity of men in the truest and most proper sense. But the converse is also true. Precisely this same grace, considered as establishing a unity between God and man, is manifested in the unity between Christ and the Church, and that too in a manifestation which has an absolute and eschatological force, and which as goal provides the basis for all other graces and their function as establishing unity in the world. For this reason there exists not merely an external similarity between the unity in love of two human individuals on the one hand and the unity between Christ and the Church on the other, but also a relationship between the two unities such that they condition one another: the former exists *precisely because* the latter exists. Their mutual relationship of similarity is not subsequent to the two but is a genuine relationship of participation due to the fact that the unity between Christ and the Church is the ultimate cause and origin of the unity of marriage.

In the light of this we can also understand that the more precise quality of the relationship between Christ as the *directing and controlling head* on the one hand, and the Church as the *obedient* and submissive *bride* on the other is not simply projected in precisely the selfsame sense into the unity of those united in love through marriage. The unity between Christ and the Church is the basis for the unity between husband and wife prior to the question of whether, and to what extent, this unity which is brought about also carries with it all the special attributes of the unity which brings it about. To the extent that the unity of Christ and the Church itself has its source in God's gracious will to bestow himself, both *this* unity *and* the unity of marriage have their basis in the selfsame grace of God, which unites mankind to God and men among themselves. To the extent that the goals of this *one single* will to bestow grace are related to one another as "cause" and "effect," since precisely *in* the will by which God intended Christ and the Church everything else is willed, this one particular effect of this grace-giving will (namely married unity) is also brought about by the other effect (the unity of Christ and the Church).

By reason of this mutual interrelationship of the two unities, the unity of marriage achieves its *full* manifestation precisely in the unity of Christ and the Church. And because of this much that would otherwise perhaps have remained obscure and unrecognised in the unity of married love can be deduced from the unity of Christ and the Church. And this remains true in spite of the caution which is necessary in adopting this approach. Thus with regard to the relationship of leadership and subordination between husband and wife in marriage Paul had already, and rightly, perceived that the basis of this was the unity of Christ with the Church, even though it may be true that the relationship which he was seeking to justify in part belonged to *that period alone*, and to that extent cannot have been a *moral demand* in the same sense at all periods. But if we were to take the same principle as our starting-point we could recognise other and similar parallels too: the character of the Cross with which both are imprinted; the irrevocability of the covenant; the provisional nature of both measured by the final and eternal consummation for which the Church and marriage are still waiting. However we cannot delay any longer in this article in explaining and rounding off this point.

Marriage, therefore, reaches upwards into the mystery of God in a sense which is far more radical even than we could have guessed merely from the nature of human love as unconditioned. Certainly all still remains hidden under the veil of faith and hope, and all this may still not be lifted from the lowly circumstances of our everyday lives. There is no question that such a truth does not take place either at a level which is utterly beyond man, his freedom, and his interior assent. There is no doubt, therefore, that those united in married love experience this reality in the same measure as they open their hearts to it in faith and love. Surely it has become clear that such a theology of marriage cannot be understood in that sense in which we introvertedly make it our own "private affair." On the contrary genuine Christian marriage has at all times the force of a real representation of the unifying love of God in Christ for mankind. In marriage the Church is made present. It is really the smallest community, the smallest, but at the same time the true community of the redeemed and the sanctified, the unity among whom can still be built up on the same basis on which the unity of the Church is founded, in other words the smallest, but at the same time the genuine individual Church. If we were able to recognise and to live out such a truth in its full significance then we could return somewhat more consoled and more bravely, in a spirit of truly Christian freedom, to our "married problems," so urgent as they are, yet almost talked to death.

46 · Indifference to All Created Things

Before we consider "indifference" as a moral requirement, as an ascetic norm for ourselves, it may be a good thing first of all to see it as in fact belonging to the essential structure of mental life. For if man is always the one who grasps the finite, individual thing in his knowledge and in his freedom in a movement directed basically towards absolute reality, towards absolute truth and goodness, in the necessary realisation of his mental life he always transcends the individual thing, he dissociates himself from it, he sets the finite, individual thing against a broader horizon, he rises above it, makes himself independent of it: he is "indifferent" in regard to the individual thing. We might say: The transcendence of human mental life in knowledge and freedom is itself that natural and supernatural basic indifference which is written into man's nature, and in face of which he alone has to answer the question whether or not he identifies himself in his freedom with this indifference of his nature, which is achieved at the roots of his mental life. Whenever we know the finite as finite, the good as provisional, the individual as contingent; whenever we tell the small truth of an affirmative judgment in virtue of affirming absolute truth; when we are free, we are in fact saying that, in the depth of our being, as ground of our being, there is an indifference in face of the finite, individual thing and that this is disowned if we do not become indifferent, that we are in fact in the process of destroying our own existence.

Ignatius of Loyola says in the *Spiritual Exercises* that it is necessary to make ourselves indifferent. What we are—for the being that we are, which is aware of itself, freely disposes of itself—is also our task. The indifference of our nature is the essential task of our life, it has to be undertaken. We must dispose ourselves for indifference, make ourselves indifferent. This means first of all that, in all that we are, in learning, enduring, going on loving, we must affirm, accept, develop openness and becoming open for the greater reality. We must keep ourselves open for what is greater, we must want to be the transcendence that we are. We never come to the end, nowhere can we finally rest, we are those who are open to the infinity of God—and this we must want to be. Not only in theory, but in the actuality of the small, bitter reality of our life. This is really difficult. We fall for the individual thing, we want to turn the particular object that we can grasp into our God, the idol of our life; we don't want to be driven out of the place where we are settled; we become mediocre; the absurd triviality of our normal life appears to us as something great, important and significant; we cannot permit anything to be taken from us, we cannot make a sacrifice, we cannot recognise the small things as small or the transitory as transitory.

Indifference as a task means first of all becoming open for the greater reality, ultimately for God. But this is not something we can take for granted, something that comes about of itself. The truth is that indifference as part of the essential structure of our mental life, if it is to be integrated into personal freedom, will be met with a mysterious resistance, which can be overcome only painfully and through the experience of something like death. There is, after all, the mystery of guilt, of sin, of egoism.

Perhaps we do not see how this sort of thing is possible; we do not know where this resistance to the indifference that belongs to our nature as transcendent really comes from; but this attempt to dispose ourselves for indifference, this forsaking of self and finite reality, this resignation, are opposed within ourselves by a deep, radical egoism. This must be overcome. Our task then is not something simple and obvious, but painful: it means something like a continual dying in the midst of our life.

The mastery of indifference, the constantly renewed effort to make ourselves indifferent, is difficult, hard, continually rouses a protest from something within us that claims to be what really matters. We are constantly under the impression—false and deceptive of course—that some particular thing in our life would make us free, exhilarated, blissfully happy; we are continually identifying ourselves with some particular thing, we don't want to transcend this, to get away from it and sacrifice it. Indifference is a task which seems to mean at least sacrifice, self-denial, renunciation and death. Each of us must ask himself where and in regard to what reality he must face this experience.

This death of sinful egoism involves courage for indifference, the courage to accept our own nature; it is in reality life lived with the incarnate Word of God. For he is pure receptivity, pure reception from the Father and pure return of reality to the Father. And he, who became man, in the dimension of his human life, receives the glory of his Father through death. Hence this indifference, apparently so philosophical, at the roots of our engraced existence and as the task of our liberty, is a sharing in living the life of Christ.

This indifference, then, is always a mystery. For in this indifference we turn from what we understand to the incomprehensible, from what we are enjoying to what is promised, from the present to the future, from what we can grasp to what we cannot grasp. It is an indifference in which a person declares that he will really take his stand solely in the unfathomable depths of God, that everything else—however much it is willed by God and therefore also to be affirmed, accepted, enjoyed and loved by us —is indeed always only that which in its finiteness rises out of an infinite depth and that which must always be hidden again in the greater and incomprehensible reality of God himself. This adaptation to indifference is therefore also a task freshly imposed each day.

We never are indifferent, we are constantly coming to be so. For whatever confronts us freshly and unforeseen, as what we experience in the odyssey of our mental, religious and Christian life, is precisely a new and unforeseen reality and must always be surmounted freshly and in a different way. This is the constantly new task, the constantly new surprise, the constantly new pain, the daily dying with Christ and also the splendour of our existence: we never come to the end of it. The God who is greater than we are is always revealing himself anew in what we have surmounted, in what we have come to terms with, in what we have freely accepted.

Ignatius also outlines the basic dimensions, the ultimate, essential dimensions for the exercise of this indifference, when he speaks of health and sickness, wealth and poverty, honour and dishonour, long life and short. Three dimensions are given.

There is first of all the corporality of existence in health and sickness: the biological, instinctive element, this inner self-assertion of bodily existence, all the impulses and instincts of our inner man. Over against this, we should have a ground in God; we should be men who, however much we accept everything and thereby fulfil ourselves, are indifferent to all this: that is we have already secured everything in the God who is greater than all.

The second dimension is self-assertion over against our personal environment, in regard to the values which are explicitly grasped in intellectual-conceptual forms: honour and dishonour, wealth and poverty. This self-assertion, too, over against the environment should be encompassed and surmounted by indifference.

The final and third factor, described as long life or short, is really the totality of existence as such. We don't belong even to ourselves. Our freedom in regard to ourselves, if it is properly exercised, consists precisely in putting ourselves at the disposal of another, so that we ourselves simply and freely accept ourselves as under control, as not having roots in ourselves, as not looking to ourselves, and in this sense are indifferent to ourselves. We perceive that we gain a footing only at the point where we break away from ourselves; that we are in possession of ourselves only when we get away from ourselves and not otherwise.

47 · Courage to Let the World Be World

Christianity, as the absolute religion of the salvation bestowed by the Creator, Redeemer, and Sanctifier of all realities, cannot refuse to teach that absolutely every reality, and each and every human activity, must be embraced by the human being's salvific activity directed toward his or her single, last end—toward that immediate community with God into which all things, each of course in its own way, are swept and absorbed. On these grounds, there can be no area of reality that is not basically *sub ratione peccati et salutis*, no area of reality not meaningful for salvation. Here the danger arises that one may think that therefore everything that is in the first instance "profane" is nevertheless thereupon directly subject to religious management—that everything can be in some measure diverted, understood in its pecularity, and dealt with from a point of departure in this ultimate purpose. The danger is that one may treat the sanctified as if it were sacralized, or at least susceptible of sacralization. In times and places where the reality constituted by human beings—their environment and the material of their deeds and woes—lay before them simply as static reality, this identification of sanctified and sacralized was far more likely to occur, but it was not practically "dangerous." The given, "natural" reality of existence was by and large withdrawn from human beings' power. As simple, raw fact, it constituted no properly religious problem. What human beings could themselves do with reality —over and above what that reality directly imposed on them (that is, over and above the struggle for existence and a primitive, very slowly and therefore almost unnoticeably changing culture and society)—was the religious itself, in religious interiority and cult. There was no area in which human beings could exercise their creativity in any very clear and forceful way except the religious area. Indeed, after all, up until the beginning of modern times the sciences were largely of religious origin and had a religious purpose. A *theoretical* knowledge of a primordial pluralism in human experience, knowledge, and behavior was had—but this theoretical acknowledgement as yet involved no very practical consequences.

There is another difficulty too—a *historically* conditioned difficulty— when it comes to the courage to let the "secular world" be really secular (without thereby denying that this secular world, precisely as such, presents a peculiar task for Christian salvific activity). From the conversion of Constantine, or the Constantinian "turning-point," onward, and through the Middle Ages, Church and Christianity de facto became accustomed to the notion that everything could be stamped directly Christian and placed directly in the service of Christian salvific activity, or at least gave the impression that it could. Of course, the Church-state reconciliation at the opening of the modern era has theoretically taught us, long since, that there is a real distinction between secular society and the Church. The Church has slowly been brought to the realization that the state is not merely the lengthened arm of the Church, reaching out into an objectively given world—that there is such a thing as a relatively autonomous area of secular culture. But up until very recent times there was simply too little "material," we might say, thanks to which Christianity and Church might have a really clear experience of the worldliness of the secular world. Even into modern times, science was developed and fostered *by the Church*, on religious grounds and for religious purposes. The school system, right up to the university, was conducted by the Church, art was in the service of religion, compensation for social inequalities was a matter of Christian charity—in a word, wherever human beings not only accepted the world as a given but began by fits and starts to create it themselves, it was in large part (at least as far as conscious goal-setting was concerned) a matter of creations of the religious spirit. And clearly, when there actually was anything else over and above this, anything secular, it was available in such narrow, such slowly expanding confines, that it succeeded in practically escaping the cognizance of the Church. Thus it was that up until our own day the Church experienced itself as the force in the world that fostered and formed nearly everything all by itself. And so it is that the Church does not find it as easy as it might appear to have the courage unabashedly to let the world be worldly, to let the world be secular.

But this courage is necessary today. Naturally, this does not mean that Christianity should flee to the abstract interiority of "pure" affect, and thus renounce all institutionalization of the religious. Secular realities and processes must be assimilated into such an institutionalization as well, since it is simply impossible to have it without them. Where it is concretely feasible, then, there can and should be such a thing as specifically Christian art, science with a Christian stamp (in the legitimate sense), Catholic universities as appropriate, genuine "confessional schools," modern communications media in the service of an explicitly religious purpose, Christian "social clubs" (in the *correct* shape and form), and so on. But again, this must not mean that everything profane and secular is to be allowed to be such simply as a grudging concession, something that in itself "should not be."

This courage also implies, in certain circumstances, a readiness on the part of the Church to "withdraw" from secular areas and tasks which up till now it has taken on with entire justification and favorable issue. Such withdrawals will most often seem to be effectuated under the de facto constraint of secular, indeed even anti-Church, forces. But even under this empirical manifestation, the withdrawal will, in its actual nature, often enough be able to be executed by the Church of its own free will. The surrender of the Papal States was a historical process which at bottom, in its ultimate character, was freely willed, since it was a result of the very nature of things. Surely there is no one today who is any longer of the opinion that the pope, in today's circumstances, ought to have such a state and could only countenance its loss "under protest."

This courage, which in certain circumstances will involve these "retreats," is called for on two grounds. First, there is a natural pluralism in human experience, human tasks and potentialities, which makes it wrong for the Christian and the Church to seek to manage all these plural realities from within the Christian faith, by a specifically Christian, perhaps actually ecclesial, manipulation. Explicit and reflective Christianity and the Church—without prejudice to the salvific significance of all dimensions of human reality—are particular realities within the totality of all realities, all of which come under the *direct* conduct only of the creative will and salvific providence of God, and not of any other instance (even ecclesial). The more the world in which the human being lives becomes a world which the human beings themselves fashion out of the pluralism of their needs, potentialities, and strivings (again, a pluralism only inadequately integrated via any reflective principle), the more secular this world will necessarily be, and the clearer will be the boundary lines given to the official Church even with respect to the immediate moral judgment of this world.

And here we have our other grounds for the necessity of this courage. Were the Church to fail of it, it would become permanently unequal to the demands made on it, and its failure to meet the demands of a task it counterfeited as its own would destroy its credibility in the eyes of the secular world itself with respect to its real mission.

The Church, in its mission and task as *official* Church, may unhesitatingly and boldly arouse this courage, since the latter does not imply that the secular world, left secular, is not a field of Christians' self-realization as Christians, is not in itself a sanctified world, is not a genuine opportunity for what is properly Christian in Christian existence. For everything human beings do (even their secular activity) in concrete freedom oriented to God, and open by God's grace upon immediacy to God, is free activity that is properly Christian (when rightly performed), and always and everywhere sanctified activity, activity with a salvific meaning. This is verified even when this concreteness cannot be immediately deduced and procured from its ultimate religious purpose. Still, it can and must be a matter of a decision ultimately signed with a religious note—even though this decision cannot be immediately urged upon individual human beings and profane society by the official Church, but must be discovered by individual Christians themselves in an existential ethic.

But here we touch on a second consideration regarding the Church's attitude toward a permanently secular world. The official Church, which must have the courage to let the permanent secular world be secular, is not simply identical with the Church *simpliciter*; and, correlatively, the secular world, which cannot be sacralized, is not therefore a salvation-less world, but one sanctified and called to sanctity. Accordingly, the Church, in its quality as the community of all sanctified Christians, must acknowledge and assume an obligation that is a specific task of the Church as such vis-à-vis this world—even if this world is the creation of human beings themselves, indeed increasingly so, so that the extent of the secular, the worldly, increases in the world. This active creation of a secular world is a positive Christian task. True, it cannot be taken on and carried out by the official Church as such, since this official Church cannot determine wholly concrete imperatives for the organization of this world, however much it must intervene in defense of ultimate Christian principles to be respected in the accomplishment of this task. But the task is not simply morally and religiously neutral. It signifies a call to the believing conscience of Christians, who (together with all men and women) must carry out this task.

The determination of the concrete imperatives of this task is the affair of an existential logic, a matter of the consciences of individual Christians and the Christian vehicles of instances of historical power (political parties, economic organizations, and so on) that seek to be guided by Christian principles and a concrete Christian inspiration. The official Church, while conceding all freedom and autonomy to the secular world, has the duty to direct attention to the Christian task and Christian responsibility it has. The accomplishment of this task is not simply a matter of blind scientific, technological, and societal causes. It means free decisions, as well, and free decisions always have a relevance for Christian morality.

If Christians make such moral decisions in this sphere of the secular world correctly (however much the correctness of such decisions may remain veiled in the risk and opacity attaching to any decision for an open future), then this too is an instance of the Church's self-realization, even though no hard and fast line can any longer be drawn between what is Church and what is only world in this area. The sanctified world, in its permanent worldliness and secularity, is a commission incumbent upon the Church as the community of all believers.

We cannot sidestep this insight by appealing to the notion that the supernaturally moral decision of Christians has no connection with the "rightness" of that decision from the point of view of the advantages of the profane forces of history operating within the world as such. To be sure, no simple, indissoluble material identity obtains between these twin aspects of human activity. A decision can be taken in good conscience, thereby having a positive salvific value before God, and yet be the wrong decision from the standpoint of the world as such. This discrepancy between subjective morality and objective appropriateness is altogether possible, given the fallibility of the human being. Indeed such a case will arise with special frequency in the area with which we are here dealing. But a Catholic theology of human activity can never approach the human being's subjective affect before God, and the material appropriateness of human behavior, as two fundamentally disparate quantities. That is, the rectitude of the moral decision oriented toward God, and inspired by God, his revelation, and his grace, offers the greater warranty or chance that the material content of such a decision will be appropriate as well.

From this fundamental thesis, we can doubtless conclude that many institutions of an ecclesial kind, whose former purpose was by and large a direct maneuvering of the world and society, need not necessarily be simply dismantled, but only reorganized in view of the new task and purpose. Many such organizations, in the most varied fields, can perform a task of the greatest significance, even where the Church has the courage to let the world be secular. They can perform the service of arming Christians with that Christian faith-perception, that discernment of spirits, and that courage which will be able to see a secular worldly task as Christian even when it cannot be enjoined by the official Church.

In the concrete performance of all these tasks, the Christian will naturally have to work in concert with all other human beings of good will, even in organizations of a profane type that are immediate vehicles for the performance of these tasks. But even this does not preclude Christians' considering *among themselves* what the concrete face of a Christian concept of these secular tasks should be. For, however much such tasks and enterprises are determined, in their broadest scope, by profane laws and considerations of a secularly empirical kind, containing nothing specifically Christian in themselves—nevertheless the totality of such creative conceptions will depend in part on whether or not that totality is conceptualized against the background of a Christian horizon, in obedience to Christian scales of value, and in virtue of God's suggestion and inspiration.

The Church has a third task of a specifically religious kind vis-à-vis this permanently secular world. It must say to this world, with the decisiveness and frankness of its faith, that the secular world is permanently under the law of sin, error, and vanity, that it is basically imperfectible on its own initiative and of its own resources, that it can never become identical, through its own efforts and planning, with the human being's absolute future, with the Kingdom of God—which is ultimately God himself, and bestowed by him under his assumption of temporal history and of human planning. The Church must unmask any and every worldly ideology that posits itself as absolute (and hence only thus becomes ideology in the strictest sense of the word) as human hybris and utopia, which not only obstruct the human being's view of the absolute future they may expect from God but wreak havoc right within secular reality itself.

It is precisely to human beings who have broken through, altogether legitimately, to creative mastery of a future they have themselves sketched and laid out that the message of sin, death, cross, and judgment must be preached. But the Church may not seek to perform this "critical task" merely by offering these human beings, on their way to creating a future themselves, its "critique"—a criticism originating from the outside somehow. It must show them how this critique originates in the concrete experience of the path to the actual secular future itself. It must tell them that the development of what has been planned always entails the growth of what has not been planned and not been foreseen. It must tell them that the sacrifice made for the future of coming generations loses its meaning and dignity, and so also its strength for the long term, when it involves dealing with human beings who are alive in the present only as material and means for the construction of the future, without regard for their own absolute value, rights, and dignity.

The Church must warn the world against utopias which are not the initiation of a real future, but a program for the shaping of a future that is unrealistic, and which therefore, in seeking to become reality, is forced to slowly correct what has been wrongly planned (so that the false ideology may "save face") and at the cost of great sacrifice and losses (as abundantly demonstrable from the history of Communism's economic and cultural policies). This manner of critical "de-ideologizing" of "ideals" and programs in the secular world can have special importance as a task of the Church, and of the people of the Church, in virtue of the fact that, wherever one truly believes with all one's heart in eternal life, in the absolute future—an absolute future for which God stands surety, and not one produced by human beings—here alone is the standpoint from which one may transcend human beings' dilemma between an absolutization of their will for the future, their potential and opportunities, on the one hand, and, on the other, despair at the imperfectibility of their own being by their own means.

Now, to be sure, the possibility of such a critique presupposes a faith that is more than mere solace and pledge from without, comfort and consolation adventitious to an existence designed on purely secular principles. It presupposes a faith that implies an attitude of genuine, primal renunciation and "asceticism" (in a really theological sense), an attitude of the "evangelical counsels," the Sermon on the Mount, and "poverty."

Only such an attitude of genuine faith can ever succeed—a little at a time at least, and time and time again—in overcoming the diabolical and culpable absolutization of secular ideologies. Of course, this protest on the part of Christianity must not only constitute a criticism of the absolutizing passion of *new* ideologies and programs for the future—of ideologies and programs recently arrived on the scene. After all, it is entirely possible for Christianity itself to have become accustomed to the sinful distortion of traditionally overcharged attitudes and institutions of a social and cultural type, attitudes and institutions whose secret passion to be absolutized it has not noticed, or not sufficiently reacted against. Thus it can happen that Christians are sensitive to what is un-Christian and inhumane in programs for the future and ideologies that have recently made their appearance, and yet basically not produce this criticism from the genuine Christian attitude of a faith that overcomes the world, but out of a conservatism sprung from habit and slothful compromise with the un-Christianity of the past.

How many things would have gone differently if Christians had taken as hard and unbending a critical stand against conditions at the beginning of the industrial age as with the utopias of classic Marxism! To be sure, a constant, even-handed inexorability vis-à-vis all ideologies, old and new alike, demands a measure of distance in the human being—the ever historically conditioned human being, for whom such distantiation is really asking too much. But the courage to allow oneself to be "asked too much of" belongs to the essence of Christianity.

The following, too, is to be observed when it comes to this criticism, this critique, as the Church's task vis-à-vis a permanently secular world: If it is to be efficacious, this critique cannot rest content with expressing itself in a theoretical and dialectical manner—always in an "on the one hand, on the other hand" approach, constantly calling for the golden mean. A critique which only did that would remain basically sterile. A critique of a historical decision still in process, one which will help determine this decision, must venture more than a mere dialectical oscillation among a number of principles to be observed simultaneously. It must have the courage to "accentuate," to state what is more urgent here and now. It must have the courage to be "one-sided," and not to wish to do everything all at once. It must entrust itself to the permanently one-sided course of history, in which the very dialectic of principles involves a temporal succession.

It has often been emphasized that the courage for such one-sidedness, which necessarily belongs to any historical decision, cannot, or can only in a very restricted degree, be the affair of the official Church, except where there is direct question of historical decisions on the part of the Church itself regarding its own life, and not decisions on the part of the secular world. But Christians must dare to have the courage for this "one-sidedness" in a positive and negative critique of decisions in the world. Naturally, the decision taken by Christians in the name of Christianity, in a critique thus understood, has no automatic, sure and absolute, guarantee that it will come down on the right side of the issue. Even when Christians seek to allow the logic of an existential, Christian decision, inspiration from on high, and the Christian instinct for the discernment of spirits to have free hand in such a critique, they may—as viewed from within the secular world—take a "shameful" position, close themselves off, by way of "reaction," to a development whose time has actually come, just as they may "progressively" identify, uncritically, with a program for the future that—again, as viewed from within the secular world —leads off in a false direction.

Such *false* criticism of the secular world is always a possibility, in both the "conservative" and the "progressive" directions. Christianity and the Church must, more than they have up until now, recognize such false criticism themselves, and when it has already been published, not attempt to cover it up, but courageously and promptly surrender it, without thinking that by so doing they are compromising the authority of the magisterial and pastoral office of the Church. But the possibility of false criticism, reactionary or progressive, does not exempt the Church and Christians from the duty to have the courage for this criticism—for a criticism which does not withdraw into a pure dialectic of being, but which involves historical decisions that are "one-sided."

Only thus can the Church really remain the *conscience* of the secular world with respect to that world, and be able to unmask, from the vantage point of Christ's Gospel, the sin that ever lurks even in what seem the most secular of events and decisions.

48 · Principles and Prescriptions

In Christian life today we have many *principles*, general norms, and few *prescriptions*, directions and instructions for the concrete situation. Not that there can be too many principles. When they are correct, there can never be too many of them, and it is right to proclaim them. It is also evident that a lot of things would be much improved if the principles proclaimed were followed and, again, that principles are not proved false because their rejection brings misfortune. Yet those who proclaim the principles should surely also ponder why these principles when preached are so little heeded. If they answer, because it is the hour of darkness and of the power of evil, they should also ask themselves why the latter is supposed suddenly to be stronger than previously and why the "ancient truths" and "unchanging principles" are of less avail. If they explain, as is after all of greater practical importance and more correct, that the historical changes of the times with their new conditions have created new problems and difficulties which can only be overcome slowly and patiently, then they must ask themselves whether they know how these new conditions and situations are to be given shape and form so as to provide a tolerable milieu for the realization of those principles, or whether once again they would only have general principles available instead of prescriptions. Viewed in this way it is clear that the more doctrinal proclamation of general principles ought to be accompanied by a statement of prescriptions.

At the same time it must be made plain that these prescriptions themselves cannot consist of principles, as is the case in our preaching and teaching, in the position adopted by the Church and by Christians in regard to concrete questions and decisions in the life of the individual and

the nation. That is why what we say often sounds well-worn and familiar, tedious, facile and almost hollow. In itself it is not. For principles
must be proclaimed. But people are mostly on the look-out for prescriptions and spontaneously take this proclamation to be intended to announce
prescriptions, as indeed it is often wrongly supposed by the speakers
themselves to be doing. People are quite right, really, to have this expectation. For the hearers are supposed to act, that is, to do something concrete,
for that is the only way fundamentals and essentials and eternal truths
can be carried into effect. But what they mostly hear is the ideal instead
of the actual model, the abstract proposition instead of a vividly depicted
actual example. Consequently we give the impression of wanting to
restore the past—and even defend this by urging that the time for the
"movements" of the twenties is now passed. Our pronouncements seem
too cautious, anxiously decanted, measured out. It is all very correct, but
rather sterile. No one clear unmistakable note. Too much golden mean.
The cart is right out in the middle of the road, well away from either
ditch, but it doesn't move on. People are proud of the Catholic synthesis
of principles that are difficult to harmonize and that sometimes seem
almost incompatible. But it is easy to lose sight of the question how this
balanced system of carefully reconciled principles actually looks in fact.
With the best will in the world, not all the actual features of our general
view of things that have to be taken into account can be fully brought out
to the same extent. A decision has to be taken to present it in a quite definite style.

For it is not the case that men with their limitations can decide from
one single principle all that they have to do and carry into effect, however much they may strive to integrate the multiplicity of their nature,
their tasks and principles in ever higher and richer unifying principles.
Inevitably a man has a plurality of principles. To respect them simultaneously is only possible by a decision, and for this, prescriptions are needed.
Yet these are often lacking, or only the old ones are proffered, and they
have already turned into abstract principles or become false, that is, historically ineffectual. Eyes are on the good old days, which of course could
scarcely have given birth to the present if they had been as ideal as all
that. Yet we are moving towards such new and difficult possibilities that
it should stimulate the hard thinkers and strong hearts among Christians,
each in his own domain, to possess not only abstract principles but also
practical prescriptions, not merely a Catholic faith but also a Christian
view of things, if we understand by this not the bare sum-total of correct
principles, particularly of natural law, but an organized body of correct
and historically appropriate practical prescriptions.

Christians in the last few centuries have come to represent the conservative principle, though that is really not something that should be taken for granted. It is not surprising, therefore, that they consider the maxims by which they in fact live as too self-evident to require much detailed discussion, or that they hold up as a reproach to their iconoclastic opponents the abiding principles. For they can demonstrate these with certainty and think, but not with quite as much certainty, that they have thereby defended the old maxims and prescriptions. Christians are on the defensive and that tempts them to defend themselves from their strongest positions. Now it is easier to cast doubt on prescriptions than on principles. Furthermore we have already seen that the Church has not in most cases the task and authority to lay down these prescriptions. Naturally it has to proclaim, for example, the fundamental moral principles of any economic system but not to recommend a particular model for a more effective economic system than the one we have. The official representatives of the Church are aware of this with greater or less degree of clarity. The Church has already had unfortunate experiences with the recommendation or defence of particular prescriptions and maxims, the alliance of Throne and Altar, for example, and has learnt caution, is afraid of saying things that would have to be withdrawn later. So there is a retreat into principles.

But that does not mean that Christians and especially the Christian laity (who are also the Church) are dispensed from the task of having prescriptions and maxims of a kind that are compatible with the Gospel and the Church's teaching and at the same time form a concrete programme of Christian activity. Simply because the Church cannot supply them ready-made and ready for use, it is far from the case that Christians can have a clear conscience even if they have not got such maxims, or that they cannot be morally reproached in this regard by the Church, even though direct ecclesiastical censure can, in most cases, only be directed against actions that contradict principles but not against false prescriptions or the lack of any in the life of the individual or the community. For example, it is only very indirectly or not at all that the Church can dissuade from a mistaken choice of profession or marriage, although this can be much more devastating than a sin, against which the Church does protest.

One might express it fairly accurately by saying that the finding and disseminating of prescriptions is first and last a matter for the laity and for the apostolate that is theirs, the action of Catholics, as distinct from "Catholic Action." Here they do not and cannot simply take their orders from the hierarchy. They should not expect orders of that kind and should not think that the apostolate of the laity only begins at the point where such commands or particular wishes are expressed, in Catholic Action for example. Here they can usually expect no direct mandate from the Church but certainly from their conscience and from God. The distinction between principles and prescriptions could perhaps also help to settle the question of the position and function of the layman in the Church, in the lay apostolate and of the difference between Catholic Action and the activities of Catholics as Catholics. If Christian lay people find and put into effect these appropriate and well-timed prescriptions, the Church (or Christendom) is operative in them, for of course they are also of the Church, yet the Church does not need to commit itself in its authoritative teaching and pastoral office. But it has to ensure, for example, that Christians do not think that they have fulfilled their duties if they are living in peace with the authoritatively proclaimed principles of the Church.

Lay people should be encouraged and educated much more than formerly to discern the will of God even in spheres where the Church cannot tell them what it is in its actual individual detail. They should be made aware that we Christians can have a duty sometimes to unite (even perhaps at the cost of sacrifice and mental self-denial), not only on principles but also on a prescription, a practical proposition, even if this cannot authoritatively be imposed by the Church's magisterium. We should learn that it may be wiser tactics to work out a few prescriptions than always to proclaim all the correct principles all together. That supplies the humility for courage to be healthily "one-sided," for it is easier by the nature of the case then to blame oneself than when one is the representative of principles. We might be more serene, more confident and have more enthusiasm and sense of mission in representing practical prescriptions than we commonly are except when the big speeches are being made. The self-assurance of the followers of Moral Rearmament might to some extent be an example. Practical prescriptions can only flourish in minds and hearts where there is proper freedom of opinion and inquiry, speech and discussion. According to Pius XII, there must be a public opinion in the Church because the lack of it would be harmful to flock and shepherd. One may well think that it is not very lively, though there are gratifying exceptions. The only defence of the inheritance of the past is the conquest of the future. But for that we need, as well as much else that is far more important, practical prescriptions, not only abstract principles.

49 · Criticism in the Church

The first thing that must be said about our subject is that, fundamentally speaking, there can and must be opposition and criticism in the Church, as one of its inner elements. Of course this critical opposition, which is part of belonging to the Church, must immediately be differentiated according to the actual facts which are the subject of criticism in any given case. A critical question about the sense of a defined dogma in the faith of the Church is quite different in kind from opposition to the Church's legal, pastoral or liturgical practices; for the Church itself declares that these things are historically conditioned and can be changed. A basic calling in question of the Church's authority in general and as a whole is something different from a protest against a concrete measure which, for example, a bishop may enforce, appealing thereby to the authority of his office.

But for the moment we will leave all these necessary and indeed highly essential differentiations on one side. They must not be allowed to obscure the basic thesis: the thesis that the Church's self-understanding and its own faith do not merely permit the Catholic to have an oppositional relationship to the Church (at least in the sense we have described), or make this unavoidable. An attitude of this kind is actually required of us.

Even as a Christian, the Christian is a human being first of all. As human being he is unavoidably and rightly a critical being; and the scope of his "criticism" is fundamentally identical with the scope of his existence. It is true that he must always be aware that critical reflection never adequately catches up with the assumptions on which he lives; and that consequently the human person, with a certain quite legitimate naivety and originality, still has the right to live according to principles which he has not adequately reflected about in a critical way. But in spite of that, man—and therefore the Christian too—is a critical being. And this also applies to the faith to which he is totally committed. Absolute commitment in faith can certainly coexist with critical enquiry about that faith in any specific individual, and the two do not have to be mutually exclusive—even though considerable theoretical and practical difficulties are inherent in a coexistence of this kind.

From its own point of view, the Church undoubtedly desires to be a power which is open to critical questioning. Its faith and the basic character which derives from that faith can be grasped only in free assent. And a free assent of this kind is possible only when the actual, specific existence of the assenting person is involved also.

The faith of the Church and the specific existence of the human person therefore exist in a permanent correspondence. On the one hand the Church is invoked by faith and, on the other, that faith is critically questioned by the believer. It is only in this way that the believer can grasp faith existentially—and because of man's historical character this is a continually new task. In the case of the true believer this critical undertaking will be continuously underpinned by an absolute assent of faith. It is borne up by a continuously renewed hope that in the future, too, this critical process will never destroy the ultimate commitment of faith.

Other realities in the Church are even more open to question, because of what they themselves understand themselves to be; for they view the Church itself as historically conditioned, as resting on human decisions, and therefore as alterable. Every member of it is empowered and obliged to help to shape this historical process of the Church, in proportion to his function and the possibilities open to him. In its fundamental nature the Church is a community of faith, faith in Jesus as the crucified and risen Lord, and in the eschatologically abiding historical presence of this faith (of course also in a basically institutional form). Apart from this fundamental character, the Church's constitution is alterable and hence open to criticism. The same applies to its liturgy and sacraments to a large extent. It applies even more to its concrete relationship to the historical, cultural and social situation in which it lives. And it applies also, naturally, to the specific and individual decisions of its office-holders.

In short, from the point of view of the Church's self-understanding, a critical attitude on the part of the Catholic Christian to it is an essential characteristic of its nature. It does not mean any weakening of its character as Church, let alone a calling in question of that character itself. This applies both to the individual and to groups in the Church, who have no need to be empowered "from above" before they can be set up. Of course in all this we must not overlook the fact that criticism cannot be the first and the last thing, either in human life or in the Church; and that criticism, if it is to be criticism of the Church from within, must rest on the basis of an ultimate assent to the Church's message and its self-understanding.

When we enquire in what direction criticism within the Church should be directed, we must remember that criticism does not necessarily have to be of an explicit and formal kind. Nor does it always have to be sustained by groups which have been formally constituted. It can also crop up under quite different names, and diffusely, so to speak.

Criticism can first of all take the form of a demand that the official proclamation of the faith make a more adequate attempt to bridge the gap between our contemporary awareness of things and the concrete way in which faith is proclaimed. This is, therefore, a criticism of theology, and of the proclamation of faith which is dependent on theology. This criticism is, of course, useful only when its demands respect the faith of the Church, its permanent identity and its historical continuity. But the boundary between permanent faith and an obsolete statement of that faith cannot always be drawn immediately and unequivocally. In this sector, too, petrified conservatism is just as possible as fashionable progressivism. This means that criticism and counter-criticism are often long-drawn-out processes which produce a sense of bitterness on both sides. We have to see them through with mutual tolerance, patience and hope; and all parties must clearly acknowledge Christianity's one and abiding faith in God in Jesus Christ.

Legitimate opposition and criticism may also be levelled at the Church's lack of commitment in its task towards "the world"(that is to say, modern society, with all its individual structures and tendencies), or at the insufficiency of that commitment or its wrong orientation. This is fundamentally important but it is often fashionably distorted. Such criticism is justifiable and necessary if the Church is to fulfil its critical function towards the world and society truly and decisively. In this sector no one in the Church—neither authority nor critics—is safe from mistaken attitudes and false decisions which can have unforeseeable historical consequences. Discretionary judgements and decisions must continually be made. The Church cannot be exempted from this task, and is even so continually exposed to the danger of blunders and errors. That explains the necessity, and the difficulty, of all criticism.

These two somewhat arbitrarily chosen examples of the direction opposition and criticism may take, show that the objects of the criticism vary considerably. When we talk about criticism and opposition, we tend to think—perhaps too much as a matter of course—of authorities: priest, bishop, episcopal conferences, the pope. Of course the authorities and office-holders are at the receiving end of opposition and criticism. But we must not overlook the fact that criticism can and must be directed towards other people as well. The Church as a whole, in its different formal and informal groups, can be the recipient of criticism. For it is not as if only the office-holders cherish attitudes and make decisions which are open to criticism. The narrow-minded mentality of individual parishes, the traditionalist theology which is animated by academic historicism rather than by the problems of human existence today, the institutions supported by the laity, which only defend the *status quo*—in short, every kind of false and anachronistic attitude shown by individuals or groups in the Church— are at least just as important targets for opposition and criticism, especially since it is not as if reactionary authorities, with all their limitations, were confronted by an enlightened laity filled with positive aspirations for the future. It happens just as often that the office-holders, together with their outlook and the decisions which emerge from it, merely reflect the mentality and attitudes of a large proportion of the rank and file of the Church. And it is by no means always certain from the outset that the critics are always right. So criticism always necessarily evokes counter-criticism.

What possible forms of criticism can there be within the Church, and what forms ought we to reject? What must be rejected in the first place is the attempt to undermine the Church, and to give it a completely new function. We may leave on one side here whether there have already been attempts of this kind in Church history, if perhaps under a different name. Today, at all events, one can notice here and there (and not only in Western Europe, but also in Latin America, for example) that people do not leave the Church, even though they reject what it understands itself to be and the substance of its faith, as this has been passed down to us; instead they want to remain within it in order to undermine it and reshape it completely. The underlying conviction here is that the Church, with its considerable membership and with its extremely powerful and differentiated institutions, still represents an immense power potential, even in today's secular societies. The idea is that, instead of patiently letting the Church die, in a long-drawn-out process, it should be altered in such a way that both it and its social power potential are placed unequivocally and solely at the service of those secular social aims and purposes which are viewed as being the right ones, with the greatest promise for the future. In other words, the aim is to reshape the previous dynamic of a vertical eschatological hope into an exclusively horizontally directed utopian power for worldly and secular changes in society; and here it makes no difference whether these goals are to be realised in an evolutionary or a revolutionary way.

We do not find these tendencies only—or even primarily—where totalitarian states put the Church (in so far as it is not already dead) at the service of their own political goals, and at most allow her a provisional right to existence in that light, preferring to make a pact with an official Church which inclines to too rash and too shortsighted a compromise, rather than to cooperate with the living and critical forces in the Church. There are tendencies towards undermining and remodelling among ourselves, in the "critical Catholicism" of the West as well. It goes without saying that the true Christian believer will reject these tendencies, and must do so; for Christian faith is faith in God and in an eschatological salvation for all. It is not merely a hope for a future, emancipated humanity which is to be realised in some transcending but untranscendental utopia.

An attempt of this kind is doomed before it starts, in the sense that it has no true chance of becoming an ultimate Christian decision of faith. A Church which, according to this view, would merely be the old-fashioned precursor of a secularised, emancipated society, is too uninteresting. It would be dead historically before it had even been modified along these new lines. And it would only be the executive officer of a secular society which has no need of a Church of this kind at all. People who stay in the Church—really only because of their individual background and up-bringing—and want to remodel it into a secular association for humane purposes, or to make it a buffer against the upholders of an established social power, would be better able to pursue their intentions usefully and effectively outside it. The Church is not a suitable medium for these aims. One can perhaps undermine parties, and try to change their self-under-standing; but the Church is not a suitable object for an undertaking of this kind, even from a worldly point of view.

If we ask about the possible forms of internal criticism and opposition in the Church, then we must not overlook the fact that there can be, and are, informal, non-institutionalised forms of opposition and criticism in the Church as well. These are ultimately perhaps more decisive than crit-icism and opposition, which see themselves as such and therefore institu-tionalise themselves. Ways of thinking and movements which—without being expressly "against" something—develop new living energies direc-ted towards positive ends, can in actual fact, through their persuasive character, exert a highly critical function, because the better and more living thing they are aiming at constitutes a silent but effective criticism of what is merely traditional.

We could give examples from the history of theology and thought, down to most recent times. Ways of thinking and conceptions have almost silent-ly made their way, in a kind of meta-historical process, and have been absorbed into the total consciousness of the Church, without having been preceded by the fierce questionings and controversies which might have been thought appropriate to the significance and profundity of these changes themselves. We may cite the absorption of Greek metaphysics into theology from Origen onwards; or the victory of Aristotelianism in Western theology in the thirteenth century; or we may call to mind the contemporary attitude to universal salvation, compared with Augustinian pessimism. Of course these changes were accompanied by struggles and crises. But compared with the extent and profundity of the process itself, these struggles and crises were trivial.

Informal criticism and opposition of great influence do therefore exist in the Church itself, and not merely in the theological sphere. We find it even more in questions of attitude, in Christian life, in liturgy, in the rela-tionship of believers to the world, and so forth. We can always have the hope that living forces in the Church will bring about changes, even when they do not expressly declare themselves as criticism and opposition.

Of course there can and must be formal criticism in the Church as well. In most cases (though not necessarily and exclusively) it will be directed against the Church authorities, and will call in question alterable structures or specific decisions and actions on the part of those authorities. To have real prospect of success, such criticism will generally be sustained by groups and not by individuals.

The actual, specific form of critical groups of this kind can, of course, vary greatly. There can be groups which exert a considerable critical function, even though their real and primary intention is directed towards positive purposes, and not criticism at all. We may think, for example, of the different religious orders which (at least in their early years) exerted a critical function of this kind. Today we may think of the various charismatic or pentecostal movements, which have become quite widespread in the United States. They do not see themselves as critical groups. All the same, they probably have a not unimportant critical significance for the Church. We may think of groups of worker priests in France, or of similar groups in Spain and Latin America, for whom social criticism plays a greater part. These groups pursue directly positive goals in secular society; but they none the less have a critical task to perform in the Church's particular situation.

It is, further, quite conceivable that critical groups should grow up within ecclesiastical institutions themselves: in parish councils, pastoral councils, diocesan clerical councils, synods, etc. The critical intention of groups of this kind, within a particular institution, will normally play a prominent part. For it is this that gives them their specific function, especially since it must be presupposed that they fundamentally endorse these institutional bodies themselves, with their advisory functions or powers of decision.

Should we (or must we) talk about parties or about groups in this context? It is largely a question of terminology. But it depends on the facts as well. We may associate the term "party" with a political grouping in a parliamentary democracy. In that case we understand by the word "party" a group striving for political power, which aims to fulfil goals which are not shared by all members of the country, or citizens of the state, and which has a permanent organisation. In that case we ought not to talk about parties in the Church. Nor should we aim to have critical groups which incline towards acquiring a monopoly of power, in the way that political parties do.

For various reasons, which do not need to be developed here, parties of this kind are hardly adapted to the nature of the Church, even though we might say that the formation of parties within it is primarily a political question, not a dogmatic one. Organised parties in the Church would lend an institutional, absolute, permanent and fixed form to religious differences. People and groups would remain permanently at enmity with one another. Ecclesiastical parties would be mixed up with political parties and different political systems. The result would be nothing less than the danger of a schism in the real sense. Consequently there were no parties at the Second Vatican Council, however distinct the various trends may have been. In all the decisions that were taken, great weight was laid on achieving a bigger majority than any individual group could produce by itself, even if that group alone was actually in a position to provide a majority as such.

A warning like this against the formation of parties in the Church is not of course intended to recommend or legitimate a state of affairs in which individuals or individual groups have no influence at all on the people who are in positions of power in it. That would really be precisely the same thing as the establishment of a particular party with absolute power, even though it rejected the name as such and wanted to give the impression that it alone was the representative of the whole, true Church.

There is, therefore, no objection to be made if groups are formed within the Church's institutions with distinct ways of thinking and aims. On the contrary, there is much to recommend it. These are party groups in a certain sense, and can provide a greater and more comprehensive flow of information among their members, can offer a better opportunity for intensive discussion, and guarantee a more regular, intelligible solution of conflicts within the institution in question. But there must be no party discipline in these groups, and no "party whips"; that would be contrary to the nature of the Church. They should have ever-open doors, should be self-critical, and should not view their opponents as enemies. Moreover, they should not, out of group fanaticism, reject the compromises which are always necessary, in view of differences of mentality in the Church. They should not be worshippers of a mere formal democracy. They should also be able to leave controversial questions open. And they should prefer to elect persons, not the representatives of a particular "party line." Otherwise groups of this kind could damage the very character of the Church. For it ought to be the very place in which social antagonisms are overcome and absorbed, not multiplied by ecclesiastical antagonisms as well.

Even in the institutional sphere the Church must present itself as the community of faith, love and prayer in spiritual unity, in free consent and concord, and with mutual open-mindedness. The Church confesses Jesus as the One who was victorious in defeat; and one of its fundamental convictions is that the goals we have described cannot be seized by force, or by means of institutions and their power. We can arrive at them only through the bold powerlessness of the Spirit and of hope. Neither should groups within the Church view its authorities arrogantly as mere "adversaries" of the Spirit, whom they reserve for themselves. They should rather try to activate the potential of hope (if we may so describe it) and to draw on that; and today this is often much greater among office-holders than resentful critics of the Church in its existing form believe. The attempt must be made. If the groups we have talked about were expressly or tacitly to be transformed into real, organised parties, then it must be feared that elements of essential importance would simply wither away, namely the living enthusiasm which is so necessary in the Church especially; the creative imagination that reaches out towards an unknown future; and the courage to think or do the unusual.

50 · Asceticism

The "spiritual life" is life with God and toward God. We are leading this life when we forget ourselves for God, when we love him, praise him, thank him. Spiritual life in grace means that we realize the inner divine life in ourselves; it means waiting for eternity in faith, hope, and love, bearing the darkness of human existence; it means not identifying oneself with this world, living according to the prayer contained in the Didache: "Let this world pass away and let the grace of God come."

All that is certainly an unforced gift of the free grace of God: especially with regard to the presuppositions and situations in which God has placed us, and which open up for us the area of our freedom even though our freedom cannot control them; we mean, for example, our time and inclinations, our character, what we have inherited, our fellow men, the social and religious milieu in which we were born, the "other things" given us by God in order that we might find him; and this free gift is also our own performance or realization, that is, the spiritual life that we put on and actualize in ourselves is at the same time the freely given grace of God.

But while praising grace we should not forget that it does not always rush over us in a wave of victory, sweeping aside all obstacles; nor is it a simple and unhindered growth; neither does it develop our spiritual life only to the extent that we suffer all in silence, leaving everything else in the hands of God. Generally speaking, the spiritual life is grace precisely because it must be painstakingly cultivated day by day; it requires constant training and drilling. In short, the spiritual life is also (even though not exclusively or even predominantly) *work, planned exercise,* and *conscious development* of the believing, hoping, and loving life in us according to the laws of nature and grace, and according to the motives of a total dedication to God. This aspect of the spiritual life is what we mean by "asceticism" in the broad sense.

Each one of us should ask himself whether or not he is an ascetic in this sense, or whether, until now, he has remained an amateur Christian, perhaps protected by grace, perhaps kept more or less on the right path by reason of his surroundings and moral code. Perhaps the greatest gifts of grace come to us where we have not sought them; perhaps God gives grace to us even though we do not bother much about it; perhaps he runs after us, pursues us through the events of our life in such a way that much later we can say to God's mercy: God has been able to bring good out of all the stupidities of my life; my laziness and indolence, my reluctance and tepidity, my stubborn attitude have not kept him from remaining by my side and putting up with me day after day. That may very well be! But it does not free us from the obligation of doing something ourselves in an orderly fashion. This "something" may be different in youth and old age, but it must have its place in a man's religious life. (An older person who has reached a certain maturity through his experiences of the grace of God, can allow himself a certain freedom in the systematic development of his spiritual life, that we cannot allow ourselves and which would be very dangerous for us.)

Asceticism in the strict sense is a part of the asceticism spoken of above, but only that part which is specifically Christian. This asceticism is Christian self-abnegation in the true sense—an abnegation which gives us positive values in this life, and not just useful things that are a mere means to the end (*bona utilia*, for example); it also gives up (preserving, of course, the proper relationship and subordination to higher values) personal values (*bona honesta*), such as marriage and the freedom to develop one's personality by disposing of material possessions that make for independence.

The Meaningfulness of Asceticism

Asceticism in this sense, at least basically and in its actual practice, cannot be deduced from the mere natural order. Nor does the natural law even suggest it. Values of intrinsic worth should not be given up in the natural order except under the pressure of circumstances. To give them up in this order would be impossible ontologically and perverse ethically. All resentful disdaining of earthly goods from the point of view of the world—because a natural ethic considers them to be cheap or dangerous or common—is by that very fact objectively false and suspect, from a psychopathological point of view, in its basic motivation. Moreover, it would undermine the true meaning and the genuine realization of Christian self-denial.

From a purely natural standpoint, it could happen that a person, by reason of special circumstances (which themselves contain the necessity of attaining a certain good, and this necessity at the same time excludes the attainment of another good), would actually be hindered from attaining an incompatible good. An example would be to give up different aspects of the present standard of living in order to train one's nature to act in harmony and in order to take the offensive against concupiscence. But this is not the meaning of the asceticism that is specifically Christian. In this regard, a person might pose the question whether or not the choice of the evangelical counsels for most men is really the "better way" to bring order into the drives in the personal whole. It is a simple fact that the evangelical counsels create new dangers. (One would be forced to draw some painful false conclusions if one wished to interpret the "heroic deeds" and the "excesses" that have occurred in the history of Christianity in this way. We cannot explain the radicalism and immensity of the penance found in the lives of the saints by appealing to a motive of self-discipline; nor can it be explained by "pious folly" or "influences of a general, historical, spiritual nature" which really have nothing to do with Christianity.) But if penance is not discipline, then we are forced to object, against every such attempt to establish asceticism, that specifically Christian asceticism (for example, the evangelical counsels) can never be established with this type of an argument. For such discipline, asceticism belongs strictly to this world. And this explanation forgets that Christian asceticism, as an essential part of Christianity itself, must necessarily partake of the scandal of Christianity and its separation from the world. Therefore, it can only be truly understood from an understanding of Christianity itself.

Since asceticism is a virtuous striving for Christian perfection, and since this perfection must be formed by charity, asceticism itself can only adequately be grasped from the standpoint of charity. For this, however, neither the difficulty of the renunciation nor the example of Christ would suffice; it would just avoid the question. For example, a suicidal offering of one's own life would certainly be "hard," but, as a fundamentally immoral act, it could never be a true realization of the love of God. And why did Christ choose poverty, chastity, and obedience as the concrete ways of realizing this love?

There must be an objective inner connection between self-denial and love. This connection consists in the fact that the renunciation of values that, from an earthly point of view, are unrenounceable is the *only possible* representation of love for the eschatological-transcendent God; for the God who is not only the ultimate meaning and guarantee of the world, but also who wished to meet us directly in love as himself. The revelation of such a love, which must always also be a quest for a return of love, is necessarily an intrusion into the isolation that the world would like to preserve; it is a rupture in which the world, even insofar as it is willed and governed by God, is reduced to a thing of only secondary importance—to something provisional, and our existential focal point is placed outside of it as the area of the tangible and the accessible.

Every naturally good act can be elevated by grace and informed by charity so that it is a co-realization of the redeeming divine love. But this does not mean that the transcendence of this love "appears" in the naturally good act. Precisely because it is naturally and morally good does it have a meaning in this world—a justification and an intelligibility in itself. God's transcendent otherness cannot be made manifest in itself in such acts. Therefore, he remains silent above the order of grace and its meaningful direction that surpasses the dimensions of this earth. Our confession of the transcendent God and of the relativity of this world, wrought by his direct gift of self to us, can only "appear" through the sacrifice of this world; this is a manifestation of faith and love that surpasses the world and its goods, even when these are of a personal nature. At the same time, it is nothing but an anticipation of Christian death— practice for it and its affirmation. For in death the totality of man's reality is absolutely put in question by God. There, in the most radical way, man is asked whether he allows himself to be disposed of in the obscure, incalculable beyond and by this "allowing" deny himself; whether he wants to understand the radical sacrifice of all "other things" from the cross of Christ as a true falling into the love of God.

If Christian asceticism in the strict sense is thus a mere anticipation of Christian death, nevertheless the throwing of oneself into the merciful hands of the transcendent God only becomes *visible* in the *freely chosen* anticipation. For death and only death is the complete sacrifice of this world, and thus the most radical possibility of faith, hope, and love. But it is also a "must" that is imposed on us by God. Our freedom can accept it in sin or redemption without affecting its outward appearance, that is, without removing its "obscurity." Asceticism, therefore, as the free sacrifice of values that should not be given up from an earthly point of view, is the only way in which our confession of the eschatological-transcendent God can "appear" in a palpable way.

The Necessity of Asceticism

That we actually make the renunciation of values that should not be given up from an earthly point of view an expression of our love for God, and in this way may and indeed must anticipate our death, can only be explained ultimately by a positive call of God (either of a general or a private nature). Supernatural love could also be realized in naturally hidden and so unapparent morally good acts (as redeeming love); and it could also be realized in the silent, patient bearing of suffering and death (as transcendent love). (Certainly, asceticism would be at least meaningful, if not absolutely necessary, as a "preparation" for such suffering, so that then death—as in the case of Christ—can become the absolute culmination of our freedom precisely in absolute weakness.)

But the clear, positive will of God in this matter is manifested in the structure of the Church. She is the primordial-sacramental tangibility of the eschatological presence of the salvation of God in the world. Accordingly, God wills that she make the eschatological transcendence of the love that constitutes her inner nature palpably apparent. This occurs sacramentally especially in baptism and the Eucharist, where a man partakes of the death of Christ and actually announces it until his reappearance; it occurs existentially in specifically Christian renunciation. Christian asceticism, therefore, is an unsurrenderable part of the Church's essence. As a life lived according to the evangelical counsels, it is not only the normal, persisting, and existence-determining norm for individuals, but it is required at all times in one form or another from all members of the Church.

Because the Church is not an ultimate guarantee that the world will make magnificent progress, because she is rather one that puts her hope in that which is yet to come, because she is the community of those men who have the courage based on faith, hope, and love to look for that which really counts in that which is yet to come, who do not try to construct the kingdom of God in this world, but wait for it as a gift of God sent into this world (a gift that will signify the eschatological elevation and transformation of this aeon), who, moreover, must visibly live their faith, hope, and love before the whole world and so become witnesses—for these reasons, there must be a self-denying, specifically Christian asceticism in the life of each and every one of us. Each one of us has many things to give up that would not be sinful to keep, that could be meaningful, beautiful, and a positive enriching of his human existence, because—especially if he is a priest—he must represent the Church, because he must live as an example for the world in a way that shows that he truly believes in eternal life, and that he does not belong to the children of this world who just happen "also" to believe in some kind of a future life.

Take a good look at the modern pagans that make up the greater part of the so-called Christian nations! In their eyes, we are at best men with a certain world view that we are more or less convinced of; for, as they say, it is our calling and we preach because we get paid for it. How can we convince the men of today that we really believe, that the Gospel is the center of our lives, that it is not just a front, unless an honest enquirer sees that we truly give up things because of our faith—things which would be utterly nonsensical to give up if we did not actually believe? We should not imagine that we can fool anyone in this matter. We are carefully scrutinized. A full measure of asceticism will be required to win the trust of the modern man.

51 · The New Asceticism

Among many other aspects of the Christian living of tomorrow which we might also take into consideration, and which are certainly also necessary, a third one has still to be mentioned: the fact that there must be a radical change in the forms of asceticism that are practised. In earlier times certain limits were imposed upon man in his activities to a large extent by the sheer force of external circumstances, by the situation in which he lived. His faults swiftly brought their own retribution and exacted their own revenge. The majority of men at least led lives that were brief and hedged about with dangers, and in which there was little or no opportunity for luxury, caprice, free time, travel, enjoyment etc. Christian asceticism, therefore, consisted in the patient acceptance of the poverty and toil in one's life which this implied, or in additional ascetical practices which were to some extent imposed from without as, e.g., in monasticism, but far less in a positive summons to a form of asceticism which was the outcome of life itself and of the actual daily circumstances in which it was lived. Under these circumstances asceticism—if it was undertaken over and above such hardships as have been mentioned—acquired the "image" of something extraordinary and heroic. In this way Christian asceticism consisted in passive endurance or else supplementary, extraordinary measures. Today man, who to a large extent has gained control over nature by his technical achievements in the sphere of medicine and all other fields of technical mastery, has to an ever-increasing extent the ability to play the part which perhaps, in virtue of his true nature, he should play. He can live without restraint and still avoid incurring thereby any of those disadvantages which used to ensue as a natural consequence upon such a course. Sexual excesses are no longer "punished" by children or by disease. The misuse of power no longer brings about its own downfall so swiftly as formerly, when a king who was immoderate in the exercise of his authority quickly incurred a tyrant's death at the hands of some assassin. The idle are no longer brought to heel under the stimulus of hunger. Medicine today rather helps than restrains the quest for enjoyment. Moderation is no longer imposed from without. Man must practise it of his own free will. And thus a new way of practising Christian asceticism is opened up, one which, precisely because it proceeds "prudently" is not so manifestly heroic or spectacular as the asceticism of former times, which took more active forms. The ascetical practices of former days had the character of that which is extra and out of the ordinary. But today ascetical practices have rather the character of freely fulfilling one's responsibilities in the performance of one's duty. Yet this is almost more difficult than the former kind precisely because it must necessarily appear in the guise of that which is manifestly the "prudent" course.

This "asceticism in the consumer society" (which, however, applies to all areas of life) is difficult. Basically, and as applied to the generality of men (we are not thinking here of those individuals in whom a certain weakness of the acquisitive instincts goes some way towards lightening the burden of making their own decisions and renders them immune to the claims of an acquisitive society with its suggestions of new needs), it will be achieved only by one who is *open to God*, and therefore can undertake in all sincerity a renunciation, which seems to be unattainable to the man who is weighed down by anxiety in the face of death. Certainly God and the state of being open to God are far from rendering one psychologically immune to pain, ideas which can be exploited in order to facilitate the asceticism so necessary in a consumer society. To think of them and to attempt to apply them in this sense would be *ipso facto* to negate them. Only where *God* is *loved* for his own sake does he also become a source of blessing. Only where an individual is *open* to the absolute future of God will he also overcome the tendency to immoderate greed, to fill his life with the greatest possible enjoyment (taking this to include power also), and so ultimately to destroy himself by sheer excess. And conversely: when man observes that moderation which is appropriate to his nature *genuinely without any thought of reward* then he is already in a mysterious sense giving his assent to God and to his absolute future even when he does not realise this.

Such is the new asceticism appropriate to the practice of Christian living in the future. It can be the new way of putting into practice that more fundamental mystery of Christian asceticism which consists in sharing in the death of Christ on the Cross, and which is offered to us because today too life still continues mysteriously to be the Passion. Today, in contrast to earlier times, this self-imposed moderation is to a large extent no longer capable of being crystallised into a general institution. But for all that it must not remain at the level of theory and abstract commandment. It must assume a form in which it can be *effective in the concrete and can provide a practical pattern of living* and, from being morality in the abstract, must precisely become "morals" in the concrete, "ethics" and good habit. This again is a major task for those secular institutes whose members genuinely do continue to live in the world: to provide examples which show how even in the contemporary setting it is possible to live a life that is moderate, self-disciplined and pure, in which one rises above that state of doubt and anxiety about death at the bottom of one's heart which makes one acquisitive and so, in the last analysis, unready also to take selflessly upon one's self genuine responsibility for the good of others in a practical and down-to-earth way, and in doing this silently and cheerfully to endure renunciations. In so acting the members of such secular institutes must be genuine, uncompromising, gentle and at the same time strict with themselves.

H·O·P·E

52 · Hope

Theology speaks of the theological *virtue* of hope. Paul lists hope with faith and love as the three basic perfections of Christian existence which "abide," which "last"—thus, which now and to all eternity constitute what makes a Christian (1 Cor. 13:13). We shall not consider here how these three theological virtues are interrelated—nor how they can be meaningfully distinguished from one another, so that for Paul, love, in contradistinction to the other two, can be the highest—nor how these three theological virtues nonetheless constitute a unity, so that, in the concrete actualization of Christian existence, they condition one another to a greater degree, and are more intimately interconnected than their scholastic distinction would seem at first to provide for. Nor shall we here address the question—in and of itself an important one—whether, despite the traditional interpretation of 1 Corinthians 13:13, *elpis* itself, hope, may also belong to the eschatologically abiding fundamental perfections of eternal life, the perfections still active in the consummation and fulfillment of Christian existence. Finally, neither is it possible in such a short space to present the biblical theology of hope. We shall have to restrict ourselves to a few propositions familiar to current scholastic theology. They seem to me to be important, indeed rather provocative. Even though at first blush they may seem to be speaking of something infinitely removed from our everyday life, we trust it will appear that very practical consequences can be drawn from them.

The virtue of hope is a *divine* virtue (as distinguished from the so-called moral virtues, which bear upon finite moral values). Together with faith and love, it determines our direct relationship to God himself. So speaks Catholic theology. What does this mean?

Here we presuppose that God as Creator—God as distinct from the world—has posited the world, and ourselves, in all their reality. All these created, finite realities, among them ourselves, stand in a relationship to their creative Ground, God. But when, in the realm accessible to our natural cognitive faculty, we experience and think anything about our relationship to God, what we experience and think is always mediated by a finite reality. God himself is only given as the Ground—abiding in himself and mediating himself via finite realities —of what we ourselves are and of what we grasp, including what we can attain of our fulfillment. God himself abides afar, in truth, and in making himself known always simultaneously erects a barrier in the very reality that declares him, a barrier that divides us from him. An infinite distance forms, keeping God and us apart.

But now Christian revelation proclaims something unheard of—indeed something unthinkable for the finite creature on its own initiative. It proclaims that the human being can reach out over this chasm, this infinite distance, and grasp for God. Hope demands God himself. Hope will have no gift of God—howsoever wondrous it be, for it will still be finite— through which God announces and represents himself. It must have God himself. God is not to invent something, in his wondrous creative power, that will make us happy, perhaps indeed blessed. He must give himself. This is the outrageous claim of the divine virtue of hope. It demands the apparently unthinkable—that God himself, through his very own reality, and not through something created and distinct from himself, becomes our destination and determination. It makes a demand that, were it not offered us by God himself, would have to be rejected, by a sober, humble metaphysics of the distinction between the infinite God and the finite creature, as blasphemous pantheism or panentheism. After all, our metaphysics would tell us, the finite cannot assume the infinite as infinite and have it become its inmost determination.

But this is just what Christian revelation says. It says that God bestows himself on the human being in the strictest sense of the word. It says that, in what theology calls "uncreated grace," God, through himself, is the human being's inmost determination and fulfillment, and that he brings this to consummation in eternity in the immediate vision of the divine reality. It is God himself that hope grasps for when it is really a theological, divine hope. Here is radical, unconditional demand, here is an optimism almost absurd in its enticement. In divine hope, one is satisfied with nothing less than the incomprehensible infinity of God himself. This hope knows that God is, and always will be, incomprehensible—that he is the eternal light, which for earthly standards of creaturely intellection is ever like an all-annihilating darkness. But it is just this infinity of God, that so inexorably appears to burst all finitude asunder, that hope reaches out for. Hope casts itself into the unquenchable fire of the eternal Godhead, convinced that it will not be consumed and incinerated there. It casts itself into the bottomless chasm of ineffable Mystery, convinced that there it will find the solitary, unquaking Ground of its own existence, for everlasting. Hope dares to reach out for God himself. It knows, of course, that a like pretension would be simply absurd were it not already borne up and supported by what it reaches for—if God himself did not reach out along with ourselves, as we long for him from the inmost core of our existence; if he did not, as theology drily puts it, warrant, enable, and empower us, with his grace, to hope for himself. Hope hopes God, through God, in God.

But this hope, which thus appears to venture the incomprehensible and the impossible—since it hopes for God himself—is our permanent overtaxing, our call beyond our strength. It would be so nice just to stay the way we are! We would be only too happy and fulfilled through what we can comprehend, measure, and accomplish by ourselves, by what suits our finitude, by an intelligible tally on the account books of our life. We want to make progress by regular increments over what we already have. We wish for a felicity consisting in an increase of the ease we already enjoy. We call for leisure time that lasts a bit longer than it does already, pleasure a little more intense than our pleasures are now. Let our successes and discoveries be a bit greater than they already are, and we shall rest content! The bourgeois people of the West and the East (who, when all is said and done, are not as different as they try to seem) long for an earthly paradise that, when one examines it more closely, is really not very different from the living space in which we have so laboriously ensconced ourselves already.

Then along comes the revelation of God, the living, free, and incomprehensible God, and demands of us that, instead of this beautiful, but really so banal, felicity for which we stubbornly hope and strive again and again despite all our disappointments, we place our hope in the infinite God. God and nothing else, really. God the nameless and incomprehensible. Are we respectfully to "let him be," on the grounds that the inscrutable should really be "left alone, and better not talk about it"? No, precisely this incomprehensible, incalculable God—and when all is said and done, really only he—is what we are to seek for, hope for, and make the solitary determining theme and subject of our existence. This divine hope by no means begins as anything like solace or consolation. It bears not the slightest resemblance to an analgesic, brewed of pious pap, that would assuage the misery of those who have to work like slaves, those whom life and our society have cheated. Instead, it is an enormous, outsized challenge. It forbids us to invent our own happiness and struggle for a paradise we like. It jars us out of all our life's evidences, plausibilities, and comfortable securities, and shoves us into the infinite darkness of God, which we can really only behold with God's own eyes.

The Christian principle of hope is by no means soothing and comforting in the first instance. Christian hope bestows beatitude only when we have abandoned ourselves to God in earnest, abandoned ourselves thanks to a strength that is no longer our own, when we have capitulated to God's incomprehensibility and his incomprehensible freedom, when ultimately (and bland religious jargon calls this the "love of God for his own sake") we no longer ask what God is for us as a stopgap and safety net, but have really accepted him, unconditionally and mutely, in the silence of our appeal. Then, and only then, does hope reach for God himself. Then, to be sure, hope *is* liberating and beatifying. Then does God's darkness become everlasting light. Then does all that is individual and finite set, and God himself breaks like day. Then does all earthly reality go down to death, and this hope itself rise up once more to eternal validation—incomprehensible though be the manner of its rising for us here—filled with the infinitude of God himself. It is of this hope against hope, the one hope without limits or conditions, the hope that hopes God through God, of which Christian faith speaks when its self-understanding is correct. It proclaims no human paradise, not even one for everlasting (that is, a paradise, once more, different from God), but God himself.

Before such a stupendous proclamation, as promise and as demand, we could well ask ourselves how, in the banal wretchedness of our ordinary lives, it could possibly come true. And then again: how can such hope have a meaning for this ordinary life, here on this earth, where, after all, it ravishes the human being away into the incomprehensibility of God?

As to the first question, one could well imagine that there would be few persons who could succeed with this act of hope, this eruption into God's incomprehensibility. One could easily think that only a few saints, a few hushed gurus in their great enlightenment, could manage to have such a theological hope—and that there could be no question of it for us poor, average men and women, who must content ourselves with life's daily necessities, and with such delights as we may be able to cull like little flowers along the pathway of our journey through this earthly wilderness. One could think that the evolution of the universe, in the dizzying succession of self-eclipses of individual realities, could indeed, in its sublimest peaking in spirit and freedom, reach right up to God, at least in principle—but that this storm of evolution in God's direction must still leave most individual realities, even the spiritual ones, the personal ones, behind, back in the unsubstantial seeming of the great dinosaurs, which stuck in mid-course and are gone. One could take an elitist approach here and view the greater part of human history itself as the humus out of which a precious few beings might actually reach the last end of all cosmic and spiritual evolution: God.

But Christianity radically rejects this arrogance of an elitist skepticism.

Whenever and wherever human beings are awakened to their humanity, Christianity says, there they attain the incomprehensible unconditionality of God himself—unless indeed they shut themselves off from this gift that is God himself. We must ever reckon with this monstrous, frightful possibility of eternal loss, this hopelessness become ultimacy in freedom. We may not make any theoretically absolute assertion as to a certain, definitive salvation for every human being. Still, we do have the right, and (*pace* Thomas Aquinas) the duty, in spite of all the horrors of human history, to hope that all human beings do indeed *hope* in such wise that they actually will attain to God himself.

This is Christianity's anti-elitism. In this respect, despite all the authoritarian constraint practiced in its history, Christianity is at bottom more democratic than any other *Weltanschauung* in history. It promises everyone eternal life, and God himself, through whom everyone has everything. But this does not answer the question how the average person, to whom such dignity is ascribed, can have access to the hope that seizes God himself. To answer this question, we must first say, quite abstractly, that this infinite hope, in which the human being bursts forth from the prison of his and her finitude, is always kindled at a concrete task of this earth. This heavenly hope is always mediated by something earthly-objective. This is how there can be a mystique of hope in the midst of the banal everyday. In that daily round, and not just in the mystical solitude of higher contemplation and ecstatic transport, occur the experiences of the Spirit, and thus the acts of ultimate hope.

These acts of ultimate hope often do not appear on the surface. We have spoken of this above, under "Experiencing the Spirit" (§ 15), for we experience in them what we Christians call the Holy Spirit of God. An experience is undergone here which is inescapable even when it is rejected. It is an experience proffered to our freedom along with a question: Do we wish to accept it, or do we choose instead to barricade ourselves up against it in a hell of freedom to which we damn ourselves? All this transpires in the routine, everyday life of even the most ordinary person. But these are all the deeds of hope, either in seed or in fulfillment. There is an everyday mysticism of hope. Divine hope is no elitist affair. It is made possible by God even for us apparently only ordinary men and women. And that is why God can demand it of us.

But the question still remains whether such divine hope, soaring as it does above all earthly things even when it occurs in life's daily round, can itself have any very rich meaning for that daily round. Before we address this question directly, we must entertain one preliminary consideration. Whether we call it hope or not, there is, in human life, such a thing as planning for an individual and collective future, a planning that is bound up with an uncertainty of success, with a less than fully manageable risk. And none the less this planning proceeds with confidence that it *will* be successful—with a greater or lesser confidence that can be called hope. This activity—which is demanded of human beings, since they cannot live by absolute, risk-free dealings alone—can, as "hazardous" behavior, meet with success or failure. It can emerge in experience of success or experience of disappointment. The will to succeed and the experience of failure are the human being's lot. Human beings must reckon with both. The risk of a given undertaking can be greater or less, and thus its success or failure will be proportionately great or small.

Now, however, when the nature of theological hope is correctly understood—and if we do not forget that this divine hope, however much it might intend God and nothing else, is mediated by the events of every day, that it must be actualized across the whole gamut of the realities of one's life, and is not just an individual, special cultic achievement of the human being—then it can be understood how not only life's dauntless deed, accomplished with a view to earthly happiness, but even the coping with the disappointment of failure can be at once legitimated and supported by this divine hope. The concrete deed in which human beings defend, fulfill, and develop their earthly life, in all of its dimensions, can be the concrete mediation of their divine hope, in such wise that they would betray their divine hope if they repudiated their earthly task. If they were to renounce a task of their private or political life because it involved risk, placed them in danger, and might end in failure—then secretly, in this cowardly abstention that will venture no risk, they would be confessing that they are unconvinced that the earthly deed that lies in ruins can and must be the realization of a hope that actually attains God. For the Christian, thanks to his or her absolute hope, there can be no risk, in a deed that is not morally abominable, that ends in definitive failure and definitive disappointment. Thus those who, in fear and secret skepticism, renounce a deed demanded of them in their private or public life, surrender divine hope as well. They reckon with the possibility of an ultimate disappointment. They seek to avoid that disappointment or at least to postpone it. They will not venture themselves and their lives, for they secretly admit the possibility of a definitive and irrevocable cataclysm of their existence. They belong to the number of those who Paul says "have no hope." One who hopes in God can venture all, since he or she can never lose God. Of course, one who risks himself or herself for other people may have God's hope even without being expressly aware of having it.

Divine hope is the strength and legitimation of the earthly deed the human being does at his or her own risk and yet in all confidence. But this divine hope endures even where no earthly calculus can soberly expect success. It endures in failure and disappointment. It is the cheap fashion today to seek to spoil the consolation people have in their hope in God in the face of the shipwreck of their earthly strivings by dubbing it an "opium of the people." Surely one should not seek to proclaim the consolation of eternity that is given in divine hope (as has certainly often happened in the Church) where an earthly effort is imposed on someone with little certainty of even a modicum of success. But there are misery, failure, and death that cannot but be the lot of the individual. When this is what one cannot abide, one can of course cheaply advertise it that the consolation of eternity and hope in God is an opium in any situation of disaster for which there is no earthly antidote. But those who have themselves been struck down with the catastrophes that offer no earthly escape can only, after all, either despair or console themselves with the thought that those who come after them, and will die after them, will have things a little easier—or open themselves to the consolation that hope in God himself gives, even where there is disaster and death. Divine hope, then, is itself both the strength to do a deed regardless of risk and danger, and consoling redemption when failure and disappointment strike or are possibilities anticipated with open eyes. Victory and defeat, life and death, are embraced, redeemed, and divinized in this single hope.

53 · Hope as the Medium of the Theological Virtues

The triad of theological virtues—faith, hope and love—need not be thought of as three virtues together, unified by a strict principle of distinction which is common to them all in the same sense and at the same level, so that they have precisely the *same* relationship *among themselves*. We do not necessarily need to argue against the correctness of regarding these three virtues as constituting a triad. We do not need to adopt this approach even though "hope" is regarded as the midterm and the common factor between the two other virtues. Admittedly in saying this we are assuming that it is not regarded merely as a *transient* modality of the two other virtues and of the "powers" corresponding to these, but rather as that property which endures in them, and which draws both equally together into one. We must not regard hope merely as standing "between" the two other virtues. Rather we must think of it as constituting the original and unifying medium between them. If we can show this then we are justified in speaking of a triad, but at the same time we do not have to conclude from its existence that hope must be related to faith and love in precisely the same way as these two are related to each other. Nor is it, ultimately speaking, of decisive importance whether the basic modality of the relationship to God as understood here is that which is called "hope" in the common parlance of everyday, or whether rather there is something which lies concealed behind this term, but which, nevertheless, this term is used to point to because there is no better one for it.

It is common practice in scholastic theology to replace the vision of this quality of hope which is so obscurely pointed to by the conceptual model according to which hope is dissolved by "possession," by the "attainment of the goal." This conceptual model is drawn from everyday experience, and from the experience of "hope" at the profane level. Initially, for instance, we "hope" for a position in life which we have not yet attained to. But once this has been achieved, once we "have" it, then we no longer need to "hope," but at most hope to retain that which we have achieved, though in that case we experience or interpret this attitude as something quite different from "hope." But what is to be said of precisely *that* basic act in which (it is called theological hope) we reach out towards God? Can we interpret this basic act too as a mere provisional attitude which will be dissolved once we have attained to that state of "possession" which itself in turn is constituted by "vision" and unifying "love"? In that case hope will be abolished as something that belongs to the past, because now there is nothing more that has to be "hoped for," but rather everything is already in our possession, and we do not even have to fear that we may lose what has been attained to, in other words we do not even have to hope that this will continue permanently. But is this line of thought correct?

In fact, however, it is questionable in the extreme—in other words basically inadequate—to take as our guide the conceptual model of "possession" in order to understand the definitive consummation of man's life, and on this basis to conceive of hope as that which is merely provisional. This conceptual model in fact distorts the special quality of man's final consummation as consisting in vision and love, and thereby too that basic modality belonging to this final consummation which is both expressed and concealed at the same time in the term "hope." This basic modality only constitutes the authentic nature of *that* theological hope in so far as it is present in the life of the pilgrim here below—and here admittedly it has a certain provisional quality. The act of attaining to God as truth in the "vision" of God in fact allows for the transcendence of this God as the incomprehensible. The event in which this takes place, inasmuch as it is made possible by the divine self-bestowal, is not the act in which the absolute mystery which is God is finally overcome and solved, but rather the act in which this truly unfathomable mystery in all its finality and its overpowering acuteness is no longer able to be suppressed, but must be sustained and endured as it is in itself without any possibility of escape into that which can be comprehended and so controlled and subordinated to the subject and his own nature as it exists prior to any elevation by grace. The act of attaining to love as love is the response to, and acceptance of, a love which, totally independent of any element in ourselves, is rather freedom in its most radically incalculable form. The intelligibility of this love is not to be found in any prior quality in ourselves which make us "worthy to be loved" (even though the love itself does confer this). On the contrary, it always depends totally and eternally on this freedom of God which is based on nothing else than itself alone. In this radical sense the love we are speaking of is, and remains eternally, "grace." The "possession" of God—if in spite of what has been said we may still use this term— is that radical transcendence of self and surrender of self which is entailed in the act of reaching out for truth into the unfathomable mystery, and it is also the radical self-surrender and self-transcendence of that love which cannot charm love from the beloved through any act of self-surrender on its part, but lives totally by the love of that which is beloved as based on nothing else than itself. It is pure act of reception and *as such* sustains the mutual interplay or *commercium* of the love involved, but is not itself upheld by this *commercium*.

These qualities inherent in the response to and acceptance of God as truth and as love have an interior unity and a common source in the one radical attitude which draws us "out of ourselves" into that which is utterly beyond our control. This "letting of one's self go" is certainly the essence of man, rightly understood *in the concrete* as already bearing "grace" within itself. Once he has discovered this nature of his and freely assented to it, man has attained to freedom in the true sense, which consists in realising himself and fulfilling the meaning of his life. And precisely this fulfilment of his nature is that "outwards from the self" attitude of the finite subject reaching out into the incomprehensibility and incircumscribability of God as truth and as love. In the word "hope" this one unifying "outwards from the self" attitude into God as the absolutely uncontrollable finds expression. Hope, therefore, represents this unifying medium between faith or vision and love (still on the way and also, even when it has achieved its "goal"). Hence "hope" does not, in this most ultimate sense, express a modality of faith and love so long as these are at the provisional stage. On the contrary, it is a process of constantly eliminating the provisional in order to make room for the radical and pure uncontrollability of God. It is the continuous process of destroying that which appears, in order that the absolute and ultimate truth may be the intelligible as comprehended, and love may be that which is brought about by our love. We would like to be those who set up God for ourselves through that which we ourselves do, acting (morally) as free and intelligent beings, and thereby having him as ours to dispose of as we will. But hope is the name of an attitude in which we dare to commit ourselves to that which is radically beyond all human control in both of man's basic dimensions, that, therefore, which is attained to precisely at that point at which the controllable is definitively transcended, i.e., in the ultimate consummation of eternal life. Taken in this sense hope is that which "endures." And this means that it also shares in this character of "enduring" which is involved in the definitive finality of the relationship to absolute truth. Hence Paul can say that faith itself "endures," even when vision has been attained to. A further point also becomes clear in the light of this, namely that the love of eternity can only rightly be understood if it is thought of as carrying the quality of "hope," so that we can just as truly speak of a *fides* and *caritas spe formata* as of a *fides* and *spes caritate formata*. Hope implies the one basic character which is the common factor in the mutual interplay of truth and love: the enduring attitude of "outwards from self" into the uncontrollability of God. Conversely we can say: where hope is achieved as the radical self-submission to the absolute uncontrollable, there alone do we truly understand what, or still better *who* God is. He is that which of its very existence empowers us to make this radical self-commitment to the absolute uncontrollable in the act of knowledge and love. One might almost say our radical self-commitment to the "absurdity" of truth and love, because both derive their true essence—quite otherwise to what we would have thought at first sight—from the incomprehensibility and uncontrollability of truth and love in themselves.

This means that radically speaking hope is not the modality of the historical process by which we pass through time to that state which is definitive and eternal, but rather the basic modality of the very *attitude to the eternal* which precisely as such sets the true advance towards eternity "in train." In the light of this both presumption *and* despair are, at basis, the refusal of the subject to allow himself to be grasped by the uncontrollability and to be drawn out of himself by it. Clearly all that has been said with regard to the ultimate nature of hope does not imply any denial of the fact that it itself, in the *status viatoris*, it bears certain properties which can no longer be ascribed to it in the eternal life in which it achieves its consummation. But these properties—the striving for the finite *within* that process in which the encounter with the provisional is still taking place—conceal more than they unveil the innermost essence of hope. For this encounter, even when we rise above it in our hope for the future, always gives rise to the impression that that which is definitive and final too will one day be possessed in the same way as now we comprehend, dominate and so dispose of the provisional and temporary benefits available to us.

54 · The Social Dimension of Hope

Certainly it is not possible to include a full treatment of all that contemporary theology and existential ontology has to say with regard to the cosmic and social dimensions of hope, with regard to hope as exercised by the people of God on pilgrimage as such and in the course of its journey, with regard to the exodus which this people is constantly undertaking afresh, quitting all situations which have become "frozen" and static in all dimensions of human existence.

Let us concentrate simply upon a single small passage in the Dogmatic Constitution on the Church, *Lumen gentium* (chap. 4, no. 35) which has for the most part gone unnoticed. There it is stated with regard to the laity that they should not conceal their eschatological hope in the innermost depths of their hearts (*in interioritate animi*), but should rather give it concrete expression (*exprimant*) in the complexities and in the framework (*per structuras*) of secular life (*vitae saecularis*). This admonition is found in the context of the prophetic function of the laity in the Church and in the world. Surely it would be to misunderstand it if we sought to interpret it merely as a moralising conclusion of a secondary kind, following from the nature of that hope which the "sons" of *the* "promise" (*ibid.*) could ultimately speaking have lived by even without "informing" the secular framework of the world with their hope in this way. Contrary to this view, the admonition contains a statement about an element which is essential to hope itself. The process by which this becomes an achieved reality involves a permanent transformation of the framework of secular life. Abstracting for the moment from the fact that "revolution" is an extremely indeterminate and ambiguous concept, we might go so far as to say that the significance of this admonition is that Christian hope is at basis a continually revolutionary attitude on the part of Christians in the world. If we interpret the significance of Christianity aright, and if Christians themselves have a right understanding of the real significance of their own commitment, then the position is the diametrical opposite of what is generally thought both within and without the Christian body. The hope that is directed towards the absolute future of God, towards that eschatological salvation which is God himself as absolute, is not entertained in order to justify an attitude of conservatism which, from motives of anxiety, prefers a certain present to an unknown future and so petrifies everything. It is not the "opium of the people" which soothes them in their present circumstances even though these are painful. Rather it is that which commands them, and at the same time empowers them, to have trust enough constantly to undertake anew an exodus out of the present into the future (even within the dimension of this world).

In reality man as physical and as belonging to the historical dimension actually fulfills the ultimately transcendental structures of his own nature not in the abstract "interiority" of a mere attitude of mind, but in intercourse with the world, the world made up of his own environment and of his fellow men. "Practice" in the real sense, and as opposed to, and radically different from, theory, is, moreover, not confined solely to the mere execution of what has been planned and so is merely theoretical, but rather consists of an opening of the sphere of action in general and an attitude in which we dare to enter upon that which has not been planned, so that it is only in practice itself that any genuine possibility is given of what we have been bold enough to commit ourselves to. Planning may be necessary and justified in the manipulation of our environment (by technical measures), of the society we live in (by social measures), and of man himself. But all this does not derogate from the element of the unplanned which presses in upon us, and does not reduce it to a mere remnant of the contents of our lives which we have "not yet" worked out. On the contrary such planning increases the element of that which is unplanned and has the effect of causing it to stand out still more sharply as the outcome of practice itself. Man himself, in the very process of breaking down the factor of the incalculable already present *beforehand* in his life, actually builds up those incalculable factors which are produced by *himself*.

Now the effect of these two elements is that in the very act of venturing upon the future which is unforeseen and incalculable in "this worldly terms" in his practical life as understood here, man realises, and necessarily must realise, his eschatological hope as a commitment "outwards from self" to that which is incalculable and uncontrollable in an absolute sense. The Christian must, therefore, impress the form of his hope upon the framework of the world he lives in. Of course this does not mean for one moment that certain specific and firm structures of the secular world he lives in could ever be such that they could constitute the enduring objective realisation of his eschatological hope (in the sense of being established as this once and for all). On the contrary, every structure of secular life, whether present *or still to come* in the future, is called in question by hope as that in which we grasp at the incalculable and uncontrollable, and in this process of being called in question, the act of hope is made real in historical and social terms.

Admittedly this is not the only way in which this is achieved. The

Christian also accepts in the "form of the world" as it passes over him those factors for which he himself is not responsible, and which he merely has to endure. He accepts these as part of the individual lot of his own personal life in death and in the renunciations which prepare for this, and it is no less true that he makes his hope real and living in this process too. A wildly revolutionary attitude, taken by himself, can be one of two things: either it implies that an absolute value is accorded to the form which the world is about to assume in the immediate future, in which case it is the opposite of hope, namely a form of presumption which only recognises that which can be controlled and manipulated, or which treats that which is not subject to our control or calculations as though it were so. Alternatively this attitude signifies despair, a state in which nothing more is hoped for, and therefore everything is absolutely negated because there is nothing final or definitive, or because nothing of this kind exists at all. But to subject the structures of this world too to constant reappraisal and criticism is *one* of the concrete forms of Christian hope which, as the courage of self-commitment to the incalculable and uncontrollable, must never hold fast to anything in this worldly life in such a way that it is as though without it man would be cast headlong into an absolute void. Hope commands man in the very moment in which, far more clearly than hitherto, he actually becomes the fashioner of his world, not only to let go of that which is taken away from him, but more than this actively to re-nounce that which, in the light of the limitless future which hope opens up to him, he recognises as provisional, and which, because of this, he can also understand to be dispensable already in this present time.

It is strange that we Christians, who have to achieve the radical com-mitment of hope in which we venture upon that which is incalculable and uncontrollable in the absolute future, have incurred the suspicion both in the minds of others and in our own that so far as we are concerned the will to guard and preserve is the basic virtue of life. In reality, however, the sole "tradition" which Christianity precisely as the people of God *on pilgrimage* has acquired on the way is the command to hope in the abso-lute promise and—in order that thereby this task may not remain at the level merely of a facile ideology of ideas—to set out ever anew from the social structures which have become petrified, old and empty. Precisely *in what* this hope is to be brought to its fulness in the concrete in an exodus which is constantly renewed in this way, precisely *what* the Christian is to hold firm to (for this too is in fact possible)—because his hope also divests the future, even within the temporal dimension, of any false appearance of being the absolute future—this is something which "theoretic" faith can-not answer as a simple deduction following from its own tenets. This con-crete imperative is not merely the result of applying the theory of faith in practice. It would be just as wrong to hold this as to say that faith as such, and by itself, transforms the general promise into that special and particular one which is only realised in the original and underivable act of hope. But this hope summons the Christian and Christianity to venture upon this imperative, underivable in each case, in which they have constantly to decide anew between whether they are to defend the present which they already possess, or to embark upon the exodus into the unforeseeable future. This is something which hope can do, for hope itself has in fact already all along achieved something which is even greater. In it man has surrendered himself to that which is absolutely and eternally uncontrollable and incalculable by any powers of his. In the power of this greater hope he also possesses the lesser hope, namely the courage to transform the "framework of secular life," as the Council puts it, and the converse too is no less true. In this lesser hope the greater one is made real.

There remain, therefore, faith, hope and love—these three. But the greatest of these is love. So says Paul. But we could also translate this: "Faith, hope and love constitute that which is definitive and final." Perhaps it has been shown that hope is not simply the attitude of one who is weak and at the same time hungering for a fulfilment that has yet to be achieved, but rather the courage to commit oneself in thought and deed to the incomprehensible and the uncontrollable which permeates our existence, and, as the future to which it is open, sustains it. Perhaps it has also been shown that such courage has the power to dare more than what can be arrived at merely by planning and calculations. Perhaps it has been shown that in the final and definitive consummation hope still prevails and endures, because this definitive consummation is God.

55 · Courage

It is difficult to say what is courage. Not because we do not know, but because as a peculiar realization of the existence of the whole person it cannot be defined as a particular occurrence distinguished from many others, in the sense of the first group of terms of which we spoke; because it is related to the totality of human existence, because it is no more open to an adequate reflection or definition than is this existence itself; because the courage that we really mean here is not courage for one thing or another that we can do, but courage for ourselves in the one totality of the human reality.

Nevertheless, it is possible to provide many hints of the meaning of courage and in this way to bring it before man's reflex consciousness.

Courage has something to do with uncertainty, with the danger of missing the reality to be actualized and sought by freedom, with decision. Certainly courage can and even should be co-existent with planning, calculation of opportunities. But courage is really required when rational reflection is faced by an obvious distance between the calculation of the possibilities of success and the deed as actually posited, a deed of whose success it is impossible to be certain before it actually occurs. The deficit between the precalculation of the goal and its prospect of success is made up in a deed precisely by what we call hopeful courage or the courage of hope. The distance between the deed as not adequately calculable in advance and the real deed is bridged by what we call courage.

The rational human being today has indeed entirely the right and the duty, in his undertakings and actions, to calculate in advance as accurately as possible and to try to achieve certainty. In advance of the deed, he must reduce the distance as much as possible up to the point at which in practice courage ceases to be necessary for the deed. So, for example, the structural engineer knows with almost absolute certainty before the completion of a bridge that the bridge will hold and that consequently no courage is required to walk across it. But in a thousand human actions the distance remains, the effect to be realized cannot be adequately calculated in advance, no adequately comprehensive knowledge of all the factors of an action is possible, and if action has to be taken courage remains indispensable. This is true even in ordinary life with its thousands and thousands of particular undertakings. It is particularly true when there is a question of *that* deed and *that* courage for the deed which are related to the *totality* of the one human existence. In what follows we shall be speaking only of this courage.

That there is and inevitably must be such a radical and total courage assumes of course that man as subject of freedom has to do, not only with one thing or another, with the thousand particular objective realities of his existence, with this partner, with that professional task, with this vacation and that individual difficulty, etc., but with himself as one and whole. The assumption we make for the notion of courage as it is meant here cannot now be justified more precisely. We assume that man as subject has to do not merely with an enormous mass of details of his life, by which he is driven or permits himself to be driven; in and through all these detailed realizations of his life he is *himself* absorbed as one and *whole*, whether he knows it explicitly or not. In real freedom man as oriented to finality is himself subject and object in one. He has not only to be concerned with a great deal and with a great variety of things in his life, he is concerned for himself as one: a task that we describe in a theological language as concern for salvation. In the varied business of his life he can forget or suppress this one and ultimate task. From being an "I" he can become a "one." This being absorbed in ourselves, being condemned to freedom, being ultimately always responsible for ourselves, is however present even as suppressed and forgotten, and comes clearly to the fore in moments of solitude and final decisions, in the invocation of a final responsibility applauded by no one, etc.

If we assume here what has just been merely indicated, it becomes clearer what is meant by that total and radical courage of which we want to speak. Man is imposed on himself in his freedom as one and whole, he is himself his one and ultimate task. But at the same time he knows that the fulfillment of this one and entire task depends on a thousand conditions and causes that he cannot wholly understand and that are not within his own power. And over and above all this he experiences his own freedom as already posited and threatened in itself, he experiences what is most properly his own in his character as subject as mysteriously alien to himself.

For both reasons there exists here in the most radical and irremovable fashion that distance between the acting subject with its capacity, its power, its means which can be calculated in advance, on the one hand, and, on the other, what has to be done in this one life's deed: the ultimate and definitive self-determination in a fulfillment of the boundless possibilities initially present in man as mind and freedom, the ultimate self-understanding that a person does not merely passively accept, but gives himself creatively in freedom. He experiences this distance, since he experiences himself at the same time as the being with unlimited claims, as the person who can never definitively stop at a restricted goal, *and* as one who is powerless, the person doomed to death, who is always fragmentary, an unhappy consciousness. This distance is bridged only by absolute hope, by the anticipation of a fulfillment which is not one's own achievement, by a hope of an absolute future as possibly and actually offered, that we call God and know originally and properly only *in* this hope.

The decision for such hope implies however also that courage with which we are concerned here. In this courage the totality of human existence is hoped for as achieved; the ground of this hope is not an empirical detail which could be completely understood and possessed; this hope is founded on the incomprehensible God, and on this God as free. Man must then entrust himself to another's freedom and accept this, not as imperiling, but as redeeming. This hope has not really anything outside itself which could serve independently as its ground and security, since the ground of hope, called God, is experienced only in hope itself. But such hope is for that reason courage purely and simply.

Before we can prove that this hopeful courage is faith in the strictly theological sense, something important must first be mentioned. We can of course objectify and verbalize the nature, content, and ground of this hopeful courage (just as we have done here and as every religion does with the aid of the most varied formulations) and realize a free act of courageous hope in regard to this reality as so verbalized. In other words it is possible to attempt expressly to hope courageously in an explicitly religious act. But however good such an act may be (and, under certain preconditions, even required) it is not simply to be identified with what we mean by this courageous hope. For in the first place it is by no means certain for man's reflective consciousness whether such an explicit individual religious act comes from that deepest centre of the acting subject from which the totality of human existence is really hazarded and surrendered, as redeeming and reconciling, to the ultimate mystery, called God. Not every religious act, however clear and well-meant, really itself disposes of the whole of existence for finality. Even if someone says sincerely, "God, I hope in you, I love you," it is far from certain that what is thought and said here really happens, that the person's whole existence moves toward God in a free decision from its innermost centre.

What is still more important, however, is that this hopeful courage can be realized very unthematically and without much reflection in the most varied free acts of life, without any attempt verbally to thematicize its nature in explicitly religious terms. If someone remains faithful to his conscience to the very last, even without reward; if someone succeeds in loving so unselfishly that in reality there is no question of a mere balance or harmony of egoisms; if someone quite calmly and without any final protest allows himself to be taken in the night of death; if the one life of a human being, despite all unceasing evil experiences and sad disappointments, opts for light and goodness; if someone, perhaps in apparently total hopelessness and despair, nevertheless hopes that he is hoping (since even hope itself cannot be established for certain as a solid fact on which further calculations could be securely based, but that very hope must be hoped for), and so on, then that courageous hope is always realized, even if it is not explicitly thematicized in religious terms. At this point man's freedom is at once identified with that hope which is the basic structure of human existence and continually offered to man's freedom throughout all the individual occurrences of life. In that very hope there is experienced and known what is really meant by "God," even if this expression is not part of the vocabulary ordinarily used by such a person.

What is courageous and final about this free hope in courage is spread up to a point anonymously over the whole course of the history of human freedom. That, of course, is not to say that explicit realizations, verbalized in religious terms, of courageous hope are superfluous or worthless. On the contrary, they can be so many ways in which this generally anonymous hope becomes fully conscious. They represent the practice of this basic hope in freedom at the heart of existence. They protect the person as much as possible from the danger of failing to make the final act of hope in the decisive moments of his history of darkness and menacing despair.

This courageous hope however is itself faith in the properly theological sense of the term. Many theologians will readily admit that this hopeful courage has the character of a "trusting belief," of a kind of provisional human form of faith properly so-called, but shrink from describing this courageous hope as itself faith, faith in revelation. They will say that this courage of absolute hope, essential as it is for a person's existence, is not yet to be described as faith, since faith in the strictly theological sense of the term is an assent to God's personal revelation, but this is not present in such a human hope as it were "from below" and thus cannot be accepted in faith.

Conversely however the theological "lay person" will perhaps be too quickly inclined to regard this hope as salvific faith, on the assumption that a person who seeks God in hope must certainly find him. This is true, but it does not answer the question raised by the theologian when he declares that faith, properly so-called, in revelation is necessary for salvation, appealing to Scripture, Christian tradition, and (when he thinks he cannot really see how this hope, this total courage, can itself be the response of faith) to God personally revealing himself.

But it can certainly be said (and it can be admitted that the merely apparently naive lay person is right in this) that such hope is in fact faith in revelation, even though only in a rudimentary form that needs to develop into its full nature. Why? First of all, it must be remembered that freedom is always also an acceptance of what is concealed, unconsidered, in a decision of freedom. Freedom is always acceptance of a "risk," always takes on more than it explicitly and reflectively intends. This is true especially of *that* act of courageous hope which is being considered here. For here man's one whole and never completely explicable existence is staked on God's incomprehensibility and freedom. Hope is centred on the uttermost reality, on everything, in fact on God himself, transcending all particular individual realities and individual goods which man encounters in the course of his history. That it is possible to hope in this way not merely for a great deal or for one individual reality after another; that hope is of God in himself; that the movement of mind and freedom, transcending all individual realities that can be grasped successively, does not in the last resort peter out into the void or need eventually to come to a stop at any individual reality, however significant, as the sole really possible fulfillment, at a "creaturely" good, but will reach God himself, the original fullness and creative ground of all individual realities; that God himself is the absolute future of our hope: these things do not amount simply to an obvious possibility of our own, but to a gift that might be refused, purely and simply grace. God himself is the innermost dynamism of this boundless movement of hope toward himself.

The very fact that God himself thus becomes by grace the dynamism and goal of our hope means that revelation has taken place. Grace, given to spirit as such, the possibility of hope founded on grace, anticipating God himself as its goal, this is revelation. It need not be explicitly grasped *as such* or explicitly distinguished from the rest of the experience of the spiritual subject of freedom, nor need it be expressly understood as distinguishable on each occasion from an isolated individual event. But this in no way alters the fact that it is a question of really personal divine revelation. It does not in fact take the form directly of the communication of certain propositions, but starts at the innermost core of the free spirit-person, opens up the latter in his dynamism toward the immediacy of God and thus gives him courage to hope for everything, that is, for God himself. When this innermost dynamism of man is accepted in freedom, when it is not diverted as a result of false modesty (implying a deep-seated secret fear of life) to a particular good as its ultimate goal, then what is described theologically as faith is *ipso facto* present.

Again, this acceptance in freedom of boundless and absolute hope must not be understood primarily as a single explicitly religious individual occurrence. When a person is faithful without any reservations to the dictate of his conscience, when in a final decision (despite all disappointments and adversities of his earthly experience) he does not reject an ultimate and absolute hope, then he surrenders in hope to the unrestricted, not wholly calculable movement of his spirit. At that point there is revelation and faith. From the Christian standpoint, what is present there is the Holy Spirit, whether this can be explained in express terms or not. This courageously hopeful acceptance of one's own existence (which is released into the salvific incomprehensibility of God and his freedom) can take place in the midst of the dull ordinary routine of the average person, since even this ordinary average person cannot avoid such final decisions, even though they generally occur very unobtrusively. Consequently such a faith in courageous absolute hope is certainly something that can occur even where religion does not occur or scarcely occurs in thematic form. Such a faith can be present even when a person, for whatever reasons, hesitates to give a name to the incomprehensible and ineffable character of his existence. Courageous hope, which is real faith, is required everywhere and is found even among those who are merely anonymous Christians. Actual faith in the full sense of the term is possible only in free hope, which is absolute courage; and, conversely, such absolute courage of unconditional hope is itself faith in the Christian sense.

56 · Perseverance

In its Decree on Justification, the Council of Trent described the teaching of the Church on perseverance in the following way:

> The same is to be said of the gift of perseverance, about which it is written, "He who has persevered to the end will be saved" [Mt. 10:22]. This gift can be had only from him who has the power to determine that he who does stand shall stand [Rom. 14:4] with perseverance, and who can lift up him who falls. Let no one feel assured of this gift with an absolute certitude, although all ought to have most secure hope in the help of God. For unless men are unfaithful to his grace, God will bring the good work to perfection, just as he began it [cf. Phil. 1:6], working both the will and the performance [Phil. 2:13]. Yet, let them who think they stand take heed lest they fall [1 Cor. 10:12], and let them work out their salvation with fear and trembling [Phil. 2:12], in labors, in sleepless nights, in almsgiving, in prayers and offerings, in fastings, and in chastity [cf. 2 Cor. 6:3f.]. Knowing that they are reborn unto the hope of glory and not yet unto glory itself, they should be in dread about the battle they must wage with the flesh, the world, and the devil. For in this battle they cannot be the victors unless, with God's grace, they obey the Apostle who says: "We are debtors, not to the flesh, that we should live according to the flesh. For if you live according to the flesh you will die; but if by the Spirit you put to death the deeds of the flesh, you will live." [Rom. 8:12–13].

It would be out of place here to comment at length on these words of the Council. But at the same time, we should realize that apprehension about the hidden future, of which the problem of perseverance is a part, is an essential moment in the reality of a finite spirit in matter. We do not live out our present life just in anticipation and projection of the future. For the future is necessarily hidden from us because of the free character of our creaturehood—free because under the disposition of God—and it must be accepted in its hiddenness. The future would not be hidden from us if we paid no attention to it whatever. It is really only hidden if we consciously venture into the unknown and consider it as in some way belonging to us. If this is our attitude not only with regard to this or that particular event of our lives, but also with regard to our whole future, which is obscure even though it really grows out of our freedom, and which, though not completely in our power, still has a determining effect on us, then we are asking a theological question about ourselves which is the question of perseverance. To raise the theological question of perseverance is the same thing as to ask whether or not a person will finally be what he now is or at least hopes to be.

The Essence and Origin of Christian Perseverance

The teaching of the Council of Trent quoted above gives us some information on this topic: "This gift can be had only from him who has the power to determine that he who does stand shall stand with perseverance, and who can lift up him who falls."

The strange thing that immediately presents itself when it comes to questioning the essence and origin of perseverance is that, on the one hand, our future will certainly be worked out by our freedom, and that, on the other hand, we are completely in the hand of God. Only when a person has experienced, believed, feared, and loved God in the absolute surrender of his whole being—and therefore also of his whole future, can he begin to realize the full meaning of God's power and freedom. We can only live in close contact with God when we believe in him as the only true love, and when we accept our future from him as a gift which, as the result of our own freedom, still really belongs to God.

It takes a consideration such as this to bring us to see how completely different God is. We could not, as it were, share our freedom with anyone else but God. If we were to share it with anyone or anything, then the inexorable conclusion would be: Either I or the other will determine my destiny. But this does not apply to God! And therefore, a person is perfectly right when he sees that the question about the future is really a question about the acts of his freedom, because he has come to realize that he cannot answer this question by himself, and nevertheless must go on to encounter the incomprehensible vagueness of the future as something really belonging to him. God is the One who gives, and His gifts are so unique that when we accept them they become our own free acts.

From a theological point of view, perseverance is efficacious grace. This is something that no theology of revelation can ignore. Protestant theology cannot ignore it, even though the Protestants frequently do not understand how it is that we beg of God something that we ourselves must do. In other words, they do not see how we can truly realize our freedom by abandoning ourselves to God in love and freedom. Actually, we effect our perseverance by seriously and constantly trying to do just that, by praying, by serving God, by using and leaving the things of this world with genuine detachment, by always being ready for the direction of God that surpasses all else. To be sure, this situation means that there is a deep and urgent restlessness in our being. Having seen this, St. Augustine asked how he could be serene before God. Then he answered himself by asking whether or not he would be more serene if he had his destiny in his own hand, or whether he should not be more confident if he knew that he was in the hand of God. To accept this situation in faith and love is salvation, and those who are perishing are not being lost because they are in the hand of God and being led by his grace, but because they have not accepted his grace and believed in it. The person who knows that he is under God's power and humbly surrenders himself to him with hope and trust—loves God. As long as he does this, he is surrounded by the grace of God. Every sin is fundamentally a drawing back from God and his direction because the sinner has more confidence in himself than he does in God. And it is mistrust of God that brings about damnation.

Therefore, our first conclusion with regard to perseverance is: Our heart can be composed and serene only in God's grace, and it can only attain serenity if it is restless in the love of God. We are not seized by a suspicious fear when we are with someone we truly love. Perfect love drives out fear. But we can also say: Perfect love effects a holy fear of God that renders us happy, calm, and confident.

Signs of Divine Election

If we were to ask ourselves whether or not there are signs of belonging to God's "elect," we would have to say that there are no signs, such as legal documents, that can be adduced as proof of certain perseverance in grace. If there are any signs of election, then they can only be those effected by our own actions, which are signs that God is working in us. Such signs are, for example, constancy in prayer, steady progress in doing good, God-fearing concern for salvation, selfless love, and so forth. We might also mention those special experiences a person has that lead him on gently and irresistibly so that, amazed, he asks himself occasionally how he escaped this or that disaster; or he might ask himself how he was able to accomplish certain things for which there was really no indication in his physical or psychological make-up.

Francis Thompson has compared the choosing love of God, which surrounds a man and pursues him down every path so that he cannot escape, with keen hounds which encircle the stag and close in on it for the kill. In this sense, therefore, there definitely are signs of election. However, they are not there to be enjoyed, but to be done. The runner may hope to reach the goal, and the one who is striving may hope that God will accomplish in him the eternal work of his mercy.

Means of Acquiring Perseverance

The question whether or not there are any means that can be employed —speaking anthropomorphically—to obtain and secure the grace of perseverance, can be reduced to the question treated above about the signs of divine election. The real answer is that such a means can be had only in doing. We could also approach this question by examining the various elements that make up our spiritual life, to see whether or not they are more suited or less suited to merit the grace of perseverance. Such an examination will certainly bring to light the fact that those forms of the religious life are useful which, by their very nature, are least apt to become institutionalized, which will normally either not be practiced at all or else will be genuinely performed, and which will not tolerate that weird, superficial no-man's-land where legal pretenses are kept up, but where the heart and spirit are not involved.

It is not difficult to point to many elements in an organized program for the spiritual life whose practice tends toward a disassociation from the personal core. For example, it is very easy to change the regular early rising into a mere habit, so that one ultimately comes to the conclusion: That which crawls out of bed in the wee hours of the morning is not a spiritually alive person, but a mere shadow who satisfies his conscience by faithfully sitting out the time for prayer. Reciting the Breviary can also easily become the performance of a merely institutional, legal "obligation."

On the other hand, it can be said of other forms of the spiritual life: If I use them at all, then I have a relatively good chance of performing them properly; if I use them at all, then I notice not only, as it were, that I have some success in them, but also that I am coming closer to God in them. On the basis of this consideration, among the many traditional devotions two can easily be singled out as important for the acquisition of the grace of final perseverance. They are the devotion to the Mother of God and the Sacred Heart devotion. These devotions must be truly interior and personal if they are to be practiced at all. This is all the more true in an age when the attraction of both devotions has suffered in the eyes of the clergy and the laity. Therefore, if Christian tradition assures us that devotion to Mary and to the Sacred Heart are practically signs of final perseverance, then that is rather easy to understand. It could be that this argument smacks a bit of theological rationalism. Perhaps we should add: The Church, which possesses the Spirit of God, knows through her supernatural instinct that God has attached very special graces to both of these devotions.

If I ask myself with all seriousness and in a truly Christian way whether or not I will remain faithful to the grace of God my whole life long right up to my death, then I must come to realize that the ultimate guarantee of this is the grace of God himself. Everything depends on him alone, the faithful One, whose love is unchangeable. Moreover, if I ask how I can know for sure whether or not I still possess the living love which is necessary for final perseverance, and which surpasses every sort of perfunctory affirmation of definitions, the Church, her glory, my office, my duties, the commandments, and so forth, then I can reduce this question to concrete terms by examining myself to see if I truly love the Mother of God.

I can also ask myself: Does the mention of the Sacred Heart of Jesus seem repulsive and tasteless to me, as words of true love are felt by those who do not love, or is it something for which I have understanding, something I am seeking from the depths of my heart, and something about which I say to myself quietly at least once in a while: "Heart of Jesus, Son of the eternal Father, have mercy on me; Heart of Jesus, kingly center of all hearts, have mercy on me"? Am I trying to understand something of this center of the world, of this pierced Heart that poured out its love into the deadly darkness of the world? If I can honestly answer myself: Yes, I am really trying to love the Lord—and that is evident in my religious life; if I can say the same thing about Mary, then I can be sure that the love of God is still alive in me, still throbbing, that it has not vanished under the pressure of daily living, that it has not been choked by formality and habit. Then I am still on the way, and it is clear that my faithful God has not abandoned me. And then he will lead me on from grace to grace until it has become final.

57 · Good Fortune and Divine Blessing

When we speak of a "blessing," we mean simply any favor of God's grace. We legitimately distinguish between good and evil, helpful and harmful, successful and unsuccessful, fortunate and unfortunate. Whether we wish to or not, this is how we sort out all the events of our private and public lives. Some of these events seem positive to us, while we regard others as negative, unfortunate. When we experience occurrences as favorable, advantageous, and fortunate, and judge them to be so, naturally we can view them simply as plain, factual occurrences—or we can attribute them to causes we ourselves can know, analyze, or change—or, finally, we can also attribute such occurrences, when they are positive, to God's causality and will, at least ultimately, and so understand them as blessing, as God's gracious visitation. The coherency between immediately tangible earthly causes and God's blessing need not necessarily be so conceptualized that these events of fortune and blessing could only occur in virtue of a further, additional intervention on God's part in order to be regarded as "God's blessings." After all, what we call intramundane causes of benediction are also ultimately God's creation—their "conspiration" lies ultimately in that will and disposition of God we call providence. We have, then, no grounds for conceiving God's blessing as only occurring where God is thought of as one who interferes, in some wondrous, unexpected way, in the tissue of earthly causes. Something can assuredly be God's blessing and still in the first instance be induced by nature's internal or external causes, or indeed by human beings' free operation. Even when blessing is regarded in this way, it can nevertheless be God's blessing.

When we beg God's blessing, when we turn to God in the prayer of petition, asking him to order and dispose our destiny to our advantage and blessing, we are not necessarily making a request for a portentous, quasi-miraculous, extraordinary intervention on God's part. Such a prayer is simply, as it were, confessing from the start that we receive and acknowledge those lucky, fortunate occurrences in our lives that are owing to earthly causes nonetheless as God's blessing.

Here, to be sure, is another consideration to be examined, and one which will lead us down to subtle, but authentic depths of our human existence. For there is something most remarkable about these external strokes of good fortune—that we earn more money, perhaps, or that we recover from a disease, or that other people oblige us with their friendliness and benevolence. All these realities, interpreted by us as good fortune, as God's blessing, are fraught with a curious ambiguity. Even in the Old Testament there was a youth who was congratulated because he had died young. And to our own day there have certainly been wealthy people who use their wealth to their own destruction. Conversely, there are diseases that can make a person earnest and conscientious in his or her inner attitude toward God and life. A good many persons may well have their gaze actually opened out upon deeper perspectives by an apparent stroke of ill fortune. In sum, we can say: All situations and events in our lives are of a curious, twofold character—they can all finally redound to our blessing or to our calamity.

And so, when we say, "Such and such has been a fortunate turn of events in my life," or "Here I have been blessed by God," we must immediately catch ourselves up short—almost as if we were a bit startled—and ask ourselves: Is what we interpret as good fortune, and God's blessing, really a blessing? When something has been given to us in this way, something that seems a good thing to us, it is not simply and automatically good fortune and blessing. It is first of all a question addressed to us—a problem to solve. What comes to us from without, in the chance occurrences of our lives, is found at bottom to be transformed into a question: how to interpret it, how to decide to make use of it, how to turn it into a blessing by handling it correctly. What is bestowed on us by the external and internal "lucky" circumstances and "chance" coincidences of our lives, over which we have no simple and direct control, is not plain and simple blessing, as we often rather carelessly and foolishly think, but material that we *use* to our blessing or mischief—depending on how we ourselves interpret it in our free disposition, depending on what further precision and determination we ourselves give it. And so ultimately everything we encounter can be for blessing or for ill. And what at first seems hard, dark, and bitter to us can actually be more of a blessing if we bear up under its demands. By our very acceptance of it in serene and resigned trust in God, we can make what at first is dark and incomprehensible into a blessing.

This being the case, we may now say that everything we meet with in life is blessing: health or sickness, wealth or poverty, pleasure or pain, life or death. All can be blessing. Of course, we can still say in prayer—making a selection, as it were—"Make me well," or, "Give me the blessing of . . . ." But we have only truly prayed when, in this differentiation we ourselves determine among the realities of our life, we know, believe, and assume nevertheless, when all is said and done, that everything in our lives can redound to our blessing. The gay and the grave, the hard and the easy, can all be, or become, blessing. And wherever we ask God's blessing, even in an altogether determinate request, let us also ask that we be given the light and strength to receive everything that comes to us, even the unexpected and the difficult, as God's blessing—to convert it, as it were, into blessing. Let us declare, in every prayer, that we are ready to have everything God sends us, everything he intends to grant us—perhaps entirely contrary to our own calculations—become a blessing for us, by accepting it aright.

58 · New Tasks of Justice

In the last General Congregation of the Society of Jesus, in which that order's goals and pastoral orientation were reformulated, it was stated that the Jesuits were to apply themselves, in their worldwide evangelization, to the promotion of "faith and justice." Now, surely this double goal might have been expected to raise a few eyebrows—and as a matter of fact, both within and outside the order, while meeting with approval, it did also arouse objections. After all, it would be easy to say that, as a religious institution for the cure of souls, for the proclamation of the Gospel, and for the missions, the Jesuit order has but one comprehensive end and purpose: precisely the propagation of the faith. Now suddenly a second purpose comes on the scene, claiming equal rights: the "promotion of justice."

What does this mean? Besides their properly religious purpose, do the

Jesuits as an order now have another purpose, a social purpose? What are they, apostles or revolutionaries or both? What has happened in this order? Indeed the Jesuits have come under the suspicion of having departed from their proper spiritual, supernatural faith-purposes and of having corporately entered upon a secularization process, in which they suddenly lay claim to a specifically secular task—which, we hear it said, actually outweighs the other in importance for them, indeed, is secretly their only earnest goal.

Such is not the case, of course. But a question is obviously raised and not just for the Jesuits. After all, this would not be so important. It is a burning question for Christian existence as such today. Everywhere in the Church we see tendencies which, rightly or wrongly, are viewed as secularization processes. No longer is there basically any faith in the supernatural world of God and his grace, we are told. God is being replaced by social critique and sociopolitical imperatives.

What is to be said about this most interesting, general Christian problem? Naturally, the answer cannot be given in all precision and depth in the space of a few pages. It is abundantly evident that Christians of all times have felt themselves somehow responsible for the world. And yet, as Paul says, their *politeuma*, their homeland, their native country, the actual core of their existence, is in heaven (Phil. 3:20)—from where they look for him to return who, as God made flesh, as Savior of the world, will, through and in his Second Coming, radically assume and perfect history, and thereby of course earthly societies too. This, the human being's total, comprehensive destiny, given through faith in Christ, will nevertheless have to be realized at different times in history, under very different conditions and circumstances, and thus this concrete life, directed toward fulfillment in God, will appear now in one aspect, now in another.

In a somewhat oversimplified and schematized fashion, then, perhaps we might be able to put it this way: Only in modern times, and especially in the very times in which we live, society's situation is no longer merely a *given* for human beings and their life. Nor again is it simply something that changes—owing partly to external circumstances and partly to what human beings themselves introduce via invention and technology—but so gradually and so slowly that its developments pass unheeded over the course of the centuries. No, today this societal situation and its transformations have themselves become an object of human activity and human reflection. Our societal situation is not only the situation in which the tasks of a human being, as human being or Christian, take place. It has *itself* become a task of the human being—a task expressly and consciously grasped, and in one way or another scientifically reflected on. Not only does the human being today do something *in* a determinate situation, but this situation, in which he or she lives and operates, is itself, again, the object of reflexive and rapidly transpiring alteration *via the human being himself and herself.*

Here, then, is a whole new situation for Christians. In the Christian life of bygone times, even when one did not flee the world, one only had a certain social *task*—one was a physician or shoemaker, or perhaps a politician or soldier, and one had to live one's Christian life in these callings, which changed, but not noticeably or reflectively, and were practically stable as measured by the yardstick of an individual lifetime. Today the change in a person's situation is quite readily perceptible even over the course of a short life. In the past, Saint Francis de Sales could write a book of direction, a book of advice, for the cultured ladies and gentlemen of his society to live by. That is to say, he wrote for Christian conduct *in* the situation of his time. Today we have to have instructions for *changing* our situation itself. You might say we need books of direction for Christians as human subjects with social obligations that include the obligation to bring about changes in society.

Here, then, arises a peculiarity for Christian living that did not present itself in the same manner in the past. This is the fundamental meaning of the demand made on the Jesuits, and any other earnest Christian, not only to live, profess, and develop his or her faith, but to take on a task with regard to justice in the world. A Christian's obligation to approach his or her fellow human beings in justice and Christian love of neighbor has of course always been a task, a fundamental Christian challenge, in every historical era of Christianity, and is the standard by which every Christian is to be judged before the judgment seat of God at the end of his or her life. It has always been recognized that God's first question at the Last Judgment will be: How did you get along with your neighbor?

What we mean, then, when we place the word "justice" along with faith at the head of our agenda, is that we have a task in society to cooperate responsibly in shaping that society's structures. To be sure, a like task, which can be labelled a "new" one, has been slow to overtake Christian awareness. But it is surely a more urgent task today than it was in the past. In the nineteenth century—after the French Revolution, then—there was an emphasis laid on a Christian's obligation to vote with a Christian party, and it was felt that the Christian thereby acquitted himself of his whole sociopolitical duty, and could obediently and humbly leave all else to the Christian government he had helped to elect. For the rest, he had simply to live his private and (private) professional life in peace and patience. Today all that has unquestionably changed. Surely the average person in a Western democracy like ours will still perform a key part of his or her sociopolitical duty, of which we have slowly become aware, by discharging his or her obligation to vote. But a good, ordinary Christian of the nineteenth century, or even of the beginning of the twentieth, knew very well what a Christian party was and knew for whom to vote. Today things are much more complicated, to say the least. Even within parties, a Christian cannot simply leave everything to the Christian intentions and the expertise of a few party leaders. Today important decisions may well be the product of an organizational structure cutting across the whole party. The party cannot be first essentially changed and then asked to make these decisions. At all events, the Christian, even the simple Christian, has a more considerable task to perform today, one which in a real sense was not present once upon a time as it is present today, and one which on that account does contribute to the essential character of one's Christian life.

Of course, all this is material for more concrete and profound theological and speculative analysis. One could and should, for example, say something about the unity of love of God and neighbor—a unity that is much more radical and not nearly as simple as the ordinary middle-class citizen imagines it to be. The average product of our religious education, if I may be allowed to put it in that way, thinks of things rather in the following manner: "Here is love of God, over here. We are to love and obey God. We are to keep his commandments. Now, one of these commandments is to treat our neighbor honorably, justly, perhaps even lovingly." The commandment of love, in this homely Christian conception, is just a portion of the application of divine obedience—a little piece of what God demands of Christians in order for their relationship to him to be peaceful, auspicious, salvific. But if we examine the matter with more theological precision, we see that although what our Christian says is true, still, on a deeper level, a right relationship with God is not only a prerequisite for an individual's authentic relationship with his or her neighbor, it is a consequence of that relationship, as well. Love of neighbor is not simply a particular precept which God has tied to the precept of love for himself. Love of neighbor, at bottom, is the manner and the primal locus in the existence of the human being in which it first dawns on that human being who God really is and how he should be loved. One could very well say that the answer to the question "Who is God?" is not only, and not ultimately, a series of theoretical demonstrations of the existence of a supramundane being called God; the answer to the question "Who is God?" is: love your neighbor—"whom you see," as John says—so that you genuinely transcend yourself in a properly incomprehensible unselfishness, and then you will know what is meant by God, even if you were never to hear the word, the name, "God." Not that love of God is just an old-fashioned way of saying love of neighbor, as certain theologians of the death of God theology and the like have maintained here and there in Germany and North America over the last few decades. No, love of God means that God in his significance as absolute summons to us to come away from ourselves, to come out of ourselves, "dawns on" human beings, is concretely grasped by them, only when they really love their neighbor, only when they do more than merely tolerate their neighbor in a selfish compromise that leaves him or her in peace in order to be left in peace oneself—only when they do more than give in order to receive. Only then is that exodus of one's own existence out of oneself and toward God—the only route to human happiness—at last under way.

Once the inner oneness of love of God and love of neighbor is thus clarified and deepened by a theological approach bearing upon existential experience; once the insight is sharpened that one can truly love one's neighbor unselfishly only when one loves God, and vice versa; and once we insert what we have said concerning the Christian's active responsibility for the transformation of the social order—then it automatically becomes understandable why one can correctly say today: Christians are obliged to actualize their faith in their lives by love directed toward the eternal God, and are obliged to make a commitment to justice in love of neighbor.

Perhaps this can all be clarified still further by pointing out that there are not only sins of injustice committed in the behavior of individuals towards their neighbor but there are fixed social structures, as well, that are unjust. For example, when someone today goes down to the corner vegetable stand to buy a bunch of bananas, it may be that the reason he or she can get them so cheaply is that the poor devils who pick the bananas somewhere in Latin America are paid such unjustly low wages by the company they work for that they are degraded to an inhumane level of life. Of course, economic and social structures are such that no one can really know what lies behind the chain of operations. We must confess, though, that we are the beneficiaries of unjust structures that signal a task, a challenge, and an obligation for the Christian who would make a commitment to justice. Here lie new tasks of justice, tasks we have never had before—tasks which, by virtue of the unity obtaining between love of God and love of neighbor in a relationship of reciprocal conditioning, contribute to the determination of our very Christian existence in its totality.

59 · The Problem of Peace

If we are to speak of peace *theologically*, then we must speak of peace with God, peace with ourselves, peace in the contacts and relationships between man and man, and within these relationships peace between the generations, the classes, the age-groups and the sexes. We should also— because this too is of concern to theologians—have something to say with regard to peace in the international sphere and of the old-fashioned idea of peace. And finally we should give some consideration, precisely as *theologians*, to that *political* peace which is implicit in the current situation, in which the tendency of world history is towards an ever-increasing and ultimately total unity. The question of how these various kinds of peace, with God, with one's self, in human relationships, in more private contacts and at the political and international levels, are related to one another is, of course, in turn, a question in itself for the theologian, for manifestly he has the impression, even after reading the scriptures, that these various modes in which peace is realised have an intrinsic relationship and unity among themselves, and that on a radical view one kind demands the other. Only the individual who is conscious in some sense of being interiorly at peace with himself, and who—as we Christians say— lives ultimately at peace with God, can truly and radically maintain that attitude which can also contribute to peace among men.

In all its dimensions, therefore, this peace—and this is something that opens up a whole range of further levels in the theology of this concept— has forms which are subject to wide variations. At a later stage we shall have to see still more clearly that the concept of "conflict" and "war" in a metaphysical sense and in terms of existential ontology, and probably also in a theological sense, is not so simple or obvious that we could react to it with a simple refusal in favour of peace as the obviously right attitude to assume. To that extent there are necessarily genuine forms of peace and true forms of conflict. And hence even from this point of view the theologian will have to exercise great prudence in his work with regard to the question of war and conflict on the one hand, and of peace on the other. Certainly there have already been times at which Christians became, to a greater or lesser extent, the representatives of the sort of quiet that belongs to the graveyard, times, moreover, at which a pseudo-*Christian* ideology was actually invoked in support of the thesis that the primary duty is to ensure that the citizen shall have quiet. And there is a modern anti-Christian ideology according to which the sole possible realistic form of peace consists in an equilibrium of fear. All this shows how widely varying in form that phenomenon can be which is so commonly characterised as peace. From the time of the Fathers of the Church onwards Christianity and the Church have always and actively concerned themselves with the question of the relationship of Christianity to the soldier's calling, to war in the concrete sense, to nationalism, to the question of conscientious objectors, and always in very varying ways and with very varying results. Today the refusal to rely on physical force is certainly on the way or is actually being pressed as a watchword within Christendom itself. This again shows how many theological problems are connected with the question of peace.

A more important idea, and one which has a quite direct connection with our understanding of peace, belongs to that which we call "power." It is manifest that Christians or theologians are not simply at one with regard to their judgments upon power. Is power something which, on any ultimate view, belongs *ipso facto* from the outset, and necessarily, to the sphere of sin? Does the basis on which power rests consist solely and exclusively in the sinful world and in the fact of its sinfulness, or is there initially a power such that, even though in the concrete conditions of the world it is always, as it were, corrupted by sin, it nevertheless has properly speaking and of its true nature a different function and a real justification for its existence in the world?

In any such question we would first have to explain what is meant by power. Now we may take this concept of "power" to mean the process in which one man is influenced by another, and the possibility which he has of determining that other's course, this act of determining his course being prior to the free decision of the man so acted upon. For my part I believe that this is more or less correct as a concept of power. Now if this is correct then we may perhaps be forced to say that the presence of some such phenomenon as power in the world is necessary, and that power of this kind belongs to the essential conditions of human living; that although—as the theologians will say—it is true that power is always sinfully misused as well, nevertheless this sinful misuse cannot on that account be totally overcome simply by adopting the attitude of an absolute renunciation of power. On the basis of a conception of power of this kind the question would then have to be raised of the inevitable existence of conflict and—in a metaphysical and theological sense—of war. On this showing the specifically *Christian* question would be more concerned with the concrete forms and manifestations of power and of conflict in so far as these could, from certain aspects, be considered the responsibility of the Christian alone. The question of how the Christian might gradually attempt to overcome this inescapable "existential" or condition of human living as defined by power and conflict in history, or at least how he can impart to history a tendency towards such a conquest through that love which in the last analysis he alone can have who knows that he is loved by God—this is a question the answer to which will only be attempted at a later stage. Here too we shall confine ourselves simply to making clear how the theological problems involved in peace become lost in a whole range of connected questions which is far broader in its extent.

A further question is how to achieve a right approach to peace considered as a theological phenomenon. In this we must not simply postulate some false utopian or romantic image of absolute rest and permanent equilibrium, something which does admittedly represent a lofty ideal in the concrete circumstances of our life, but which, nevertheless, does not provide us with very much force with which to realise it. And if this is the case, then at the same time we must seek for that concept which, in terms of theological meaning, constitutes the opposite pole to that of peace. The moment, for instance, one formulates the theological concept of concupiscence it carries with it *ipso facto* and in each case the further idea of an interior dissatisfaction on man's part, a state of inward conflict, a plurality of the forces within him of which, ultimately speaking, he is not in control, and which he cannot reduce to any state of definitive integration. What is being spoken of, therefore, is a "war" and "conflict" of man within himself, and this involves as its counterpart the opposite idea of peace with himself that comes through God and from God.

The theological and Christian problem of peace is further associated with the question of what the idea of "peace" is really intended to conjure up. What does it mean to conceive of this as "the order of justice," seeing that "order" and "justice" are, and continue to be, in a certain sense extremely obscure concepts? What does such a concept of peace signify when we raise the question of a *dynamism of history* which will certainly not be held at any one specific point in an equilibrium of power, of social relationship, etc., which is wholly predetermined? What must we say with regard to peace seeing that the question of a theology of revolution can be raised and that the young people precisely are today inclined, even in their Christian representatives, to invoke a Christian watchword to the effect that under certain circumstances revolution may be necessary. This in itself is, of course, enough to indicate the question of how a theology of history on the one hand and the theology of peace on the other are related to one another since they are two factors which can be taken as having a necessary connection with one another and so reveal a further range of theological problems into which the question of peace leads us.

Today the peace which we seek in the international sphere is dependent to an extraordinary extent upon the growing unity of the history of the world, upon a situation of secularism in the sphere of culture, of society, of the state and of politics, and also upon the rationalisation and technical manipulation of the world. And in view of this it is obvious that any question of the theology of peace invariably implies also something in the nature of an enquiry into the theology of the worldliness of the world, the unity of contemporary world history in general, a theology which consists in analysing the contemporary situation in world history and the factor of the rational and the technical in human living. This is turn entails a further and almost incalculable range of problems associated with the question of the theology of peace.

Properly speaking if the theologian sets himself to consider the question of peace he must also consider his theology of justice and his theology of love, his theology of the mutual relationship between justice and love. He must enter into a problem which, in current theology, is once more becoming very clear: the problem, namely, of how we should conceive of the unity and the distinction between love of God and love of neighbour upon an originally and authentically Christian conception. Undoubtedly the question of peace is not wholly unconnected with the Christian message of love of neighbour, and this love of neighbour has manifestly something to do with that which we call the love of God for us and our love of God. In the biblical concept of *agape* the various aspects of both kinds of love are already indissolubly interconnected. According as each theologian views the love of God and love of neighbour as a unity he will undoubtedly modify also his concept of that peace which is achieved through this single love of God and love of neighbour.

In fact a further problem which arises for theology is that of Christian and secular humanism, and this too in turn has connections with a theology of peace. Is there such a thing as a unity between men such that they become one in their humanity and one in their humanism? Is there a material content belonging to a humanism of this kind such that in it Christians and non-Christians could be at one, so that on this basis they could achieve a common concept of what they really understand by peace? These too are problems and questions which are evidently not so easy to solve, and which can serve in turn to throw light upon the whole multidimensional character of a theology of peace.

60 · The Theology of Peace

On any showing "peace" as presented in the Old and New Testaments is one of the most important religious concepts. *Shalom* in the Old Testament signifies, ultimately speaking, a state of wellbeing, of having overcome an evil of some kind. It therefore signifies a state of good fortune, precisely a "being whole," so that a man can salute his fellow with the greeting *Shalom*, "Peace be to you." And even on this basis this state of "wholeness," precisely in those cases in which it is applied to an area involving human relationships, also acquires the significance of peace, and is therefore translated in the Septuagint as *eirene*. In this connection, however, we must constantly keep clearly before our eyes the fact that this specifically Old Testament concept originally had a far broader, deeper and more comprehensive meaning than that which we attach to the term "peace" today, thinking of it in a sense that is based on politics or merely on human relationships. This peace in the Old Testament is, of its very nature and right from the outset, something that has to be supplicated from God, because without God there can be no peace. And in the Old Testament prophets Jeremiah and Ezekiel peace in this sense precisely becomes the key word for what is central to the content of salvation in all its aspects, and as such also becomes in the case of Isaiah the key word for messianic expectation. Because of this peace already comes, under certain circumstances—by including, as it were, protology and eschatology within a single conspectus—something approaching the restoration of the paradisal peace which was destroyed by original sin, and on this view the Messiah is the *princeps pacis*, the prince of peace. But even here peace is, once more, interpreted as the all-inclusive content of salvation.

In the New Testament too, therefore, the Christian message (Eph. 6:15) can be called the "gospel of peace," that peace of which God is the author and Jesus Christ the mediator. Peace is, then, that which is mediated by Christ in the Spirit through a new creation as the fruit of the *Pneuma*, so that *he* is our peace. And this peace is regarded as the peace which exists between God and men (Rom. 5:1). Hence peace then ensues between men but in such a way that this peace is also really and effectively the appeasement of that interior conflict which has arisen in man through sin.

On this basis we might pursue the concept of peace through all departments of theology. When we came to consider the doctrine of creation we would have, as it were, to regard the openness of the creature to salvation, the ability to be saved, the possibility of attaining to its own "union with God" as peace, as well as the counterpart of this from God's side. In Christology, when we speak of the plenitude of grace in Christ then Christ is precisely he who is in his own person this peace between God and the world, and from whom the new order of the world as reconciled with God is initiated. In any presentation of ecclesiology we might wholeheartedly follow the Second Vatican Council in viewing the Church as, so to say, the sacramental sign in history, the historical manifestation, of this self-utterance of God which unites the world with God and in itself, and so gives it peace. In a presentation of ethics peace could be regarded as the goal at which work for the kingdom of God is aimed, and in a presentation of eschatology we could speak of a hope for the eternal rest, and in that case once more this peace would be being regarded as the content of eschatological hope.

We must now turn to a further point and attempt to say something on the theology of peace and of the peaceable attitude or state of mind. A thesis might be formulated, however untimely it might sound, which would not give a very Christian impression and yet perhaps would be extremely Christian: the *"conflict" which is a "war" so long as this world in which we live endures, so long as the "kingdom of God" is not made present by the act of God himself—is an abiding reality, and insuperable "existential" of human living.* In spite of this the *Christian*—in precisely the same way as mankind in general—*has an abiding task to create peace,* and so both must constantly be expressing the demand that humanitarian principles shall prevail.

This thesis derives from a realism that is Christian and anti-ideological. As has already been said, any genuine Christian theology can and must recognise the inescapability and the necessity of that which is called and is power. Every individual is, to a certain extent, in virtue of his very existence, and in the very act of his self-fulfilment within the general sphere of existence common to all men, one who alters the situation of freedom, the sphere of freedom open to his fellow, restricting it in some measure prior to any agreement on the latter's part. After all this is, more or less, what power means, and a power more or less of this sort is unmistakably present. Of course the Christian will always recognise that this natural "existential" of human living, which is inevitable and which, therefore, since man is not merely sin, is perfectly legitimate, is *de facto* always conditioned by sin as well, in other words by the sinful uses to which this inevitable power is put. But if such a power is present not merely in the sphere of our private lives, in which we mutually restrict the field of liberty open to one another, but is present also in the dimension of society and of peoples, then it is quite impossible for Christianity, maintaining as it does an anti-ideological realism of this kind, to escape from something like a war in this sense, that is to say conflict or contradiction. For the situation is that many human lives, each of which is multidimensional in itself, are in process of achieving their self-fulfilment in many ways. All of them exist within a single finite sphere of freedom, and therefore necessarily mutually restrict one another within this sphere of freedom. And it is this that constitutes the exercise of such a power, which ultimately speaking cannot be guided or controlled by any earthly authority. The reason for this is that any such central and totalitarian administration, or any division of this single sphere of existence of the kind that this would imply, would in fact represent the greatest exercise of power, in fact the most radical use of force by man.

When applied in an anti-ideological sense, therefore, Christian realism soberly recognises the existence of power and therefore of conflict as one side of human living. It does not raise this power to the status of an ideology or accord it an absolute value. It precisely does not want this power to be administered by an ultimate and central tribunal within this present world. It is, therefore, against any ideological or any practical monopolisation of this power, but at the same time it also recognises that it is inevitable that there shall be something in the nature of conflict, contradiction and war. The Christian, therefore, is sufficiently realistic to take his stand in principle at a point halfway between a total rejection of power, an absolute hostility *towards* it on the one hand, and an attitude on the other in which power is accorded an absolute value raised to an ideology and monopolised.

The Christian is *in principle* opposed to both extremes, for ultimately speaking they come to the same. For the absolute abrogation of power and of the conflict or contradiction ensuing from it, the abrogation of a situation of struggle in general, would be possible only through an absolute monopolisation of power, and this would precisely be absolute tyranny. The Christian cannot agree to any easy compromise, but must maintain a genuinely central position between these two extremes, because precisely in virtue of his awareness of his own creatureliness he must recognise from the outset that he, the individual, *must not* set himself up as the absolute representative of God in the world, since he *cannot* be this. A further reason is that neither the Church or state on the one hand, nor any different body on the other, representing science or some other finite concrete entity in the world, can or should set itself up, as it were, as absolutely acting in God's place, and so as having absolute authority to decide how the sphere of freedom should be divided between men.

The Christian's attitude is that any attempt to develop the ideal of an absolute peace in this present world into an ideology would imply the death, the end of history, a fellahin culture or rather lack of culture, and precisely the state of absolute tyranny. In other words the sober anti-ideological realism of the Christian, who takes due account of conflict, contradiction and war, provides what is precisely the sole genuine possibility of coping with the problem of war and conflict in general in a manner that is fully *human*, because any attempt at radically abolishing conflict and war would precisely imply the ultimate in tyranny, the most extreme concentration of power.

Nevertheless the Christian has the most solemn duty and task, and one which radically and vitally affects his salvation, of restraining this inevitable conflict, of inculcating humanity, and, to the utmost of his power, of avoiding it. Obviously he has also, as one who knows about sins and in fact about his own sins, a critical attitude towards power and authority. He knows that this authority is one of the forces in the world which are indeed created by God, but which, nevertheless, can at the same time constitute the greatest possible temptation to man to put them to a wrong use and perhaps actually to rebel against God by means of them. To that extent he has always the task of bringing humanitarian standards to bear upon the struggle, just as, for instance "blood feuds" and individual acts of retribution against private enemies have actually been eliminated from our society today.

When, therefore, it is asserted that theology, on the basis of a sober Christian realism which is anti-ideological in character, maintains that power, and therefore conflict too—that is war in the abstract sense— cannot be eliminated this obviously does not mean that the old and seemingly immovable forms in which power has been customarily applied in the past need always remain the same as they were, or even that we can allow them to do so. The opposite is true. Precisely the struggle against these forms of war, forms which are still less than human, must be conducted precisely in the light of the anti-ideological realism of the Christian with its capacity for sober criticism.

Now if we ask as Christian theologians how and in what way this effort or this task to achieve a humanisation of the struggle and of power is to be conducted, then what first comes to mind—at least as far as Catholics are concerned—are the two Christian key words of "justice" and "love." It is in fact stated in a noteworthy manner in the Second Vatican Council that peace is not the outcome of any human dictatorship or a balance of power between opposing forces, but is in a true and proper sense the work of justice. Now obviously we cannot here embark upon an attempt to present a theology of the nature of what is here meant by justice and love considered as the means by which the conflict is to be humanised. This would go beyond the scope and the limitations of the present consideration. Thus only a few indications may be made at this point.

It could in fact be said that peace exists where "each individual is accorded his due" in justice. Certainly some kind of description of justice could be given by explaining the phrase *suum cuique*, but in that case what is right and fair for "each individual"? The question still remains, how can we in this one finite sphere of freedom, attain to that equality in which *no one individual* receives less than his due. Justice is constantly in danger of stopping short at the level of an organised egoism, and thereby, once more, providing the occasion for that conflict and war which has to be overcome and humanised. Whereas justice says, in a certain sense: "to each according to his due," "Let me have what is mine and you keep what is yours," Christian love says: "What is mine is yours."

Now certainly if we wish to remain realistic as Christians we must always keep clearly before our eyes the abiding fact that justice and love are two distinct entities. In this concrete world in which there is a pluralism even of virtues, justice cannot simply be elevated into that love which never counts the cost to itself, and which is self-forgetful in such a way that all the Christian would have to do for everything to be well would be to practise that prodigality, that self-forgetfulness of love, in which he no longer sought to assert any claims on his own behalf. There remains too a pluralism in our Christian attitudes which itself cannot adequately be integrated or elevated into a higher synthesis—for instance precisely that of love. This is a pluralism which, in a true sense, must be endured by the Christian so long as this present age lasts. This sounds terribly abstract, yet it is an extremely practical matter.

Certainly there is and must be that love in the life of the Christian in which he abandons himself, renounces himself, surrenders his own rights, allows his fellow to have his way with him, achieves the folly of power-lessness, and really rises above the level of organised self-interest to the folly of self-abandonment according to the model which God has set before him in Jesus Christ. But Christian love as applied in the concrete in all that plurality which cannot be controlled by man, and which is to be found even in the virtues belonging to man, also means precisely that under certain circumstances it can be not merely a possibility, not merely morally permissible, but an actual duty for man to establish that kind of justice which at some specific point precisely does not put into practice the holy foolishness of love, but rather seeks soberly, intelligently and empirically to create conditions in which rights may be distributed between all concerned. This is what is so fearfully difficult and at the same time once more what is utterly realistic and down to earth in this Christian attitude.

If I may so express it, it cannot reduce love to justice. Love is, from the Christian point of view, really something different from the intelligent organisation of human living such that each receives at least a portion from the cake of worldly prosperity. Love is really something more like the element of madness, of the improbable, of that which does not pay, that through which we continue to be the ones who do the paying and in which we let ourselves be exploited. Love is, therefore, something too in which we are bold enough to make experiments—of the kind, for instance, which our politicians are always so frightened of making.

On the other hand, however, we cannot turn Christian living into some kind of marvellous and blessed paroxysm of love in which we strip ourselves of all power. This task of coming to terms with both aspects *for the sake of peace* is one that is incalculable and that changes according to the changes in the particular situation concerned. It is the task of the Christian, and one for which, ultimately speaking, neither the churches nor the letter of the gospel can supply any readymade or concrete formula. Admittedly the Christian will again and again have to tell himself—in the spirit and meaning of the Sermon on the Mount—that in a true and ultimate sense it is his duty to keep his eyes fixed upon the folly of God on the Cross, and so in all cases of doubt, whether at the individual or personal level, or at the collective and political one, to opt for the folly of love in that situation in human life in which he is placed in concrete history, which makes demands upon him and yet all the time remains ambiguous. And yet so long as the age of this present world lasts justice, so sober, realistic and hard as it seems, and even when it involves the use of power, whether in private or in public life, can precisely be the earthly form in which an extremely selfless love is embodied, which perhaps even for the sake of another may have to find courage enough to appear as though it were devoid of love.

A further point must be added to this: the experience of man shows again and again that mere justice, however strict it may be in not claiming more than its due, always fails, is always reduced to absurdity and, taken by itself, can never provide a basis for peace.

The sphere of freedom open to us in our mode of living becomes ever more restricted and, from the point of view of sociology, ever more complicated systems of dividing it are required. Because of this it will become, in a certain sense, ever less possible to establish solely as an end in itself an ideology by which to divide this sphere of freedom realistically in order to create peace. The world is a place in which all men are, as it were, justified in living and claiming their own due, and in which they actually seek to assert their own sinful egoism. But this world will become more and more the danger area in which a highly explosive mixture is present. And the more we seek to divide this restricted sphere of living in an equable manner the less peace will prevail. Wherever this sphere of human living is growing ever narrower, and wherever a frenzied will to be just asserts itself as an absolute, there naturally and inevitably an ideology will come into force and will proclaim intolerantly and again and again as a fresh message that there is nothing to wish for, no peace and no justice to achieve, unless it yields power and "right" to a single absolute autonomous totalitarian centre to determine what is due to each individual, and thereby to achieve a just distribution of the one source of prosperity to be found upon earth.

Man after all is not an animal, and even in the empirical world belonging to him there is a vital need for that folly and mystery of love. But when he comes to this point the Christian asks how man can really manage, in a manner that is fully justified, to renounce something to which he has a right or at least supposes that he has a right. I know that regrettably I am forced to speak in very abstract terms, but I believe that thereby we really are attaining to a point of central importance. There is much that an individual can renounce simply because, for instance, he wants to be left in peace; because under certain circumstances he may feel that egoism as practised by a group of two or of many is of greater advantage than being egoistical in a more primitive, solipsist or individualistic sense. But in the human living of the individual and also in political and national life moments will arise again and again in which something should be and has to be renounced such that the renouncing of it no longer benefits the renouncer, where, as it were, he feels himself threatened and injured in the most personal claims which he makes upon existence. Precisely in the Protestant theology of the Reformation period great emphasis was laid upon this, and in the Catholic theology of the natural law perhaps too little attention was paid to the fact that here, in these matters, there is a difference—we cannot examine it in greater detail at this point—between the private sphere and the political and national sphere. But in this case the situation is such that we have to entertain that love which is capable of renouncing that which seems to belong to one as a necessity, a necessity of life, and even a necessity of salvation. And the question is what resources man can find within himself really to achieve this.

Among this world's goods I can only as a last resort renounce that which seems to be a necessity of life if I am conscious of being so radically loved by someone that that which is mine is constituted by the infinite fulness of life that is his. Thus, as it were, in him and in his love is to be found the only place in which I can give way and allow my fellow his due within this present world. And this is precisely the point to which any rationally organised and intelligent egoism no longer extends. On the other hand a man cannot, in any true sense, adopt a position of sheer paradox by taking his fellow more seriously than himself, and ultimately speaking he can only take himself and his fellow seriously, and concede something to him which is truly his, if he is conscious that both he and his fellow are already at rest in, and encompassed by the infinite land, in the infinitude of love and freedom, in peace with God. Only then can there no longer be any question of whether I have this or that, whether I am a little more or a little less fortunate, more or less solitary. Here peace with God, his love bestowed in the event of his self-utterance, becomes that which opens the way to and makes possible that other love which is also precisely that which opens the way to peace among men.

Obviously this is not to provide a formula which, if it were applied in this sense, would bring the world once and for all into a condition of peace, that is of a sheer absence of disagreement. In fact all this takes place in a changing history. All this takes place in a synthesis which is ever new, and which has to be discovered in ever different forms, between a love which commits itself and offers itself and a justice which asserts itself even rightly so that under certain circumstances this love can even initiate the use of force or even revolution and a state of "non-peace." Thus it can be a correct view that the first duty of the citizen is unrest. All this is possible if love accords justice its right and proper status, confines it within this proper status, and commands. If the just man is conscious that he can and should be the man who hazards himself and commits himself, the man who dares to make experiments, then this will only be possible in the hope that in this process which is still unfolding—not through the efforts of men but through the deed of God—the kingdom of God is actually present, and in it that peace which surpasses all understanding, a peace which is no longer built upon a synthesis of the kind of which we have been speaking, always unstable, always to be established afresh, or upon a precarious balance of all the elements which constitute human living in the here and now so long as history is still unfolding.

It is obvious that against this background of theological considerations we ought, as men and Christians, to set ourselves to consider specific problems which are necessary in this world as we experience it in the concrete: as a world of hunger, of illiteracy, of atomic bombs, of ever increasing inter-involvement on the part of nations and the histories belonging to them; the world of the technical mastery and the media of communication of the present, of the present needs of man and of the population explosion. It is necessary to consider these specific problems in order thereby to preserve and to establish something at least which holds out some prospect of a tolerable peace. What, therefore, is the final impression which the Christian as he exists in the concrete will receive precisely from the sort of theological considerations set forth above? He may think that he can leave them as they were before. He may think that precisely because he has to be one who loves and serves selflessly, one who has to work out his own salvation in the concrete reality of his own existence, he must apply himself to the concrete and contemporary questions regarding peace. And in that case we agree with him. After such theological considerations the theologian as such once more returns to the ranks and leaves to Christians as men with concrete human lives to live their due place and their task which he of course for his part also recognises as his own.

61 · Charism and Suffering

A charism always involves suffering. For it is painful to fulfil the task set by the charism, the gift received, and at the same time within the one body to endure the opposition of another's activity which may in certain circumstances be equally justified. One's own gift is always limited and humbled by another's gift. Sometimes it must wait until it can develop, until its *kairos*, its hour, has come and that of another has passed or is fading. This painful fact is to be viewed soberly as an inevitable consequence of there being one Church and many gifts. If the words are taken seriously and not emptied of meaning, "many gifts" implies that one person has a gift that another has not. How could that other person show an understanding of a gift that is only possible to its possessor who is called to exercise that precise function in the Church? Even supposing we had all the goodwill and tolerance that we could or should have, it would still not be possible to show another and his gift and task that understanding and enthusiasm which he expects and is tempted to claim his mission justifies and requires. Outside the Church the man with a mission may, of course, be misunderstood and persecuted, but he can flee to those who esteem him and recognize his mission and a community can be founded and centred on this mission. In the Church this is only possible to a much more limited extent, for example by the founding of an order or similar social structures in the Church which are legitimate and derive part of their meaning and justification from this need for social response to a new mission. In general someone in the Church who bears the burden of a charismatic mission to the Church and for the Church, must remain in the circle of his brethren. They will tolerate him when things go well but perhaps reject him and in any case show little understanding of him. The authenticity of a charism, which after all is for the Church and into the Church, not out of her, is shown by the fact that the person so endowed bears humbly and patiently this inevitable sorrow of his charismatic endowment, builds no little chapel for himself inside the Church in order to make things more tolerable, does not become embittered but knows that it is the one Lord who creates a force and resistance to it, the wine of enthusiasm and the water of sobriety in his Church, and has given to none of his servants singly the task of representing him.

Two observations must be made on this theme of the burden of a spiritual gift in the Church. One is, that to suffer opposition to the charism within the Church is no proof against the mission from above and the authenticity of the gift. Certainly the Church has the right and duty of discernment of spirits even to the point of completely rejecting a claim that this or that spirit is from God. But that does not mean that every contradiction, delay, distrust that is aroused in the Church or its authorities against a charism is itself a sign that this prophet has not been sent by Yahweh. The criteria for distinguishing between the legitimate opposition of the Church to a deceitful spirit and false enthusiasm on one hand, and the painful resistance of the Church to the mission of its own Spirit in a true "prophet" on the other, are known in their main features and need not be expounded in more detail here. They are the rules which the Church and its theology lay down regarding its teaching authority, its various levels and their binding force, and the equally discriminating rules about ecclesiastical obedience. In this respect another thing must be said. To apply these rules correctly in more difficult cases is itself a charism, a special gift. For who can tell always and at once, precisely and definitely, when self-defence of a charismatic mission against the mistrust, difference or hesitation of holders of ecclesiastical office, of even against their actual opposition, is a sign of higher charismatic insight and fidelity to his own mission, and when an attitude of illegitimate revolt against ecclesiastical authority? Why, for example, were the Jesuits right in acting as they did when they resisted Pius V's attempt to impose solemn choir-office on them? Why were they not breaking their own rules of thinking with the Church? Why was it a praiseworthy action on the part of the representatives of devotion to the Sacred Heart not to allow themselves to be put off by the rejection which they first met with from the Holy See? How often can one really remonstrate with the competent authority with petitions, pressure and so on, without by that very fact offending against the ecclesiastical spirit? When is as minimizing an interpretation as possible of an ecclesiastical prohibition, in order to continue to preserve as much room and freedom of movement for an endeavour that has the appearance of contradicting it, quite definitely compatible (as even the practice of the saints shows), with an ecclesiastical spirit, and when not? Such questions show (and that was their only purpose here) that it can itself be a special gift given only to the humble and brave, obedient yet independent and responsible saint to discern where the burden of opposition to a mission is the cross which blesses a genuine mission and where it is a proof that the endeavour has not its origin in God. There too it is clear that it is not possible completely to comprise in plain rules of law the stirrings of the Church's life, that a charismatic element remains.

The second thing to be said about the burden of a charism is that the inner necessity that links charism and suffering in the Church, of course gives no patent to the authorities, and others devoid of special gifts, to be lacking in understanding, and blind and obstinate. Sometimes one has the impression that there are people in the Church who infer from Gamaliel's words (Acts 5:38 ff.) that the authenticity of the Spirit is shown by its not being extinguished by the most frivolous and malicious opposition from other people, and that consequently they have the right to put the spirit to the test on the largest possible scale. Of course, it is not possible to extinguish the Spirit in the Church, God sees to that. But it is quite possible for a human being by his sloth and indifference and hardness of heart to extinguish a true spirit in another. Not only is it possible for grace to be without fruit in the person for whom it is intended, through his own resistance, but it can be given to someone for another's benefit—it is then called *gratia gratis data* or *charisma*—and remain without fruit because rejected by the person for whom it was given, although it was faithfully received by the one who received it on another's behalf. We must not be Jansenists in our doctrine of the charismata, either, and hold that all these special gifts must be given as *gratiae efficaces*, infallibly producing their effect. There are also gifts which through men's fault remain without effect for the Church. Gamaliel for that matter drew from his maxim the contrary conclusion to that of the people we have in mind. He inferred that one must be as tolerant as possible towards a spirit whose origin one cannot yet clearly make out. Ecclesiastical authorities cannot, therefore, do wrong on the grounds that a spirit will triumph in the end even against their opposition, if it really comes from God. Otherwise they cause suffering beyond what is unavoidable, do wrong to God, to those endowed with spiritual gifts and to the Church.

Anyone even slightly familiar with the history of the Church knows of sufficient examples of suffering of that kind by those gifted by the Spirit. St. John of the Cross was thrown into a horrible dungeon by his own brethren, St. Joan of Arc died at the stake, Newman lived for years under a cloud, Sailer of Ratisbon was denigrated in Rome by another saint, Clement Maria Hofbauer, and only became a bishop when it was really too late, Mary Ward was for a long time in the custody of the Inquisition and yet, of course, she was right about her mission, nevertheless. In the controversy about the nature of the love of God, Fénelon was disavowed, not without reason, by Rome, but his adversary Bossuet who seemed to have triumphed was not much nearer the truth than his less powerful opponent. In her foundations St. Teresa of Jesus, certainly to her great sorrow, had to undergo much persecution on the part of ecclesiastics, and use much ingenuity and many ruses in order to succeed. From the beginning of the Church down to the present day there have been great and small instances, of these and similar kinds, of the sufferings of the charismatic individual, and there will continue to be. They are unavoidable. They belong to the inescapable "necessity" of suffering by which Christ continues to suffer in his members until the end. And he willed that these his members should also cause one another to suffer.

62 · Experiences of Oncoming Death

There is something like an experience of death even when there is no question of suffering and sickness in the proper and ordinary sense of the terms. The transcendental constitution of man, who in all his mental achievements of knowledge, freedom, production and in all other intellectual-personal achievements aims at a particular categorial object and at the same time (even though generally only unthematically) surpasses it, produces to a continually increasing extent the experience of the finiteness of his milieu and environment and thus, too, of himself and consequently that "disappointment" as a basic mood of our existence which the preacher in the Old Testament described in radical terms at an early stage. This very experience itself is a presence of death in which all the "disappointing" individual realities of life perish and thus the finiteness of the subject itself becomes a matter of radical experience. Here there is an experience of dying inwardly that is not an individual occurrence here and there in the course of life, but a basic mood permeating all things, whether the latter is accepted in freedom and resolution or not.

This basic mood makes itself felt as warning and herald of death whenever suffering, failure, and the like are experienced, as something that even an average, everyday consciousness regards as what ought not to be. All this (which need not be presented here in detail in its thousand shapes) is every time a partial death, no matter what attitude a person takes toward it. Something perishes that the person judges to be possible, realizable, and desirable, and yet he is deprived of it. Hence the theodicy relevant to suffering in the world, possible only in the hope inspired by faith, is an element in the theodicy of death, and vice versa. At the same time we should be under no illusion that bravery, rationality, and so on could *so* remold and transform all these disappointing experiences, that the "maturity" of a person could be so effective and assured and thus the success of "heroically" coping with death could be established. Consequently there will be no attempt at this point to produce (once again) a theodicy of death in terms only of an unconditional surrender of man to the incomprehensibility of God in what in the last resort is a self-evident hope; it would in fact be nothing but the understanding of faith, hope, and love in regard to God's incomprehensibility in face of death, before which alone the meaning of these basic Christian achievements can be made radically clear. This is true then also of that *prolixitas mortis* which consists in suffering of every kind in individual and social life.

This infiltration of death is felt most clearly in real (that is, dangerous) illness, for it is the danger of biological death as directly perceptible.

That is why in the Old Testament also death through sickness as distinct from a smooth fading out of life at an advanced age was regarded as particularly hard and problematical and liberation from sickness as a special mark of God's favour. Even apart from all the discoveries of modern psychosomatic medicine, sickness is distinguished as a total human phenomenon and not merely as a disturbance of man's biological dimension, because in the light of our very ordinary experience (even though not clearly verifiable in every individual case) it threatens and reduces even man's intellectual and free subjectivity, diminishes or withdraws from man the possibility of reacting to it, so that this helplessness of the subject itself is an element in a really human and not merely biological sense. But in this way and not as a purely biological disturbance sickness points and tends toward that endpoint of life in which man as a whole is deprived of himself and his sovereignty, and which we call death. The experience of a sickness rendering the whole person helpless up to a point itself shows that human death is not to be identified simply with clinical death understood in terms of natural science with its immediate causes. By its individual peculiarities also sickness proves to be as such preeminently *prolixitas mortis*. The impossibility of completely foreseeing and manipulating sickness; the helplessness into which it thrusts us; the special, remote relationship to society, into which it forces us; the solitude and the curtailment of possibilities of communication; the weakening of the capacity for active self-direction; the permanent uncertainty of any interpretation of its "sense" and its causes within the total structure of a human life; the burden it imposes on the people around the sick person; the withdrawal from an efficiency-oriented society; the sick person's experience of being useless to others; the impossibility of integrating sickness meaningfully into a plan of life, and many other peculiarities of sickness make it a herald of death.

In the light of this constant presence of death in the whole course of life Christian wisdom has always been aware of a *memento mori*. If and insofar as dying and death amount not only to a purely passively endured happening at the end of life, but also to an active deed of man, and if this act, as we said, cannot be located simply at the moment of the advent of death in the medical sense, then for the Christian, coming death cannot be something which does not concern him "for the time being," something that he might now suppress as much as possible. Within life he has to live with death. This happens primarily and fundamentally through all those accomplishments of freedom in which a person accepts with resignation the finiteness of his milieu and environment and of himself in hope of the incomprehensible and thus abandons the attempt to regard as absolute anything that can be experienced in itself; this sort of thing happens also when someone simply accepts as unanswerable the question of his ultimate identity and his relationship to God as sinner and (as he hopes) justified before God. This ultimate acquiescence, too, is an anticipation of that "night in which no man can work." But, in addition to these basic, even though unthematic realizations of a *memento mori*, in Christian life and in the life of the Church there is rightly an explicit remembrance of the prospect of death. There is no need to describe here in detail these ways of keeping death in mind, of explicit preparation for death, of organizing life with an eye on death, etc. Despite their derivative character, they are of great importance, since in the light of man's nature the reflex thematicizing and practising of basic realizations, which, whether accepted or rejected, are in any case inescapably present in human life, is of great importance for the very reason that it renders more secure retrospectively the true and radical acceptance of these basic realizations by fundamental freedom and because man is bound in principle (of course, only insofar as it is possible) to make these things secure.

In history of the Christian life and also in the history of the life of mankind as a whole there can be found obviously varying styles of dying. The method and custom of a particular society presents to its individual members a definite style of dying, to be preferred as right and proper, at least for the "normal" case. In Christendom, too, there are such "rules for dying" and they have not always simply remained the same. In particular a certain style of dying was expected from those holding important positions in the Church, a style in which their rank, their responsibility for others, their Christian faith, could be presented as an example. Formerly, a Christian died within his family circle, said goodbye there, blessed them, had a few last words to say, asserted his orthodox faith and his Christian hope, etc. It is very different today, when, as a result of thrusting the sick into the impersonal atmosphere of public hospitals, dying has largely become styleless. This may be deplorable and need not simply be accepted as inevitable; but it is part of that lack of style (that is, shapelessness) which we accept as belonging to death and thus also to dying, which in the last resort is beyond our control. The individual styles of dying possible to a Christian and up to a point being successively eliminated in the course of history need not be described here in detail. Their alternation and the continually changing concrete circumstances of dying, which determine this style on each occasion, are also part of that radical uncontrolability that is proper to death. Thus all that remains to be noted here in theological terms—as distinct from those of a (perhaps ecclesial) cultural history of dying—is that the Christian is bound to the Christian Church's style of dying in the "normal case," that is, when the concrete possibilities are available and can be realized without recourse to extraordinary measures, insofar as he is "bound" to die in an explicitly Christian way. Concretely, this means that he is expected to receive the last sacraments. An attitude of this kind, in which there is also realized an indispensable readiness to accept death, is present (to put it circumspectly) according to general Christian feeling also when the dying person can regard himself as being at peace with God, as justified, and thus the last sacraments are not for him the obligatory mode of sacramental reconciliation with God and the Church. The exact form of this obligation to an ecclesial "style of dying" can be examined in a work of moral theology.

63 · The Ambiguity of Death

The death that a man must undergo is ambiguous in a terrifying way. First of all, it is a participation in the death of Adam, and as such the revelation of sin and despair. And secondly, our death is also the participation in the death of Christ, and hence a participation in the advent of redemption from sin. In this sense, it is the incarnation of that faith that saves. Looked at from the outside, and this can be true even of the experience of a man who is dying, both of these meanings seem to be the same. According to the way each person accepts and endures this ambiguous and puzzling fate, whether in despair or in faith and love—therefore does he die either the death of the first sinner or the death of our Lord.

Our death is a culmination of the unrepeatable *onceness* of our personal human existence. The Epistle to the Hebrews (9 and 10) applies this *hapax* (onceness) to the death of Christ. Also with regard to its onceness, man's death cannot be practiced ahead of time. We cannot study death perfectly before experiencing it. Man goes through it once either rightly or wrongly without the chance of correcting himself. This is so true that what we call heaven or hell is the result with absolute finality.

Despite this onceness, there is such a thing as a real preparation for death. St. Paul says that we die our whole life through (2 Cor. 4:7ff.). It remains true that death is just the way life was, and that a person only concretizes in this death the full meaning of the "detachment" spoken of in the Foundation of the Exercises. Therefore, in a very true sense death is actually anticipated in every moral act in which the higher and more distant goal is preferred to the lower, nearer, and more pleasant one.

Through the intrusion of death from without, and through the rupture of existence which essentially characterizes death, indifference is, as it were, forced on us whether we like it or not. Now absolutely everything is taken away from us. Now, even if we are in a good hospital and have all the necessary drugs, we are suspended with Christ between heaven and earth and are excluded from human society. But death is especially the end from within myself: It is my final act.

We can also consider the weakness involved in death in an Adamitic or a Christian way. Death is either that impotency which is the ultimate result of the sin that took hold of Adam, or it is a participation in the self-divestment of Christ that was never so great and so extensive as it was in his death on the cross.

We might think of the loneliness of death. A dying man is pitilessly lonely. No one can do anything for him. We can share our life with others, but not our death! But the loneliness of death is especially a being-alone before the hidden, living God: It is either the blessed abandonment of Christ, or the unholy expulsion into the outer darkness that is eternally impregnated with hate.

The onceness of death implies also its finality. In death, I am really at the end of the rope. There just is no life after death in the sense that my human existence then "keeps right on going" more or less the way it is now. Death means a radical and questionless existence with or against God. Therefore, the finality of death is the last decision. To this extent, man's death is also his judgment.

64 · Jesus Christ as the Meaning of Life

Before we speak of Jesus Christ as the meaning of life, we must make some clarifications. By "meaning," we of course do not intend particular individual connections among particular, concrete realities, in the manner of, for example, the recognizably "meaningful" connection between a bird's ability to fly and the construction of its wing—or even the insight that a given particular artistic experience, for example, has a meaning in itself, one that legitimates its existence apart from simple serviceability for something else. By "meaning," here, we intend the one, whole, universal, definitive meaning of all human existence. We presuppose that it is at least possible for there to be such meaning—that it is conceivable in nature and that it can be realized in the act of existence.

This presupposition is not a simple evidence. An agnostic or skeptic will say that human beings do indeed constantly undergo the experience of partial purposefulness and meaningfulness when they set themselves goals and realize them or strive for results which they consider to be positive or gratifying and pleasurable. But, our objectants will add, we cannot find and attain total, definitive meaning. Life ultimately melts away into emptiness, spills into the void. The search and demand for a definitive, all-encompassing meaning is senseless from the start.

The Christian is convinced of the contrary. He or she believes in the possibility of a comprehensive actualization of meaning, and believes that this actualization is the task of his or her own liberty, through the fulfillment of that human history which is the story of human freedom. At the same time the Christian believes this comprehensive meaning to be the gift of the one we call God—and that indeed it is only in positing an all-embracing fullness of meaning that it can dawn on anyone what is meant by the word "God."

It would take us much too far afield to undertake to establish this basic conviction of Christians and to defend it as deserving of credence. Nevertheless there are two observations we must make concerning this total or global meaning.

First, it is immediately evident that the total, all-encompassing meaning of existence, which fulfills every requirement of a search for meaning, cannot be patched together of partial meanings. The search for a fulfillment of meaning would then yield nothing more than an endless series of partial meanings. Each would offer only the ever unfulfilled promise of a total fullness of meaning. The Christian seeks total meaning "outside the course of history," as everlasting life bestowed by God himself—even though this fullness of meaning is at the same time the eternal fruit of this history, in which it of course arises. Thus the Christian requires a meaning that must needs render all other possible answers unthinkable. The Christian answer is a "transcendent" one—and yet its validity is that of the only total answer for concrete living, for the life we have to live here and now. We may in no way blissfully consign the hope for eternity to the mystics and the dreamers, as if this earthly task of ours could suffer no changes under the influence of metaphysical dreams like those. For when, in earnest faith, we really and definitively "open up to God" and his eternal life as our only hope, then our relation to the realities and tasks of this world *will* undergo a change—and a liberating, unburdening change at that, a change that bestows on us the clear vision of the wide awake. But this, again, is something we cannot examine more closely here. Still we must hold firmly to the fact that our search for meaning, here and now, however surely its goal may be the God who overwhelms our practical experience, is not a question for idle speculation: it comports altogether real and tangible consequences.

Conversely, nevertheless, it is emphatically true that our global search for meaning does have God as its object—a God who is not a matter of our everyday experience, especially in the form in which that experience is so narrowly shaped and molded by the spirit of modern empirical science. And yet, even in the presence of these limits and this narrowness, the problem of a metaphysical-existential (hence also in some way empirical) experience of God is far from deserving of a negative answer.

Second, this God whom Christianity declares to be the fulfillment of the search for global meaning is the incomprehensible, impenetrable Mystery that can never be manipulated, and this he remains for all eternity. We cannot offer the basis for this proposition here. It shows why human perception is ultimately simply directed toward this mystery but "shatters" when it encounters it, if we may so speak, and only thus finds its fulfillment. But here we must simply presuppose the Christian conviction that God's incomprehensibility remains everlastingly mysterious. When all is said and done, the human being can approach this incomprehensibility only in loving surrender and not by a perception that would drag the Perceived before some high tribunal charged with the perceiving of all reality.

But if God is the infinite Mystery that can never be comprehended, then the global search for meaning encounters a curious crisis. We cry for meaning, total meaning. And it is right that we should. In doing so, however, we are tempted almost involuntarily and unreflectively to understand this "meaning" as something "penetrable and penetrated," something illuminated and hence lighting up the darkness of our existence. We cry out for light, and unconsciously think of this Light, which is to illuminate all things and make them meaningful, after the fashion of our own lights, with which we go groping about in the dark. We think something is "perceived" or contacted by our knowledge only when the whole grid of all its little interconnections can clearly be seen, and the thing itself can now be inserted into the larger grid of our needs and inquisitiveness. But this is just what God in his incomprehensible mystery is *not* "all about." What our experience of perceiving the Incomprehensible constitutes is precisely *not* the pitiful leftovers of a perception that "sees through" things but the ultimate and primordial essence of perception itself.

When it is a matter of the total and definitive sense of human existence, and when this sense is to be the incomprehensible God, meaning becomes mystery, and we must surrender to it in mute, adoring love in order to approach it. This utterly different, unexpected signification makes no sense that we can see through, grasp, and bring into subjection. This sense is the mystery that closes *us* in its grasp. Its beatitude is bestowed on us only when we affirm and love this holy mystery for its own sake and not ours, when we surrender, and not when we surreptitiously seek to make God a means of our own self-affirmation.

With the above as our point of departure, the question must now be broached whether and how Jesus Christ is the Christian response to the human search for meaning.

The proper and ultimate response to the search for meaning is of course God, in the way that we have just indicated. Now inasmuch as we understand Jesus Christ to be the eternal Word of God, the proposition "Jesus Christ is the ultimate answer to the human being's search for meaning" is identical with the proposition that God is this answer—God and no one or anything else. But this is manifestly not what is meant by the proposition "Jesus Christ is the answer to the human being's search for meaning," for this would be nothing new, nothing particular or proper, nothing specifically Christian. Surely by "Jesus Christ" we mean the eternal Word of God. But we mean the eternal Word of God precisely *qua* incarnate, "become flesh," as John puts it—precisely as having entered into a real, substantial oneness with the whole human reality of Jesus of Nazareth.

Thus we are asking to what extent this Jesus of Nazareth, as a human being with a concrete human history, as someone died and risen, has what we shall call a constitutive significance for the sense of our life as total meaning. This will not simply coincide with the proposition that the eternal Word is the meaning of our life. Hence Jesus Christ, in his human reality and history, cannot be just as fully the global meaning of our existence as God is *qua* God.

This line of questioning is evidently of basic importance for Christian faith and life. On the one hand, Jesus Christ in his humanity is not simply identical with God. He is one with God in the hypostatic union, but the hypostatic oneness in which we believe simultaneously expresses the distinction of the human and the divine reality. On the other hand, only God can be the human being's ultimate goal and meaning. It is surely an urgent question for Christians to know more precisely just what the humanity of Jesus betokens for the actual salvation—the total meaning—of the human being.

To be sure, this question is answered over and over again in Scripture, in Christian tradition and proclamation, in formulations that partly complement and partly simply repeat one another. Thus God is said to have assumed, in the incarnation of the eternal Word in Jesus of Nazareth, humanity in its entirety, and thus by taking on our nature to have entered into solidarity with all humanity. Or: the eternal Word has redeemed us in the passion and obedient death of his human history, as it is through these that he has made satisfaction to God's everlasting justice and thereby become the ground of God's salvific will—the basis for God's addressing to us, in spite of humanity's sinfulness, his forgiving grace that is himself. Or again: Jesus of Nazareth is in some way the historical event that is not only supported and maintained by the eternal, transhistorical God, like any other history, but the event in whom God himself deals with the world on the stage of history, suffering its tragedy with it to the end. Or finally: through the obedience of his passion, as the absolutely innocent and lovingly pure one, Jesus Christ has opened for us the way to the Father, for he has entered into absolute and complete solidarity with us.

These expressions and conceptions of the salvific meaning of Jesus Christ—of his constitutive meaning and function for the total sense of our existence—are but a few of the many such formulations that may be found.

Now, the soteriological declarations of Christian tradition may be divided into those which we can range more or less under a "pure Chalcedonianism," and those which would be more likely to go under "neo-Chalcedonianism." These are merely abstruse, technical theological formulations for the following. Many theologians understand the oneness of divinity and humanity as the ground of salvation so emphatically *as* oneness that, while maintaining the Chalcedonian doctrine of the nonconfusion, or noncommingling, of divinity and humanity in Jesus, they nevertheless proceed to regard Jesus' history and lot as the history and lot of God *as God*. Thus they interpret the Chalcedonian dogma in the manner of Cyril of Alexandria: God has suffered; the eternal Word of God has himself undergone our condition and our death and thereby our condition and our death are saved and redeemed; the Word of the Father has personally taken on our condition, with its mortgage of sin and death, and thereby redeemed it.

This neo-Chalcedonian salvation theory has its representatives in theology today as well, although to be sure they generally do not make explicit appeal to neo-Chalcedonianism itself. Its expressions and propositions belong per se to Catholic Christianity's deposit of faith, for they contain, as far as they go, the *communicatio idiomatum*—the doctrine that everything that can be said of Jesus as a human being is also predicable of Jesus-Christ-who-is-God (not "insofar as he is God"!). But a fine distinction, difficult to discern and yet of far-reaching consequence, arises in this neo-Chalcedonianism as we have just described it, the moment these expressions are read in the sense of a pure Chalcedonianism, which insists on the nonconfusion of the two natures.

The neo-Chalcedonian presentation would, while respecting the mystery, understand redemption as a matter of God's having suffered, God's having died, and thereby having redeemed us. While not forgetting that we are dealing with a mystery here, the neo-Chalcedonian understands the expression "Jesus was obedient unto death" of the divinity itself, as well as of the humanity. A representative of pure Chalcedonianism, however, while continuing to maintain the hypostatic union of divinity and humanity in Jesus will insist here that, in this union of divinity and humanity, the nonconfusion must also be safeguarded. Death and finitude belong only to the creaturely reality of Jesus. They remain "this side" of the infinite distance separating God and creature; they remain on the creaturely side of the one "God-man." The eternal Word, in his *divinity*, can undergo no such historicity nor any "obedience unto death."

Pure Chalcedonianism is ever wary of the other soteriology, fearing it will make the surreptitious transition from a *communicatio idiomatum*, a communication or exchange of concrete attributes (in the two natures), precisely to an *identity* of concrete attributes (of both natures). We would then have the eternal, impassible God, who transcends all history—in a spirit of gnosticism or Schellingism or what you will—suffering in himself, suffering as God. We would be positing the redemption of our condition as occurring in virtue of a transposition of that condition to the interiority of God himself. Pure Chalcedonianism, while maintaining the hypostatic union, and thereby the validity of the *communicatio idiomatum* (but understood in a Chalcedonian way), will emphasize that finitude and death are the prime constituents of the condition from which we are to be redeemed—that we are redeemed from them by their being Jesus' condition as well—and that in him they can indeed be rightly predicated of the Word too, because of the hypostatic union, but not in such a way as to posit this subject and predicate, the eternity of the divinity and the passion of the humanity, in an identity. The dogma of the hypostatic union expresses a unity, a oneness, that is unique, not occurring elsewhere, unknown to us in any other instance, and including within itself the distinction and nonconfusion that was proclaimed as dogma at Chalcedon.

But then the theologians of pure Chalcedonianism are left with the question as to how this oneness of God and the human being may be the bearer of a function and meaning for redemption. The question remains how we are redeemed, if God has burdened the human reality of Jesus with our existential condition of guilt and death. Jesus' lot is God's lot in a true sense. But this lot, this history and condition, leaves God's own life, with its transhistoricity, impassibility, and innocent beatitude, untouched. God's reality and Jesus' creatureliness remain "unconfused," uncommingled. The pure Chalcedonian will always hold that it is God's impassible, holy blessedness that has "formally" redeemed us—not something earthly and finite that has been speculatively introduced into the interiority of God *qua* God. He or she will say that Jesus' death, however it is ultimately to be explained, can alone be the reason why, and rationale how, God gives us his own blessedness as our own. It cannot in itself be ("formally," then) this redemption.

Our rather lengthy excursus here on neo-Chalcedonian soteriology is not intended as a denial that the doctrine of the hypostatic union is the basis of the soteriological meaning of Jesus' history and a necessary element in salvation itself. But the question remains whether an understanding of christological dogma, including the hypostatic union, would not be better served by an approach from just the opposite pole from that with which traditional theology begins: whether it would not be better to begin not with Jesus' divinity, not with the hypostatic union, and thence proceed to the reality of salvation, but to begin with the soteriological significance for us of Jesus and his history, and there begin our search for an understanding of the meaning of the hypostatic union.

The path we are proposing, then, leads from "Christ for us" to "Christ in himself." Let us put it very simply. The hypostatic union will be understood here as the presupposition, perhaps not a very readily clarified one, for what we experience in Jesus: that he is the last, irrevocable word of God's forgiveness and self-bestowal upon us. The Christian dogma of Jesus as both God and human being will be understood as a formulation of Jesus' unique, irreplacable meaning for salvation for us, and the hypostatic union is thereby the presupposition inseparably contained in this proposition about Jesus' meaning for salvation.

In order to present Jesus' unsurpassable and definitive salvation-meaning in a way we can grasp, let us start out quite "from below." Here is a human being who lives in an attitude of matchless nearness to God—someone who lives in pure obedience to God and at the same time in unconditional solidarity with human beings, regardless of how the latter may behave toward him. This two-way solidarity, with God and with human beings, is maintained by Jesus unconditionally, to the limit. The historical outcome of this for Jesus is his death—in which he definitively and totally surrenders to God and God's incomprehensible disposition, while steadfastly maintaining his unconditional love for human beings as well. In this plunge into the helplessness of death, however, he becomes the definitively Affirmed and Accepted One, *and* this is how he is experienced by us: as the Risen One. (This is the Christian faith, going back to the experience of Jesus' disciples and of the Church, and we cannot undertake an express legitimation of it here.)

Thus the fate and person of Jesus have a special, proper meaning, above and beyond their ordinary human character. This Jesus proclaims that, with himself, the definitive, irrevocable address of God's forgiving and self-bestowing love is present—that the Kingdom of God has irrevocably come, that the victory of God's forgiving love in the history of humankind is complete and irreversible insofar as God himself is concerned. And in God's definitive acceptance of Jesus through his resurrection, Jesus' claim to be the vehicle of God's definitive self-communication to the world, despite its sin and finitude and mortality, is legitimated and sealed.

But then, in his self-interpretation, in his death, and in his resurrection,

Jesus is the matchless, definitive word of God's testimony to himself in the world. If we understand this to the hilt, we have the traditional doctrine of the substantial, hypostatic union of the Word with the human reality of Jesus. If we accept Jesus as God's irreversible, definitive self-bestowal on us, thereby we shall be confessing him as the consubstantial Son of God.

How is this to be explained? Any creaturely, finite reality emerges from a broader field of possibilities. Alongside this reality there are other, non-contradictory possibilities which could be, or could have been, realized as well, or instead. In this one actualized possibility alone, God, its free creator, is never definitively committed. Everything finite and historical, considered as such and in itself, is subject to recall, is ever the object of a divine liberty that never posits itself absolutely, as indeed it is unable to, through this finite thing as such alone. Therefore any revelation in which God objectifies and manifests his will through a finite word or historical event remains, *a parte post*, open, subject to revision, and provisional.

Nothing simply finite is capable, as such and in itself alone, of signifying and transmitting to us an unsurpassable communication of God. It is ever provisional among the infinitude of God's opportunities and the sovereignty of his freedom. Thus if God communicates his self-affirmation to us as an irrevocable and definitive self-affirmation, then the creaturely reality through which he does so cannot simply stand at the same distance from him as other creaturely realities. The creaturely reality must in this instance be God's own reality, in such unique wise that God would be effectively cancelling *himself*, were he ever to surpass it in virtue of its creaturely finitude.

Only a finite reality that is assumed by God as his own reality can make God's commitment in the world irrevocable. The revelatory word of God to us, when it is to be unsurpassable, must be God's own reality—else it will remain trapped in the conditionality and surpassability peculiar to things finite. A mere prophet can surely speak in God's name. But the finite message he or she communicates by deed and word can only proclaim something that is open *a parte post* and surpassable. To put it in biblical terms: Only the Son who *is* God's word, and who announces it not in mere finitude alone, can be the definitive, ultimate, no longer surpassable prophet. But Jesus claims to be God's definitive, unconditional, irreversible self-commitment, and this self-interpretation and claim of his are endorsed and confirmed by God through the definitiveness of his existence, in death and resurrection. Accordingly, his human reality, with its historicity and finitude intact, must be not merely *posited* by the God of the other world, but must be that God's own reality—however difficult we may find it to discern whence it comes that a divine reality that is God in

identity can be distinguished from a reality of God that is God by acceptance—that is, in oneness, but without being one and the same.

If these considerations are correct in their basic intent, despite any imperfections they may comport in their formulation, then we can say: Jesus
is the consubstantial Son of God; his human reality, without prejudice to
its genuine, free, human subjectivity, is that of the eternal Word of God—
for Jesus is the irrevocable, unsurpassable, and definitive self-commitment
of God to us; and this he can only be as God's consubstantial Son.

Now it is clear how altogether possible it is to have a Christology that
begins with the experience of Jesus, that begins "from below," that experiences him as our salvation—that is, that encounters him as the historical
experience of God's self-bestowal. From here we can proceed quite readily
to the metaphysical propositions of classic Christology. The proposition
that Jesus is God's definitive self-commitment to us, and the proposition
that Jesus is the incarnate Word of God, are interchangeable, provided
only the first proposition be taken in radical earnest, and the second be
understood in a Chalcedonian, and not monophysitical, sense as being a
proposition about the true *oneness* or *unity* of the Word and the human
reality of Jesus, and not as a proposition of simple identity.

There is an ascending, or "low," Christology—a Christology that begins with the human Jesus—that complements the classic descending, or
"high," Christology of God become a human being. The former clarifies
how and why a seemingly innocuous relationship of unconditional trust
in Jesus can be charged with the whole of classic Christology. It shows
that such a relationship is altogether available to the ordinary Christian
who is not a professional theologian, and that indeed it can be expected of
him or her. To be sure, it is desirable that such a Christian have a certain
acquaintance with the formulations of classic Christology, and if he or
she is educated this is to be expected. But if he or she finds this a difficulty
and experiences, shall we say, a "metaphysical overload," he or she need
not consider himself or herself a poor Christian, or one of doubtful or-
thodoxy.

If a Christian can trustingly and confidently say: "In Jesus of Nazareth,
in his life, his teaching, his catastrophic death, his victory (which we call
his resurrection), God has given me himself"—his forgiveness, his own life,
above and beyond all finite fulfillment—if a Christian believes that this
self-bestowal of God's is unconditional, irreversible, and definitive for his
own part, and that it can never be superseded or surpassed in some new age
to come—for indeed, as God's last word it *can* no longer be superseded—if
a Christian is engaged and committed to this in a free outpouring of faith,
and allows this matchless hope more validity than all doubts, skepticism,
and reservations—then he or she is an orthodox Christian. This Christian

experiences classic Christology existentially. This Christian finds and accepts Jesus, actually understood, and rightly understood, as his or her salvation.

65 · Eternity from Time

Scepticism in Regard to Eternal Life

There can be no doubt that belief in eternal life as a consequence of survival after death has grown weaker in the consciousness of modern people. This fundamental doctrine of Christianity, scarcely affected at first by the Enlightenment from the eighteenth century onward, is now questioned, or at any rate has lost its place among those things which mainly interest people today. It is true that at all times there have been some who thought (as they put it) that death is the end of everything; but the conviction that man lives on into a definitive permanent existence was generally taken for granted and firmly established in the public mind, at least among Christian nations, but also far beyond these, even though the ideas of this life after death were and are very diverse. Today, even among Christians, what was once a basic Christian conviction is largely threatened. There are Christians who are sure of the existence of God and who lead lives according to the tenets of their religion, but who do not think it necessary to show any great interest in the question of an eternal life that is not simply identical with life here and now.

Of course, the fact that this scepticism in regard to eternal life exists in modern society does not mean that it is justified. Faced by the essential and ultimate questions of human existence, we cannot hide behind the prestige and allure of popular opinion at the present time. The lofty and sublime persuasion of a few can be the truth that holds for all, even though there are not many who acknowledge it. The ultimate truths are not found in the popular press, nor are they established by thoughtless chatter in a public house.

Of course, it can readily be admitted by a Christian that the ways of presenting the idea of the perennially valid truth of eternal life are more inadequate than is necessary or avoidable, obscuring rather than elucidating the real meaning. Among these unsatisfactory ideas of eternity is that of a never ending time running on into infinity. Up to very recently preachers have too often made indiscriminate use of this idea with reference to the eternity of hell. But even modern physics knows that in order to express certain facts or realities of the physical world without getting lost in mathematical abstractness (which is also incapable by itself of bringing out what is really meant) we must work with very inadequate ideas, perhaps even with several apparently mutually contradictory ideas, which, however, can bring home to us only together up to a point the meaning of the reality under discussion. If this sort of thing happens even in physics, people today ought really not to be put off (as they so readily are) by the fact that in the sphere of religion, also, more or less apt terms and ideas (for example, in regard to eternal life) can be worked out only imperfectly and arduously.

Within our present scope it is, of course, not possible even to a slight degree to make clear the existence and nature of the eternal life awaiting us. Here and now we are attempting to draw attention only to one point from this immense theme: that is, that we experience eternity in the present time in a way that constantly eludes reflection and can learn from this that the eternity which emerges through death out of the present time and becomes definitive cannot be conceived as a continuation of time into eternity.

The Tyranny of Our Concept of Time

By way of preparation for our main reflections, it must again be made more clear what are the difficulties that arise if we understand eternity "after" death as the unlimited continuation of time. If we understand eternity (which is the definitiveness of our life, emerging in time) as the running on of time with one section coming after another, each to be filled out in a new way and each different from the others, then, of course, all the semiclever and semistupid questions arise that tempt today's semiclever person to regard belief in eternal life as incredible, if not downright ridiculous. For then he can ask what is to be used to fill up these ever new periods of time. Will it not gradually become boring if, as devout people think, this never stopping conveyor belt of time has its individual parts stacked again and again with the same thing, with the eternal glorification of the infinite God by his creature's praise? Why then is there no opportunity in this ever continuing time for the damned to be converted, change their outlook, repent, and thus turn their hell into heaven? Are they prevented by a God who, in a final act of despotism, refuses to accept a change of mind on the part of the lost, although there would be place for such a change and it could happen at some point in these ever continuing times ("aeons," as they are called in Scripture).

If eternity is conceived, then, as time open to infinity, have not the world, man and his history always ahead of them that which is not yet (in other words, that which can find its place only in a future space of time), and is not heaven the very thing that may not enter into this scheme of ever continuing, continual succession in time? But if it is to go on forever, if everything that exists is no more than the starting point for attaining what is to come, and so on and so on, is not the eternity of this kind of time the damnation of Ahasuerus, the wandering Jew, doomed always to roam, without ever finally arriving anywhere? Under the tyranny of this concept of time, is not the eternal heaven dissolved into an eternal hell, and vice versa? It is easy to see how dangerous and pernicious is the idea of eternity as an endless running on of time.

In order to get out of this difficulty we can, of course, in the first place say quite appropriately that a notion of eternity can be formed with the aid of a negation, excluding from the notion of the real, the permanent, and the definitive the element of sequence, of succession, of one thing after another. This method of forming a new concept by the negation of certain aspects of the present concept is not always illegitimate in principle. It is a method that is often unavoidable. With its aid a blind person, for example, can form an idea, if not a visualization, of colour and consequently gain the assurance that there are colours, even though he has never seen them; he can also hope, although blind from birth, that perhaps one day he will see. But it is a method that also has its problems. How are we to know in the concrete case whether what is conceptually grasped can really exist, even when a particular element of what is experienced is excluded by a negation of this kind? In our case can there really be something permanent, if we exclude from its notion the succession that exists in all the enduring things that we directly experience?

Hints of an Eternal Reality

In order to gain further confidence that there can also be something permanent and eternal which is not subject to the domination of endless succession, let us take a closer look at our experience of time and (so I think) discover there something "eternal": that is, at least something that is not simply in the "now," in the mere moment of time, perishing and giving way to something else that is different from what went before, replacing this, only to be itself replaced and thrust into nothingness. We are considering the paradox of time itself which lives in secret from an eternity.

A kind of permanency in time appears at three levels. There is the necessary permanency of any reality (what we used to describe as "substance") which persists while sustaining the alternation of qualities, phenomena, and occurrences. There is mental experience which combines past, present, and future in a unity. There is free personal decision which, by its very nature, does not permit what it has posited purely and simply to disappear into the void of nothingness. Let us look again a little more closely at these three hints of something eternal in the world of our experience.

The Totality of a History

Time appears to us in the first place as a chain of individual occurrences stretching forward and backward into infinity, with each occurrence replacing the one before it and itself disappearing to make way for what follows. But at the same time, even though we are much less attentive to the fact, we are sure that these changing phenomena replacing one another are nevertheless manifestations of something permanent which (at least for a longer or shorter period) persists as the same reality, sustaining the changing appearances, bringing them together into a totality, into a history, which is in fact one and does not disintegrate or crumble into a dust of pure individual moments. Something of this can be seen, for instance, in the history of a flower, continuing in varying stages from the seed until it finally withers. Or we may consider our own life history from beginning to end, in which every moment is different from the one before it and yet each is a determination of one and the same reality, which persists as the same throughout this changing history, and, as one and the same, claims for itself all these alternating moments. These identities, lying behind the alternation and contents of the moments of time and thus holding together the infinitesimally tiny elements of time, shaping out of the dust of these elements a greater, structured history, cannot as such share the quality of time itself as it divides and passes away, if they are to fulfill their task of sustaining and unifying time. If time is to make sense as a greater unity and more definite shape, as history, there must be something that we always take for granted in ordinary life and that is not simply the succession of moments of time flashing out and then fading again. There is in time something that is not identical with time itself. This something may perhaps need to expand over time if it is to be itself, but it is not identical with this extension in moments of time. Even what is properly temporal contains more than time: at least something that persists and gives a unity to time in historical temporal shapes.

Mental Experience

This supra-temporal element in time becomes still more clear when we reflect on the way in which time is unified and shaped in the mental process of experiencing it. Time is not simply there; it is experienced by us, not by merely submitting to its sequence, but by confronting it, gathering together past, present, and future and mentally binding them into a unity and shape which is more than the pure succession of time where the next moment triumphs over the last by annihilating it. Someone observing this mental unifying of time, this interruption of time's course, might retort sceptically that this time so unified, in which bare succession is eliminated, this time that "stands still," ceases to run on, and consequently does not run out, is nothing but an *idea* of time, and the subject reflecting on time in this way is hopelessly borne along and passes away in real time. But, if time as such is nothing but the flow of time atoms, each of which extinguishes its predecessor and is then extinguished by its successor, how can it be unified meaningfully and truly (even if merely "in thought") into such instant time-configurations, into a history of meaning and structure, unless there is more to time itself than mere passing away?

And, even more importantly, how is the thinking subject, conferring unity and shape in time as it runs on, to be understood as capable of doing this? How can a thinking subject of this kind create a time that stands still, even merely in thought, if it is completely dependent on flowing time for its own true being, when thinking itself is also a reality, and thinking and what is thought are mutually dependent? No, if and insofar as there is a thought of time, something happens which does in fact occur in time's course, but as an event which has a peculiar superiority over time, an event intimating eternity, since the thought that thinks time is not simply time's subject.

Free Decisions

Eternity is experienced in time itself most clearly when the intellectual subject in man makes a free decision which concerns and involves the one and entire person. We cannot analyze decisions of this kind in all their dimensions here. That would take too long. All that we can say is that there are free decisions in man, involving the person's total self-disposal, for which he bears an ultimate, inescapable responsibility, a responsibility which he cannot shift off to anyone or anything else, neither by a psychology seeking to break down the ultimate character of man as subject nor by social sciences seeking to reduce man to a pure effect of social conditions. But (and this in the long run is unavoidable and inexorably occurs at certain points, whether there is any very explicit and theoretical reflection on it or not) if someone says as he proceeds to act, "I am inexorably and inescapably responsible for this, there is nothing in the last resort to which I can appeal to relieve me of responsibility," he can simultaneously think and say, "Not that all this is so important or so bad. For when the end really comes I can always take refuge in the empty void where no one can reach me any longer, neither the voice of conscience nor any world history nor God." No, ultimate personal decisions, at least when they involve a life in its totality, are irrevocable, they are truly eternity coming to be in time.

Of course, if we had time to do so, we would have to ask here about the possibility of repentance and conversion within the continuing course of the time and history of man, we would have to bear in mind the essentially dialogic character of human freedom, to which God assigns a decisive role in this history of freedom. But none of these things would remove the basic fact, rooted in the nature of this freedom and its inextricable responsibility, that freedom in the last resort (and, indeed, freedom alone) wills and posits finality and unrevisability, that this implies the finality, the eternity of the existence of this freedom and consequently does not permit this freedom any flight from responsibility into the void. Here time really creates eternity and eternity is experienced in time.

Accepting Incomprehensibility

There may perhaps be some doubt as to whether our suggestions provide adequate illumination for the understanding of that eternity which we as Christians hope to reach as our definitive life after death. But I think that these suggestions at least show that it cannot be said that each and every thing within the range of our experience is so exclusively and solely temporal that we can think meaningfully of something as real only by thinking of it either as existing simply here and now and then disappearing into the void or as a reality consisting merely of an unlimited number of moments of time continuing always without end and incapable in principle of offering any scope for a decision of freedom that posits a real finality. Both these ideas (that is, of time as ending in the void or of time as never ceasing) are equally incompatible with the Christian belief in eternal life. And neither of these ideas can appeal to the actual experience we have of time if we unhesitatingly permit the *whole* experience to speak for itself.

These merely tentatively outlined considerations must, however, allow us to draw a few conclusions for concrete life. First of all, even in this way, it becomes evident that we cannot positively imagine here the concreteness of our eternal life. We know, it is true, that it will be an existence and life that has God himself in himself as its content, a life that implies love, limitless knowledge, supreme happiness, and so on. But how all this can be experienced in the concreteness of a state beyond time, what is that meaning of transfigured corporality, eternal fellowship with the redeemed, and so on: this is something we cannot concretely imagine or picture to ourselves here and now. We Christians need not be disturbed today if we can scarcely summon up the courage to see it all as depicted from Scripture to Dante, and even subsequently. For we are actually going into the unknown, the unimaginable, and, properly speaking, know only that it is filled with the incomprehensibility of God and his love and that it is final. It is sufficient to accept for ourselves now the incomprehensibility of our eternal life and nevertheless to go on hoping and trusting. Our experience of time (which is always a mysterious experience of something more than time) certainly gives us the right not to hold suspect as empty speculation our "no" to time in the concept of eternity; but it certainly does not relieve us of the decision to say this "no" to time in our "yes" to eternity. Thus it leaves our life one of faith and hope that must still wait for the definitive end and has no power triumphantly to exhibit it before the fact.

Victory of God's Love

In the third case of eternity in time, which we considered briefly, it becomes clear, if we look closely enough, that our eternal life, however much it will then be filled with God himself, will be the definitiveness of that moral and free act of our life in which (beyond all the dividedness of time) as one and whole, we made ourselves the persons we wanted finally to be. But if our eternity is thus nothing but the now definitive history which we ourselves freely made, then we can see with both horror and supreme delight the immense grandeur, depth, and density of those acts in which our whole life is involved. Of course, in our life there is a great deal of routine and superficiality that is unavoidable, in which freedom occurs without bearing any trace of finality or eternity. If, however, there is such a thing as eternal life at all, if it is not merely something different added to our temporal life and likewise stretching out over time, if it is truly the finality of this present life of freedom which fittingly comes to a final and definitive consummation, only then can be seen the unfathomable depths and the richness of our existence, of that existence which often gives the impression of consisting of nothing but banalities. Where an ultimate responsibility is assumed in obedience to a person's own conscience, where ultimate selfless love and fidelity are given, where an ultimate selfless obedience to truth regardless of self is lived out, and so on, at this point there is really in our life something that is infinitely precious, that of itself has the right and reality not to perish, that is able to fill out an eternity, that actually deserves not merely to be rewarded (a misleading expression, savouring of selfishness) by perpetual eternity but to claim this as its most authentic right, as its most intimate nature.

This is the dignity and potentiality with which we human beings are endowed—all of us, not merely the great geniuses of mankind, not merely a Buddha or a Socrates, but all of us, even though there are far too many who seem to be terribly mediocre, mayflies, as it were. But the truth proclaimed by Christianity is that in this time (apparently stretching out endlessly, in order to reproduce in an eternal recurrence always the same thing and always that which perishes in the eternal cycle of coming and going), whenever life is lived in faith, hope, and love, eternity truly occurs: eternity which does not come only to depart, which persists and (this is what matters) is such that its persistence means supreme happiness and not hell, since it has received God himself and thus is really worthy of being definitive and forever. Of course, in principle, it must be firmly maintained that man's history of freedom can also produce a person's similarly timeless definitive perdition. But what Christianity really proclaims as essential is not the equal possibility of these *two* ways of passing from time to eternity, but the victory of the love of God who bestows himself in and through our freedom: it points to the cross and resurrection of Jesus as to the event of this now manifest victory of God's love. This love is the cause and guarantee that our brief time, which passes away, creates an eternity which is not made up out of time. If it seems that we perish in death, since the dead do not become perceptible again anywhere where time goes on, this is merely a sign that eternity, born from time, is something other than what can readily be seen here and now.

List of Sources

1. *Our Christian Faith*, pp. 160–79
2. *Concern for the Church (Theological Investigations XX)*, pp. 144–53
3. *The Shape of the Church to Come*, pp. 21–25
4. *Faith Today*, pp. 9–18
5. *Faith Today*, pp. 27–37
6. *Our Christian Faith*, pp. 23–25
7. *Entschluss* 37/9–10 (1982): 6–11, trans. Robert Barr
8. Previously unpublished, trans. Robert Barr
9. *Grace in Freedom*, pp. 127–32
10. *Theological Investigations XVII*, pp. 235–40
11. *The Priesthood*, pp. 5–10
12. *Theological Investigations XVI*, pp. 235–40
13. *Theological Investigations XVIII*, pp. 174–76
14. C. Albrecht, *Das mystische Wort* (Mainz 1974), pp. vii–xiv, trans. Robert Barr
15. *The Spirit in the Church*, pp. 11–22
16. *Christian at the Crossroads*, pp. 52–55
17. *Christian at the Crossroads*, pp. 55–59
18. *Christian at the Crossroads*, pp. 62–69
19. Previously unpublished, trans. Robert Barr
20. Previously unpublished, trans. Robert Barr
21. F. X. Arnold et al., eds., *Handbuch der Pastoraltheologie*, 2nd ed. (Freiburg 1970ff.), II/2:63, trans. Robert Barr
22. *Christian at the Crossroads*, pp. 75–80
23. *The Priesthood*, pp. 52–63
24. *Theological Investigations X*, pp. 158–65
25. *Christian at the Crossroads*, pp. 70–74
26. *Handbuch der Pastoraltheologie*, III:530–35, trans. Robert Barr
27. *Grace in Freedom*, pp. 215–18
28. *The Love of Jesus and the Love of Neighbor*, pp. 69–71
29. *The Love of Jesus and the Love of Neighbor*, pp. 16–24
30. *Theological Investigations XVIII*, pp. 158–70
31. *Theological Investigations III*, pp. 93–102
32. *Mary, Mother of the Lord*, pp. 23–31
33. *Theological Investigations XIX*, pp. 88–92

34. *Entschluss* 36/1 (1981): 4–8, trans. Robert Barr
35. *Entschluss* 35/1 (1980): 7–10, trans. Robert Barr
36. *Spiritual Exercises*, pp. 210–16
37. *Theological Investigations XIX*, pp. 150–58
38. *Theological Investigations XIX*, pp. 119–22
39. *Spiritual Exercises*, pp. 205–9
40. Previously unpublished, trans. Robert Barr
41. *Handbuch der Pastoraltheologie*, I:164–71, trans. Robert Barr
42. *Wagnis des Christen* (Freiburg 1974), pp. 134–36, trans. Robert Barr
43. *Entschluss* 35/11 (1980): 4–8, trans. Robert Barr
44. Previously unpublished, trans. Robert Barr
45. *Theological Investigations X*, pp. 213–21
46. *The Priesthood*, pp. 30–35
47. *Handbuch der Pastoraltheologie*, II/2:36–45, trans. Robert Barr
48. *Everyday Faith*, pp. 135–41
49. *Theological Investigations XVII*, pp. 129–38
50. *Spiritual Exercises*, pp. 69–76
51. *Theological Investigations XVII*, pp. 19–22
52. Previously unpublished, trans. Robert Barr
53. *Theological Investigations X*, pp. 248–51
54. *Theological Investigations X*, pp. 256–59
55. *Theological Investigations XVIII*, pp. 215–21
56. *Spiritual Exercises*, pp. 278–84
57. *Entschluss* 36/5 (1981):4–5, trans. Robert Barr
58. *Entschluss* 35/6 (1980):4–7, trans. Robert Barr
59. *Theological Investigations X*, pp. 371–77
60. *Theological Investigations X*, pp. 377–88
61. *The Spirit in the Church*, pp. 68–72
62. *Theological Investigations XVIII*, pp. 230–34
63. *Spiritual Exercises*, pp. 89–91
64. *The Love of Jesus and the Love of Neighbor*, pp. 51–61
65. *Theological Investigations XIX*, pp. 169–77

Acknowledgments

Christian at the Crossroads (*Wagnis des Christen*, 1974), trans. V. Green,
© Search Press Ltd, 1975 (London: Search Press/New York: Seabury Press,
1975)

Everyday Faith (*Glaube, der die Erde liebt*, 1966), trans. W. J. O'Hara,
© 1967 Herder KG (London: Burns & Oates/New York: Herder and Herder,
1968)

Faith Today (*Im Heute Glauben*, 1965), trans. Ray and Rosaleen Ockenden,
© (London/New York: Sheed and Ward, 1967)

Grace in Freedom (*Gnade als Freiheit*, 1968), trans. Hilda Graef, © 1969
Herder KG (London: Burns & Oates/New York: Herder and Herder, 1969)

Mary, Mother of the Lord (*Maria, Mutter des Herrn*), trans. W. J. O'Hara,
© Herder KG 1963 (New York: Herder and Herder, 1963)

Our Christian Faith: Answers for the Future (with Karl-Heinz Weger) (*Was
sollen wir noch Glauben?* 1980), trans. Francis McDonagh, © Search Press
Ltd, 1980 (London: Burns & Oates/New York: Crossroad, 1981)

Spiritual Exercises (*Betrachtungen zum ignatianischen Exerzitienbuch*, 1965),
trans. Kenneth Baker, S.J., © 1965 by Herder and Herder, Incorporated
(New York: Herder and Herder, 1965)

The Love of Jesus and the Love of Neighbor (*Was heisst Jesus lieben?*, 1982,
and *Wer ist dein Bruder?*, 1981), trans. Robert Barr, © 1983 by The
Crossroad Publishing Company (New York: Crossroad/London: St. Paul
Publications, 1983)

The Priesthood (*Einübung priesterlicher Existenz*, 1970), trans. Edward Quinn,
© 1973 by Sheed and Ward Ltd (London: Sheed and Ward/New York:
Seabury Press, 1973)

The Shape of the Church to Come (*Strukturwandel der Kirche als Aufgabe und
Chance*, 1972), trans. Edward Quinn, © translation, S.P.C.K., 1974
(London: S.P.C.K./New York: Seabury, 1974)

The Spirit in the Church, "Part I: Experiencing the Spirit" (*Erfahrung des
Geistes*, 1977), trans. John Griffiths, © Search Press Ltd, 1979; "Part II: The
charismatic element in the Church" (*Das Dynamische in der Kirche*, 1962),
trans. W. J. O'Hara, © Herder KG 1964, 1978 (London: Search Press/New
York: Seabury Press, 1979)

Theological Investigations III (*Schriften zur Theologie III*), trans. Karl-H. and
Boniface Kruger, © Darton, Longman & Todd Ltd, 1967 and 1974
(London: Darton, Longman & Todd/Baltimore: Helicon, 1967)